RETAIL RACISM

PERSPECTIVES ON A MULTIRACIAL AMERICA SERIES

Joe R. Feagin, Texas A&M University, Series Editor

The racial composition of the United States is rapidly changing. Books in the series will explore various aspects of the coming multiracial society, one in which European-Americans are no longer the majority and where issues of white-on-black racism have been joined by many other challenges to white dominance.

Titles:

Melanie Bush, *Breaking the Code of Good Intentions: Everyday Forms of Whiteness*

Amir Mavasti and Karyn McKinney, *Middle Eastern Lives in America*

Katheryn Russell-Brown, *Protecting Our Own: Race, Crime, and African Americans*

Victoria Kaplan, *Structural Inequality: Black Architects in the United States*

Elizabeth M. Aranda, *Emotional Bridges to Puerto Rico: Migration, Return Migration, and the Struggles of Incorporation*

Richard Rees, *Shades of Difference: A History of Ethnicity in America*

Pamela Anne Quiroz, *Adoption in a Color-Blind Society*

Adia Harvey Wingfield, *Doing Business with Beauty: Black Women, Hair Salons, and the Racial Enclave Economy*

Angela J. Hattery, David G. Embrick, and Earl Smith, *Globalization and America: Race, Human Rights, and Inequality*

Erica Chito Childs, *Fade to Black and White: Interracial Images in Popular Culture*

Jessie Daniels, *Cyber Racism: White Supremacy Online and the New Attack on Civil Rights*

Teun A. van Dijk, *Racism and Discourse in Latin America*

C. Richard King, Carmen R. Lugo-Lugo, and Mary K. Bloodsworth-Lugo, *Animating Difference: Race, Gender, and Sexuality in Contemporary Films for Children*

Melanie E. L. Bush, *Everyday Forms of Whiteness: Understanding Race in a "Post-Racial" World*, 2nd edition

David J. Leonard and C. Richard King, *Commodified and Criminalized: New Racism and African Americans in Contemporary Sports*

Maria Chávez, *Everyday Injustice: Latino Professionals and Racism*

Benjamin Fleury-Steiner, *Disposable Heroes: The Betrayal of African American Veterans*

Noel A. Cazenave, *The Urban Racial State: Managing Race Relations in American Cities*

Cherise A. Harris, *The Cosby Cohort: Race, Class, and Identity among Second Generation Middle Class Blacks*

Louwanda Evans, *Cabin Pressure: African American Pilots, Flight Attendants, and Emotional Labor*

Kristen M. Lavelle, *Whitewashing the South: White Memories of Segregation and Civil Rights*

Ruth Thompson-Miller, Joe R. Feagin, and Leslie H. Picca, *Jim Crow's Legacy: The Lasting Impact of Segregation*

Mary K. Bloodsworth-Lugo and Carmen R. Lugo-Lugo, *Projecting 9/11: Race, Gender, and Citizenship in Recent Hollywood Films*

Tsedale M. Melaku, *You Don't Look Like a Lawyer: Black Women and Systemic Gendered Racism*

Michelle R. Dunlap, *Retail Racism: Shopping While Black and Brown in America*

RETAIL RACISM

Shopping While Black and Brown in America

Michelle R. Dunlap

ROWMAN & LITTLEFIELD
Lanham • Boulder • New York • London

Published by Rowman & Littlefield
An imprint of The Rowman & Littlefield Publishing Group, Inc.
4501 Forbes Boulevard, Suite 200, Lanham, Maryland 20706
www.rowman.com

86–90 Paul Street, London EC2A 4NE, United Kingdom

British Library Cataloguing in Publication Information Available

Library of Congress Cataloging-in-Publication Data

Names: Dunlap, Michelle R., 1965- author.
Title: Retail racism : shopping while Black and Brown in America / Michelle R. Dunlap.
Description: Lanham : Rowman & Littlefield, [2021] | Series: Perspectives on a multiracial America series | Includes bibliographical references.
Identifiers: LCCN 2021018210 (print) | LCCN 2021018211 (ebook) | ISBN 9781538137123 (cloth) | ISBN 9781538137147 (epub)
Subjects: LCSH: African American consumers. | Minority consumers—United States. | Race discrimination—United States. | Retail trade—Moral and ethical aspects—United States. | Customer relations—Moral and ethical aspects—United States. | Shoplifting—United States—Prevention. | Stores, Retail—Security measures—United States. | United States—Race relations.
Classification: LCC HC110.C6 D846 2021 (print) | LCC HC110.C6 (ebook) | DDC 381.3—dc23
LC record available at https://lccn.loc.gov/2021018210
LC ebook record available at https://lccn.loc.gov/2021018211

Dedicated to
Antron McCray, Kevin Richardson,
Yusef Salaam, Raymond Santana,
and Korey Wise . . .
the exonerated Central Park Five.

A portion of the author proceeds from the sale of this book are automatically donated to the Florida Education Fund (FEF) McKnight Doctoral Fellowship Program. Since 1984, the FEF has had the mission of addressing the underrepresentation of African American and Hispanic faculty at colleges and universities by increasing the pool of citizens qualified with PhD degrees to teach at the college and university levels.

. . . Ms. Reeves kept talking to us the way you told me white folk would talk to us if we weren't perfect, the way I saw white women at the mall and police talk to you whether you'd broken the law or not.

—Kiese Laymon, *Heavy: An American Memoir*

CONTENTS

PART II: INEQUITIES

PART III: TRAUMAS

PART IV: PHILOSOPHIES

PART V: CONCLUSION

PREFACE

Like most people, I have all kinds of philosophies or personal theories in my head. One of them is that sometimes God allows things to happen to us or to those we love because He knows that our passion about resisting it will inspire us to not only survive the catastrophe but also create something out of it. Some choose to create art, offer testimony, start after-school programs, take on leadership roles in government to make new laws, become doctors or lawyers or teachers, start social movements, make documentaries and movies, or write books. Write a book, that's the route I took. Normally I write about human developmental issues, such as college-student community engagement and learning, racial identity development, adolescent development, social worker perceptions and misperceptions of African American families and child discipline, and a variety of other diversity issues. However, a marketplace incident happened roughly twenty-five years ago that so bothered me that it changed my life and eventually shifted my focus to this book. This is not just my, or my loved ones', story, or the story of the people telling their stories, but it's a story of U.S. white supremacy structures and of Black and Brown folks' survival. It's a collection of true stories that exemplify what countless numbers of Black and Brown people are facing from moment to moment. This book initially was inspired by an incident in the mid-1990s when a very smart, beautiful, Brown, eight-year-old beloved extended family member went with me to run an errand at the mall. While we were there, he got the bright idea to steal two $1-packs of sports cards. He was closely observed by the store manager, who got my attention and called the store owner right away. I apologized profusely, and asked the store manager and owner if I could pay for the cards. As I was pulling the money out of my purse, I assured them that the parents would deal with this when I take him home. But to my shock, the owner threatened to call law enforcement. Being a relatively new full-time professor, I had been reading a series of books for my upcoming child-development classes that spoke of how children need to be free to make mistakes and need to experience natural consequences so that they can learn within safe, supportive environments. The books spoke of how children learn more through personal experiences than exclusively through verbal instructions, and how rather than being punished, they need to be given room to explore, make mistakes, and learn from those mistakes. Thus, they need to be able to safely roam and explore their environments and learn through mishaps and natural, supportive, constructive consequences. The problem with such child-development philosophies is that there is a failure for many experts to realize that the "natural" consequences for the little Black and Brown children tend to be much more life-altering and even deadlier than those of the vast majority of White children—even for identical offenses. In fact, it has been well-documented that little Black children, no matter their gender, are perceived as older and more dangerous than their White counterparts of the same age. Often, Black and Brown children are inappropriately treated as criminals before the first sign of puberty has even initiated itself. Therefore, Black and Brown children and teens are easily blamed for things they did not do, or are held accountable for infractions for which White children typically would not be held accountable.[1] As an example, let's juxtapose such findings with the interview in this book where a young White woman shares with us her cognitive dissonance and even her lecture to her White sixteen-year-old younger brother when he was *not* processed into the criminal justice system upon his being confronted by police after stealing a $40 wallet. Instead, the store and police called his parents on the phone and released him with no charges whatsoever. Black and Brown people's experiences and observations tend to vastly differ from the kindly phone call from a police officer. For example, just recently, police were called and guns were pulled and held on a family and their children after, unbeknown to the parents, their four-year-old picked up a doll from a dollar store.[2] These are not at all new experiences, they are just more easily documented now, as millions saw the video recordings of this family being traumatized as they prayed that they and their children would not be shot and killed.

So, on that day at the mall, many years ago, with my new PhD in hand, and with my head filled with mainstream ideas concerning psychology and child development, I could not even fathom that someone would call law enforcement on an eight-year-old. In disbelief, I naively asked the owner if he was serious about calling law enforcement. "You mean his parents would have to get a lawyer and all that for an eight-year-old stealing baseball cards?!" I asked incredulously while holding the phone. I could not even imagine. The owner likely was angered further by this sincere response, which he may have perceived as not stereotypically gendered enough nor stereotypically Black-submissive enough, as he, the store owner, was holding all of the power at that moment. His response to me was that he "would call the police on a five-year-old for stealing a bubble gum," and he promptly instructed the manager to call the police. I am not sure whether that was a punishment meant for a too-uppity me or a punishment meant for my young relative, but I do know that it was my young relative who suffered. Not at all suggesting that it's right for a child to steal. However, it certainly wasn't anything that could not have been resolved within a few seconds by my paying for the cards and by asking his parents to counsel him at their home on the matter.

Nonetheless, we found ourselves surrounded by the store managers, the mall's security guards, the city's police, and state troopers—some of them with their hands placed not far from their gun holsters, which may have given the impression, real or not, that they were ready to pull and shoot at the drop of a hat even for a little eight-year-old Black child. I looked over at the little fellow and observed that he had literally disassociated from or left his body. He had taken his "self" to the ceiling or some other remote but safer place, I guess, as only a shell of himself seemed physically to be standing there as the various police stood all around us. I was trying to fully perceive that all of this was over two small packs of cards for which I had begged to pay, but to no avail. As I tried to process all of this, it seemed that everything was in slow motion, with the slow, stretched out, distorted voices of the police officers and manager, with their heads turning and looking at the little one as if they were seeing a six-foot-tall, stout, grown man stupefied, holding a bloody knife in his hand, but frozen in space where they could gawk at him, and occasionally at me. This young, African American second-grader became a criminal justice case in the juvenile system in that district, and was processed for larceny from a store. I was told by the officers that had I not been standing there (for example, if I had been upstairs browsing at the record store where I often was), that my beloved young relative would have been carried off by the police to a juvenile detention center, ninety minutes away. His parents, and many others among their and my circles of family, our communities, and friends, believed that had this young relative been a little White child, he would have had more humane, age-appropriate options. He would have received a good talking-to by the store manager, maybe a phone call from security to his parents or a warning, along with being made to pay for the cards—but not processing into the criminal justice system. This system is known as the preschool-to-prison pipeline. A few days later the primary parent called the owner of the store to request a meeting to discuss the incident and was stunned to be told by him that he "does not meet with criminals and their families."

Over the years, I took note of how that incident impacted that child and his parents' rearing of him. From that point, one of the parents seemed to become significantly much stricter and more protective of him, not wanting to let him out of sight, almost to the point of protectively suffocating him. This particular parent also became much firmer and somewhat militaristic in discipline, out of fear of the bigger threats that obviously could await a Black child outside of the home.

Also, since that time, I myself have taken greater conscious note of a lifetime of my own discomfort in consumer marketplaces. For example, memories of my own anxiety when I was an older child and teen in many consumer marketplaces, and the burden of always keeping my hands visible, and making sure that I did not make any moves that could be mistaken for stealing. I've also found myself noting the way that various stores' and other consumer personnel addressed me, made assumptions about me, and treated me; their treatment often varying with my hairstyles, the professional formality of my clothing, or who was present with me, be they White, light-skinned, or dark-skinned in complexion. These kinds of marketplace incidents were like water is to a fish—you may not really think about them until something drastic happens, like the time I came home to find that my one fish had jumped out of its tank and died. The little fish, I suspect, finally knew as she was dying what water was. Watching this young relative dissociating as police held their hands a little too close to their guns for my comfort was like watching that fish lying on the ground, flopping and grasping for water. I knew plain as day what marketplace racism was then. It had reached a tipping point for me, to the point that I could now more clearly see it and name it, just like that little fish knew that life-sustaining water was missing from its nostrils, fins, or whatever parts fish use to survive when water reaches them. Being able to name it, as well as seeing countless incidents and catastrophes reported in the news and other media about it have helped me know how serious it is. Studying it also through books, journal articles, and news accounts written about marketplace racism, and by having the daunting privilege to personally hear stories and traumas gleaned from extensive interviews that I conducted with victims across the country, has allowed marketplace racism (also known as retail racism or "shopping while Black") to now have a well-formed, nameable body and face, and it is a significant thing! It is a huge monster that continues to create anxiety, traumatize, and otherwise negatively impact many people of color just as it has for centuries. The only difference—to use a famous Will Smith phrase about racism—is that "it's now getting filmed."

So, this is the polluted water in which many of us live and breathe on a day-to-day basis. Going to the mall, shopping for clothes, paying a bill, riding an airplane, making an insurance claim, or even just trying to live with our families in peace at home. Many of us are surrounded by racism so deeply that sometimes we as a society have gotten used to it to the point that we can't clearly see it. Or, alternatively, we've learned to function within it, and in doing so, some of us unfortunately are either dying from it or dying trying to escape it.

The pandemic seems to have offered us an opportunity to see this "polluted water," that has encapsulated many of us for centuries, with greater visual clarity. Maybe because many of us have been quarantined and have been watching the news like never before, or maybe because some events have been so shocking that they are unbelievable. One of the most striking and traumatizing to our nation occurred on the date of May 25, 2020, after a young man in Minneapolis, Minnesota, walked into a convenience store with his buddy. Reportedly he was intoxicated and also tried to spend a counterfeit $20 bill to make a purchase. The clerk called the police to report this. Just minutes later, that young man, George Floyd, was dead. Although it was not the intention of the store staff to see anyone die over a $20 bill, apparently less than exemplar consumer conduct combined with historically unchecked white-supremacist law enforcement practices caused a trip to the store to end in the nine-minute-and-twenty-nine-second murder of a young man who was loved by his family, multiple communities, and now the world over. The tragedy of George Floyd's death by a police officer's knee in his back gave us a real-life horror. It visually documented what Black people have known and experienced either in person or vicariously for five-hundred years. But this time, it was brought visually and devastatingly into full detail to as far away as online signals travel within the universe.

Ironically, on that very same day, another Black man, Christian Cooper, was partaking in his love for birdwatching in Central Park and had the police called on him by a woman premeditatedly dramatizing as if she were being attacked after they had words. In the weeks leading up to these two events, there was Ahmaud Arbery, Breonna Taylor, and so many other tragic victims—and all of this in the midst of a mishandled Covid-19 pandemic. The deaths of 318,000 U.S. victims by the end of 2020, and nearly 600,000 as we approached the middle of 2021—consisting of disproportionate numbers of Black and Brown people—seemed to be too familiar of a theme, as many families and communities dealt with bereavement overload, trauma, and vicarious victimization.

With the onset of the pandemic, I found myself extremely thankful to still have a job when I observed that so many suddenly did not. After more than three decades of teaching in-person, fall of 2020 was my first full semester of teaching remotely. During that semester, I was blessed to teach an "Introduction to Human Development" class with twenty-eight brilliant first-year undergraduate scholars, who were rigorously riding the waves of the pandemic themselves. Although a predominantly White class, they were somewhat of a diverse class as well. There was a reasonable mix of Hispanic, African American, Caribbean, and Asian students. To my surprise, I began to find that teaching in a pandemic has been both a challenge and also a blessing, in that it seems that my students hear me differently over Zoom. Perhaps also I am a somewhat different professor over Zoom, as I teach from home. Home is where I raised my children and cried and fought to protect them from a world not built with them in mind. Home is where I have emotionally worked out many of these struggles and helped my children to work out theirs. So, my mind is focused a little bit differently as I teach from home within the context of a pandemic that, God forbid, could kill me or anyone at any given moment. Thus, in this new remote mode, I found myself teaching a bit differently and listening quite differently—and the listening overwhelmed my heart at times. So, as we were nearing the end of our first fall semester in a pandemic, I was teaching on the topic of factors that we can build on within children, families, and communities to help strengthen collaborative community work. In talking about this, I mentioned the preschool-to-prison pipeline. In my courses I often discuss the preschool-to-prison pipeline that exists for many youth, (no) thanks to the kinds of inequitable practices, even in stores and other public spaces on which this book will focus. In our lecture, we were focusing on the importance of governmental structural and systemic support of grassroots community programs to help preventively strengthen children, families, and communities that have been disenfranchised throughout generations. My students and I were connecting the preschool-to-prison pipeline to the lack of structural and systemic support of underserved communities. After

I further explained how the preschool-to-prison pipeline is the system of structural and systemic policies that move large numbers of Black, Brown, and poor children straight to law enforcement and incarceration at a young age, one of my students, Shamar, spoke up on the Zoom. Initially I had difficulty hearing this intellectually engaged young man of color from a large Midwestern city—a city about which many observers have inaccurate, stereotypic notions. Not hearing him clearly, I asked him to repeat himself. He said, "The preschool-to-prison pipeline is real. . . . We can even skip this and go like [straight] through to the preschool-to-grave pipeline." "Oh, oh, my goodness. . . . Yes!" I exclaimed, as I was a bit emotionally overwhelmed by the truth of his comment. Shamar continued on:

> A lot of parents of color [where I grew up] understood that the preschool-to-grave pipeline is real and pushed their children to take advantage of their education and any extra programs or supports they could find. . . . Because, like, I literally know [those] who are in jail right now, or who have died or who have been there for like such a long time, because they weren't able to grab these opportunities. . . . Because the environment that they live in is an [underserved] environment where a lot of leaders of color have high [burdens]. . . . [This is all] portrayed in the media in different ways. You can focus on changing the outcome of the situation, or you can focus on preventing the situation. Some policy-makers don't get that the day you don't have preventive educational community programs such as Big Brothers Big Sisters, tutoring, mentoring, etc., then you are going to have to focus on the outcome of the situation such as prison or death. . . . I think preventive programs are imperative.

Shamar's comments hit me extremely hard, especially as I thought of all of the perils of 2020 and beyond, and the racist, victim-blaming ideologies that were being promoted throughout these times (and for decades and centuries). When in reality, the systemically racist structures have set disenfranchised communities up to fail, and then blamed the victims. Shamar was eloquently pointing out how in his world, many youth live in such precarious and structurally neglected and overly policed communities that they end up in the grave either during or before getting to the prisons that were premeditatedly and systemically built for them. His sharing helped the class to further understand how serious and even critical these issues are.

The real-life experience of a beautiful little Brown child going into a store and taking two packs of sports cards and having multiple police agencies appear and process him into the criminal justice system, rather than his chaperone being appropriately engaged and allowed to pay for the cards, is an example of how the preschool-to-prison or preschool-to-grave pipeline can get started in a child's life. Such devastating consequences for a young child's slip-up becomes many children's norms—being over-policed, over-penalized, treated as criminals before they can even get past the second grade, all of which move them straight into the school-(or preschool)-to-prison pipeline, or worse, the school-to-grave pipeline, as Shamar reminded our class. The year 2020 has been a year like no other for illustrating the preschool-to-grave pipeline, and, hopefully, we will never see a year like it again. George Floyd, Ahmaud Arbery, Breonna Taylor, and many other unnecessary deaths, the nationwide backlash over protests, the many videos of African American consumers being harassed while shopping, the health disparities and Covid-19 casualties in the United States and throughout the world, the terrorist insurrection at the Capitol, and the targeting and killing of Asian women service workers, all speak to some of the horrifically tumultuous events of 2020 and the first half of 2021.

Many have thought of shopping, especially pre-pandemic, as an all-American, leisurely activity for everyone. However, for Black and Brown and a vast array of disenfranchised people, shopping has always been exceptionally stressful and full of elements of precarity and danger. Let us not forget that George Floyd's life ended brutally, violently, and vulgarly over an incident that started in a store—when a police officer used that incident as an opportunity to treat him viciously. In the pages ahead, although the incidences are nowhere near as physically or emotionally violent as that endured by George Floyd, nineteen insightful people, several talented poets and spoken-word and visual artists tell the story of their pain, their frustration, the occasional use of humor in coping, and the creativity of victims within the Black and Brown consumer-marketplace experience. These materials reveal that even in the third decade of the twenty-first century, we still are in need of a world where everyone's truth is valued and responded to. It is my hope that this book will help to tell more of the reality concerning what the marketplace is like for many Black and Brown people. I hope that it will help those who are unaware, to acknowledge that this problem exists and, further, that change is needed. I hope also that this book will serve as a resource—that it will help move people from all walks of life and at all levels of power to be further inspired either toward making change or toward demanding change.

In sum, this book is what I have done with my pain when more than two decades ago I had no ability to help a beloved child learn in the manner in which a child should have been able to learn. It's the vehicle for change that God has inspired in me for placing my anger and passion about these matters. It's my allowing Him to take what was meant for bad, and hopefully having it be used for some goodness. I hope that these stories will greatly matter to many, as Black lives, and the quality of Black and Brown lives, do matter. May the diverse, incredible voices—heroic voices—who tell their stories through different forms of media, be a resource that gives us strength, that blesses us, and that propels us to greater change so that every day, mundane, leisurely, and fun activities like shopping can feel more like whatever normal is, even post-pandemic; not predominantly just to the privileged, but to everyone.

INTRODUCTION

I go into the convenience store with my twelve-year-old son and my seven-year-old nephew. I've just picked them up from school and they are hungry. The store is our pit stop on the way to the local public library to which I had promised to take them. We all selected a snack and drinks and headed to the cash register and sat our items on the counter. Hungry, beautiful Brown boys are excitedly smiling, just waiting to grab their stuff and get to the car to start snacking. The young White lady asks me, "Cash or EBT?" (Electronic Benefits Transfer Card, also known as welfare or food stamps). I am familiar with EBT, and I am not saying that I'm above using it if needed. It's that I'm thinking what happened to the "debit" and "credit" options as well? And why? And I'm getting a little heated. Thank God Pastor prayed for everyone in service yesterday, so I calm myself down while all of this happens internally within a split second. To protect my emotions, I play dumb and respond with, "What's EBT?" She looks surprised—in fact a little shocked—and she replies, "It's food stamps." I then say, nice and loud, "I'LL BE PAYING WITH ***DEBIT****!" And I swipe my card with the most delight ever, grab my bags, grab my boys, and walk away!* (personal journal entry, Michelle R. Dunlap, March 24, 2014)

One of the most vivid stories my father has told me concerning his upbringing in the 1940s and 1950s involved the consumer marketplace. My father is biracial, and through no doing of his own, he is someone whom strangers easily assume to be White. He told me a story of when he was a young teen of thirteen or fourteen years old. He, his African American father (i.e., my grandfather), and a friend of my grandfather's (also African American) traveled from Detroit to West Virginia by automobile to see relatives there. As they were passing through Ohio, their car experienced a flat tire. When my grandfather and his buddy pulled off the road and into a gas station to get the tire repaired as my dad slept in the back seat of the car, the White attendant took one look at my grandfather and turned this proud man away—refusing to assist him at all. Using a combination of half-desperation and half-creativity, my grandfather drove the wobbling car up the road a bit. Grandpa got out of the car and removed the tire, and awakened my father. Then he gave his young teenager some money to pay for the repair, instructing him to roll the tire up the road back to the gas station to request assistance. My father did just that. The attendant, having not seen or noticed my father earlier sleeping in the back seat of the car, and assuming that the teen was White, obliged him right away, kindly fixing the tire and sending my dad along his way. Dad rolled the tire back up the road to where my grandfather and his buddy were waiting. The men reattached the tire, and all three were back on their journey to West Virginia in no time! While sharing this memory with me, Dad explained this was "everyday life" for him, his White mother, and his Black father in that era. Thus, even *marketplace* experiences like this one were "just a way of life" as he describes it, for him and his parents. We may say to ourselves that things have changed a lot since the 1950s. Surely marketplace experiences are much more equitable, comfortable, and enjoyable for people of color since that era—or are they?

MARKETPLACE RACIAL PROFILING STILL HEAVILY EXISTS

Unfortunately, marketplace racial profiling still exists. Marketplace racial profiling is when, in consumer environments, apparent African American, Indigenous, and many cultures of people of color (i.e., BIPOCs, or Black, Indigenous, and People of Color) are examined more closely for criminal or other negative behavior than their White or White-appearing counterparts displaying identical behavior. Such profiling is associated with marketplace discrimination or inequitable treatment, which is when staff or administration subject an individual or even a community to different policies or procedures than their White counterparts or communities exhibiting identical behavior. Discrimination based on race, gender, disability, religion, or any protected category is illegal, even in a marketplace. However, at the beginning of the third decade of the twenty-first century, the high number of cases being brought forth for marketplace racial profiling suggest that "consumer discrimination remains a problem in the U.S. marketplace."[1]

In a 2017 survey of African American New Yorkers, 80 percent reported having experienced retail marketplace inequitable treatment[2] or "the practice of racial profiling in retail settings," known in the research literature and colloquially among people of color as "Shopping While Black."[3] Such experiences can include being unjustly suspected of, accused of, or arrested for stealing; disproportionate monitoring; being subjected to unfair or inequitable treatment, such as being refused service or charged higher prices or greater interest rates for products; having the police called over nothing; or being physically or even mortally harmed by staff or other customers for no legitimate reason. Thus, people of color go shopping for goods and services just like everyone else, but besides those goods and services, they often also return having received a plethora of racist experiences. Because of these kinds of experiences, the consumer marketplace can be an anxiety-provoking place of constant discomfort for a disproportionate number of people of color. Not only are such experiences extremely stressful, but they make the retail marketplace a much more unpleasant venue for many people of color than the consistently leisurely and enjoyable one that the media and popular culture portray. A 2007 survey sampling of Philadelphia area residents found that African Americans were ten times more likely than their non–African American counterparts to experience such profiling; men were twice as likely to experience it as women; higher educated respondents were more likely to report experiencing this marketplace profiling than their less educated counterparts; while income showed no correlations with this phenomenon.[4] Another study actually tested how frequently different-race research teammates posing as "customers wanting to try on a pair of sunglasses" would be closely monitored. The findings revealed that staff were more likely to carefully watch and follow the Black and the male "customers."[5]

The 1866 post-enslavement period federal court legislation was supposed to ensure that consumers are treated equitably. The legislation reads, "A dollar in the hands of a Negro will purchase the same thing as a dollar in the hands of a white man."[6] Nonetheless, very few consumer racial profiling cases have succeeded up until now because of their difficulty to prove. However, as technology and information-sharing is improving, the ability to prove these cases are gaining potential as we saw, for example, with the notorious 2018 Starbucks-video case in Philadelphia, which was swiftly settled out of court. Studies and other types of documentation concerning this topic, spanning all continents, reveal that disparities in consumer treatment exists not only in the United States but also in other places throughout the world.[7]

THE IRONY OF MARKETPLACE RACIAL PROFILING

Although African Americans have been for centuries—and continue to be—one of the most economically disenfranchised groups in our nation, ironically, we manage to contribute in excess of $1.2 trillion annually into the economy.[8] Thus, in spite of being only 12 to 14 percent of the U.S. population and having an individual net value that averages only one-tenth of our White counterparts', we continue to be a group that contributes incredible amounts of financial resources to the national economy. We also are one of the most generous categories of people, with African Americans being known for sharing what we have. Our donations tend to be 25 percent higher than our White counterparts', and with "nearly two-thirds of Black households making charitable donations, totaling $11 billion a year."[9] Because of the extended family kinship or collectivist nature of Africana cultures, if our nondocumented giving were tracked, the giving figures likely would be exponentially higher. Further, people living in poverty as well as people of color are subject to exploitive business practices in our communities.[10] Prices are inflated, interest rates are hiked to unbelievable proportions, and the quality of products are diminished. In these poor and Black communities, businesses, advertising, and billboards are composed disproportionately of liquor, marijuana, pawn, and gun-trade promotions.[11] Poor and minoritized (i.e., made to hold a minority status) youth, adults, and communities are exploited through marketing campaigns and businesses such as rent-to-own companies and check-cashing kiosks that capitalize on the vulnerabilities of the disenfranchised who may lack transportation and thus mobility, have fewer economic, savings, and loan resources, less education, and more compromised health. In spite of these facts and the support of the consumer marketplace by people of color, past and recent current events suggest that inequity, discomfort, and even trauma have never ended for people of color engaging in the consumer marketplace.

VENUES AND PROFILES OF MARKETPLACE RACISM

Unlike the stereotype that many have of retail settings (leisurely, fun, friendly, etc.), such spaces often consist of "sites where anti-Black bias is made evident, requiring Black shoppers to navigate racial hierarchies while procuring goods."[12] Secondly, Cassi Pittman argues that the profiling and discrimination experienced by people of color in consumer-marketplace landscapes "alters the experience of shopping, arguably raising the costs and reducing the rewards derived from consumption [and preventing it from being] a form of leisure [and] changing the meaning and status attached to goods."[13] The truth of Pittman's arguments is clear within the many recent accounts reported in the media, as well as within the in-depth interviews of this book.

IN STORES

Marketplace racial profiling and incidences of inequity from over the years have been, and still are, daily, widespread, and innumerable for people of color. They extend to every marketplace venue imaginable, including shopping, dining, educational, medical, traveling and vacationing, walking or transporting to or from engaging in the marketplace, contracting, sports and leisure activities, banking, and other marketplace businesses. For example, a couple is suing a large retailer in Maryland for four million dollars for allegedly wrongly accusing them of shoplifting.[14] A high school student on a school assignment at a Colorado mall was wrongly accused by another shopper of stealing a wallet.[15] A store clerk reportedly called the police on a college student for being arrogant and Black.[16] A woman in Texas was reported to have been shot and killed by a security guard on suspicion of shoplifting.[17] Reportedly, people of color, mostly Black, have been shot and killed by store staff, security, or police over suspicions of stealing a $4 bracelet,[18] an energy drink,[19] soda,[20] beer,[21] a cake,[22] etc. Twenty-one-year-old Emantic "EJ" Fitzgerald Bradford Jr. was shot and killed by law enforcement in an Alabama mall while he was trying to protect strangers after mayhem broke out in the mall. Law enforcement say it was an accident, but his family says that it was murder.[23] At a far opposite extreme, a suspected White supremacist was arrested peacefully in an El Paso Walmart after horrifically massacring twenty-two mostly Hispanic shoppers between the ages of fifteen and ninety, and injuring another twenty-four.[24]

Upscale retailers in Maryland, Missouri, Oregon, and throughout the country have been publicly called out for calling police on teenagers who come to their stores to shop in preparation for their proms and other occasions.[25] Community protesters are reported to have temporarily shut down a neighborhood store after a video showed an employee kicking one of its Black customers.[26] Several videos have been posted online documenting fellow customer-strangers eavesdropping on people of color in grocery stores, commenting on their use of food stamps, their personal conversations, and unleashing negative, stereotypic notions about them.[27] A business owner in Michigan was reported to have apologized for spitting on a Black man over a dispute regarding a parking space as he was trying to patronize a nearby business.[28] Two employees in Illinois were fired for calling the police on a Black woman over a coupon dispute.[29] In a Massachusetts grocery store, a White man called a Black woman's two young sons "profanity-laced racist epithets."[30] A nine-year-old boy in New York made worldwide news when he and his mother and siblings visited a neighborhood bodega only to have a White woman vehemently, but wrongly, accuse the young boy of grabbing her backseat.[31] Many people think that such incidences are both new and rare, but they are not, as people of color have experienced these incidences for decades and even centuries—if and when we were even allowed in such establishments—and the incidences are too numerous to count.

IN RESTAURANTS

Such incidences extend to dining venues as well. For example, a Minnesota couple complained and a national restaurant reportedly apologized for using photos of lynchings for their table décor.[32] Applebee's restaurant reportedly admitted to racial profiling at a Missouri restaurant and issued an apology.[33] Several restaurants have admitted to or publicly apologized for either making Black patrons pay in advance or for calling the police to ensure that Black patrons pay, to settle disputes over coupons, or just out of fear grounded in no reason, sometimes resulting in large settlements and employee firings.[34] An Oklahoma restaurant owner is reported to have claimed that he refuses service to "freaks, faggots, the disabled, and welfare recipients."[35]A Muslim high school student in Illinois was harassed by a customer at a local restaurant who yelled racial comments at her, and told her that if she "doesn't like this country, leave."[36] A White man is reported to have faced hate crime charges when, during an altercation with a Black man, he yelled, "Shut up, slave!"[37] A Black comedian is reported to have been awarded a $6,000 settlement (for his favorite charity) after a server commented that she "doesn't like serving Blacks."[38] In a story that had worldwide reach, two men were arrested in a Pennsylvania Starbucks coffee shop, and later settled for $200,000 to donate to youth entrepreneurs. In Tennessee, a White man shot and killed four Black and Hispanic patrons in a Waffle House restaurant before being tackled by a fifth patron of color.[39] A young woman requesting a plastic fork with her Waffle House order had police called on her and was brutalized in the course of being arrested.[40] In Minnesota, a group of Somali teens were asked to leave a McDonald's restaurant when a White man exited while reportedly pulling a gun on the youths.[41]

IN OTHER MARKETPLACES

Similar and numerous incidences have been reported concerning travel and transportation, medical, educational, recreation/leisure, contracting, banking and loans, and community marketplaces. Even with many online options and a pandemic, shopping and otherwise conducting business in the consumer marketplace still is a part of the day-to-day experience of many people in the twenty-first century. Conflicts with protective masks aside, shopping is an experience that the majority of people in the Western world, and especially America, may not expect to be overly complicated. But, what does that experience look like and feel like to people of color in the twenty-first century, compared to, say, that of my grandfather whom I mentioned at the beginning of this chapter? And how might those experiences still relate to the concept of microaggressions even in these modern times? Both historically and currently there are greater complexities to moving about in the retail and consumer marketplace than some might expect—even as simple as having to show more ID to make a purchase.[42] Studies suggest that African American consumers report feeling profiled in consumer marketplaces ten times more often than their White counterparts,[43] and the vast majority of African Americans feel that they have experienced racial profiling or other disparate treatment in retail stores and other consumer marketplaces.[44]

Other studies have reported that in the not-too-distant past, it was *common* for store employees to instruct their staff to closely monitor, in particular, their customers of color.[45] These incidences and other findings suggest that whether shopping in stores, waiting, walking, parking, traveling, getting medical care, contracting, or any number of other things that we do in our day-to-day lives, at any given moment stress can arise from being treated without the respect, trust, and dignity that is deserving of any human being. Some recent reports suggest that how people of color are treated in service domains such as schools, medical care, and so on, can be influenced in part by how much providers have in common or how well they can relate to their students, patients, or clients. For example, some studies indicate that practitioners may provide greater care and compassion to those with whom they feel a cultural connection.[46] Thus, the less connected that service providers or staff feel to diverse categories of people, the more likely they may be to treat those groups in detached and less-than-empathic ways.

CONSIDERATIONS FOR MARKETERS

These all are serious issues for the marketplace to consider, both for ethical and financial reasons. The marketplace is currently losing White customers who are not accustomed to these traumas, so how much faster may they lose their consumers of color? Research is showing that African American customers already disproportionately outpace their White consumer counterparts and a variety of other racial and ethnic groups in online internet usage and some categories of online shopping.[47] Could racial profiling trends play a role in this greater engagement online? While research indicates that African Americans shop more, it also suggests that we spend more time online, which could include online shopping.[48] Even before the pandemic, retailers found that "something has gone missing in American commerce," which has been "in a funk,"[49] with it tending to find significant dips especially in face-to-face shopping[50] resulting in many famous, and even long-standing, stores closing.[51] Unfortunately, this trend has only increased since the pandemic. At the same time, on a larger, structural level, unfair business practices aimed at people of color and the less privileged have come under fire in recent years. For example, it is commonly known that people of color often pay more—and a much greater proportion of their income—for their basic needs such as food, cars, housing, utilities, and appliances.[52] For example, African Americans who make up roughly 12 percent of the U.S. population also constitute 31 percent or almost one-third of the rent-to-own industry customers.[53] Likewise, because automobile retailers have been charged with making people of color pay higher base amounts and interest rates for automobiles than their White counterparts, the Justice Department has been examining the fairness and equity of car loans and rates.[54] This is reminiscent of the redlining practices that occurred for many decades, making it very difficult for African Americans to buy homes rather than renting, the impact of which is still significantly felt today in the poverty rates for African Americans.[55]

What role could Black and Brown consumers and our dollars be playing in the decline of stores and malls across the country? African Americans and many people of color tend not to be passive marketplace victims, but rather we are creative protestors, and protesting with our dollar is one of our greatest strategies.[56] Nonetheless, back to the question posed earlier: how much have things changed for people of color in the marketplace since the 1950s when my grandfather, father, and their friend traveled to West Virginia and could not outright get a tire repaired? Surely, marketplace experiences are much more equitable, comfortable, and enjoyable for people of color since that era—or are they? In order to more completely answer that question, we also need to examine the larger contexts of Black and Brown life in American society and beyond. What we see in the marketplace is an extension of the overall quality of life that often exists for people or color in America.

The kinds of incidences that we see above are a reflection of minoritized life in America, both historically—since colonization, genocide of Indigenous tribes, violence toward and enslavement of Africans beginning more than four hundred years ago, postenslavement violence, oppression, and exploitation of a variety of minoritized groups—and currently. While many people would like to believe that prejudice, stereotyping, racism, and discrimination are no longer an issue in our society, most people of color and allies, and many scholars and daily news reports, assert that our country is still deeply plagued by and divided on racial issues, behavior, and understanding.

Thus, BIPOCs' marketplace experiences are embedded within the larger context of history and life in a society that was developed, honed, and prospered on White supremacy, racism, and racist ideology, also known as the "White racial frame."[57] The White racial frame consists of all of the ways, means, and rationalizations that have propelled White supremacy and its many forms. The overarching presence of White supremacy among the governmental structures and systems that surround people of color, mean that White supremacy can impact each individual in a unique and complex way, depending on the multiple categories or layers of vulnerability that one holds (e.g., race, gender, sexual orientation, economic status).[58] Because of the many forms of violence that can accompany White supremacy, the marketplace, or even society in general, have never been considered safe spaces for most people of color. For example, many incidents that resulted in the brutal lynching of Black humans, and sometimes other minoritized people and allies, began in the consumer marketplace. This is so true that during the Jim Crow period and since, Black consumers have had resources such as the Green Book to help us travel safely from one marketplace to another, including hotels, restaurants, and so on.[59] The creation of a Green Book also further illustrates for us that African Americans and other minoritized groups never have been passive consumers, but have found ways to resist our exploitation any way that we could. However, the difference between the past and the present is that BIPOC shoppers' options have increased exponentially with the growth of technology, the internet, customer feedback and networking, do-it-yourself (DIY) educational videos, and so on.[60] Unlike in the past, people of color and allies now have the capability to video record the very abuses that we have experienced since the days that we either were dragged onto enslavement ships as involuntary minorities, were otherwise colonized, or whatever other means we experienced arriving here. For example, based on recent news accounts stemming from videos of racist incidents, the National Association for the Advancement of Colored People (NAACP) has begun issuing travel advisories for certain states and areas of the country, as well as for airlines, because of civil rights violations.[61] Given the disproportionately large contribution that African American and other minoritized peoples make to the economy, these kinds of measures should be a significant concern for many marketers. But first, there should be concern because equitable treatment of customers and other clientele is a moral and ethical issue, and is the right thing to do, no matter how much any group spends. Secondly, there should be concern because businesses can lose their customer bases due to negative reviews, video exposures, negative reporting, boycotting, and other sanctioning. Thus, as businesses are discovering, they can find themselves at risk of closing down.

HISTORICAL AND CURRENT WHITE SUPREMACY

The shopping-while-Black or retail racism conversation is one subset within the larger issue of Black experiences in predominantly White-controlled environments, White supremacist spaces, or spaces of color where White supremacist ideologies have been internalized. In these spaces, most White people themselves are not our enemy, but internalized, structural, or systemic White supremacy is. White supremacy is defined here as the normalized notion that whiteness is better; more trustworthy; superior; worthier of notice, acknowledgment, or respect; and more capable of the ruling of society than blackness and other racial statuses. It includes the maintaining of the exploitive powers, structures, violence, laws, and economics that have created and maintained the oppression of Black and Indigenous people, especially, as well as other people of color, the poor, and those otherwise disenfranchised. "White allies" are people who work in collaboration with African American, Indigenous, and other historically disenfranchised people to resist and remediate these personal, social, economic, and policy patterns that undergird White supremacy. According to the FBI, White supremacy, at its extremes, poses a "persistent, pervasive threat" to the United States and its national security,[62] and we saw evidence of that with the terrorist insurrection at the U.S. Capitol on January 6, 2021.

The structural underpinnings of White supremacy always have been, and continue to be, a tremendous, constant threat to the socioeconomic sustainability of families of color. Because of more than four hundred years of White supremacy, it would take a Black family about 228 years to catch up to the accumulated wealth of the average of their White counterparts, and that's with the Black family doing everything to some kind of unknown perfection in conjunction with society not negatively impacting anyone in the family with unfair or inequitable laws, policies, and so on.[63] The prospects for most Indigenous tribes may be even worse. This means that no matter how hard people of color work and do all the "right" things, individual perpetrators and the currently existing systemic structures contribute heavily to social ills, such as poverty, health disparities, and, our main focus here, marketplace racism. Even people of color can internalize White supremacist ideologies and contribute to the marketplace racism problem, such as a clerk or security officer of color assuming that a Black or Brown person is more likely to steal than a White one. Even one brush with the law can add decades to the 228 years that it takes to catch up.

Because marketplace experiences also are within the larger context of maneuvering in spaces (roads, sidewalks, etc.) in order to get to shopping and other marketplace venues (such as hospitals, educational institutions, etc.), at times this book will include the experiences that can happen before, during, and after marketplace experiences per se. In order to get to consumer marketplaces (other than online ones) one often has to leave the relative protection of one's home, enter transportation spaces, and then further navigate entering and engaging with the marketplace venue, exiting the venue, and returning home. At every point of engagement there can be risks, as will be shared further.

Retail racism finally is becoming a human resources and public relations issue as documentation methods have improved. For example, some perpetrators of racist behaviors have gotten fired from their jobs, and increasing numbers of businesses have had to pay out large settlements for the discriminatory behavior of their staff. Even so, as a society, even in the latter half of the second decade of a new century, many components of society, and marketplace businesses in particular, still have a long way to go when it comes to understanding racial issues and their day-to-day impact on traditionally disenfranchised groups and individuals whose true stories tend to go untold, unheard, unnoticed, or not validated. Many are still unaware of the impact of our nation's severe systemic economic, education, employment, incarceration, health, and mortality disparities that exist between Black people and White counterparts in our society[64] or are not interested in working collaboratively to ameliorate them. For example, Black health disparities outpace those of White counterparts sometimes by decades in every major disease, especially those exacerbated by stress. Home ownership rates and property values are disproportionately less than our White counterparts, which is the number one way that families accumulate wealth, educate their children, and prepare for retirement. The educational terrain for youth of color is so problematic that it has come to be known as the preschool-to-prison pipeline, or as my student Shamar calls it, the preschool-to-grave pipeline. In all, the traditionally disenfranchised are far from economic, health, and quality of life parity with their White counterparts, and it shows from the prenatal period, throughout life, and all the way to death and dying. Thus, this is the context in which the minoritized shopping experience is embedded.

To add to this, many people of color find that they are racially profiled in their day-to-day activities, and fear being singled out and accused of things that they did not do. Studies have indicated that there is good reason to feel that way, with African Americans and Hispanics being not only more frequently searched, charged with a crime, and arrested but also more likely to do prison time for identical crimes as their White counterparts, and for longer periods.[65] These trends are mirrored among youths of color but are considerably bleaker statistically, especially for boys of color.[66] Assuring us that these statistics are not happening by accident, nor completely by the fault of youth and adults being incarcerated, a recent Department of Justice study has found that some municipalities have targeted African Americans to bring them into their court systems with the primary purpose of increasing revenue.[67] In one case, a judge was sentenced to twenty-eight years in prison for selling mostly Black or poor "kids for cash" into the juvenile incarceration system to economically benefit himself and the prison industrial complex.[68] The preschool-to-prison pipeline, inequitable justice system, and the prison industrial complex have prompted social philosophers of our day, such as Bryan Stevenson, to conclude that, "slavery didn't end in 1865, it just evolved."[69]

The wider contexts for historically minoritized life in America help to explain why flying on an airplane, walking to or from the store, making a small or major purchase, browsing, dining, or stopping for gas or snacks at a convenience store can be so frequently traumatizing for people of color. There seems to be a frequency and randomness to the bizarre things that can happen when the people serving or waiting on us may perceive us as a stereotype or statistic rather than as a person. But it is not as random as it may seem to those unfamiliar with it. For those from traditionally disenfranchised groups and our allies, it is already understood that even today these experiences are common and are the result of the perpetuation of the history, practices, and policies created early in American history from its White supremacist roots, White supremacist nurturing, sanctioning, harvesting, and perpetual fruition. The inequities, stress, and trauma that it engenders even today are illustrated in the stories told in the parts and chapters ahead.

TWELVE OBSERVATIONS CONCERNING RETAIL RACISM OR "SHOPPING WHILE BLACK AND BROWN"

Below are some key elements of what I have gleaned concerning retail racism based on the nineteen interviews that I conducted and more than five hundred news articles, in addition to books and journal articles, that I have collected.

1. Marketplace Racial Profiling Is Felt Early in Life

People of color, even from a wide range of socioeconomic backgrounds, often know from a very young age that they are suspected and are being watched in consumer marketplaces, thus adding to minoritized children's daily stresses and burdens. Research also shows that African Americans experience retail racism most significantly, but are not the only minoritized groups impacted by it.[70]

2. Marketplace Racism Throws Life-Altering Nightmares into the "American Dream"

It's been said that racial profiling is just an old problem under new scrutiny. Thus, for many minoritized groups, the marketplace still can be a place of angst, anxiety, disparity, and trauma because of the negative and inaccurate stereotypes believed of Black people and other people of color being untrustworthy, out of control, or dangerous.[71] The bottom line is that the consumer marketplace often is not the place of community, fun, and leisure that more privileged groups may find it to be, if it ever was for the minoritized. Therefore, compared to other forms of discrimination, this can be an exceptionally insidious and burdensome form of racism for Black and Brown people, no matter how much success one achieves.

3. Over-Monitoring of Black and Brown Bodies Is an Overarching Issue in the Marketplace

As the stories shared in this book will reveal, the diversity of shoppers and their experiences in consumer marketplaces vary widely. People of any particular "race" or background who are discussed in one story may behave as a perpetrator, and in another story may behave as a victim, and yet in another story may behave as an ally. The collection of stories reveal that it's not races who are our enemies, but rather the internalization of supremacist ideologies combined with the holding of power to enact or execute such ideologies upon people which can impact their quality of life and put their well-being at risk. The interviews also suggest that there is a complicated paradox where Black and Brown people feel both invisible and hypermonitored within the marketplace at the same time. Meaning that marketplace personnel may seem to vacillate between the two extremes where BIPOC shoppers may be ignored when needing assistance, but overly monitored when not needing assistance. Such incidences may be resurged by variations in contextual and political climates. For example, with the increased militarization of law enforcement and the resurgence and tripling of hate groups and hate rhetoric in America in the past twenty years,[72] people of color can feel greater tensions concerning being invisibly ignored, or at the other extreme, being scrutinized as if holding criminal tendencies as we try to conduct our day-to-day affairs. Heightened surveillance of people of color exacerbates the negative and inequitable tendencies that already exist, even in malls, convenience stores, and other consumer marketplaces. Some have explained these trends as being caused by the historical and ever-present fear of Black people and other people of color.[73] This fear prompts culturally skittish or fragile White people to closely monitor and easily overreact if people of color take the same comforts and liberties within public and other spaces that White people take (such as, get comfortable at a coffee house and chat for an extended time before ordering, or even terrorize the U.S. Capitol in large numbers).

4. People of Color Are Not at Fault for Marketplace Racism

It's not the fault of the victims of racism that this social problem still exists but rather the intentional and unintentional perpetuators of it are responsible. Also responsible are the oppressive systems of White and wealth supremacy that help to foster, incubate, and perpetuate racism. People of color are not naturally overly cautious, anxious, and agitated, but our circumstances often give us good reason for wariness. Thus, the victims are not the problem: the oppressive systems, ignorance, and stereotypes that perpetuate racism are. Therefore, people of color are not positioned here as a problem being addressed; rather, the hurtful behaviors of those who view people of color inaccurately are the problem. Also, if shopping and other day-to-day consumer experiences can be this complicated, imagine how disproportionately challenging other aspects of life can be for BIPOCs, like holding down jobs and advancing in careers. At the same time, it is acknowledged here that BIPOCs are not the only people who experience these oppressions, but we are the only ones who experience such oppression with the question of whether the color of skin or perceptions of race played a role, rather than other factors such as personality, economics, skill, and so on.

5. Nonetheless, Society Blames People of Color for Our Victimization in the Marketplace

People of color often do not feel free to talk about these incidents outside of our own groups as much as we should—for one, for fear that we won't be believed by those who should be putting a stop to it. Beyond recent high-profile marketplace experiences, there may not be widespread societal awareness of racism in the marketplace as a systemic, daily issue with which many minoritized people are dealing. Perhaps when victims do not talk openly about these experiences it's because of the negative and inaccurate stereotypes of our supposed mistrustfulness and paranoia. We are so often blamed by society for our own victimization that when we tell those outside of our own groups of our mistreatment or even call out for help, we run the risk of being blamed or even penalized for it. There have been numerous cases of people of color calling out for help only to be blamed for their circumstances and even arrested or killed. For many people of color, having law enforcement get involved is a gamble—it's the luck of the draw as to the frame of mind of the officers one will encounter, from the very compassionate, supportive, honorable, and equitable to the furthest extremes from that. For example, it is alleged that a young Dallas woman called police for assistance when being beaten in a parking lot by a White stranger, only to find herself getting arrested once police arrived.[74] Public attention to this, and law enforcement embarrassment over it, resulted in her charges being dropped. These misperceptions of us as untrustworthy, paranoid perpetrators rather than victims of other people's inappropriate or violent behavior may make people of color sometimes feel that, somehow, we are responsible for or have invited the victimization that we have experienced, or worse, that no one will care even if they have the power to do something about it. Further, just as marketplace victims of racism or discrimination are not talking publicly about it as much as we could, neither are the marketplace staff, members of law enforcement, nor other potential shapers of it. Perhaps the marketplace staff who perpetrate against shoppers of color, or otherwise victimize them, do not talk about it because they are not aware of the implications of what they have done or do not care. On the other hand, if they are aware, but they themselves are not directly impacted by it, held accountable, or punished for it, why should they care? Nonetheless, everyone has a responsibility to become more aware of this issue, as it is posing a health risk to people of color and perpetuating racism and discrimination in our society—even while people of color are spending our hard-earned money or otherwise investing in the marketplace. Such consumer disparities in the marketplace may create or exacerbate health issues like any other microaggressions that contribute to the significant health disparities that we see for people of color.[75]

6. Marketplace Racism Negatively Impacts Health and Quality of Life for the Entire Family

Thus, the cumulative, insidious, microaggressive impact of retail racism is a heavy weight emotionally burdening people of color, our allies, and our extended communities. Such experiences can seemingly randomly (and not randomly) turn a lovely, happy, mediocre, or even already difficult day, into a grand horror that can ripple out to the entire family and community. As one example among too many that can be recounted, a lovely couple and a host of their friends visited a hard cider orchard where a Black man had intentions of proposing to his future bride and celebrating with their closest friends. Such a lovely event reportedly turned sour and was cut short as the proposal was interrupted by staff three times with accusations of shoplifting, requests to search the Black participants but not the White ones, and threats of calling police because it was alleged that the future groom or his friends had stolen a T-shirt. The moment of a lifetime was certainly marked by the random racist wrecking ball, if not completely ruined by it. There is at least one story of the nineteen in this book that to some extent mirrors this one, where one of the happiest days of a person's life was completely ruined by false accusations, police presence, and fear of arrest, or worse—over nothing. Thus, people of color and allies of communities, cities, states, regions, and nations may experience trauma after trauma through the racial profiling incidents that continually occur in the marketplace. Because of our often collectivist, extended-family kinship styles, if we aren't personally experiencing marketplace profiling incidents, we may feel as if we are, as we hear about what other victims are experiencing across the country.[76] Each time many of us hear about an incident, we know that it could have been us, our child or children, our parents, or our partners, and maybe tomorrow, God forbid, it will be. Thus, marketplace racism adds stress not only to the individual victims of it but also to the families and even communities near and far who absorb the impact right along with the victimized individuals. This is known as vicarious, secondary, or linked trauma.[77]

Therefore, for people of color, the consumer marketplace experience is a clinical health, psychological, human developmental, and community health issue.[78] In addition, it also is a law enforcement, marketing, human resource, and societal issue, all of which impact or risk both daily and long-term "quality" of life for adults, children, teens, and elders.[79] Thus, retail racism continues to "creat[e] a health crisis of enormous proportions."[80]

7. There Is a Special Burden on Parents Rearing Children of Color

Sending Black and Brown children anywhere outside of the house, be it to the store, the mall, or the bank can be stressful, if not for the children, then for their parents who worry about them. Parents of color often lament all of the repeated orientations that they must give their children and teens before they go to a store, mall, or other consumer venues so that they do not bring unwarranted or additional attention to themselves. This is a burden to which parents of White children often cannot relate. Black and Brown parents want their children to be free to come and go, but simultaneously, there often is an effort to protect them from all of the potential horrors that may await them. In other words, even potential marketplace experiences complicate the parenting of many Black and Brown children. Further, some studies reveal that parental stress is significantly increased when parents become aware of the experiences of discrimination that their children experience.[81, 82]

8. There Are Other Vulnerable Populations and Overlapping Communities in the Consumer Marketplace

Elders and other categories of vulnerable people may be especially at risk for exploitation and violence in the marketplace. For example, in New York, an eighty-one-year-old White woman was dragged by her hair and thrown down to the ground by a woman, also White, who had cut in line in front of her and did not receive the elder woman's admonishment about it well.[83] Similarly, a thirty-year-old Black woman attacked a ninety-two-year-old Hispanic man as they both were on walks in the community marketplace.[84] An elderly Black woman was attacked on a subway by a younger Black man.[85] Likewise, in comparison to their straight counterparts openly LGBTQIA+ traveling consumers are not as safe to travel the world, with some countries not considering even the *killing* of an LGBTQIA+ person to be a crime.[86] Thus, individuals who are LGBTQIA+ still at times have to contend with a lack of accommodations, safety, and appropriate protections in the consumer marketplace, which may make it more difficult to experience the marketplace as the pleasant place that it should be.[87] People who are differently-abled also have their own share of inequitable treatment in the consumer marketplace. For example, a man in Iowa was reported to have been denied the use of a wheelchair to return to his car, prompting public outrage.[88] Some people of color intersectionally cross these categories, and therefore may experience an additive, multiplicative, or exponentially greater burden as they try to maneuver in the consumer marketplace. So, while this book will focus on racial marketplace experiences, it may be important to remember that other vulnerable classes of people likely also experience disparities in monitoring, inequity, and trauma in the consumer marketplace, and often these categories of people fit into multiple groups of vulnerability.[89]

9. Marketplace Racism Involves Wrestling with Powers and Inaccurate, Negative Stereotypes and Delusions in Other People

The systems and structures that allow racist privileges, practices, policies, and discrimination to occur also have some history and roots in delusional beliefs not founded in reality. These delusional beliefs and behaviors create prejudices that cause people to respond to individuals with no real prior evidence in order to continue to support their beliefs and actions. A great deal of the memory-telling that you will hear in this book are illustrations of that, where someone's perceptions were distorted by negative, inaccurate beliefs and stereotypes, causing them to behave in an unfounded, outrageous, and often racist way (that is, with enough power to negatively impact someone's life). Some practitioners are suggesting that racism should be treated as a sickness or mental illness, while some fear that would make people feel even less accountable or less responsible for such behavior. The point is, people of color and allies often regularly deal with behavior enacted toward them that may be grounded in unfounded, negative, and inaccurate stereotypes and inequitable policies and practices, and it is very, very taxing. Even my asking participants and poets to tell their stories for this book was a lot to ask of them. But in the interest of trying to make the world a better place, they opened their hearts and burdened themselves once again, to try to share their experiences and educate people on the extra burdens of marketplace racism. After all that they have endured—and we are only hearing a small slice of their lives and experiences—they are heroic survivors in my eyes.

10. Marketplace Racism Impacts White Institutions and People as Well

There is a vicarious impact on White and other allies who observe marketplace disparities that can be brutal and burdensome to the psyche. That is, the marketplace can reinforce a sense of White supremacy with which some may already struggle if they have have not yet questioned stereotypical and racist beliefs in general and consumer marketplace disparities specifically. Therefore delusional, supremacist notions within the marketplace continue to be reinforced from one generation to another because they have not been questioned, and that can't possibly be healthy for people or institutions. Interestingly, when *minoritized* individuals wittingly or unwittingly adopt White supremacist notions and stereotypical and/or prejudiced ideologies about our own groups, it is called internalized racism. However, it likely does not contain the traditional government-sanctioned power to systemically harm beyond oneself and to wherever one's social capital extends. In either case, reinforced are notions that White people are more intelligent, organized, trustworthy, and so on, than people of color. The reinforcement of such notions has made it possible both historically (e.g., enslavement), and currently, for White-dominated groups, institutions, and structures to execute power, rights, values, sense of superior worth, and inequitable policies at the expense of the regard for the historically less privileged, including in the marketplace. The adoption of supremacist ideologies is not healthy for those deluded by and acting on them brutally or microaggressively, and is especially unhealthy for those exploited and otherwise victimized by them.[90]

11. All of the Contexts Surrounding the Marketplace Can Be Dangerous

Seemingly every aspect of the marketplace experience can be exceptionally risky for people of color. Getting to and from the marketplace, entering and exiting, and so on. Nowhere may be emotionally, if not physically, safe. A Black teenager was stopped and handcuffed by police when he was riding to the store with his White grandmother, as the officers allegedly assumed that he was robbing her.[91] Seventeen-year-old murder victim Trayvon Martin walked from the store where he bought an iced tea and a bag of skittles, and was apprehended by a "neighborhood watch" vigilante who shot and killed him.[92] Eighteen-year-old unarmed Michael Brown was making his way from a local store when he was shot and killed by law enforcement in Missouri.[93] Twenty-three-year-old Elijah McClain died after going to the store to purchase an iced tea for his brother when, for no good reason, he was apprehended by police and placed in a chokehold and then given a sedative by paramedics that sent his body into cardiac arrest. Predating the 2020 horrific knee-to-neck-chokehold murder of forty-six-year-old George Floyd as he exited a store in Minneapolis, was the 2014 killing of forty-three-year-old unarmed Eric Garner by authorities who applied a lethal chokehold as he stood and then fell in front of a Staten Island beauty-supply store.[94] Unarmed Levar Jones, who was attempting to visit a local gas station, was shot while obeying a state trooper's order to get his license.[95] Thankfully Jones managed to survive the shooting, and the officer involved was one of the relatively few in these kinds of instances to actually be charged with a crime and stand trial.[96] Similarly, seventeen-year-old unarmed Jordan Davis was shot and killed on his way home from the mall, as he and his friends sat in a car listening to loud music in the parking lot of a convenience store, when a passing motorist became angered by the music.[97] Even in 1955, fourteen-year-old Emmett Till was within the marketplace when he stopped at a diner for a soda, resulting in false accusations of flirtation by a White woman and then lynching by White supremacists who apprehended him and then killed and brutalized him beyond recognition. John Crawford was a customer in a Walmart when he was shot holding a toy gun merchandise item.[98] Twenty-eight-year-old Markeis McGlocton had just exited a local store and was standing in the parking lot when he tried to intervene with the perpetrator who was verbally assaulting his fiancée over a parking space. In the course of that, he was gunned down and killed by the perpetrator.[99]

This is just a minute sampling of an extensive list of incidences that occurred before, during, and after shopping. Thus, whether we are on our way to the marketplace, coming from the marketplace, stopping to eat or snack in the marketplace, waiting in or near the marketplace, are inside or outside of the marketplace, or whether it's in the 1700s, 1800s, 1900s, or within just the past few years, the marketplace is not yet safe for Black people especially, and other people of color. Not only might some personnel behave in racist ways, but so might consumers, passersby, and so on.

12. Black and Brown People Didn't Create Marketplace Racism and Shouldn't Have to Be Overly Burdened with Fixing It

Trying to resist personal and systemic racism takes a lot of energy, and often it is those most burdened by its impact who have the task of trying to fix it when it is loaded upon and constantly surrounds people of color, and that is not fair. Further, like other types of racism, for individuals addressing marketplace racism, it involves reliving the impacts, possibly over and over as one continues to tell, write, and otherwise report the details of it. Therefore, it is retraumatizing. Then add to that the vicarious trauma of hearing and seeing other people experience it over and over.[100] All of this creates a great emotional burden for people who are victims of it or have connection with victims of retail racism. For example, I still can recall in 1991 hearing of the murder of fifteen-year-old Latasha Harlins, who died within a Los Angeles neighborhood bodega. She was a teen girl who went with money in her hand to purchase a drink, but was shot to death by a Korean shopkeeper who thought she was stealing.[101] The aftermath contributed to the breakdown of many alliances between Black and Asian communities at that time. Latasha is so etched in the minds of Californians and people throughout the world that she has been the subject of songs and poems performed by Tupac and Nas. Then, add to traumas such as that, a very long series of staff, customer, security, law enforcement, and passerby killings of Black people, and it's like the whole Black community is in a constant state of trauma. What's particularly frustrating about trying to address racist policies, procedures, and behaviors, is that it involves dealing with perpetrator assumptions, cognitive processes, and mental health processes, such as unfounded White fears and fragility that may be difficult to identify, quantify, prove, or document.[102] Allies who are White also may be psychologically impacted to some degree by racism in the marketplace experience. However, allies who are White often have a greater ability to decide when and how racism issues will impact their lives, whereas most

Black and Brown people do not have this choice. Nonetheless, when White allies are committed to intervening, they may experience backlash for it. In the "Barbeque Becky" incident, a White woman confronted another White woman about her behavior toward a group of African Americans in the recreational marketplace (at a park), but she later received criticism for it.[103] At the now-infamous Starbucks incident, a White person videotaped and tried to interrupt the inequitable treatment of the two men who were being harassed and arrested. Reportedly, she also experienced harassment in the aftermath for the stance she took in the incident. This may come as a surprise to some, but not to people of color who are accustomed to such backlash for speaking up against racist behavior. Nonetheless, it is said that "White silence is White violence," because such silence creates the conditions for racist practices. The stories and other materials in this book suggest appropriate White ally roles—being present, using one's voice to speak up and question what is happening in an effort to help advocate for those being abused, advocating for equitable policy and system change, absorbing, getting their hands dirty in the racism "mess" too—a mess that wasn't created by Black people, and therefore Black people should not be overly burdened with trying to ameliorate it. But most times we are, and that leaves an additional heavy burden on us. In spite of its unfairness, many people of color remain resilient in the fight against injustice, but it can be at a high cumulative cost to health. It will be obvious throughout many of these stories the spirituality (not to be confused with religion) that is common within collectivist cultures from which most of the people of color in the book come. Collectivist cultures are those ethnicities that tend to center on the extended-family kinship network, as opposed to the Western mainstream of the nuclear family. While there are individual differences among Africana, Indigenous, Latina, and Asian cultures, as a whole, in spite of religious differences, the tendency to rely on spiritual strength as a protective mechanism will be apparent in many of the stories even though it was not solicited as a factor. Spirituality is often overlooked as a possible resource by those working with collectivist cultures.[104] Nonetheless, it is an important one that always should be listened for as a survival mechanism with which counseling and other methods of intervention for thriving can be interwoven. Whatever resources people of color use for surviving racism, however, is no substitute for our nation making the elimination of inequity and racist practices and systems altogether its top priority.

These twelve observations evolve out of the personal memory-telling, poems, and reflections shared in this book, news accounts, and past research.[105] The memories told in this book matter because they can help bring greater awareness and understanding of these additional burdens that often exist for consumers of color as we interface with the marketplace. This greater awareness is useful both to the people of color and allies who may have grown used to it, may be weary of it, who may want to resist or fight it, or to those who never had to think about it but would like to help change it for the better.

THE SIGNIFICANCE OF THE DAY-TO-DAY STRESS THAT BIPOC LIFE IN AMERICA ENTAILS

Besides many people not understanding the severe structural disparities that exist for Black people especially, there also is not an understanding of the day-to-day stress that Black and Brown life in America entails.[106] It's been estimated that the potential for experiencing racism, racial profiling, and discrimination imposes an extra 25 percent daily energy drain on African American people.[107] Thus, there can be added burdens and costs to the African American psyche of always having to worry about being wrongly accused of something, or of simple tasks suddenly becoming complicated because of other people's negatively stereotypical, and possibly delusional, perceptions. It's been estimated that those extra day-to-day worries and microaggressions may cost people of color their emotional energy and short- and long-term health. The shocking health and mortality rates among African Americans and other people of color would certainly help to support those hypotheses. At least one scholar has suggested that to live Black in America is to be in a constant state of "mourning" due to the constant and random race-based minor and major losses that Black Americans experience and observe in their lives.[108] Years of research by various academics have examined and documented the day-to-day stress that trying to safely get around—or at least without incident—can take on people of color. These kinds of daily "hassles" and incidents are known as "microaggressions" and tend to be commonly experienced by people of color, and especially African Americans, in American society.[109] Such microaggressions often are carried out by White people who have internalized and failed to examine and critique stereotypical and racist ideologies, who therefore consider themselves colorblind and far from prejudice or racist behavior. Research has been shown since the mid-1980s that colorblindness is highly associated with prejudiced opinions and negative evaluations of minoritized people, as well as with micro- and macroaggressive behaviors.[110] Micro- and macroaggressions toward people of color can contribute to BIPOC health disparities involving increased stress, alarm, exhaustion, depression, post-traumatic stress disorder (PTSD), physical health challenges, hypervigilance, wariness, distrust, anger, fatigue, or hopelessness.[111] As an example, a college student who had police called on her apparently for no good reason as she ate her lunch in a dorm lounge, was significantly shaken by the incident to the point that she experienced difficulty sleeping, among other challenges.[112]

THE PURPOSES OF THIS BOOK

To get an understanding of how retail racism may play out in the consumer marketplace, I traveled distances to collect memories. Thus, the purposes of this book are threefold. First, to bring awareness to this issue for consumers and marketplaces by offering a tapestry of what shopping and otherwise moving about and engaging in the consumer marketplaces may look like for people of color. Second, to increase sensitivity to this issue for all involved. And third, to provide some of the steps and resources that have been taken in an attempt to interrupt, disrupt, or ameliorate the inappropriate handling of consumers of color. To an extent, this book is about not only shopping and other market engagement, but also living in America, surviving and making sense of experiences, and what to do about them.

The experiences shared in this book through a few different formats illustrate that for people of color there is that ever-present hazardousness to, and yet a creativeness within, life—even to something often thought to be as harmless as shopping. A profile of the disenfranchised shopper experience is told in-depth and in the voices of those who personally have experienced it. Therefore, hopefully this platform will help readers hear, connect to, relate to, and understand some of the added complications and stresses through which many people of color try to navigate in the course of shopping or otherwise engaging in the marketplace. Further, the hope is that the experiences of racial profiling and other microaggressions (and beyond) shared here will help to bring greater awareness to the challenges that minoritized people of a variety of racial, ethnic, cultural, gender and sexual identities, ages, socioeconomic and educational backgrounds, professions, and geographic locations, have faced as they have gone about their business in the "free" consumer marketplace. These memories are intended to provide connection, validation, and support to victims and families who have encountered marketplace profiling, while also further sensitizing readers to the prevalence and impact of such profiling. Those impacted by marketplace profiling and discrimination, and/or who want to stop it, are likely to find validation and support. While accomplishing these purposes, readers also may find this to be a book of heart-wrenching, yet often heartwarming and humorous, true stories that hopefully will help to change the way that people think about everyday racism and its deleterious impact on people of color and, thus, the rest of society.

This book is not intended to bash, indict, nor condemn any race, group, the marketplace, nor hardworking store staff, police, other officers of the law, nor any other occupation. It is not intended to bring dissention among consumers or marketers, retail, business, other consumer industries, nor the law enforcement agencies that secure them. However, it is intended to challenge them, because some, and far too many, have abused their power by ascribing to misinformation, negative stereotypes, and inequitable and sometimes racist structures, policies, and practices. There obviously are many venues where every person who walks through its doors are treated with dignity, respect, and value—businesses that make the marketplace feel to everyone like the supportive, even fun, leisurely place we read about in books and see in commercials. However, there seems to be some gaping holes in the marketplace experience for people of color as indicated by numerous research studies, and by the memory-telling in this book. Thus, we are here to talk about and listen to stories about some of the challenges and problems; therefore, what is shared in this book is not always pretty, nor warm and fuzzy. But hopefully, this collection will bring greater awareness through in-depth voices, to help further inform, inspire, and challenge everyone who reads it to work toward disrupting dysfunctional patterns that make the marketplace physically or psychosocially inequitable and even traumatic based on race and other categories. Sometimes these interviews reveal the severe psychological and emotional toll that microaggressions take on the lives and health of people of color, often on a daily basis—including when we attempt to spend our hard-earned money, support our local and national economies, and acquire the food, clothes, and other products and services that we need for our survival. The examples offered above, as well as the incidents reported in the interviews, represent just a tiny fraction of the likely incalculable number of racial-profiling incidences, situations, macro/microaggressions, and emotional processes that abound for people of color who have engaged in the consumer marketplace. Hopefully this collection will help to inspire policy changes so that the consumer marketplace can do better in terms of physical safety and emotional climate for all of the humanity engaging with it.

METHOD OF THIS BOOK

Nineteen true stories were collected in the form of face-to-face testimonies collected over the past several years from interviews with real people who told of their experiences, which occurred mostly in department stores, but also in restaurants, banks, laundromats, pharmacies, hotels, on buses, at a festival, and at an insurance company.

The nineteen interviewees and several other contributors share their experiences predominantly through interviews, but also through spoken-word and poetry, illustrating the intellect and broad diversity of this group. The voices shared range in age from seventeen to eighty-five. The participants include cis women, cis men, openly straight people, openly gay people, openly queer individuals, and some who did not mention their sexual or gender orientation in the course of talking. They are from a wide diversity of backgrounds and walks of life, socioeconomic groups, and ethnic/racial backgrounds, with the vast majority being Black, including African American, Indigenous/African American, Caribbean Black, and Black/European Biracial. Other memory-tellers are Asian, Latina, and White/European American.

The interviews took place in seven different states within the United States, comprising of locations predominantly in the Northeastern United States and New England, but also in the Midwest and the South. The interviews took place in-person between 2008 and 2019. These brilliant minds speak of experiences that caused mild agitation, to circumstances that resulted in the need for psychological therapy and prescription medication. Interspersed between their stories are the spoken-word/poems regarding entering, exiting, or engaging within marketplace experiences. The poetry reveals the lack of respect to Black and Brown bodies of all ages experienced while shopping.

In terms of method, the interviewees were recruited using the "snowball" strategy where invitations were disseminated across the country through a wide variety of networks, and those networks and recruits led to other networks and recruits. Most of the interviewees speak of incidences that have occurred very recently, while other interviewees speak of incidences experienced in the past decade or even earlier in their lives. All of the interviewees offer their reflections on how they make sense of profiling experiences within the context of our society, as well as personal or community steps that they have taken to protest or otherwise resist such profiling.

ORGANIZATION OF THIS BOOK

This book is organized in a way that allows readers to move around it in whatever order works for you (if you are reading for pleasure) or for your instructor (if you are reading for academic purposes). You can start wherever you or your instructor (if applicable) feel most comfortable or most interested, or you can read in the order that the book is written. If you are reading for pleasure, introductions and interviews can be skimmed, skipped, or revisited as you feel necessary—if you would like to read the interviews in a particular section first or in a particular order, you can. One section of the book does not depend on the other sections of the book, and the same holds true for the interviews. Although each interview has multiple and overlapping themes with one another, I have loosely organized the stories into four sections by predominant themes consisting of either "Monitoring," "Inequities," "Trauma," and "Philosophies." The themes are not mutually exclusive. For example, trauma may overlap with being monitored or experiencing inequitable treatment.

The audiences for this book include victims and disrupting allies of consumer marketplace racial profiling, over-monitoring, discrimination, and trauma. It also is intended as a resource for leaders and staff of law enforcement, security, sales and marketing, management, human resource, and public relations, and other administrators, staff, human resource trainers, diversity trainers, trainees, and anyone. Teachers, professors, and other educators may find it of interest as a resource for illustrating how something considered a symbol of fun, freedom, and relaxation in the Western world can be a source of racism, discrimination, and trauma for those who tend to hold the least power in our society. Storytelling, or what I sometimes call memory-telling, is one way that people begin to listen to and hear those who have tended to be invisible or relatively voiceless in the past.

At the beginning of each interview, I offer a few of the things that went through my mind as I prepared for the interviews, as I drove to the interviews, as I met the interviewees, and as I later tried to assimilate or reorganize my processing of them into my mental and cognitive processing. My goal is not to negatively or inaccurately stereotype anyone but to pull readers into my experiences of preparing for and meeting the participants. Thus, I may share my initial assumptions; not that my initial assumptions were at all correct—which in itself is a lesson in the need to keep our minds open as we try to hear and understand people. As you read the stories, if you find yourself wanting assistance with the processing of what the memory-teller is sharing or experiencing, you might return to the list of my twelve observations in this introduction. While not exhaustive, it may assist you in your processing if, by chance, you find yourself wanting some guidance. I purposely did not chop up these stories to interject my perceptions throughout them, so that you could experience the storytelling the same way that I did.

Each interview went far beyond what I was asking. Those interviewed spoke from their hearts, with a level of trust and engagement that surprised me. They knew why I was there—for truth—and they gave it, each in their own way. But each going far beyond the marketplace incidents they experienced and into the greater contexts that surround those incidents. At the end of each of the four sections there are interview-derived lessons and suggestions for consumers and marketers. These are suggestions for interrupting the negative trends that are discussed throughout each section. The collection of these nineteen stories, nine poems or spoken-word pieces, and artwork and photos reveal that consumers of color are not passive. But rather we tend to be strategically selective in our actions, and therefore active, creative, resourceful, and full of wisdom and sometimes humor in our resistance and coping. These four sections reveal brave, wise, creative consumers in spite of the anxiety, stress, sadness, anger, frustration, and psychological trauma that these stories reveal the seemingly innocuous marketplace can engender. These insightful memory-tellers, spoken-word poets, and artists have opened their hearts to allow us to see even deeper into and beyond the recent headlines, as we consider the experiences of consumers of color, in their own words.

I

MONITORING

Black and Brown bodies commonly feel closely watched in stores, malls, and other businesses and marketplaces while, paradoxically, often also feeling ignored for customer service at the same time.

The Big Eye, By Kenneth Watts

POEM 1

Alfreda Recalls Marshall Fields

Tara Betts

For Ida B. Wells-Barnett while shopping

Before the city was pared into juicy cuts
for some and chewy scraps for others,
before laws drew gates around where
you could go, Mother always had taste.

Stationery, simple jewelry, tailored dresses.
She glided across the floor, even beyond her
fifties, which marked when she bought
the shorts for Father.

Waiting, waiting like an invisible
woman on a floor full of clerks
until she draped underpants across
her left shoulder and marched to an exit.
Finally, a floorwalker broke her pace.

My mother, suspected shoplifter,
held out boxers with a smile.
Yes, I'd like to purchase these.
Thank you for your attention.

INTRODUCTION

Over-monitoring involves being assumed untrustworthy by marketplace staff or security and being constantly prowled or surveyed by them as if you will take from and exploit others—therefore always a suspect. For example, eventually prompting protests that shut the store down for days, a lawyer and her teen daughter were recently reported to have been arrested after being targeted by staff at a clothing store who followed, interrogated, and had them arrested related to suspicions that they were shoplifting. One of the alleged victims, attorney Nancy Bedard, remarked that shopping is just one of a long list of things that Black people are not free to do in our society. "It's while we're shopping, drinking coffee, sleeping, selling cigarettes. . . . The fact that you're Black alone is suspicious."[1] Another example of monitoring involves a Kansas teen who was accused of trespassing by staff at a movie theater and was arrested allegedly for the way that his pants fit him.[2] Other examples abound. It was reported that in one region, Black consumers often had to show receipts in urban Lowes stores, but not in suburban Lowes stores.[3] Safeway employees in California are alleged to have prompted five police officers to come to their store on suspicions that a fair-skinned Black man shoplifted, and rather than accosting a fair-skinned Black man, the store employees targeted a Black woman and her children. The adult victim, Erika Martin, noted, "They don't even see the type of person it is; the darker the skin, the more frightened they become. . . . To be honest with you, I don't see it ending . . . and it's very scary."[4]

Bryon Ragland, who is a nine-year Air Force veteran, a Washington state court-appointed special advocate, and a visitation supervisor, had the police called on him by the yogurt shop in which he was supervising a parental visit.[5] Some commentators are questioning why there is such a great need to often call the police on people of color, amounting to using the police as "personal racism valets," and thus subjecting people of color to possible risk "based on nothing more than the word of a White person whom [a person of color] made uncomfortable."[6] In one situation, police were sent to a customer's home with a no-trespass order simply because he questioned store policy when, reportedly, it was the cashier who behaved inappropriately with his response to the customer.[7] Even some police are getting frustrated with unnecessary calls on Black and Brown people.[8] Instances, too many to recount here, abound—even while living at home (e.g., Breonna Taylor), while walking and driving to and from consumer marketplaces (e.g., Tony McDade), while in school and at work, while seeking medical care, traveling, while engaging in sports and leisure activities, and while engaged with banks and seeking loans.[9]

THE IMPACT OF DISPROPORTIONATE MONITORING

Most people of color and allies are not surprised by such headlines, as many of us already know very well that Black and Brown people are differentially monitored or watched while we shop or otherwise conduct business in the consumer marketplace. It makes us feel uncomfortable, unfairly targeted, and even anxious. What does this do to a young person? What does this do to an elder? What does a lifetime of such messages do to a person's psyche and health? The five forthcoming stories suggest that such behavior imposes a heavy burden for people of color. People of color know throughout our lives that we are being watched, so much so that we find different ways of handling it, from ignoring it, to humorously responding to it, to boldly confronting it. Some people of color make forays into the marketplace as briefly as possible, as articulated by many of the interviewees in this book. We may avoid marketplaces altogether by sending less concerned loved ones to do necessary shopping, or, alternatively, by shopping online. At the other extreme, some shoppers or consumers in the marketplace may feel totally ignored or invisible, as will be noted in some of the upcoming interviews and incidents discussed. So, there seem to be the extremes of invisibility when BIPOCs need assistance on the one hand, but a hypervisibility or constant monitoring to be sure that BIPOCs do not steal on the other hand. It's a crazy-making paradox for those stuck on the receiving end of it when attempting to shop or to otherwise conduct business in the consumer marketplace.

The extra scrutiny that people of color, even youth, experience is par for the course within many realms of our society. Racial comparison on juvenile criminal justice statistics supports the belief that Black youth especially are monitored more closely and processed into the school disciplinary and criminal justice systems.[10] Statistics from the Department of Justice indicate that for many crimes, compared to their White counterparts, children of color are not only significantly more likely to be arrested and found guilty, but they also are more likely to serve jail or prison time, and for significantly longer periods for identical crimes.[11] Research studies also are finding that Black youth are perceived both by police and civilians as significantly older and more dangerous than their same-aged White counterparts.[12] To many, this seemed well-demonstrated in the case of twelve-year-old Tamir Rice, who tragically was gunned down by police, reportedly within seconds of their arrival, while he stood on a playground holding a toy gun.[13] Statistics and research findings for adults indicate that similar perceptions hold true for Black adults, especially for Black men, who often are misperceived as exceptionally dangerous in comparison to their adult White male counterparts.[14]

RESPONSES TO DISPROPORTIONATE MONITORING

Racial profiling is defined as the targeting of people based on their apparent group membership such as race, ethnicity, gender, sexual orientation, religion, socioeconomic status, and so on rather than based on their behavior.[15] Recent arrest, prosecution, and imprisonment statistics strongly illustrate that people of color are more likely to be monitored, profiled, arrested, convicted, and serve time than their White counterparts for identical crimes.[16]

Recent studies suggest that racial profiling of people of color begins even before reaching elementary school in spite of socioeconomic status. In a Yale Child Study Center study using eye-tracking technology, it was revealed that teachers tend to monitor, expect, and perceive children who are Black as more problematic, out of control, and so on. Further, these ways of seeing Black children start as early as preschool age, when teachers already have differential and subconsciously negative expectations and perceptions compared to their White student counterparts.[17] For that reason, teachers tend to watch Black children, especially, much more closely for misbehavior than they do their White pupils. Attempting to ignore race (i.e., colorblindness) makes matters worse. For example, among service providers such as social workers and teachers, the more one ascribes to colorblind ideology, the greater the tendency to see fictionalized children of color as aggressive and out of control.[18] For many people of color, shopping in a predominately White world tends to be a complicated and anxiety-producing activity that can make one feel extremely vulnerable to being misperceived, maltreated by staff and other personnel, and inappropriately confronted by security and law officials. Thus, for many people of color, like in many social settings, the marketplace can be an anxiety- and stereotype threat-provoking place where one can tend to feel over-scrutinized, treated rudely, and easily accused of stealing or some other wrongdoing.[19]

Over the years, instances also have been published recounting investigations, and sometimes millions of dollars have been litigated or paid out to individuals falsely accused of shoplifting or otherwise victimized by racial profiling in the marketplace.[20] More than a few settlements have involved incidents at upscale clothing and accessory stores. In one incident, a woman was offered a settlement with the Louis Vuitton store at Saks Fifth Avenue, when the clerk processing her purchase called the police on her and accused her of fraud.[21] In another incident some years ago, a young Black man, Alonzo Jackson, was awarded $850,000 in damages by a federal district court in Maryland. His two friends also were awarded $75,000 each after an incident where Mr. Jackson was made to strip himself of a shirt that he wore into an Eddie Bauer store because it was assumed that he had stolen it.[22] Two Black women sued Toys "R" Us for $200,000 each, alleging that the store was exclusively requiring customers of color to show their receipts for their purchases.[23] Similarly, two cases in Minnesota were settled out of court for the amounts of $20,000 (Marshalls) and $5,000 (Walgreens) when customers were profiled, mishandled, and wrongly accused of shoplifting.[24] Wet Seal stores settled discrimination charges with three Black women managers who cited employee discrimination, including the store explicitly giving the message that they wanted to cater to White, thin, blonde-haired, blue-eyed clientele, which seemed to translate into other clientele being overlooked.[25] A nineteen-year-old African American college student filed a lawsuit against the New York Police Department (NYPD) and Barneys stores because he was arrested, cuffed, and jailed by local police after purchasing a $350 belt.[26] Likewise, a twenty-one-year-old African American nursing student sued the same store and the NYPD after being harassed by law enforcement when she purchased a $2,500 handbag.[27] Barneys paid $525,000 to settle these two cases.[28] In 2018, five retailers in Portland,

Oregon, were slapped with five lawsuits for $500,000, $500,000, $250,000, $100,000, and $55,000 for following shoppers of color and unjustly accusing them of stealing.[29]

Affluent Black shoppers assert that their socioeconomic status does not prevent or protect them from the tendency to be racially profiled as they go about their business in the world.[30] Even shoppers of color who hold celebrity status are not exempt from being profiled and overly monitored while engaging in the consumer marketplace. For example, world-syndicated talk-show host Trevor Noah has talked about his run-ins trying to get about in the community.[31] Black billionaire Bob Johnson reportedly had difficulty cashing a check in a Florida hotel.[32] An HBO television actor, Robert Brown, filed a racial profiling lawsuit against NYPD and Macy's after being accused of credit card fraud and being handcuffed and jailed when he purchased a $1,300 graduation gift for his mother.[33] Former Miami Hurricanes football player Steven Marshall and his fiancée Zuleyka Bremer sued Regions Bank after they were embarrassed, humiliated, and detained while being accused of trying to open an account with a supposedly fraudulent check.[34] Beloved mega-celebrity Oprah has been no stranger to such profiling. In the past decade, she has experienced demoralizing experiences both in Paris and in Zurich. In Paris, she was rudely refused entry into a store, and in Zurich, her request to look at an expensive purse was denied because the clerk assumed that she would not be able to afford it.[35] Academy Award–nominated actress Gabourey Sidibe is reported to have had a similar experience over a pair of eyeglasses at a Chicago boutique.[36] Former President of the United States Barack Obama stated that he had been "followed in a department store."[37] Reverend Al Sharpton has made similar comments and has taken this issue on as a major cause.[38] In a *CNN* commentary, sociopolitical comedian W. Kamau Bell has delineated how he has been kicked out of at least two coffeehouses, one of them on his birthday while sharing with his wife a children's book he had just finished writing.[39] Three accomplished actresses of color allege that they were arrested in Atlanta for staying in a restaurant restroom for too long.[40] Even Santa can't catch a break—at least not the African American Santa. While there is a high demand for Santas of different racial and ethnic backgrounds,[41] there often is a great deal of backlash when he presents himself to the public. For example, immediately following Minneapolis' Mall of America's recent presentation of their first ever Black Santa, an avalanche of hate mail, comment wars, racial epithets, threats, and boycotts ensued.[42]

Similarly, there is a plethora of incidents involving individuals of color who hold law enforcement positions, who themselves have experienced profiling or racial-related monitoring and related incidents in the consumer marketplace. For example, a Black retired corrections officer filed a lawsuit after an incident occurred when he went into a grocery store to buy cooking oil. The retired officer was shocked to be apprehended and beaten by police even as he tried to tell them that he was a corrections officer. The officers had mistaken him for a Black suspect who weighed an estimated hundred pounds more than the retired corrections officer, and allegedly they responded to him by saying, "You're no f_____g officer!"[43]

VOICES OF THE OVER-MONITORED

In spite of the misperceptions and accompanying constant monitoring, what speaks to the creativity and resilience of the traditionally disenfranchised spirit is the selective, humorous, and diverse range of confrontational ways that people respond to such surveillance. In the pages ahead, an African American reverend speaks of an ironic full-circle lesson that one security monitor eventually was taught. A Latina college administrator speaks to the many complications she experiences as she attempts to enjoy the art of shopping, only to often have it cut short by the anxieties with which she has to contend at the hands of store personnel who stereotype and constantly watch her. A queer White man shares his observations of shopping with his friends of color who are overly observed in ways that he is not. A retired African American senior citizen speaks of the way that a White couple robbed a restaurant of large amounts of food while not being monitored because managers were too busy watching her. And lastly, a former African American political leader octogenarian tells of the many ways that she has been watched and treated differently while engaging with various businesses, and her regret that things seem not to have changed much in her entire lifetime. Thus, in sum, you will find presented a small slice of diverse stories that will further give understanding to the extensive monitoring experienced by many people of color, and the painful emotional toll that it takes.

MISPERCEIVED

"Oh Reverend, I'm So Sorry" (Alton's Story)

Alton's[1] story is about his reflections on covert monitoring in a discount department store. As I prepared to meet with Alton and hear his story, I found myself feeling a little nervous. While our paths had crossed briefly in the past, I had never had an extensive conversation with him, and, after all, he is a reverend. I was no stranger to Protestant or Catholic clergy, having grown up the granddaughter of a staunch Catholic maternal grandmother, the granddaughter of a Methodist paternal grandmother, and the granddaughter of a Pentecostal step-grandfather who was not only a preacher, but his denomination's diocese Bishop of five states. So, I felt familiar and prepared for whatever Reverend Alton's tradition might be. It's just that having grown up from the age of six with my Bishop-grandfather as a major influence on my life and someone that I respected to the ultimate and adored to all ends, I felt particularly honored that this reverend would not only be a part of this collection, but he seemed very concerned about the issue and eager to tell his story. I was to meet him and his wife at their home at 5 p.m. on a weekday.

The Reverend is an African American man in his early fifties, clearly educated, and very eloquent in his speech. He appeared as if he might be very athletic, as if he may have played football or basketball in his youth, and now perhaps he camps, hunts, or fishes in the outdoors in his midlife years. And of course, I could be wrong about everything in my head at that moment. I knew that he has served as a local pastor for many years, but I did not know that he also was a pastoral counselor for two secular facilities. He is college-educated, including two master degrees, one of which was his seminary degree.

Upon meeting Rev. Alton's wife, I had the impression that she might be from a culture different from his, as their dialects differed from one another quite a bit, as well as their race. She seemed kind, confident, and comfortable. Whether it was her turn to cook or she did this all the time, she seemed to enjoy the role of hostess. She was just finishing a pan of lasagna and taking it out of the oven. She warmly asked if I would like to join them for dinner. I hadn't planned on that, but how was I to refuse? To be so warmly greeted, given such hospitality, and offered lasagna, I could not turn it down!

As we ate together and chatted about their children and grandchildren, I realized that their company was as good as the food. When dinner was over, they escorted me into their living room. It also was warm and cozy. The Reverend placed a cup of coffee for me and one for himself on the table, while his wife brought in a small plate of cookies that looked as if they were home-baked. She sat the plate down on the table. She then excused herself, letting me know that she had some things to tend to, and she warmly hugged me as she exited. I could hear her stepping away as I was soaking in my gratitude for this kind family—and I was studying the cookies as the Reverend was shifting in his seat, properly positioning supportive pillows behind his back. Then suddenly everything was still and quiet. I pulled my eyes away from the cookies, and looked over, and the Reverend, using a gesture with his hands, said, "Shall we begin?" I smiled and said, "Yes, of course," as I pulled out paperwork from my folder I was carrying, turned on the tape recorder, and our process began. As he spoke, I reached over and grabbed a cookie and listened intently.

In the words ahead, Rev. Alton speaks of his experiences, both old and new, of being followed by store staff as he attempts to shop, and he offers his creative solutions for dealing with such annoying experiences. Paradoxically, his methods allow him both responsibility and freedom at the same time, which is not a balance easily reached on the fly when we are at the brunt end of both unpredictable and unfair marketplace practices. Rev. Alton also talks of the responsibility that he feels for addressing his concerns to store and corporate management. He feels that doing so is important, so that those who do not have the same resources as he does can be empowered and treated with more dignity in the future.

Rev. Alton shares his story and insights . . .

* * *

I clearly recall a situation where I experienced discrimination while shopping. I can't remember exactly the store, [but] it was [a discount department store] right in town. It was in the nineties, somewhere thereabouts that time. It was a store where I like to go and just sort of tool around because my way of shopping is to just go and look around. I'm probably an impulse buyer, but not in a gross way. But I'll look around and see if I find something, and if so, I'll buy it. I like to do that, and that's how I get new things. I was in this store, and I was just sort of going through and looking around at different things, and I noticed that I was being followed. And that's not atypical, because that is always on my mind as I am going into a store. It's not atypical in that I'll just presume that's going on, and almost at a paranoid level where I know that someone's looking at me somewhere. You just know—Black folks know that we are targeted for surveillance when we go into stores. But this time the person was just so horribly awkward at it. They were not good at all! I would be going down an aisle, and they'd be just sort of trailing me. And I would look up, and I'd see them down in the aisle going around. They were just sort of classless about it, and it offended me that they were just so inept. I think I may have been there after work hours, so I may have had my casual way of dressing, especially during the summer, with just sort of a T-shirt and a pair of jeans or something like that.

I'm just going through and looking around, and I see the person. Usually I can maybe let things go, but I didn't want to just let this go this time. So, I went up to the person and without cussing or anything, I said, "Look, will you do me a favor? . . . If you're going to follow me around, at least be good about it." I can chuckle about it now, but at that time my tone was, "Can you just hide a little better, or something?" Actually, to be more specific, what I did was I went up and introduced myself to him. See, this is the way I'll handle things. I said, "Look, my name is Reverend [Alton]. I'm a Chaplin at [a local facility]. I'm not here trying to steal anything because that is not anything that I have in mind. And, if you're going to follow me, at least do it a little better because it's just embarrassing both for you and for me."

In reaction to being followed, I was presenting to him my annoyance around it. Some weeks later it turned out that the guy was a deacon at a church I had been invited to preach at. It was an all-White congregation and all, and a good time of fellowship. I finished my sermon and thought no more about it. But he saw me, and afterward when we met he said,

"Reverend, I am so embarrassed." But I was embarrassed also. I initially was a Black man in the store who's going to steal everything!

When reflecting on my life, I count myself blessed by God just with my background. I went to a little prep school, and then to college, and to [a very prestigious Ivy League school]. However, those sort of external things don't mean a darn thing. However, in terms of the structure of our society, folks will look at these things and accord some level of respect or whatever the heck you want to call it. For myself, I couldn't play the game. I'd try not to go around and say I'm Reverend [Alton] from [a local facility], because when I would, people would get foolish on themselves and probably accord clergy more than they should. But because I have something of that status, situations like that in the store don't really touch me. I can sort of see the humor and the foolishness of it for myself. I am sort of insulated from someone else's foolishness because they really don't have any power over me; I'll just leave the store and say to myself, "You fool, I've got money, and I'll go spend it elsewhere." I'll be nasty enough at times to go tell the manager, "You're losing money, and I'm somebody who spends money."

None of us are ever separated from a situation like the one I recounted, and such a situation is crushing no matter who you are. I'm sure you've heard Oprah and the whole thing where people say you have situations that remind us that you're Black, or will say you're just another n[_____] and all. We have things that remind us of that, and we have some of the external stuff to get beyond that. Like Oprah has that whole wallet! But there are folks that don't have that, whose life is devastated. I am speaking of those who are already harmed by things in life, and then they also have an experience like that, that just continues to dehumanize them. I get upset with things like that, not so much for myself, because as I said, I can move beyond that and sort of like play the game with someone. "Oh, Reverend [Alton], I'm so sorry, if I knew that was you, I would not have done that." I'll go and sort of hang out in casual attire; this is one of the things that I like to do. And I will think, "I'm glad you didn't know that it was me." So then, you come around and you discover just how wrong you are, and how wrong you can be. But there are folks that don't have it like this that get trashed on! It just angers me—for the folk who are trashed on and are just harmed by that.

I also get upset with the power dynamics that exist. And there's a better way of putting it, and I like putting things in a better way. Having some idiot who is completely unworthy come and harm the humanity of someone of far greater human worth is so . . . just so wrong. It's distressing that someone with the most wonderful, open, generous heart can have someone come and treat them inhumanely just because of the color of their skin. For example, a few years ago, I was making a substantial deposit into the bank, and it's the bank I have done business with for a long time—fifteen, perhaps twenty years. When I went into the bank to make the deposit, I was told that there would be a five-day hold put on the check, to which I said, "Fine." Actually, at that time, my wife who is White and my kids were making similar deposits at the same bank. My wife went to another branch and was told there was a two-day hold. And when we got home, we were talking and comparing. And they were teasing me and saying, "ha, ha, ha; you got a five-day hold on yours!" and were sort of joking around. And then they started saying, "What is going on?" It turned out that it was supposed to be only a two-day hold. So, we went back to my local branch to talk to the person who placed the five-day hold. And this is the stuff that sort of burns me; they say, "No, no, no, this is what's going on." And they justify the five-day hold for "this and that" reasons. And we said fine, knowing that she was wrong because over at the other branch with my wife, the person that she talked to said, "No, this is not it." So, the next day we went down and actually talked with the branch manager to get clarification on their policy. She also started to backpedal by trying to give a variety of excuses that did not hold water, excuses that did not address that it was because I am Black. After the manager did her [explaining], I actually wrote a letter and contacted someone in the corporate office about the situation. [The bottom line is that] banks operate on money. And they treat people who are dealing with money nicely. I was not being treated nicely. When we went up to the corporate office, they went down and bit the manager's butt somewhat. She gave me a call and tried to give a flimsy apology, but it never really [felt genuine].

These kinds of situations take a lot of energy, and therefore it's draining. I don't want to minimize any of it, because it is angering. It's just an awful situation for anyone to experience, and to muster yourself to deal with. However, I'm in a situation where I can go down and know how to deal with the system on a matter, and to some degree I can have a little bit of fun twigging the system in a situation like that. And knowing how to articulate to "the Pope" and with clarity, I can say what's going on. I know when I'm getting shined off, and I am able to call it that and to press things. I can deal with it and handle it. I can be in a situation where I can put out the energy, and I'm going to be okay with it. But again, it disturbs me because I know that there are brothers and sisters around that are not able to do that. And that's the treatment that happens to them also. They may not be able to go down and deal with the system, or they will not feel that they can go down there and talk with them. Or they'll go down and try to sit and talk with the manager, and the manager will—as they tried to do with me—blow you off and essentially say you're wrong, you're crazy. And we never go away buying it, but we will go away saying, "What can I do, and why even try?" And that burns me!

[But] what works for me—and this is just in my situation—we have power as shoppers because we're spending our money. And when we are ill-treated, we can express our power by going and spending our money elsewhere. We will make that decision for ourselves. But before we do that, and as we do that, we should at least find the powers that be to express our concerns. We can go to the powers that be or to the level above them—perhaps even to store management at the corporate level. We should find someone to express our concerns to. We can say, for example, "Because of the ill-treatment of one of your workers toward me, you're losing money. . . . And I'm going to talk about you like a dog. . . . I'm going to tell folk what you've done, so you're not just losing my money, but you're also going to lose money from others in the community."

For me, it really is personal advocacy, but I also see it as not just for myself, but also for other things that are going on. For me it's almost part of our name [as ministers]. That is the prophetic aspect of my ministry. I have to [advocate], and bless God. I just thank God that I'm in the position and in the situation where I can do that, and not in the situation—which I have seen—where you are so disempowered by the system that a clerk can make a judgment about you that will be seen as being more powerful than any response that you can make. And it causes you to say, "I have got to just keep away." Also, I can just be an ornery person, it's sort of fun for me! One of the things God has blessed me with is that He has put me in the position where I can respond, and almost have to.

MISTRUSTED

"So I'm a *Suspect*, and It Makes Me Feel Terrible" (Balbira's Story)

Balbira's story is about overt monitoring in upscale department stores. As I prepared to meet with Balbira, I thought about the fact that the people in this book represent just a very tiny sampling of the innumerable experiences people may have about the minoritized shopping experience. Balbira is a Latina educational administrator in her early forties. We met for the interview at her home, which was a long drive for me, but a pleasant one. Her home was small but pristine. Therefore, you could eat off of her floors if you had to do so, as my grandmother used to say about some peoples' homes. This meant that Balbira's home was so clean that if for some bizarre reason you needed or wanted to, you could just plop down and eat your dinner from anywhere in the house—even on the floor—and it would still be sanitary. It was apparent that she liked fine, delicate things like white carpet, crystal, and other things that at my house full of rambunctious children and pets could have easily gotten roughed-up or broken. Therefore, as I walked into her lovely home, I kind of chuckled to myself at the thought of my whole crew of children, nieces, nephews, and godchildren coming to visit. While introducing myself to her, I was envisioning what would fall first, how badly it would be broken, and while cleaning it up, what would be the next item to splatter. Laughing within myself helps me to relax. Most people would not know that I am a well-disguised introvert who has had to learn to adjust to a life that has constantly thrust me in front of people. But there's all kinds of little tricks that I play, such as comical visioning, to help myself relax. So, in I went into Balbira's lovely home, thinking in exaggerated terms about my own upbringing and that of my own children and extended family, and what shape this house would be in when we were done with it. It made me smile quite a bit, and she returned the smiles just as much as we warmed up to each other. We sat at the coffee table and chatted a little before getting started, which I always do to try to get comfortable with the interviewees, or memory-tellers, as I call them. I could see that we both had some things in common, especially with us both being academics and apparently, earring fanatics. She also seemed that she was trying to get comfortable with me as well, so as we both shared a little bit of our congeniality with each other, we seemed to settle right down and were ready for work. I pulled out my paperwork and tape recorder and we got started. I intermittently sipped on the tea she had brought in earlier as I listened intently to her tell her story.

In her interview Balbira discusses her experiences with high-end stores while living in the Northeastern United States and as far away as the West Coast. She shares how intimidating she has found these stores when being followed by store staff, and the extremes that she has gone to try to stereotypically appear to be someone who does not need monitoring. Her experiences vary from being completely ignored when needing assistance, all the way to the extreme of being followed and monitored every second. She also discusses how she has learned to protect herself from the stress of all of this. She speaks of how she taught herself to ignore and cope with such monitoring and to avoid taking it personally. Ever the educator, she expresses her thoughts about the importance of diversity training for retail marketplace staff and security personnel. Most importantly, she illustrates that no matter how successful a person of color may be, they may struggle with experiences of unwelcome and lack of entitlement to the same space that their White counterparts may take for granted.

Balbira shares her experiences . . .

* * *

When I was growing up, I was poor—in fact, I was dirt poor. We needed to take advantage of every government program that was available to be able to survive as a family. I come from a family that was poor-working class and off-and-on welfare. Compared to what my parents had, and compared to how I grew up, I would be considered rich now. I work as [an educational] administrator. . . . If you ask [my family] where I am financially, to them, they would say I am rich. But I'm not rich. But compared to what I came from, and what they know, I am rich. My mother is still living on social security, and my father has passed. It's just a big difference—the income disparity is enormous. I have a pension plan and I have extra money that I invest. Every time I get a raise, I put that money toward my investment. I'm also financially looking at my future. And I save money in other accounts, so I'm not frivolous with my money. I sort of take care of everybody, but I make a pretty high salary. And I own a property. In fact, I've owned several properties. So I'm business savvy as well, and I'm financially savvy. I try to make sure I do save. I'm very good with the shopping—I keep a look out for the clearance and the sales. I like good things, but I will wait a couple of months until it drops in price. If it's not there, it's not there; but if I find it, then I'll pick it up. But with everything going on in the world, I'm going to be low-middle-class soon. With oil and food, and everything's going up. And I'm alone, and I'm still carrying all this by myself. So, it's easy to get bumped down.

I recently had [a] shopping experience that [was particularly] disconcerting to me. I have had several throughout my lifetime, but [this one was very] recent. I took my sister and my mother with me for a walk at a local mall. My mother was in the area shopping, and I came back to pick her up after half an hour. My sister suffers from [an illness]. You can tell that by looking at her, so I was taking care of her. I put my coat down to help her pick [out] what she wanted, and I put it in the cart. There was this man who was standing nearby, and all of a sudden he turned blue in the face. He followed us around everywhere. It was so obvious that he was security. It was obvious that he wasn't buying anything; he didn't have anything in his hands; he wasn't picking up anything. Here I was being followed by security. He probably thought I was going to wrap something up in my jacket and steal it. I got so mad that I almost told him, "You are so poor at what you do—it's so obvious—you need to stop following me around. . . . I am not going to steal anything." I really wanted to speak up, because after a while it was obvious. He was trying to follow me around, watching to see what I was putting in the cart.

So, I'm a suspect, and it makes me feel terrible. It makes me feel terrible because on average when I go out, I'm usually well-dressed, I'm always well-groomed. Always. I never walk out of the house without earrings—even if I'm just going to buy a cup of coffee. And I always have some earrings on that tend to be something good—a pair of gold earrings or something, no matter how plain I may be. And you can look at me and tell I'm not destitute. To walk into a store, regardless of what the store is, and to be made out to be someone who could potentially steal feels horrible. And that's just not something I've ever done. I could see if at one point in time I had stolen. I may feel that I should be followed. But I don't have any of those tendencies, so I wonder what is it about me or what is it about my mother—my seventy-two-year-old mother—and my poor sister who looks like she's very ill—who even gets winded just walking around. What is it that we're going to do that was so threatening that I need to be followed around in a store? I think it's just because we're people of color—just simply because we're people of color. I think that's all there is, and there's no other reason. There was nothing I was doing; I wasn't acting unusual; I wasn't doing anything unusual. I was being helpful to my sister who needed help with the shopping she needed to do. Perhaps he just didn't have anybody in his area whom he needed to address or whatever, so he focused on us. I don't know.

I don't know how they go about doing their business. I don't know how they pick and choose who they follow, and what they do and don't do. It's also happened to my older sister who's a legal secretary. There was also another time, some years ago, when I went into a [high-end store] on the West Coast, and I knew I didn't have any business in there. However, I was approaching it like a museum really, because I knew it was expensive. I definitely felt like, "Oh, this is out of my league." I happened to go up to the floor that had gowns, suits, and merchandise like that. They had really beautiful things. So, the first thing I looked at was like five-thousand dollars. I remember looking at it, and the expression on my face probably gave me away, like, "Whoa! . . . Time for me to get moving here!" So, I did not linger too long on any one item. I just kept looking at particular items, and I was enjoying myself. And the next thing you know, I had somebody sort of next to me. I felt like it was this lady, and then it was this man. They seemed to be together, but they were looking at things separately. And I was thinking, "What is this man doing looking at these gowns?" I guess if he was with his wife and they were together, I could understand. But I saw them together, and then they were separate. Perhaps they were watching me from different angles, I really don't know what they were doing. But I found it sort of odd that they stuck around me. And there was this whole feeling like I was definitely being watched. And I just started moving. It was a big, huge floor for shopping, there were a lot of items there, and I was just looking around, taking my time. And then I started thinking, well I can't afford any of this stuff, and there's nothing even just for fun to look at. There was nothing really in my sizes—everything seemed to be sizes 4 and 8. They don't tend to make fancy, couture clothes for women that are top heavy or anything of the sort. There are just very, very petite sections in very expensive stores for some reason—and that's another thing. But, I just sort of decided to move along and keep going.

I went to another section, and I started looking at suits. And I'm looking and checking out the prices. Again, I couldn't afford it, but I was thinking maybe I'd come across something or maybe I'd find the clearance sections. So, I'm just looking at sales, and I'm in there trying to figure whether there is something in there that I could buy that would fit. I've always been like a 12 or 14, and I'm top heavy, so I always have to buy separates. And if I ever want to buy something really fancy, it's always tight, so I have to look really hard. I'm searching, and again, these two people just sort of popped up! I'm like, "I just saw those people about fifteen or twenty minutes ago over there, and now they're over here." So, I moved quickly, but I wasn't being methodical about the sections I was going through. I looked, and there they were again. Then I decided nothing in this section, and it's all too expensive, so I need to go on to the next section. I move to the next section, and here they are again. Again, and again, they get right into my view.

I had another experience in Miami shopping at one of those expensive shops in [a specific] mall. I went to buy a perfume for my sister, so I was testing them out. I decided which one I wanted, so I was standing there. And this lady clerk saw me standing there, and she just ignored me—she just completely ignored me! I felt she was ignoring me because she assumed that I didn't have any money, and that I wasn't going to buy anything. So, I just stood there and waited for her because I had made a selection. She came over and asked, "What size do you want?" She immediately suggested the smallest size. She said, "You want this small size?" And I said, "Can I see the different sizes?" She told me about the others—the bigger ones. And, I said, "Well, I'll take the mid-size one—I'll take that and I want two of them." She said, "Oh, you want two of them?" I said, "Yes, I'll take two because I want one for my sister and one for myself, because I really like it." And that was like the surprise. After she had ignored me to the point that I was getting ready to leave because I just felt like this lady doesn't even care to help me, and I felt like I needed to say, "Can you help me?" She saw me standing there—there was nobody else at the counter. I was there with a friend—but it was just me and him. I think she really thought I was just there to sample the smells of perfumes, and that I wasn't going to make a purchase.

As I think back to my first experience with these kinds of stores, I knew as soon as I walked in there [that] the store was not like anything else I had ever seen. You could see the richness in it, in the decoration, the people, everybody looked like a model, even the workers. I don't remember any minorities, the workers were all White, and [again] they all looked like models. They looked as if they had been handpicked out of some magazine to just work there. And there was just an immediate sort of ambiance in the store—just everything about it. The way it was laid out was just so . . . perfect. The decorations. The people. You knew you were in the very expensive, very high-end, very exclusive place to be. I approached it as I would a museum. I'm coming in here to just look around because my impression was that there's nothing in here I was going to be able to buy. . . . These were not the kind of stores I'd been in.

Now I'm not as intimidated, so I haven't adjusted my shopping, and I haven't changed [due to racism]. I like shopping—it's sort of a hobby for me. . . . I'm not going to adjust that because that's something I enjoy doing. [However,] I'm more cognizant that if I'm going to be shopping high-end in New York, I want to dress up in quality merchandise. I wouldn't wear sweats, or I wouldn't wear jeans or anything like that. I would dress—not in a suit necessarily—but a cashmere or corduroy suit, or something like that. It would just be a quality whatever—a quality pair of pants and a dress shirt, and a sweater, and a good coat. I also would wear a good pair of shoes and a good pocketbook. I would wear items that match, and I would not wear a spoiled old thing that's there for comfort, unless it goes with a dressy outfit—I'm just cognizant of that kind of thing. I'm now much more mature than I used to be when I shop. Now I just take my time. I'm not going to rush, even if people want to watch. They can do whatever they please. I know what I'm not going to do, so I don't worry about it. It does bother me, but I don't allow my being followed or whatever to interfere with my shopping. I love to shop, so I try not to pay attention to [monitoring] unless they make themselves obvious to me. I just go about my business, although I know that I'm being watched and followed. But I don't address them. I figure they're doing their job and whatever way they were trained to do their job is what they feel they need to do. If they don't know how to do their job well enough to not be identified and noticed, then that's foolish on their part because obviously if someone knows they're being followed they're not going to steal. So, they're not going to catch anybody anyways. That's pretty much it, as far as I'm concerned.

I just think that in the retail industry, more needs to be done to train people on issues of diversity and how to go about doing their work. I understand from TV that there's a lot of laws and thefts, and they've come up with a lot of new technology and different ways to keep people from stealing. This is something that's a real problem with the retail industry. But there's got to be a way to train and sensitize people in reference to how they treat everybody, and especially how they treat people of color as they do their job. They must be trained on those techniques instead of just picking out somebody or making people feel uncomfortable. They don't have to be so obvious about it. I don't know any other way to put it—training is what is needed.

MORTIFIED

"My Sense of Gravity Knows Where Your Center of Gravity Is" (Chad's Story)

Chad's story is about his observations of monitoring in a pharmacy and beyond. Chad is a White ally who is humorous, charismatic, and self-described "queer" in his early thirties. He also describes himself as a transplant from the Northwestern United States, now living in a big city further east to work on his master's degree. He seems characteristically quiet in a crowd. But when in a small group or one-on-one he seems to open up, and it doesn't take much to see that he is a sensitive ally to the historically disenfranchised.

We recently met at a social science conference where we were all living in a hostel for a couple of days already, on a one-week stint. After a jam-packed second day of classes, we first officially met late one evening in our dormitory's main lobby where I had gone to look for anyone with a corkscrew. My own suitemates and the suitemates from across the hall had randomly designated me the corkscrew finder, so off I went in search of someone with one. Chad was sitting in a folding chair at a table in the main lobby, quietly working on his laptop—most likely doing homework, of which we had plenty during our conference. He was warm, friendly, and didn't have a corkscrew. Nonetheless, he was brilliant at opening a bottle without one. He solved our problem using one of our hostel keys—a handy trick he says he learned as an undergrad.

While working on opening the bottle, we chatted and asked each other about our careers and work. When he learned that I was writing a book on shopping while Black, he became very animated. Right away he passionately told me of some of his experiences of privilege and observations of discrimination, and I determined that I must ask him for an interview. I asked him, and without hesitation he said, "Yes!" We decided we would touch base with each other in between conference classes the next day to schedule a time, and we did.

In this interview, Chad offers his experiences and insights on how to listen to and be an ally to people of color, and he offers these insights through the lens of his recent shopping experiences and observations. He reveals shopping privileges that he has been able to take for granted all of his life—that he has observed repeatedly to not be available for people of color. He shares his experiences as he juxtaposes them against his observations of the many complications that his friends of color endure while shopping. In the course of speaking, he shares also his perceptions of how some people of color treat other people of color, suggesting the adoption or internalization of racist assumptions.

Chad shares . . .

* * *

I'm thirty-two years old, and I come from like a middle-class, government-working family. We moved around a lot all over the country, as my parents followed the promotions. Typically, I grew up in White regions, White towns, White neighborhoods. Some regions had Asians and Natives, but it was very segregated. Then [after high school], I went to undergrad at [a small liberal arts college in the Northeastern United States], where it's more diverse, but still pretty segregated. I was in [the arts in college] and guess who does [the arts at small, private liberal arts colleges]? All the White kids. It was really diverse, and everyone sticks to their groups. I would say at my undergrad college 30 to 35 percent of the students were students of color, and maybe more if you include the international students. The surrounding town was diverse, and the whole state has struck me as pretty diverse. But going to [that] college was the first time that I actually saw what I would call racial-class segregation, or segregation by [simultaneously] race and class where the Black people are poorer, and the White people all live on the seaside, like that old-money thing. Whereas in the [Northwestern] part of the country, once you are over there, it feels more like a more even playing field—or that's the perception anyway. Growing up [as a young child in the Northwest], I encountered Native people and a lot of Asian people, but very few

Black people. In the state I lived in, I can't think of one Black person that I knew, and I lived there for more than a decade. When I lived in [the Southern Mid-West], the county I lived in for four years during middle school was very White. I would do the community [arts], and every now and then and there might be somebody [of color] from like the other town over. And then for high school [in the most northern Northwest] where we had moved to a town of 30,000, I participated in arts programs and maybe only three [participants] were Black.

As a White person, the only time that I [myself] have experienced discomfort in the consumer marketplace is when I don't fit it in, and I can think of only one situation where that happened. My parents moved to a town in the Midwest, and they lived near a really suburban, really fancy, midwestern lake town—it's an art-galleries-and-fancy-shops type of town. It wasn't discrimination based on my being White, but I definitely was feeling unwelcomed because I didn't look like the rest of their typical White males. I was wearing Chacos [hiking sandals], jeans, and just didn't look like a [White midwestern] kind of guy who in this town tends to wear a suit or a button-up shirt tucked into jeans and nice shoes, with that kind of church-going White, suburban look, kind of thing. I just remember a sense that my questions were alarming them—what [items] cost or where they were. It was the only time that I felt like . . . watched. When I asked [the clerk] where something was, the woman said it was by this other thing that I was near. And then she said, "You had your ha—." But she stopped herself, but it was clear to me that she was referring to it being near something that I had my hand on, and she gave away that she was watching me. That's the only time that I ever felt that—and I think it was because I did not fit the mold of that particular town. I didn't look like the White people that they expected me to look like. Nor did I talk like the White people they expected me to talk like. I didn't match their class idea and that kind of thing.

[Unlike that,] yesterday, I walked a mile and a half [from our conference site] to the laundromat—in the "bad" (making air quotes) side of town. It's the non-bubble, or the real [non-college, part of town]. It's pretty diverse, but not as diverse as the university population here. I went to the laundromat. While I was waiting on my laundry I wandered over to [a large franchised] drugstore nearby to look for a measuring cup. There's a young couple, a man and a woman, probably in their early twenties or late teens. They were off to the side—by the door [of the interior of the drugstore]. The older White woman who was ringing me up—I could just sense and observe her awareness of the couple. I observed her not really looking at what I had, but looking over to the side near where the couple was, but not directly at them. I saw her brow was furrowed, kind of very concerned-looking. She was making a very stereotypical concerned storeowner face. She didn't look at them directly; she did not ask them what they were doing. She had rung them up earlier, I guess. She almost finished ringing me up as they left, and I saw her turn and just watch them leave. To my eye, their behavior was pretty mundane. They did not seem like they were hiding anything, or looking sheepish or looking suspicious in any physical way, other than the fact that they were two young Black people in the drugstore. I've observed that before—seeing a White cashier like, just watch people, and me being aware that you are only watching that person because they're Black.

In [the large, metropolitan town where I currently live in the Northeastern U.S.], in every other store I am greeted by [predominantly White] staff with open arms and great adulation and kindness. When I shop with friends, they tend to be female, and I have noticed differences when I am with my Black female friends. I also lived with a roommate for five years [in the same town] who was a Black woman, and I don't remember specific instances, but we definitely had a different sense of what it meant to be shopping [when I was] with her. We would see more direct, immediate engagement with her from [staff]. So, like, she had to establish herself and they had to establish themselves with her right away, as a way of either keeping track of her, or assuring her they weren't racist. She's about the same age and level of education as me, African American, and we would shop in a White and diverse, more expensive section of town. When I would go into stores with her or with other Black friends, in general, I noticed that I have a stronger physical perception of the cashier or retail people's awareness of where we are. Whereas, as opposed to when I go into a store alone, I feel like I can kind of breathe. I don't get the sense—that animal sense—of another human animal knowing where I am right now. So, I feel freer to move about the space when I am by myself. But when I am with a Black friend, I feel a level of eyes on me or monitoring that I don't feel when I am by myself. I don't think that it's as direct as that little White lady in the drugstore, but it does feel like that animal, my sense of gravity knows where your center of gravity is. Even if I am over here folding a thing, I can feel if they are watching. Anytime we go to a bookstore, or [brand name clothing] shops—when I go into those kinds of fancy-schmancy shops with my friends of color—I just as a human animal have a much bigger perception of being watched—be it [either] directly or peripherally without any direct, mean, or apparent/[overt] surveillance of us. Whereas when I am alone, I can basically wander anywhere I want in the [entire] city and not feel that same [sensation of being monitored]. I perceive this difference in how my former roommate and my other friends of color and I are monitored, even if we are not standing right next to each other. So, if my roommate was in one part of the store and I was in another, I have the gut memory that she typically was watched more than I was. A lot of these retail staff jobs are held by women—and I hope that this isn't a latent sexism—but I do see a lot of concerned White women faces as I like think about this.

And if it wasn't the negative, I'm watching you like a hawk, then it was the opposite, taking care side. Like, "We're going to really make sure that you feel really safe here and that you feel okay here and that you know that I'm not racist and that you are welcome in this store." That's just my gut talking about it. But it's much sooner to connect the retail worker and us, than it is when I go into the store alone. I can go into a store and be left alone, and maybe five minutes in someone will say something. But the greeting, and the follow-up questions—"Do you know we are having a sale on such and such?"—that kind of customer engagement is always more immediate when I am with my friends of color.

[With respect to these observations and my role in them,] I think that my development [as a White ally] is a combination of having been brought up in a liberal household that valued—well I was taught—about blatant racism and that kind of stuff early on. I think that [it was that] in itself, combined with curiosity. [For example], in my current graduate program, it's very easy for me to say something that is a microaggression. [For example, recently], something happened where I said something, and I was able to hear [feedback about] it. I was like, "Oh God, I didn't know . . . I understand why . . . me . . . that [what I said] hurt you." I think there's something about the curiosity and general ethos of fairness, and hoping that I could treat people the way that I want to be treated. And [knowing] that I don't have all the answers and information about all of these systems that I am enjoying [and what they] are built on. I think it's a combination of those [curiosities] that make me feel different from other people of similar cloistered upbringings.

[At times] it's so frustrating trying to keep track of what you're supposed to—what's a microaggression, what's an appropriate thing—it's a moving target. That's uncomfortable for me as a White person, but being on the other end of that, I know, is way more uncomfortable. It's more of a frustrating inconvenience for me to try to learn what to say, and I'm okay with that. Being in acceptance that if I am engaging [with others] I will say the wrong thing at some point, and I will ruffle someone's feathers at one point. I can trust that if I do that, I [can] accept how I was brought up—in terms of being cloistered away from Black culture and encountering it for the first time mostly in my twenties and thirties and just knowing that I will make errors.

I don't think that there's a retail worker who either doesn't have bias about people of color in America or at least about people of color on the east coast of America, or who [alternatively] doesn't worry about their own perceived bias. There just seems to be a lot of awareness about where people of color are at any given moment in the stores. Whether it's fear of them shoplifting or fear of their own fear about being perceived as too watchful or concerned over them. Whereas with me, [other White] people don't even think about me unless they see me looking at something expensive, and then I may get attention.

I also can think of two instances where Black or Latina cashiers in [the Northeastern United States in a very diverse section of a large, metropolitan city] with a minority White [population] extended greater privileges to me. For example, at one of the crabbiest, worst post offices in [that section of the city] with lines that are always long, almost all of the customers are people of color. There was this instance where I went in, and I knew I had post office business to attend to that required me to wait in the long line, but I also had another very quick question that involved a package. The shorter line was not the appropriate line to do both things, but I went to the shorter line anyway. When my turn came, I walked up to the [clerk] and I said, "I have this question about this package, but also I need this other thing." She was a middle-aged woman of color between the ages of forty and sixty. I just remember that the way she treated me was way different from the way that she had just berated or wouldn't help or couldn't help or whatever somebody [of color] who was in line right before me. But then she was totally willing to help me and was charmed by me, and I wasn't even trying. Her behavior was like, "I am going to go out of my way, and we are going to get you out of here quickly." My gut feeling picked up on this [disparity]. My instincts [perceived] that I am not bringing anything to this encounter other than my whiteness and my maleness—that's the only thing I am bringing here. I'm coming to you with a direct question, and you are letting me have what I want without me going out of my way to be super friendly or asking for favors or bargaining or being mean or whatever. This happened four or five years ago, but it is still with me because it was the first time that I can recall palpably realizing that the only reason I am getting what I want is because I'm White and male. I have no proof of that of course, but I was the only White man in that post office. And I think it also was because I knew that there was nothing else that I was bringing to the table but that. I wasn't being particularly cordial or negative, I was just being direct and kind, but not annoying or saccharin or bossy—to my eye of course.

Another situation involved a bank [clerk]. So, you don't get change from a bank. What I mean is, you can't go into a bank and get change for like a bus or something like that unless you are a customer of that bank. This happened two days ago [as I arrived via] the bus for this conference. The train had taken me to [one town], and then I was getting the bus to [this next town, for the conference] but I needed change. [To get change] I went to the nearby bank. There was a Black woman clerk between the ages of thirty and forty-five, and I asked, "Can I get change for the bus? I have a twenty." She [first] looked to the side, and then said, ". . . That'll be okay" or "That'll be fine," as if it was breaking the rules. I have no idea what the policy is for [that particular] bank, only my experience of banks usually saying "no" to that kind of thing. Because of [her] words, I realized [to myself], "You just heard me asking if I can break the rules." And she let me.

MANAGED

"Fried Chicken!" (Dana's Story)

Dana's story is about the wrong people being monitored while partaking in a franchised restaurant buffet. It's about the obliviousness that some people have about the distorted stereotypes that they hold in their minds about Black people. For this reason, I am obsessive about myself and my children getting receipts for our purchases—in case some venue takes it upon themselves to think that any of us did not pay for something.

Dana's memory-telling reminded me of a story that a Hispanic colleague used to tell me. He said that in his community, the White, Black, and Latina youth would work together to steal from stores. The youth of color would go into a department store first, and the White youth would follow several minutes later behind them. While the store staff would be busy watching the youth of color, the White youth would fill their pockets and backpacks with candy, school supplies, clothes, and anything else needed. Then the White youths would leave the store first, and then the youth of color would leave. They would all assemble right away at a central location and split their bounty. The truth is that many people of color and White allies know what the deal is concerning the presumption of guilt when it comes to shopping and many other aspects of minoritized life in America. And likewise, there still are many people who have no idea that people of color, and especially Black youth and adults, are more likely to be assumed guilty and monitored more closely—all of which brings us to Dana.

Dana is a vibrant, African American woman in her early seventies, living in the South. She recently had had an experience in an all-you-can-eat restaurant where she was being heavily monitored by staff as she dined, while her White dining partner and other White customers were not being monitored at all. I had heard about the incident from her daughter, and we laughed about it—sarcastically. But under our sarcastic laughs, like most sarcasm, there was pain. As women of color, we both have felt the pain of being carefully watched from a young age and even into our older ages as we have gone into consumer marketplaces. Likewise, we also have perceived that not everyone seems to have that same burden of being frequently or differentially monitored imposed upon them, as noted earlier. Dana tells the brief story of, even at her age, being monitored closely by management, who ironically were Asian, at an all-you-can-eat-buffet while a White couple ate the restaurant clean out of a good portion of its menu. She also speaks of the demoralizing discomfort that this experience caused her. Ironically, all of this seemed to go on underneath the awareness of her White dining partner. Dana illustrates for us what an unknown number of White people may believe and apparently some voluntary immigrants may internalize—that there is a greater tendency for people of color to be dishonest and a greater need for us to be both watched and controlled. This tendency for significantly greater scrutiny from White people and sometimes other minoritized people, is an added burden that many Black and Brown people carry throughout life. My question always is, what do these added burdens cost many Black and Brown people over the course of our lifetimes?

Dana speaks . . .

* * *

I had this experience [recently when] I had a [White] friend visiting from [the Midwest]. We decided that we would stop at [a fast-food franchise] for dinner. They had a nice little buffet there, so we decided that's where we would eat. We decided we would go to the back because it was quiet, so that we could talk. She was visiting from out of town, and we hadn't seen each other since high school. The last booth was taken, so we decided to sit at the second-to-last booth. There was a [White] couple, probably in their fifties, sitting there, and they were already eating. They had a huge stack of bones, so they had eaten a lot of chicken. The wife went up and got some more chicken—another huge stack of chicken—and that disappeared very rapidly. Then the husband went up and got another huge plate of chicken, and they ate that. This was the second plate that I saw of bones that they had consumed from eating all of this chicken—and they repeated this several times. On the last incident, when they were finished stashing and eating chicken, the woman was sitting in the center of the booth where she could face the [check-in/check-out] counter. The man had his back to the counter and the door. The last time they went up, they switched places—the man sat on the edge of the booth on the opposite side, and the woman moved to the edge of the booth. Then I noticed that every time they would just gracefully get up and go [get chicken] was when it was busy, when customers came in. This time, several people came in at one time, and that's when they got up and just quietly strolled out of the store. I don't know how, they were such a small size couple, [or] rather, on the small side. To me, I don't know how they could consume that much chicken. The lady had quite a large bag, and it was all filled with chicken [also].

I could see them stuffing the chicken into their bag. I was facing the last booth and the glass window [they sat next to]. It was like the glass was real shiny, and I could see everything that was going on from the glass window that goes outside. I could actually see—I could just look there. I couldn't see what the man was doing because his back was to me, but I could see everything that the woman was doing because she was facing me. When I went up to get some more chicken, she also came up, and she was just as cordial and friendly, and sounded very intelligent. I wouldn't say that they were homeless or anything like that. I would say that they were people who didn't need to consume and take such excessive amounts of chicken. They were small people, and not overweight by any stretch of the imagination. I just don't know where they put it, I don't know how their stomachs were large enough to hold so much chicken. But [again], her purse was large enough where it could hold a lot of chicken, and it did (chuckling).

There was a couple managing the store—only two people. The lady, she was at the counter, and the other was in the back cooking and replenishing the food. It was poetic justice to me, because the manager at the counter was suspicious of me—eyeing me when I went up and asked her if there were some more rolls—she didn't like it. She snapped that there would be some more up in a minute, like I was taking too much or something. I just had a very uncomfortable experience [with her reaction]. I had just witnessed the other couple, what they were doing with the buffet, so that was a very, very interesting experience.

So, this story is twofold. For one, how did they consume so much chicken—and how were they going to deal with all of the chicken that she had in her purse. I felt that if that was a frequent occurrence, [that restaurant] wasn't going to stay in business very long. And secondly, I was very uncomfortable and I felt like, as a minority—a person of color, that she [the owner or manager] was just suspicious [of me]; she really didn't want to give me any food. I was the only minority customer. The owners or managers also were minorities—I would say, far Eastern Indians. But all of the [other] customers were Caucasian, even my friend was Caucasian. I was the only Black customer in the restaurant. I felt that they were suspicious anyway, and were stereotyping Black people. She made me feel very uncomfortable and unwelcomed in her restaurant. She was hesitant to give me [an additional] plate, and the eye language, the body language, and then definitely when I went up there to ask her if there were any more rolls. The eye contact, and the way she said they [the rolls] would be up later. This was in a diverse neighborhood, but all the customers were Caucasian. Welcoming, friendly, courteous, she [the owner or manager] was not. And like I said, there was only the one man in the back cooking and bringing up the food, replenishing the food on the buffet, so that made it kind of hard [for them] to keep up with everyone. But I was very uncomfortable, and I felt very unwelcomed.

MISTOOK

"I Was Hoping to Live Long Enough to See Major Changes on Earth" (Eleanor's Story)

Eleanor's experiences of being monitored across age, socioeconomic status, and professional success are shared. Eleanor is a young octogenarian and prominent leader in a local community in the Northern United States. In fact, she's someone that I have idolized for many years for her compassion for youth, her vision for change, and her outspokenness. With both of us being educators and community activists, it seemed that our paths have crossed often, even when attending conferences outside of our states. It was at one of these conferences that we were able to connect about my idea for this book.

Eleanor seems to always be surrounded by people younger than her. I don't know whether to call us fans, or mentees, or groupies, or what. But for her, I suspect that her mission may be to grab our ears and lend hers to us every chance she gets with the mission of mutual encouragement, sharing of inspiration, and, most importantly, passing on the torch to the younger generations. So, it was in one of these moments where a few of us were standing with her and chatting and catching up on our recent endeavors, current goals, and desired missions. In sharing these things among us, I mentioned to her that I was working on a book about Black and Brown experiences while shopping and such. She connected right away with this topic, and began to tell us of some of her rather vivid experiences. Knowing how busy she is, I was reluctant to ask for an interview, but I pushed myself to put the idea out there. So, when those circling her had moved on to find food and it was just her and I, I asked her if she would be willing to share some of her experiences and insights for my book. When she responded that she would, I forgot for a moment where we were and halfway screamed out with happiness. I let out enough of a gleeful squeal that several of the conference attendees turned their heads to see what was going on. I raised a hand to let them know that all was okay, and then I put my arm around this lovely role-model and walked her to her next session of the conference, joyfully brainstorming with her on a date for me to take the journey up to her home to interview her.

Upon meeting with her, I found that Eleanor seemed to have a great need, even an extraordinary passion, for telling her story. I found myself enthralled as she spoke. I thought quite a bit about her values on the ride home, and the legacy she has built for the younger generations, maybe at the cost of her daily comforts. And I said to myself, "That is a true hero!" This true hero, Eleanor, tells of her experiences being monitored in stores no matter how well-known she was or how much of a leadership position she held within the predominantly White community where she lives. An African American woman of leadership, she is a long-time community activist and retired educator. She also served in the highest of political leadership roles within a rapidly growing, bustling community. But she illustrates, through her memory-telling, that no amount of achieving can protect a Black person from colorism, internalized racism, the eye of suspicion and monitoring, over "helpfulness," or alternatively, invisibility, any of which may follow us. She also shows us that it is important for us to be aware of the pain that we may feel in public spaces, but to be as strategically constructive as we can in how we choose to respond to it.

Eleanor shares her story . . .

* * *

While thinking about experiences while shopping, well as a former [Black woman political leader in my region], I was well-known in the community. When I would go shopping, I found the same discrimination that I had a lot of other times. There would always be this store person shopping along with me. I could always notice that it would be the same person. [So] many times, I was being watched—this lady would shop when I shopped. She wore the same clothes, and she would come shopping when I would, moving along the same way I did. After four or five occasions, I finally said to her, "It's amazing that we would be shopping at the same time, all the time." She looked at me and said, "It is surprising." That was the normal kind of the thing when I would go into a store. The reason I knew they were watching me is because it was the same woman all the time; she would carry the same little pocketbook under her arm, and she would become familiar to whatever store I would go into. I also find there is some store person who comes right over to ask, "May I help you?" Even if I say "No, I am okay," they still linger around. That not only happens here, but it happens here—and there. Senior citizens, whenever they go in a big grocery store, we find somebody moving along with us. This happens almost everywhere. As a [political leader] it became difficult because people stopped me to talk about their problems. They thought, here she is, and I will tell her what my problem is. I was sympathetic. That meant I didn't get a chance to get to try the clothes that I bought. I decided to go shopping when the store was about ready to be closed since there would be less people, but then I noticed they were watching me closely because I was in the store. But when people in the community stopped me, I would have two or three outfits that I had picked to try on, but I didn't get time to try them on, so I ended up buying all of them. I couldn't go when the store was full of people, and I couldn't go when the store was closing.

The store nearest to me is right here in the shopping center where I could go to find clothes, underwear, and household goods—whatever I needed, I could find there. That store would close at 9 p.m. and I would go around 8:30 p.m., thinking I could shop. But, once again, there always would be this person watching me down the aisles. I would not engage with them, but they were always there. It became a really conscious thing with me, and I hated going shopping. And if I went out to the mall, that's even worse. From one shop to another, somebody would stop me, so shopping was really difficult. I was really conscious of that "shopper" hovering close by—it didn't matter what I did, there was somebody hovering as if they were shopping—they tried to look like they were shopping. It became so obvious that for almost two years, I didn't do much shopping. I tried, but it became an obvious thing. I didn't tell them who I was. I didn't do things to make much out of it, I would just leave.

But not only in the stores, it also happened in the streets. Most shops in this town would put things outside on the street sidewalks and in the shopping centers. If you were Black and stopped, you would see somebody immediately come outside and wait on you, but they didn't do that for other folks. I am not sure that White America was aware that we knew what they were doing. I don't know, maybe they needed to do it. Maybe there was shoplifting, I don't know, but it was obvious to me that they were watching Blacks. There was one of the stores that had a signal where if you didn't go to the store often, you wouldn't realize that they were triggering the signal. I went often enough to the store to know—they would make this announcement over the intercom. I went to that store often because I wouldn't finish shopping, and I would have to go back. I would hear this message, it would come from the intercom, and it would be the same message. I learned going in and out of this store often enough that this message would come when there was a Black person shopping in the store. It wouldn't be a name of the person, but somebody "report to area so-and-so." I can't remember what the wording was, but it was so obvious because it was the same wording all the time, and the wording would "designate" the same so-called area of the store. Instead of two girls coming over to peruse, there would be three girls. It was so obvious that I learned the signal. I didn't think that it was a coincidence that I would hear this signal. I never thought of memorizing it, but I could always recognize it.

Although I never was stopped, I kept on thinking that I was going to be stopped at some moment. For example, once, I bought something with one of those tags on the material, and I didn't notice right away that they forgot to remove it. It didn't set off the alarm, so, later, I was curious about that. I couldn't wear the dress because it had the thing on it. So, I took it back to the store. When I went back to the store, the alarm went off. They might have thought I had stolen it if I didn't have the receipt. . . . I am sure it would have been a problem. I would have had to verify how I got to do this, and how I got out of the store with this. I always keep the receipts. I save them four or five months, because I have a box where I keep them.

So, I became aware of them watching me. If I had something in the cart, I might say, "I don't think I will take this item," for fear of someone thinking I would try to steal it. I had one lady say to me, "Listen, we better get these items out of your cart because we don't want them to think that you are going to steal them." She was a clerk there, and she was helping me to get the stuff out of my cart. She realized that they would think a Black person was stealing something—and that just happened recently! I had a couple of hats and a pocketbook that I really needed, and I had them in my cart. She said, "Let's take them out of the basket because we don't want them—the store personnel—to think that you are stealing them." She just took the things and put them behind the counter. She didn't realize that I felt she might have said that because I was Black. She probably knew that they were checking all Blacks. I just look back over it, and I notice it now. I still notice it, but it doesn't bother me that much.

One of the ways that I cope with these things is that I don't go to the same store that often, and I don't go at the same time [of day]. Before, I would shop right before the shop closed. Now, I go at different times. So, it's not as obvious to me. I don't go often enough to recognize the people. . . . I don't think it has changed simply because I travel with senior citizens in this town. We always go to exclusive shopping centers and areas to shop. When I walk in the store, there is an absolute change in attitude, and a change of clerks who assist me in particular. Usually, I am with the senior citizens, and they are [almost] all White. There are only three of us [Black people], and we don't shop together because we are different ages and we like different things. However, when I walk in the store, I get special attention—they come over to say, "May I help you?" Now, there are thirty-four of us, and we are moving around the store, but I get the special attention. Why would they pick me out? There are more than thirty of us, and we are moving in at the same time. There are maybe three clerks in the store, and I am getting this special attention because I am Black. I look like other senior citizens. . . . We all wear just sweaters and jackets, and I don't dress any different than the others. These are senior citizens who are retired people just like me. Most of them are retired professionals, and we just go on trips together. A lady arranges the trips and it's easy for us to go shopping. There's no difference in us; none whatsoever. Except that immediately I get help! We are all acting the same, we all look the same, except I'm Black. We're acting the same; we all get into that store; we scatter out to see what it is we like; but invariably, I will get attention right away. "Can I help you, may I help you, what would you like?" And I get this attention. The first question that comes to my mind is, "Why is she helping me, and why isn't she helping the other ladies?" Ha, ha! And I pass it right off, because I know why she's helping me. She wants to see what I'm going to pick up. She wants to see what I'm going to buy, she wants to watch, there's no question in my mind.

I have a basic background from childhood because I lived in the South where light-skinned Blacks had better opportunities because their White ancestors saw to it that they went to school, got college degrees, [and that] they were professionals. So, they had more funds, more money and they were treated differently. And even though you had a very, very dark-skinned Black man who had even more money, a finer car, his kids looked as good as the light-skinned ones, but they were invariably treated differently. I've just known that because that's the way I've grown up, and I knew that that's how you're going to get treated. Even in the shopping situation, the Black ones are immediately circled and watched. . . .

Even today the lighter-skinned person is being treated better and faster and kinder and waited on [more quickly] than a darker-skinned person. . . . Now if there were two of us Blacks, and one's dark and one's light, they would follow the darker one first. Discriminatory attitudes that have come over time haven't changed very much. Black people themselves will treat you differently [also]. Even if you were in a store where Blacks are in control, the Blacks will wait on the White-skinned person first. That's history, they've grown up doing it, and they're still doing it. I can't say I don't know why, but I wish I didn't know why. But I do know why, and I could write a book. And I don't think it gets any better. Sometimes I have to demand my waitress to do some things. I can go and ask them, can I have some more coffee? And the waitress will fold napkins for another minute or two, and bring me that coffee whenever she feels like getting it. With the other patrons, they're going to get that coffee; "Would you like some coffee, would you like some coffee?"

Over the years, I have noticed that men tend not to pay as much attention to how they get treated. However, my [deceased] husband used to tell me they follow him around the store too. Even back then, he had to prove one time that he bought the cigarettes he had. He had to go back to the store to prove he had bought the cigarettes. Because I've gone out to dinner with a gentleman, and if I say, "I don't like this salad dressing, waitress could you bring me something else?" he would say, "Why won't you just eat your dinner and stop complaining?!" But I'm never going to eat anything I don't want, and I'm never going to eat anything that's not right. I've waited too many long years to [now] just take any kind of service. But I think men aren't as fussy. But changes don't get made if you don't complain.

I was hoping that I would live long enough to see some major changes in the Earth. I traveled all over the world—Australia, London, Paris—and we get mistreated there too! However, we were treated very special when we were in Africa—we were treated very special because we were guests—and Americans—and things like that. But I had hoped I would live long enough to see a change, but I still think it's going to have to change. Economic systems and things change. The South has changed, but most people in the North don't know that. The South has been forced to change because of the economy. The bus boycott in Montgomery started the change, so when you go to the South now, you're treated like royalty because the Southern merchants have become aware that money has become important and that money is the major way to success for them. The North hasn't come to that realization. That's why lots and lots of people are going south and businesses are moving to the South. I just hope we are going to have some changes up here. I am not optimistic about it, and that's the part that's scary; we are too complacent. We used to think that we are going to go to the North and get treated better, but it is very different in the South. You won't know that until you take a trip to the South. In the South, the welcome mat is out—service is there, because they have gone through poverty. They have gone through the depression years and they know that money is important.

[Growing up in the South], I can remember from [as early as] age two, that my father was a very strict man about Whites and Blacks. We grew up knowing that we had to be protected from what might happen to us out there. So, I knew from the time I was two or three, that I was different, and that the world was going to treat me differently. I grew up knowing that, I went off to college knowing that, and I went into the work world knowing that. That's why I can pick up on discrimination—without even talking to you, I can look at you and tell when you're going to discriminate. I see so much discrimination here in this [Northern U.S.] region, and I try to stay out of it. But sometimes I have to speak up. I've known it all my life, and I know it when I see it, and it's obvious to me. It's not an accident that I can sense it, I just know it's there, and I know what's going to happen. With that, you kind of know how to steer yourself away from it. I steer around it, and I know how to change it when I see it, and sometimes I can change it before it even happens. If I am in a situation where I know the Black person's going to be mistreated, I can just walk up and get in front of that situation, and change it, and let the establishment know that I know what's going to happen here. I do that often. For example, if I go into a restaurant and there's a line of us, they will want to seat me and take me past ten empty tables, all the way down to the end, in the very back of the restaurant—all the way to the back wall. And I might say to the waitress when I get there, "Oh why did you have to pass all those tables to bring us down here?" And she'll say, "Oh we have to allot the spaces out to the waitresses." While we were sitting there eating, the place may fill up completely. There wasn't a vacant space in the place, and we ate our dinner, and we came out, and I laughed. I said to myself, "Wasn't that something, I could have sat at the first table." But that is what happens to you, when you are unaware and you follow the waitress, she will take you to the back wall.

Last winter a White girlfriend and I went to a [regional] vacation spot. She and I went together, and she did not believe what was going to happen to me. I said to her, "Let's go and I will show you what will happen to me." When we arrived, we went to a hotel and we were heading to get checked in. She still didn't believe what happens to us minorities. So, I said to her, you check in, and I'll check in, and let's see what happens. We went to the hotel desk and the lady signed her to the room. She got to me and she assigned me to a room. The room she assigned me was all the way on the other side of the hotel that was closed-off. There was no heat in there. They weren't even using it for the winter. They put her in another place. The attendant told her that she could park her car right outside the room. When the attendant got to me, I asked, "Where do you park your car?" she said, "There is parking space two blocks up, you could take your car up there and then come back down." We checked in at the same time! Now, once I moved in, I called her and she asked, "Where are you?" I said, "I am over here in the section of the hotel that hasn't been used for the entire winter." And I called them [about the heat] and they said that they have been working on the heat. And then, finally, I said, "Send that young man to get my bags, I am going to check out." When the young man arrived, he said, "What are you doing over here? . . . We haven't used this room the entire winter." I told him, "Well, take me to another room," so he arranged for the lady to put me in another room. The next morning we got up and got ready for breakfast, and we went down to this fancy restaurant we were supposed to go to. The waitress took me way over by the kitchen, and put me at a little table in a nook there. But my girlfriend, she put her over by a window. I was just letting her see what could happen. They didn't know we were together, but she had the experience of her life. She didn't believe it. She was born and bred right here in [this region], and she could not believe all the things I was telling her that were happening to me up here. Okay! Let's go, and I will show you what is happening.

Well, this happens to me all the time as I travel. If I travel with a group of White people, they will put me in a room right under the staircase or the elevator or next to the plunger. [Now] my friend just says, "Let's just sit down and have a cup of coffee and wait for them to change the room," [because] they already know that when I check in to a hotel they are going to have to change my room. Now, I did that for five years. I traveled with a [a group from] all over the United States. We traveled to all first-class hotels—and they would invariably put me under the staircase, or under the elevator or next to the laundry room. I don't get bitter. I don't get angry. I don't wait till later. I confront it right then and right there.

THINGS THAT PART I'S STORIES CAN TEACH CONSUMERS AND MARKETERS

STRATEGIES CONSUMERS MIGHT CONSIDER TRYING

- Be aware that in addition to the joy, freedom, and fun that can accompany the consumer marketplace experience, it also can come with anxiety, upset, pain, energy drain, and negative emotions, especially for people of color and other disenfranchised people. When finding oneself aware of the pain, when it occurs, it should be treated constructively—by reaching out to resources and deciding to what degree you are electing to attempt to address it.
- If the personnel you are speaking with in order to try to address the matter are not interested in your concerns, then you can diplomatically confront or address your concerns up the ladder to the manager(s) of the store, the division, the agency, or the corporation, and so on. First, communicate the reasons that you, your family, your friends, your community, and so on, engage with their business, and then communicate why you are disappointed with your most recent experience(s). It may be helpful if you also can make clear what you are seeking in terms of a remedy (e.g., an acknowledgment, an apology, a refund, a credit, etc.). I often have found myself saying the following: "I am having a problem with an issue at your store, and I am hoping that you can help me to get it resolved."

- You can inquire about the store, division, agency, or corporation policies and ask where you can find a copy of those policies in writing.
- If you have a "funny bone," sometimes humor can be used to get your point across (e.g., "Feel welcome to take pictures of me while you follow me around").
- Rather than changing your shopping patterns, some consumers change how they think about their shopping or other consumer experiences. For example, some consumers view the heavy store monitoring as foolish and ignore it, as long as severely inappropriate boundaries are not crossed. Others turn it into a game (e.g., "cat and mouse"), or challenge themselves to see how quickly they can go into the store, shop for what they need, pay, and exit. However, the downside of using this as an exclusive strategy is that it puts all the burden on the consumer and does not impose any challenge to the establishment to change.
- You can consider each situation in terms of whether you should resist poor service, racial profiling, and so on, if not for yourself, then for the benefit of those in the community who may not have the same wherewithal or resources for advocating for themselves or others as you may possess.
- You can seek an online survey or write a letter to the managers all the way up to the corporate offices, with a cc: to all of them.
- You can write an online review on sites such as Yelp, Angie's List, Better Business Bureau, and so on.
- Before you visit stores or other businesses that are new to you, you can look for credible reviews online to see if there are complaints or concerns that you also would find annoying if those things happened to you.
- As a form of protest, or just for the sake of your health, you can consider otherwise adapting your shopping behavior, for example, by grocery shopping, clothes shopping, or banking online, while holding the same standards for online transactions as you would any other transactions (e.g., courteous customer service).
- If you monitor your comfort and sense of health and wellbeing in marketplace environments, as well as the energy that it takes to speak up when concerns arise, and find that it is taxing to your health, you might take self-care action. You might benefit from engaging in self-care practices, such as relaxation, yoga, meditation, prayer, counseling, therapy, or other supports, when these environments have added more stress to your day or week than is healthy for you.[1]

- If you have the transportation options, time, and resources, you could possibly choose not to shop in stores or businesses that treat you, your family, or your community inappropriately or that do not contribute to the upkeep and betterment of the very community that supports and keeps its business thriving. Unfortunately, not all consumers have the resources for this option, but for those that do, this may be an option to consider if you haven't already practiced it.
- You might examine the reading resources and suggestions at the end of the other parts of this book.

STRATEGIES MARKETERS MIGHT CONSIDER TRYING

- Retailers and other marketplace businesses are becoming increasingly vulnerable to consumers' online options. Consumers have more options than ever, including African Americans who spend more than a trillion per year in our economy. Therefore, considering whether your business's or franchise's climate(s) is welcoming and equitable for everyone is more important than ever.
- Be aware that high-quality, ongoing or regular (as opposed to one-shot, quick-fix) diversity training is needed for stores and other retail marketplaces, divisions, agencies, and corporation staff at every level, as well as for all security and other law enforcement personnel.
- Be aware that ongoing diversity training that is not focused just on learning about "the other folks," but rather is inclusive of ongoing examination of one's self is extremely important. Diversity training that does not facilitate serious consideration and examination of one's self is counterproductive. Self-examination and self-reflection may include implicit bias explorations, racial identity development explorations, social-location work, intersectional examination, and so on.
- Be aware that although many consumers have come to expect it, they still do not like and even find it from a young age emotionally painful or anger-provoking to be negatively or inaccurately stereotyped, inequitably or unjustly suspected, or singled-out for surveillance, being followed, or otherwise treated as criminal. Many people of color and allies have a personality, disposition, or interest in justice and activism that rightfully does not always allow such things to slide. Therefore, eventually your corporation is going to have a potential public relations nightmare if you don't move proactively.[2]

- Be aware that many people of color are burdened by daily, weekly, monthly, annual, and generational microaggressions that have a cumulative impact over time. Many people of color may at times feel barked at, pushed around, snapped at, mistrusted, ignored, or otherwise belittled in the marketplace by staff or other customers. Some scholars have estimated that this adds an average additional 25 percent burden of emotional weight to most people's of color functioning on any given day, whether it is obvious to others or not. This can create hidden or visible anxiety, anger, discomfort, and other emotions in people of color who do not need your store or business to further add to these daily burdens.
- Be aware that many people of color are concerned not only for how they and their families are being treated, but also for the treatment of those with fewer resources to address the situation. As current events have illustrated, mistreating one person of color may ripple out and have the vicarious impact upon national or international communities of people of color and allies being offended and withdrawing their support from your business, which can translate into huge profit losses for your business. However, in spite of profits, treating consumers equitably both in theory and in practice is the right thing to do.
- Be aware that it has been well documented in research literature that people of color tend to be very sensitive to and perceptive of the emotional climate in an environment. Therefore, people of color may be very quick to pick up on being served, not served, or overserved because of their looks (e.g., race, skin-color, jewelry, style of clothes, designer labels, etc.). This is painful and offensive to many and may drive your customers away, which can translate into lost opportunities for your business and negative publicity. Unfortunately, the more vulnerable customers may not have as much of a choice or any other options, but they too are developing resources for resisting marketplace abuse.
- Some people of color have expressed that they have adapted to negative marketplace experiences by avoiding them, which also translates into lost revenue for businesses and aborted opportunities to build community.
- When any consumer comes to express to personnel or managers their concerns, those concerns should be taken seriously and followed up with in a timely fashion, no matter what socioeconomic status, age, gender, race, ethnicity, LGBTQIA+ status, religion, and so on, the consumer appears to be.

- Research studies involving eye-scan technology have shown that as early as preschool, children of color are disproportionately monitored in comparison to their White counterparts.[3] School discipline and criminal justice statistics and a plethora of current events suggest this disparate tendency continues throughout life, even in the consumer marketplace. Therefore, it's advisable to not be so busy watching the people of color and poor consumers and staff in your stores and businesses that you miss the White and economically privileged folks who may be stealing.
- You might examine the reading resources and suggestions at the end of the other parts of the book.

MONITORING

Reflection Questions and Related Readings

1. Having now read the first part of this book, or portions of it, what would you add to the list of twelve observations offered in the introduction, concerning the nature of marketplace racism?
2. What can everyday citizens do to help themselves not rely so heavily on stereotypic notions when engaging with people or making decisions about them, especially in consumer marketplaces?
3. What steps can citizens and the marketplace take to resist, disrupt, or otherwise ameliorate or eliminate inequitable surveillance and other marketplace practices?
4. Responsible engagement with others requires reflection. What do you need to do or what can you do to think further, more responsibly, and more critically regarding the consumer of color shopping experience and the history and contexts that surround it?
5. What questions, comments, thoughts, and further processing do you still have to do about each of the stories that you read in this section? Who can you partner with to work together on getting a better understanding of what you have read? On what appropriate resources can you draw?

RELATED READINGS

Eberhardt, Jennifer. *Biased: Uncovering the Hidden Prejudice that Shapes What We See, Think, and Do.* New York: Vintage Press, 2019.

Johnson, Guillaume D., Kevin D. Thomas, Anthony K. Harrison, and Sonya A. Grier. *Race in the Marketplace: Crossing Critical Boundaries.* New York: Palgrave MacMillan, 2019.

II

INEQUITIES

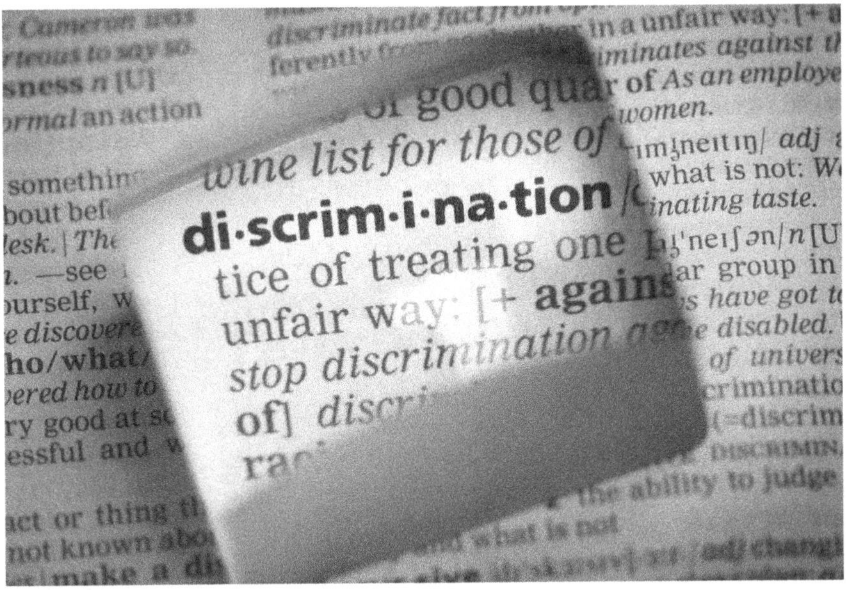

Not everyone experiences stores, malls, and other businesses and marketplaces in the same way.

ineskoleva/iStock/Getty Images

POEM 2

Internal Dialogue

Micah E. Lubensky

Attention Safeway staff:
As of immediately, all grocery clerks
must shut down their register and lock it with a key
if they need to take the two steps down the check-out counter,
away from the register,
in order to bag the groceries of the tall biracial man in aisle 5.
Once you have bagged his groceries,
and he is on his way out of the store, you may
then
return to your register
and unlock it with your key and 15-digit passcode.
Thank you, and
have a nice day.

Why did he just . . .
. . . is this happening to me?
In this Safeway
where I've paid
for more than four years?

I know I did not hear
any special announcement,
but why this sudden change
of checker comportment?

Beyond closing the drawer,
was it necessary to
SHUT DOWN the register?

. . . It's 3pm, bright as day . . .
There's an elderly couple in line behind me
(but they sure look like they're gonna pay),
and people all around—everyone can see.
I'm not wearing a ski
mask. No tattoo on my forehead saying
GIVE ME ALL YOUR MONEY . . .

The only bulge in my pocket
is my too-small wallet
which he saw go back into my pants
and it's just my car keys in my hands . . .
Well, I've got a nail clipper on my keyring that I didn't explain . . .
I know I can't bring that on a plane since September Eleventh,
but I didn't think it would cause Safeway employees to feel threatened . . .

So why did he shut down his register
to take the two steps to bag my beans
when I have never
in all these years seen
any checker
do that here before?

Did my hair scare
him? *Look out, beware!*
Again my crazy coils must've foiled
my unknown plot to shoplift. As if:
"Boy, I'd
make out like a king
if I nab the scrilla from that
checkout ringer
and oh they'd never catch me
as I try to flee
through the doors to the lot
where my getaway car must be hot
to fly me to my ghetto home
(yeah right, in THIS all-White suburban domain)
. . . where I could count all the dough
that I nabbed from the sto' . . .

what, a grand total
of $329? or
whatever is in your big box?"

. . . Chil', please!
I have NO time for a life of crime,
nor any intention to fulfill your fearful,
personal, racist unmentions of what I would do
to your store and you.

And on top of it all, now I'm even more pissed
that I went through all of this
just to dismiss
that it wasn't anything I did
or that my behavior was remiss.

So, without a word, nor the slightest sign to deceive
I snatch my bag of generic garbanzo beans
and leave.

And do you know
that I stood outside the door of that store
with my bag in my hand
looking back inside
for the proof I was right!

He did *not* close down when he stepped over to snare
the groceries for the next, dear old pair.
Nor did he shut down for the woman after them.
. . . Nor did *any other* checker shut down
    while I stood there in the door watching,
        with my big frown.

If there is a new policy,
it certainly is NOT applied consistently.
In the past 15 minutes, it was only used
with the one customer of African descent
who came to pay for his groceries.
If there is no new policy, that was just
nasty discrimination, whether or not it was his intent.

Either way, I'm *OFFENDED* and won't go
to that checker anymore.

If I hadn't been so shocked, I should've complained before
walking out the door.
Well, from now on I'm ready whenever I go to that store.
If I get treated like that, I'm calling the manager out on the floor.

POEM 3

Two Friends

Lisa Mallory

We are two friends.
We like to shop, and go out to eat, and talk, and laugh, and share stories.
She is everything I could want to be.
She is accomplished, and funny, and beautiful, and smart, and caring.
And she is very patient with me.
She knows that I am still learning.
And some of what I am learning is horribly ugly.

One day we are out shopping.
My friend and I walk over to a cosmetics counter.
She plans to buy some perfume and get the free bonus gift.
While she makes her purchase, I step away to look at something else.
I feel a presence beside me and turn to see a sales clerk.
"Can I show you something?" the clerk asks, smiling.
"No, I'm just browsing," I reply.
"Some of these scents are really beautiful," she says.
"No, I'm just here with my friend.
She, actually, is the one who is planning to buy something."
I turn and walk back towards my friend.
At this point I haven't realized what is going on.

I walk all the way around the counter and then notice that the clerk is still behind me.
Meanwhile, my friend is standing alone, still waiting to make her purchase.
"The lipstick in the bonus gift would look really nice on you," the clerk continues.

Her white face is smiling and helpful.
She is **so** willing to be of service.
As I tell her again that I am not planning to buy anything, my friend still waits.
"The lady over there is interested in buying something," I tell the clerk.
But she makes no effort to even walk over to my friend.

I feel a cold stab in my heart as I suddenly realize what is happening.
I want to protect my friend, but I can't.
I feel angry and powerless.
God, forgive me, but I feel such hatred for this sales clerk.
This is not a documentary on television.
I am standing in Macy's at Perimeter Mall, and this is real.
This sales clerk is a shiny, white example of the very, very ignorant.
I am humiliated to be associated with her in any way.
All we have in common is our race.

Another day my friend and I are on our way to lunch.
"There's the book mobile," I say, as we pass a parking lot.
"I remember the book mobile," my friend replies.
"Oh, that's cute," I answer.
"Yes," my friend says. "When I was little, I used the book mobile.
Black people ***had*** to use the book mobile.
We weren't allowed in 'white libraries.'
The book mobile came every two weeks.
We were only allowed to check out five books at a time,
And I always read all mine within a couple of days."

I suddenly feel like crying.
The book mobile isn't cute any more.
I am haunted by her story and I think of two little girls.
They both had long pig tails and they both loved their mothers very much.
They liked to read, and dream, and think about what they wanted to be.
But even if they had been the same age and had lived in the same city,
They maybe never would have been friends,
Because the little black girl and the little white girl couldn't go to the same places.

One afternoon, my friend and I go to the Fox Theatre.
I arrive early, so I spend a few minutes looking around the lovely lobby.
A smiling white face greets me and invites me join the Theatre's guild.
He is **so** proud to represent the Theatre.
Beaming, he tells me that "The Theatre is an ***important*** piece of history.
It has such a regal past and it's a place of ***'fabulous'*** tradition."

When my friend arrives and we take our seats, she tells me more about the Theatre.
This is not my first visit to the Theatre, but it is the first time I hear of its ugly past.
My friend tells me something the Theatre representative must have "forgotten."
She tells me about what it was like to visit here when she was little.
African Americans could only enter the Theatre through one side door.
And they could only sit in one small balcony section.
And they could only sit in that section if white people weren't sitting there.

My heart is heavy.
The beauty of the Theatre now seems an oppressive facade.
The truth is shameful, and there is no way to unring the bell.
I thank God for my friend's gentleness,
For her patience when I am still sometimes surprised by the ugliness,
And for her ability to separate me from the others.

INTRODUCTION

One of the most frustrating aspects of minoritized life, besides being watched or monitored incessantly, can be experiencing that one's daily existence is subject to different rules and policies than one's White counterparts. This can take the form of more or greater misperceptions, differing economics, rules, policies, procedures, and fewer protections than one's White or more economically secure counterparts. Thus, inequitable treatment involves differential treatment or discrimination based on perceived group membership. Thus, the minoritized are often subjected to inequitable, discriminatory practices, behaviors, and policies in shopping venues that leave us singled-out, upset, in protest mode, or even catastrophically devastated.

INEQUITABLE TREATMENT IN THE CONSUMER MARKETPLACE

One of the common themes expressed in this book by the people of color interviewed across the country about their marketplace experiences is that of feeling that they are not treated with the same freedoms, rights, dignities, and privileges as their White counterparts in the marketplace. With this heavy burden of seemingly random, yet often paradoxically predictable, differential treatment comes having to make decisions at any given moment about when, where, and how to respond when feeling that one has been treated unfairly when dealing in public spaces such as marketplaces. For example, if you are asked to present identification when making a credit card purchase, but the White person in line either immediately before you or after you was not asked for ID, that can leave a person of color feeling upset, singled-out, and unfairly treated. People of color may feel in a quandary concerning what to do about it that won't result in being further targeted, mistreated, having the police called, or thrown into jail for speaking up.

Further, numerous consumer allegations and complaints involving inequitable treatment that extend broadly outside of the walls of department stores, grocery stores, and malls to other areas of consumer life are found in the media. One of the more popular venues for inequitable consumer-related micro- and macroaggressive behaviors are restaurants and other eating establishments. For example, a man shouted racial slurs and spit on a couple of color as they stood in line at a Seattle Starbucks.[1] Spitting on Black people historically has not been a rare occurrence, and still occurs to this day in restaurants, grocery stores, and other marketplace settings.[2] Now that it can be documented on videotape, those who spit on people to demean them, even after work hours, are tending to lose their jobs, as it is a very poor representation of any workforce. Further, studies reveal that White people proportionally are more likely to engage in such assaults of BIPOCs than the reverse.[3]

In another restaurant incident, a party of twenty-five customers allege that they were asked to leave a Wild Wings Café in South Carolina because a White customer felt threatened by them.[4] The wife of a White House correspondent blogged about what she perceived as racial profiling and discrimination. She charges that when she dropped her husband at a correspondents' dinner and then forgot her keys and tried to retrieve them from him, she was treated in a way that made her feel suspected and racially profiled, and she was not allowed to retrieve her keys.[5] An African American woman was beaten by a White man unknown to her and called racial epithets as she was exiting a Cracker Barrel restaurant with her seven-year-old daughter.[6] In another dining-related incident, internet-surfing customers at a restaurant franchise were subject to a WiFi network named "N-----s Go Home."[7] Similarly, in other places around the country consumers have observed WiFi signals such as "F--- All Jews and N-----s."[8]

TRAVEL AND TRANSIT MARKETPLACES

Another common marketplace venue for microaggressive-and-beyond incidents has been in traveling spaces. Therefore, traveling continues to be exceptionally stressful for many people of color, and with good reason.[9] For example, a stranger was sentenced for slapping and yelling racial slurs at a crying biracial toddler while sitting next to the child's mother on an airplane flight. The stranger was both fired from his job and sentenced to eight months in jail.[10] A Black woman doctor was barred and blocked from assisting a fellow passenger on an airline flight because flight personnel would not believe that she was a doctor.[11] A grieving, twenty-year-old professional athlete was escorted off of an airplane for wearing a sagging style of pants,[12] while it has been alleged that White passengers are allowed to fly even in their underwear with no questions asked.[13] An Asian doctor sitting in his seat was brutally dragged off of an airline flight because the flight was overbooked, and no one volunteered to give up their seat.[14] In another incident, a woman was alleged to have been called "a fat n____r" on an airplane.[15] For several years, Black women were being routinely subjected to TSA (Transportation Security Administration) searches of our hair and hairstyles when going through security in airports, which made many of us feel singled-out and violated.[16] Profiling is still an issue even in the new millennium on trains where an eighty-three-year-old Black woman and ten of her bookclub mates were thrown off and initially banned for laughing and talking too loudly.[17] Three young African American women were attacked by a man wielding a knife as they exited a train in what some are insisting was a racially motivated attack. One of the women, Nia Wilson, died as a result, and family, friends, community, and White allies have been critical of the handling of the case.[18] Even when walking to buses, passing neighbors' houses to get home after school, or trying to solicit help from neighbors after a car accident, youths have been shot, as were fourteen-year-old Brennan Walker and fifteen-year-old Vernon Marcus Jr. Nineteen-year-old Renisha McBryde was even killed.[19] Youths of color approaching neighbors' homes, for example to fundraise for their schools, have had guns pulled on them and have even been held at gunpoint until police arrived.[20] Decades after the firm stand of Rosa Parks, public transportation has still revealed itself to be burdensome to people of color in terms of microaggressive challenges at times. Even getting to school as consumers of mass or school transit can be problematic as youth of color on their way to and from school and school-sponsored events have been targeted. For example, reportedly three sixteen- and seventeen-year-old basketball players in Rochester, New

York, were arrested while "waiting while Black" for a school bus to take them to their scrimmage game.[21]

STREETS AND PARKING MARKETPLACES

Streets, parking lots, and spaces near stores and malls are another venue for inequitable, microaggressive behavior and beyond. For example, the father of a Mexican American woman was reportedly berated by an irate woman who hit his car with her door. The woman yelled statements to him in front of his daughter and young granddaughter such as "Go back to the country you came from! . . . You people are stealing our jobs. . . . I don't know where you Pakistani, Middle East people come from!"[22]

PARKS, RECREATION, AND LEISURE MARKETPLACES

Engaging in parks, recreation, and leisure also can be precarious or at least inequitable and unjust. For example, unarmed thirty-one-year-old Dontre Hamilton, who suffered from schizophrenia, was shot fourteen times in the back by a law enforcement officer in a community park as he fled a police officer who was never charged for the shooting.[23] Unarmed Walter Scott was both tasered and shot in the back and killed by a police officer as he fled through a park after a routine traffic stop for a broken taillight. It is argued by his family that Scott feared going to jail for unpaid child support and therefore ran. Another horrid event involved a White mother and her two teenage sons hurling racial slurs at an African American teen while also trying to drown him as he fought for his life.[24] Thankfully, they did not succeed. Pool swimming sites also have had a past and recent history of posting racist signs that were far from welcoming of people of color.[25]

MEDICAL AND SOCIAL SERVICE MARKETPLACES

Doctors' offices, hospitals, and other medical consumer facilities can be inequitable as well. For example, an African American nurse of many years was forbid by a young child's father (and subsequently the hospital administration) to care for a baby to whom she was assigned because the baby's father did not want any staff of color handling his child.[26] Related to distrust of people of color as caregivers, a study in the *Journal of the Ameri-*

can Medical Association reported that Black families are three times more likely to be reported for suspected child abuse compared to White families who present with children with identical injuries.[27] Child protective services across the nation show similar disparities in their report rates.[28] Therefore, people of color tend not to have the same level of trust in the medical and social service systems as their White counterparts, and therefore may not be as willing or as eager to engage with them, which may translate into negative health outcomes.[29]

BANKS, BARS, AND ENTERTAINMENT

A simple stop at the bank can turn into a major complication if you are woman, Muslim, and wearing a hijab—in fact, you could be removed from that bank for wearing your hijab.[30] An expectedly fun jaunt to a local club to dance with friends could become emotionally complicated and extremely disappointing if you perceive that there is a cover charge for Black patrons, but not for White ones, as was reportedly the case with a Michigan venue.[31] Such incidents have occurred in all realms of the consumer marketplace, including, for example, county fairs, casinos, bars, banks, while walking or sitting, and in the course of trying to conduct almost every kind of day-to-day business one can imagine.[32] And oftentimes they can involve security, police, and other law enforcement if one is not quick to comply with whatever unfair policy or procedure is being demanded at the time.

RESIDENTIAL AND FAITH-BASED MARKETPLACES

Even one's own rented or owned property spaces have not been immune to these kinds of incidents. For example, a lesbian Dominican and El Salvadoran couple in the San Francisco area trying to park their car near their home were stopped by police and allegedly ticketed for no reason that they could discern.[33] Fay Wells, "a graduate of Duke, MBA of Dartmouth, and president of strategy for a multinational corporation" with a very slight build, found herself surrounded by seventeen police and roughly handled in her own home in Santa Monica when a White neighbor called to report a supposed burglary at her apartment.[34] A White woman harassed and blocked her Black neighbor from entering his apartment building, believing that he could not possibly live there. The videotaped incident prompted her employer to fire her.[35] Police pepper-sprayed and apprehended a fostered

Black youth in his own home when White neighbors mistook him for a burglar and called authorities.[36] Twenty-six-year-old Botham Jean was gunned down in his own home by an off-duty woman police officer who entered the wrong apartment and took him to be an intruder.[37] Twenty-eight-year-old Atatiana Jefferson was killed in her home by a police officer after they were called by a neighbor on their nonemergency line for a welfare check.[38] Twenty-six-year-old Breonna Taylor was shot, received no medical care, and died in the course of a search warrant being executed at the wrong location while she was sleeping in her home. Thirty-year-old Gregory Hill Jr. was reportedly killed by police inside of his own garage when they were called to the house for a loud music complaint.[39] Black people have had police called on them for gardening in their yards,[40] making phone calls outside,[41] and picking up trash in their own yard.[42] Thirteen-year-old Darius Simmons was murdered by a White neighbor while taking out the trash.[43] Black and Brown people showing up for babysitting or engaging with their White counterparts in private or public spaces may get the police called on them as well.[44] Even faith-based venues—which are homes away from home for many—are not the safe havens that they should be as churches, mosques, and synagogues continue to be bombed, shot up, and otherwise threatened, even while occupied.[45] Some have questioned whether there is any place where Black children and adults can just breathe safely.[46]

THE EXTRAORDINARY BURDEN ON PARENTS AND THEIR CHILDREN

As mentioned earlier, the perilousness of the consumer marketplace places an additional, very heavy burden of stress on parents of color and their youth as they try to prepare them at an early age for a world that at any moment can be inequitable and unkind, if not abusive and otherwise dangerous, toward them.[47] Trayvon Martin's mother, Sybrina Fulton, puts it this way:

> I feel that our kids have to be careful now, because now we have to have the conversation with our kids about do you walk fast? Do you walk slow? Do you even walk at all to the store to get a drink and some candy?. . . I want them to be able to walk down the street, but I don't want them to be afraid that somebody's going to see them as a target. Somebody may see them as a burglar. And he was no burglar. Trayvon was no burglar and neither is Jahvaris [his brother]. . . . I would tell them to be safe. Be safe and just try to make it back

home as quickly as you can and as safely as you can because you don't know what the other person's intentions are.[48]

These concerns have been echoed often by parents across the country as they lament all of the rules and burdens that they place on their children of color to try to keep them secure and get them back home safely from civic and consumer marketplaces.[49]

VOICES OF INEQUITIES

In this section, an immigrated Asian/Indian-American man speaks of his consumer marketplace experiences as he immigrated to the U.S., and the different ways that he made sense of them while also coping with heart-breaking humiliations. A young African American woman college student speaks of her difficulty growing up, struggling with the pain and anxiety of going into stores because of how closely she would be watched, and trying to express her discomfort to her mother. An Indigenous and African American man speaks of his experience in a record store where he was assumed to be there to steal. An Asian man speaks of his experiences as a graduate student riding buses and using a laundromat. Taken together, these four memory-tellers further elaborate on the pain and emotional toll, as well as the added burdens, creativity, and resourcefulness that often come with engaging in the consumer marketplace with its various inequities.

INDICTED

"It's Not for Sale" (Graham's Story)

Graham's story is about the potential complexity and inequity of minor transactions in the post-9/11 era. There are experiences that members of minoritized groups have in the marketplace that seem to be geared toward asserting to us that we are "outsiders" who do not belong and that we have no control in the situation. If we question this, we may be seen as a threat, and we may even have security or the police called on us. Social critics speak of the calling of police on people of color as a power move to keep us in check when we dare to question the service we have received, our charges or bills, our coupons, and so on.[1] There seems to be a fear of Black people especially, but also of other people of color who dispute these things. One of the most powerful ways to dismiss someone in the marketplace, or to render them unimportant or invisible, is to refuse service to them. And then, when people of color get upset at this, staff get very uncomfortable. The next step is to assert one's power by calling security or the police. Countless examples abound in the news, so much so that some writers are calling the police the "personal valet" of White people, who use calling the police or threatening to call police as a control measure to assert authority rather than as a safety or legitimate law enforcement measure.[2] I have experienced this myself. For example, on my return home from air travel, a long-term parking lot clerk at the airport threatened to call the police on me when I questioned my bill. Had my seven-year-old, exhausted from our trip, not been sleeping in the car, I would have welcomed her to call the police. But I did not want to risk my child's comfort, nor traumatize him, with the fact of someone calling the police on Mommy, so I paid fees that I should not have, in order to quickly resolve the matter before my son was awakened by the situation. The next day I tried to make complaints about the clerk's behavior, but to no avail. Thus, at any given moment in the marketplace, we can be reminded that we are invisible, unimportant, powerless, or nonexistent, and that if we speak up about it, we could end up playing an unwelcome game of police roulette. This next interview will illustrate this dynamic of knowing that if we make a fuss, it could turn into something uglier. Graham tells the story of his immigration experience as a young man in the Midwest, as the backdrop for his post–September 11th experiences living and shopping in a large metropolitan city on the East Coast. These are experiences that, reflecting on them almost two decades later, still have left him internally struggling with his sense of dignity, respect, and self-worth as the world doesn't seem to be changing for the better fast enough.

Graham is a forty-nine-year-old immigrated man, originally from India, who works in the healthcare administration industry. Upon meeting him for our interview, he struck me as very warm, friendly, prepared, and organized. In fact, he seemed even somewhat eager to start speaking of his experiences in the consumer marketplace, perhaps because of his busy schedule. Being the manager of a nonprofit, he also may have been motivated by the fact that he has so little of his time available. Therefore, he may be used to cutting the nonessentials and getting right to the business at hand. We met in a somewhat sterile-looking conference room at the community advocacy facility where he worked, and within five minutes I was already recording him and taking notes. His ability to get us right to the point was at no cost to his seemingly kind personality or cordiality, and without my being made to feel rushed.

Graham's story shows us how easily people of color can be dismissed or otherwise rendered dangerous, or at least invisible, in the consumer marketplace. Further, his story shows that these experiences create pain, anger, or disillusionment as we try to recover, still years and decades later.

Graham tells his story . . .

* * *

I'm going to be fifty [soon]. I'm not that old. I'm the director of [a health care program]. I've had about eighteen years of schooling, and a master's degree in business administration. I come by way of many, many cultures. I was born in [a particular town in] India. I've been in the states since the late 1970s. My story [first] concerns how I became an American citizen.

Well, I was living in [the Midwest] in the early 1980s, and I went for my immigration interview. Now, they don't let you become a citizen right away. They make you wait. And I waited. And when I was ready, I went, and I filled out my application, and I told them I was ready to become an American citizen. Well, they do a lot of insulting things to you before you become a citizen. It is part of their way of testing you. One of the insulting things that they do is they bring your wife in with you, just to make sure you're living together and that it is not just a marriage of convenience. And they'll ask you questions to see if you're really married. Questions like, "What did you have for breakfast?"—fundamental things to see if you get your stories right. They interview you and your wife separately. One of the things [about me is that] I'm a conscientious objector—[that is,] I don't believe in fighting. I don't think there is anything worth fighting about, and I think that it is un-Christian to kill. [Therefore,] I really don't like the military. Now, when you become a citizen, you renounce your [original] citizenship and become a [U.S.] citizen. When you become a citizen, you're supposed to swear to [at least one of] three things: that you're going to bear arms; that you will serve as a noncombatant; that you'll work under a civilian administrator that will assign you to specific duties. . . .

So, I am sitting at my interview. I was very confident, and I told them, "Look, I don't want to serve in the military in any way shape or form, because no one is going to tell me when I'm going kill somebody. . . . You know, that's really not my thing." And this guy who was a [very high-ranking attorney] for the state—one of the big muckety-mucks over there, he started giving me a really hard time. He said, "What kind of a citizenship is this that you are looking for?" I said, "Look, I don't know, if you don't think I am eligible for it, then I am not eligible for it, but I am telling you these are the terms under which I will be an American citizen." And according to what I had understood, and what I had read, you have to choose one of these three things. You could choose all of them, [or just] one thing. And I said, "Well, I know civilian administration, I can do that. . . . In fact, that's what my job is . . . trying to provide health services in this environment. . . . I mean, there's nothing better than something like that." Well, [the interviewer] posed a hypothetical question to me and said, "So, what would happen if we asked you to work in a munitions factory?" And I said, "I couldn't do that." So, he says, "Well, there is your answer. . . . If you are not willing to serve under civilian direction in a civilian administration, then you are not fit to be an American citizen, and we'll see you later." So, I left. Now, very fortunately for me, my wife had taken off [because] I told her to come back after a couple of hours. So I was stuck waiting over there only a half an hour into my [interview]. I went into the library, and they had a huge immigration library. I went to the front desk, and there was this much older lady, maybe thirty or forty years older. She said, "What's the matter with you?" So, I told her my position and she said "Really?" Then she went and flipped through her index files and she said, "You want to know what? . . . Go, from this section to this section, go and take a look and see what's there in the library." So, I went and there was case, after case, after case, after case, of people who are conscientious objectors who have taken citizenship. And I even came up to a point where I found a case where the Supreme Court had ruled and said that it was illegal in the process of testing for citizenship, for there to be a posing of a hypothetical question. And I took that case and I walked right into this guy's office and I put it down [on top] of his desk, and I said, "You asked me an illegal question." And he had to concede that. . . . So then later on when I had to swear, I took a partial oath. When you pledge to become a citizen you have to raise your hand saying that you agree to become a combatant of this land. [But in a case like mine], you have to raise your hand to say "noncombatant. . . ." Then when you pledge they say, "Will you serve under a civil administration?" and I said, "Yes, I will do that, yeah."

This is the thing that scares me: The people who are the custodians of our nation, they aren't those attorneys. They are the librarians! These are the people who look out for us! I was quite resigned to the fact that I was not going to be a citizen. This was not a citizenship that I would really get. [But] I am very proud to be an American. I consider myself to be probably more American than some Americans that I know. But, I really feel that this is a country that really is the land of freedom—where you can choose the kind of freedom you want, and the freedom you believe in.

I also remember [the day of 9/11] when we started getting the reports. I remember we had our auditors who had come from New York, they were sitting in the office, and when I heard that a plane had flown into that building, I just couldn't help it, I said, "Those bastards!" And these [auditors] said "Well, it could be an accident, you know?" and I said, "No, it's not an accident!" And then sure enough, the second plane hit, and these auditors were worried because they were from the financial district. In those days I used to commute [quite a distance] between my home with my wife and daughter, and my job. About a week after 9/11, it was the birthday of one of the people with whom I work. Now in that county there is a [donut] store where they have the best donuts, and it is really the best place. I've been going there since the early 1980s. Now, I used to bring donuts to work just to improve my ratings. Anyway, it was [my coworker's] birthday, and I decided, "You know what? I'm going to go pick up a cake." So, I leave early in the morning because it takes about an hour and a half to get to work, so by about seven o'clock I have to be in the car. So, before seven o'clock, I show up, and they're there because they are located pretty close to the train station, and I stood in the line, and the line [slowly] creeps up. I've been seeing the woman [proprietor there] for more than twenty years. Yes, twenty years I have been shopping in the same place. They have these great chocolate cakes, chocolate cakes with coffee, and chocolate cakes with raspberries in them. And the cakes are lined up in the display. So, I said, "Hey, can I have this cake over here?" She says, "It's not for sale." So, I said, "Well, how about this one?" And she says, "It's not for sale." And I say, "How about this one?" And she says, "It's not for sale." And she turns her back on me, and she goes to the next person. She was a White woman, [perhaps] the wife of the owner, and maybe five, six, or ten years older than me, and she just totally dismissed me. She turned her back on me, and she went to the next person. And I just didn't know what to say because I had gotten the sense that she did not want to serve me.

I looked around at the people over there, and they all had different kinds of "masks" on. I don't know how to describe it. They didn't see what happened, and they didn't hear what happened. It's like this other mask that they have on. And you [yourself] have a mask on also. And when we're in line, it's like "Don't touch me. . . . Don't come too close to me. . . . Don't be near me." You are a single fact, a single event. You're the only one there. The rest of it is just a machine. It refuses to see your individuality. It refuses to recognize your self-worth. It just sees you as being, and you are not recognized really for what you are. You're just in the way. And I needed to get out of line, and let the other person be served. I was so confused, so I just left that place.

Two days later I told the people at work because I just felt like I needed to talk to somebody, and they were absolutely outraged because they know me. And they know there's a difference between India, Saudi Arabia, and Yemen. And even so, there's a difference between one brother and another brother. You shouldn't treat one as the other, because they are to their own.

But this is something that's unresolved for me. It's not complete. It's not something that's just packaged. I have this thing inside me, and it's still alive—the hurt from it, from that incident. I had some anger from this, because I feel like, even still, that I . . . should have done something. I should have stood up. I should have made my stand. I should have done something really dramatic. . . . It's not worth holding this anger . . . it is an anger that turns on itself. It turns on itself and destroys you. It's the kind of anger that insidiously eats you on the inside. So, I just walked away. I got into my car and drove to work. I drove about an hour and a half. The pain was a feeling of betrayal. For years and years and years and years, you know, this woman was behind the counter, had served me, with a smile, without any feeling, without any hostility. I gave her my money, I took advantage of the fine donuts she had, for twenty years!

So many people lost their lives that very same day, on 9/11. There was a Sikh, and they shot him in Arizona. He was pumping gas. Some kids driving by, and they just blew him away. That's a much more dramatic event. But hearing this kind of xenophobia that emanates from that one single episode, on both sides of the Suez Canal. It's not just on this side of the Suez Canal that reacted. You've got the same thing going on on the other side of the Suez Canal, exactly, as a mirror image.

I couldn't get [my coworker] a cake. It was my coworker's birthday. I felt like this is part of the damage that was created by 9/11. Not on the same scale [because] no one lost their lives. It's just part of the continuing concern—unnatural concern about the strangers in their midst and who the people are who are coming. . . . I don't want to be defined like that either. In a way, I don't want to be defined at all. I have a name—you can use that. You may not know how to pronounce it, but you can use that. You should understand me by my works, and not by [whatever] your skewed vision is.

I will never go back to that store. However, I've encouraged my family to go back to that store because when you look at it in all its honesty, her act was an act of ignorance. She couldn't differentiate between her fear and who I really was. So, she was doing this thing to protect herself. The reality is, does anybody really see you, except for the Lord? I mean, fathers don't know their daughters, and daughters don't know their fathers, so how do I expect this person from across this county to know me?

This is something that cannot be reconciled now. Unless we actually staged an event where I can go back to [the donut store], and I can open that door and walk through that door, and I can meet that woman and I can ask her to serve me. It could happen, if I wanted to let it go. It would be very risky, and I would be the one carrying the risk. But the fact of the matter is this: As a Christian, I am supposed to be taking risks. This is fundamental: Jesus took the ultimate risk. But what does Jesus ask of us? He asks of us to take that risk. He says, "Love thy brother." "Love your neighbor." "Turn the cheek." He says, "Render onto Caesar what is Caesar's, [and] render onto God what is God's." What is that about? I think he's saying, "You know we are supposed to love." And in loving you are taking the ultimate risk because you are offering your heart and you're saying, "Okay, go ahead, take it." And you can put your heart out there, and some people can spit on it. But does that mean you should hold it back for yourself and say, "No, I'm not going to let that happen"? Or does that mean you should get out of there? Does that mean I should walk into [that donut store] again and say, "I'm back for my cake"?

There is a lesson over here that needs to be learned. There is an action that is left over, and maybe it is just talking about this [to make it public]. But I think there is something else that needs to happen. You may look at it as somebody else needing to improve their performance: the salesperson improving their performance in a particular way and being more sensitive to customers. [But] I think inwardly, because I'm stuck in this issue, and this is something that I need to work on.

I feel as a minority man in the environment, that it is open season. People can go ahead and take as many shots as they want at you. So, there are some things that haven't changed at all. So, I should not be lulled into that false sense of security. Because I feel [a lack of security]—I felt it after 9/11, but I really don't care anymore. I feel that people can't really see me for who I am, and if they still think that I'm somebody who needs watching, then go ahead [and watch]. If you have time to do it, look and see, and keep looking. You're not going to find anything there. I have felt a lot of scrutiny. I have felt it wherever I go. This is part of my mask, because people sometimes like talking to a package. They respect a tie.

After 9/11 I think a lot of things changed for me. My thing was, "Hey, look. I don't want to make any waves." After the elevated concerns in the environment, I was oversensitized. And this is again the machine. You are against the machine. You are just one particle, a little thing, and you've got the whole machine against you.

How can I really come to terms with [this incident] unless I reenact it and we actually find a different outcome? But I really suspect there's something over here that really blocks my energy, which makes me stick over here, which means I haven't learned my lesson. I think I have a story here, and I need to write this story out. I can feel myself turning away from that line and walking out. And I can feel the shame of not standing up and not saying, "What's the matter with you? . . . What part of me do you really not understand?" [Instead, I] just melted away without leaving my mark or turning that cheek and saying, "This is what Jesus must have felt." Or even just saying, "What? . . . This is really not worth my time to address this ignorance at this stage." . . . I would say, "You should never forget your voice." And you can use your voice in some very surprising and confounding ways. So, whenever you have the opportunity to use your voice, and to use the strength that God has given you in your voice, use it with kindness. . . . And rely on your cultural [upbringing], I think that's your basic factory settings. Do what Momma says. You should listen to what Momma says, and do what Momma says.

INTIMIDATED

"It's Really Painful for a Kid" (Janisha's Story)

Janisha's story concerns her depression and anxiety, inspired by bodega and corner store inequities, starting from a young age. Her story suggests the idea that shopping while Black is a human developmental issue that threatens the self-security and self-esteem of youth—at least until they can understand that they themselves have not caused this, but that rather it's due to prejudices, racism, and structural forces outside of their control. Janisha's story illustrates the threat that the disparate practices of the consumer marketplace can pose to the emotional development of a child, teen, and young adult.

Janisha is a twenty-one-year-old African American woman and a senior in college who is from the New York City area. On the day that we were to meet, things had been so busy on my end that I almost canceled. I had taught three classes that day, and one of the classes was exceptionally intense given that we were discussing pediatric HIV. So, it was one of those days, where my first class consisted of helping my students grapple with the many nuances involved in the development of some of the most vulnerable children and families on Earth. By the time my last class was finished, although the other two weren't on nearly as heavy topics, I was quite emotionally drained. I considered calling Janisha to ask if we could reschedule, but getting an interview is like going fishing. In other words, interviews are not easy to come by, and when you get one, you do not want to risk losing it. So, I went to my office to try to decompress for a bit before making the extended drive to meet with this young woman. First, I went across the hall to the kitchenette in the building where I work, and I made myself a cup of decaf with stevia, and two shots of sugar-free hazelnut flavoring. I went back to my office, closed my door, and sat down at my desk. I closed my eyes, and took a sip of the coffee, which was a bit too hot. I sat it down on my desk while I tried to lean back in my chair with my eyes still closed. I took in a deep breath. "Breath in slowly through the nose," I said to myself, "and breathe out even more slowly through the mouth." I did this about seven times. With each breath, I tried to exhale anything that was worrying me. With each breath, I visualized things that I could not control floating away from me. When I opened my eyes, I looked at the clock, and thirty minutes had passed! Darn it! I fell asleep. I grabbed my bag with the notebook and informed consents, my tape recorder, my purse, my semi-cold coffee, and I was out the door. The walk to the parking lot to get my car was just a short distance, which is a blessing on a college campus. I jumped in and set my GPS, and off I went. I managed to meet Janisha pretty much on time, maybe because she herself was running roughly ten minutes late.

We met at her campus library and walked to what turned out to be a very small, very quiet room that she had reserved. Janisha seemed to be a very dignified young woman. She greeted me warmly, with an ease and maturity that seemed characteristic of someone a bit older than the age of twenty-one. She seemed very familiar with the library, and escorted me back to the reserved rooms where we found ours right away. As Janisha engaged in small talk, I could detect a very subtle Caribbean accent, I guessed of either someone who immigrated perhaps during the elementary school years, or even perhaps a second-generation child with parents who immigrated at a mature age, thus likely holding on to strong accents. I later learned from Janisha that her father was indeed an immigrated Caribbean who came to the United States to pursue his education.

Janisha took it upon herself to let me know that as a student, she had already participated in a number of interviews, so she was familiar with the drill and ready to proceed. Again, I could see that this young woman was as poised and confident as might be expected for a person twice her age. Noting her comfort with the situation, I prepared my papers and tape recorder, and we jumped right in.

Janisha shares how shopping while Black has been a challenge since she was a child. It also has become a problem for the next generation of her family, thus further highlighting the burdens that it presents to developing children who experience it. She also describes the ways that she has learned to cope or compensate for the discomfort she feels in the consumer retail marketplace. Janisha tells her story, speaking both as a consumer, and as a grocery store sales associate. She told of being unwelcomed, of not feeling good enough, and of the impact on her self-esteem. She also goes on to discuss how this negative legacy is impacting the next generations by discussing her young teen nephews and their experiences. And finally, she also offers recommendations for moving up the chain of command when trying to resolve suspected discrimination—from cashier, to manager, to store manager.

Janisha speaks . . .

* * *

When I was younger, I used to go into a [small grocery] shop, look around, and see what's new. I first noticed my discomfort in [these] stores when I was about nine . . . [at a nearby] twenty-four-hour gas station. I went to get a small milk and a bag of Doritos. So, there was this woman. She was behind the counter, and I was right beyond the counter. I was like, "What's going on?" She moves with me every time I move. That was the first time that I noticed, and it really shocked me. The next guy I went to buy something from also insisted on watching me. After that, I was like, "I got to do something to minimize this . . . perhaps get something and get out!" But I always felt mad. I always wanted to say something, but I was reserved. . . . It doesn't mean I don't like to shop, it's like, "Man, I got to get out." It's not a pleasant experience, and it required a change. When I was younger, I [even] had to tell my mom, "I don't understand why they are always [hovering,] following me around the store." I figured my mom would go up to them and tell them that she is a good kid, she goes to church every Sunday, she knows her ten commandments, and so on and so forth; but she didn't do that. She was like, "there are some people who know you really well, and some who think they know you but can't change their minds about what they think they know about you and how they feel about you." I would have rather had her go up to them and talk to them to see what happens, but she always treated it like a feeble attempt to change something that couldn't be changed. Maybe it was something with her past experiences. She never really went into details, but she says, "Yeah, there are situations where people have known me, but they still didn't trust me. . . . And I know I was able to deal with it because I know who I am." My mother was born in a town in New England, but her parents are from [the South]. She definitely has a bit of the southern flavor to her. "You just have to deal with those things, strive, and just brush the dirt off your shoulders," she says. I think it's something that she felt, and the [down South] background that she was coming from was really different. It might have been a situation where that kind of behavior was really common, and she just felt that it was something that she had to get used to. She knew it was something that I was going to see a lot.

After a few incidences [and as I grew older], my attitude was, "I don't need to know what is new [in the store inventory] . . . . Maybe I will hear about it, and then I will get it [to buy]." Especially when you are going into a shop where it seems they feel you are not even supposed to be there. It's just the perception out there—that minorities aren't supposed to be there—that minorities don't belong in expensive shops. "What are you doing here, you aren't supposed to be here?" At first I didn't understand; I am a great person, I come here and say "Hi," and I am wondering, "Why is this person following me around?" It was degrading. I was there every day, and there was no reason for them not to trust me as one of their customers. And I thought, what else could it be? Is it that I am a middle schooler [now]? Do a lot of middle school kids steal from them and they just see me as another middle schooler? Or is that I am Black? I told my mom, and that is what she said: "It's because I am Black." I was like, "Oh, that's not fair because everybody in the neighborhood is Black, where is this coming from?" I especially didn't expect it from another person of color, even if they are from another country. I initially had looked at it as a Black/White thing. In real life it exists. [But] the differences between people of color was really disheartening.

As I have grown older since middle and high school, I have noticed a change in the stores. I have noticed that with corner stores that are owned by [immigrants], it is very blatant—that "Yes, we are watching you and that is just how it is going to be." I would say this is true for any person of color who enters their store. But being that I grew up shopping mostly in a neighborhood of predominately Black people, I don't know if they treat a White person any differently. . . . For example . . . there is the corner store that I frequent, and they know me well. But every time I go in, they kept on insisting that they are watching me. They kept their drinks all the way in the back, so you would have to walk all the way down just to get a drink. And if you are indecisive about what you wanted to get, they would just come there and stand by the counter and just look around and stand there. Any time I had to go to that store, I would get what I wanted right away because I didn't want to feel awkward. Once you are browsing around, they think that you are going to steal something.

But once I got older, around late teens—seventeen, eighteen—I realized they tried to make it less obvious. But when you are young—I would say, as long as you are in the middle, early high school age—they really don't seem to care. It's like, you don't have a say. They literally walk with you around the store. It's really painful for a kid. But once you get older, I guess, they fear retaliation in the form of a verbal dispute, so they try to look at the mirror [instead]. [So,] no matter where I go [to shop], I just decide what I want so that I can quickly leave. It's just like I have to know what I want, and if they ask me, "Do you need help?" I say, "Yeah, I need this, this, and this," and I am ready to go [home]; because you believe that you are not welcome. It's like, if you are there too long, they start to suspect things, so you just make a list. I follow the list strictly. If I like something extra, I just grab it and I am out. I really don't want to put myself into a situation where somebody might start feeling a certain way about me or that I am doing something wrong. I become really conscious of that, and just so I don't look like I am doing wrong, this is what I do—I shop fast. It may seem fast, but actually it's a more slowly-but-surely, more planned-out, way to shop. If I had a big incident, I don't know what I would do. This way, I think I have done everything in my power to minimize encounters.

I've also noticed that as a minority, you won't get assistance as quickly—at least this is with myself. Some stores, I don't even really shop there, but I am always at the clearance rack. At those upper-scale stores, I don't even look at the expensive stuff because I worry about being followed around. And then I'm being asked "Can I help you?" one too many times. It's definitely the store itself, it changes your confidence level. I know, when I go to economically lower-end stores, I feel a little bit more comfortable there. On the other hand, if it is [an upper scale department] store in the mall, it's blatant, "I am following you around because you are Black." There is this feeling I get that they think I might not belong there because I am Black. In my perception, I just don't want to be there. Black people may reason it out that if I am not trusted at the corner store, what are they going to think about me here in the upper-scale store?

While finishing college, I also work part-time as a grocery store cashier in my hometown. It is definitely a moderately large franchised grocery store that is serving an increasingly diverse Black and Latino inner-city population, but also a mostly White university population nearby. As far as the cashiers and team captains, yes, there are people of color; but as far as the administration there are maybe two people of color, making up around 5 percent of the management. As a cashier, I have noticed that most of the security guards and the people who monitor the cameras, they tend to do a pretty good job of detecting people who are stealing, but they don't seem to discriminate much. They seem to have a better way of looking at things and figuring out who is stealing what. But the actual people who work there, like the store managers, they seem to be more suspicious of their Black customers. Just because something needs to be returned at the service desk by the Black customer, they will give the customer a hard time. Then the customer complains. I remember a specific incident, it was a woman who came in to return some cans of formula. We tell all our customers that they can't return it. This particular woman, she was White and she stood there forever and she wanted to speak to the manager. Now usually, all of them want to speak to the manager and the manager usually says "no" to the request also. But I guess, given her age—she was in her upper forties—and the fact that she was short, and she was pleasant, and she went "But I didn't know. . ." in a helpless kind of way, [the manager met with her]—but she had no receipt and she admitted that. The manager at the time said, "Let her have the refund." We couldn't really do anything with it, it was expired—we can't resell it, yet she was still able to exchange it. And there have been other situations where people of color have come in with the receipt, shown that they have bought it with cash, it wasn't expired, and they would say, "No, we can't exchange the formula."

The big issue of observing people returning things has made me conscious of when I go to return things. It's like, do I want to return this and go through the havoc of other cashiers asking a whole bunch of questions? Even if I have my receipt and everything, are they still going to give me a hard time? I just feel the inner anger of "What if"? But other than the staff's reaction to the customer when returning things, I would say the department doesn't discriminate much racially—but they definitely do this age thing in that they watch the children a whole lot. It's hard to tell whether they watch the White kids because the White kids usually are less likely to come in the shop without their parents, because most White people are coming from outside of the city. Whereas a parent of a Black kid would send their kid to pick up some bread and butter. Store management tend to watch the kids a lot—especially if they enter the area where there are, for example, goods for your nails and stuff like that.

My nephews, ages thirteen and sixteen, complain all the time about this. My nephews, they definitely pick up on those kind of things. They wouldn't refer it to as tone, but they would just say, "It was the way she was talking to me," and then they would mimic it.

I definitely tend to feel that the corner stores of the inner-city neighborhoods are definitely more likely to treat Black and Latino people differently [than Whites]. I don't know if the stores have diversity training. I will definitely say, my store doesn't at all. I find it very interesting because I definitely feel that the managers and all those workers in general should have some diversity training. Here you are in the center of the city, and it feels like there is no diversity training. The corner stores, parent-owned, family-owned, mom-and-pop shops, it's like they don't have that kind of stuff such as diversity training, and of course they come with their own prejudices when they are in their store.

As a worker, I have to figure out what a worker should do [for example, when asked by a customer for a refund]. . . . There seems to always be the administration saying, you have to do this. You don't know what else to tell the customer. But as a person, I would definitely advise the consumer to talk to more than one person. Don't take "no" from that one cashier. If that one person is being unsupportive, ask him or her to let you speak to the manager. If the manager of that department isn't talking to you, or doesn't want to listen to you or isn't giving it to you, then you should go a step further. Don't stop at the cashier. The manager might be the cashier's best friend because they work in the same department. Go to the store manager, and make a big fuss. Not in a hostile way, but definitely make a case. Say, for example, "This is what I am trying to do, this is what happened, I am a loyal shopper, and I would appreciate it if you can do this and such." Ultimately, it will be a success.

INSULTED

"Every Kind of Cracker That Nabisco Makes" (Tamir's Story)

Tamir's story is about the inaccurate and stereotypical assumption of the Black man as a thief. Relatedly, I was speaking with a Latina friend recently, and we were commiserating about how we learned from an early age not to appear that we could be stealing anything in a store. From a young age as we entered stores, we knew that we were suspect. Thus, to this day, we are careful about going into our purses while we shop, as well as about engaging with our cell phones as we take them in and out of our purses, and even having concerns about things like putting a tissue in our pocket or our purses. Perhaps everyone feels this burden, but it doesn't appear so to us, as we see Caucasians doing all kinds of things with their purses, pockets, shopping bags, and so on, in the marketplace that we would never do. Anyway, knowing that we may be considered more likely to be a suspect, we try not to do anything that would draw even more attention to us than what we already have on us.

I also am reminded of a story a mature-aged African American PhD professor colleague from the South shared with me wherein he was shopping, and security approached him requesting to search him, as they suspected him of stealing. He told them that if they would like to search him, then they must call the police and have the police search him. He went on to say that if they do not find anything, they can rest assured there is going to be a big problem for their store, alluding to a lawsuit. He stood there and waited for them to answer. They decided not to bother him, and he was allowed to walk away. Tamir's story illustrates how easy it is for people of color to be considered suspicious by some of the personnel observing customers and how that translates into inequitable treatment.

Tamir is a fifty-two-year-old African American and Indigenous engineering inspector in the New England area. Upon meeting him, I realized that our paths had crossed in the past when we both had served on a community governing board some years prior. We were two of only three people of color who sat on that rather large board, and he was leaving the board as I was entering it. We laughed when we realized that we already were familiar with one another, having known each other by face but neither of us so well by name. Tamir had a big smile, and he greeted me as if I were his sister, as many Black Indigenous people do with one another before any words about one another are spoken. Sometimes mixed heritage people just recognize one another, if not through our physical features, then through our spirits. So, once we had a chance to actually meet each other again—but one-on-one—and sit down and talk with one another, we felt a kinship immediately. He asked me right away if I was of Indigenous heritage, and I told him of my multiracial background: African American, Irish, French, and Indigenous. As soon as I said Indigenous, he broke into a smile. I returned his smile, as a sibling would, and I knew in that moment that he was my brother. There are words, experiences, emotions, exclusions, silences, and traumas that do not have to be explained. Sometimes common-ethnicities or mixed-cultures people already understand our likely common experiences without explanation, again, like similar-aged siblings who have grown up in the same household. Memories of the cultural traumas and survival of the past can get passed down within us from one generation to another somewhat like cultural DNA. If individuals are in touch with that within themselves, then sometimes they are in touch with that among strangers they meet who have similar backgrounds. So here I was sitting with my new brother, about to interview him. And I knew he would remain my brother whether I saw him again right away or in the distant future.

Tamir speaks of his recent experiences being monitored in a new and used record store. Unlike the previous stories in this book, in addition to being closely watched, Tamir also blatantly was accused of stealing. Having worked hard all of his life, beginning right after high school, he felt particularly insulted that someone would think that he would steal. He speaks of the inner strength and self-restraint he found himself relying upon as he attempted to deal with the situation. His story illustrates that many people of color know exactly what is going on when we enter consumer marketplaces. Any human might steal; however, BIPOCs should not be treated as if we are *disproportionately* more likely to steal. We should not be assumed to be thieves. Again, the marketplace may be so busy watching people of color that they miss some of the White people who are indeed stealing.

Tamir tells his story . . .

* * *

Recently, I happened to be in the local record shop. I have the tendency to carry a newspaper with me at most times, and I happened to be in the store and I was looking through the CDs. Well, in order to have access to the CDs a little better, I rolled up my newspaper and put it in my back pocket. At this time, one of the attendants, a White guy probably about twenty-seven or twenty-eight [years old], came over to me and said, "I'll put that behind the back desk." I said, "Put what?" He said, "The CD that you just put in your pocket." I took out my paper, and I said, "Nah, I don't do that." I knew it was expected of me because I had earphones on, and I more or less was dressed in hip-hop fashion. But he never said, "I'm sorry." He said, "Oh, I thought you did." So, I continued looking through the CDs, and waited for him while he was in the middle of a conversation with someone else. I turned to him and said "Oh, by the way, this would be a good time to apologize," which he did. I was a little mad, but since now the Lord is in me, that's the first thing I think of. He has changed me, because if I were like I was before, I probably would've ended up getting arrested—especially since I was right. But I ended up making a positive out of the situation. I let him know his mistake, and I left out the door smiling actually. But it was all because of his misconception of what he saw Blacks as, and that was the basic story.

I guess that since I have changed it was good and bad that—well nothing's ever bad having the Lord in you—but I was frustrated. But the Lord helped me get over my frustration because as I said, I would've called him every kind of cracker that Nabisco makes, more than likely. But I refrained from that.

One of the things was that, as I recall it, I was the only minority in the store. And as I said, he rushed over when it wasn't that long after I had put the paper in my pocket that he appeared, and basically accused me of stealing a CD. So, it could have happened to a White guy, possibly, but more than likely not. I was almost ready to really blow then. But as I said, I brought him to another level. Maybe he even expected me to react violently, or whatever. I think even he was surprised when I basically made a joke about it because even I said, "Since you're standing around you can come over and help me with finding this CD." Which I didn't actually need help, I knew what I was going to get, but it was another way of diffusing the situation and making him see what a fool he really was by his actions. And hopefully it won't happen to some other minority that goes into the store. The [initial] lack of apology, it added insult to injury.

I would've ended up getting arrested if I just let my reactions flow, if I didn't take that moment to come up with that creativity. Using my creativity, I was able to get some kind of satisfaction. There is no doubt about it, my creativity, timing, and everything was part of [it]. The thing of waiting for him to be in a conversation with another customer, and then asking for my apology, was part of it also. I couldn't describe the other customer to you at all. I wasn't thinking about the other customer when I basically ordered the associate to give me assistance as he was standing around doing nothing behind the counter.

Maybe I should've done more in the sense of having things documented, or something like that. But at the moment I didn't see where it warranted jeopardizing his job or discipline or anything. I felt that just being brought on the carpet by me was enough. From there, I left it as it was. I've come to terms with the incident, and it's over for me.

That was the main incident. I mean, everyone has had staring, or has been followed and certain things. But like I said, I wasn't in the Lord then, and they would've been right following me, or whatever. But this was an instance where I was totally [innocent]. I wouldn't do anything like that—it was not even on my mind, particularly because of my age and [with not stealing] being one of the Lord's commandments. But I was offended, and the old me might have been inebriated. I might have been good and drunk, and I might've did [sic] something stupid—not necessarily as far as stealing something. But I might have been just loud, obnoxious, [behaving as] one might consider an adolescent, even though I was well beyond my adolescent years. I can honestly say that I've been incarcerated, and I've talked to different guys in there, and some guys are supposed to be in there. I'm just saying, comparatively, sometimes you are looked at and followed and it is more than a "I think they're going to do something." Even before they know that you're stupid drunk or something like that, they would follow you—just because. They would recognize skin color first.

[In terms of coping and responding], the one thing I can think of is, be courteous. Treat the staff as you would like to be treated. That's not to say that it's going to stop the situation, this isn't a way to stop it. We should act as a customer and be able to go, and get, and pay, for the goods we purchased. [We should not] have that reverse outlook on the [staff] person and say, yeah, well I know he's this. [But instead,] give him the chance to go ahead and at least act courteous or whatever they're going to do. Don't assume automatically, until you know something does happen. Because, we can [have the tendency to] go in with an "I know what they're going to do" type of attitude.

INVALIDATED

"I Am the Minority, the *'Foreigner'*" (Hart's Story)

Hart's story is about the anti-Asian immigrant sentiments expressed and experienced on buses and in laundromats. When engaging in the consumer marketplace, sometimes more privileged people violate the comfort of people of color through their words or aggressive actions, as if a person of color is less worthy of that space they are taking up.[1] I can recall being harassed by a White woman train employee as I slept after I had hastily tied a scarf around my hair to protect it. She put her hands all over my legs, thighs, and arms to wake me up to her brashly demanding my ticket receipt. Awakening to all of this drama, I felt disoriented and could not locate my ticket receipt within the three seconds that she seemed to be expecting. As soon as she stomped off, I located my ticket receipt, and I posted it where she could easily see it if or when she returned. Return she did, but with a Black woman security guard in tow. I showed them my receipt, and they both marched off, seemingly angry with me. Once I gathered my wits about me, I walked up to the dining car to ask the staff if I could speak with the person at the highest level of being in charge on the train. In about ten minutes, a train conductor came down to the dining car to meet me, and I described the situation to him. He called for the employee who created this problem, and although she was not really willing to hear me out, the conductor made her listen to what I had to say. I explained to her that I felt violated, criminalized, and disrespected, and I told her why.

When engaging in consumer marketplaces, sometimes we are treated inequitably, or otherwise inappropriately, by personnel or even other consumers. Thus, other customers may come into the marketplace holding White supremacist and internalized racist ideologies when dealing with their fellow customers, which can create additional layers of stress for people of color engaging in the consumer marketplace.[2] Hart shares two examples that illustrate this.

Hart is a thirty-six-year-old Asian professor on the tenure track at a college in the southeastern United States. He is the colleague of a colleague twice-removed, who is a colleague of mine. In other words, he is many "snowball" throws away from me, but that did not stop us from connecting during his travels to New England. We met at the campus library where a conference was being hosted that he was attending, and where he also was making a presentation. I had to travel almost two hours to get to him, and I arrived in enough time to catch the last twenty minutes of his lecture. Our plan was to meet immediately following his lecture when he had roughly an hour before he would have to attend a roundtable related to his research. Walking briskly, we hustled over to the library, asking for directions from passing students along the way. Once we arrived, we realized that neither of us was familiar with the inside of that library, so we stopped at the front desk for information. We explained that we needed a quiet space for an interview. The (apparent) student behind the desk understood right away, and she gave us a key to a locked room that would be straight down a hall behind us. She emphasized to please not forget to return the key before heading out because a guest during the last semester forgot and they had to get a new key made. We gave assurance that we would, and I asked Hart if he would be responsible for the key as I held it out, and he quickly grabbed it as we scurried to the quiet room.

When I asked Hart what made him interested in participating in the interviews about minority shopping experiences, he explained that like many Asians, he considers himself an ethnic minority within the United States. He further explained that he finds himself being discriminated against in the consumer marketplace because of his minoritized status. He tells of his experiences in consumer venues as he shares with us his shock, confusion, and heartbreak just trying to do laundry and ride buses within the marketplace. His stories give a profile of the White supremacist entitlement that some consumers may have, and how they may make demands of minoritized consumer counterparts based on their sense of entitlement.

Hart speaks . . .

* * *

I was born in [East Asia], and came to the United States in the late 1990s for graduate school. When I was a graduate student in [the northeastern United States], I would go to the laundromat. [While there,] I sometimes met people who approached me and said some things I didn't like. For example, I remember a middle-aged White man wearing glasses came up to me and said, "I need a job." At first I didn't know what [he meant]. But clearly, he was insinuating that I was taking his job away. Even though I was a grad student and a teaching assistant, and I don't think he was able to teach [my particular discipline]. But still, that is what he was insinuating. It was surprising because [that college town] was supposed to be a really liberal town, and it is one of the so-called latte towns. A latte town is where upper-middle-class people come to drink coffee. So, it was surprising. I didn't know what he meant at first, but when I realized what he meant later, I felt really stupid. [I felt stupid] because basically he was insulting me, but I didn't know that he was insulting me. When he told me he needed a job, I had no idea what he was saying, so I didn't really respond. I was just looking at him, [and] asking, "What are you talking about?" Then I realized that he was insulting me. It didn't take a long time to figure out what he meant—he wasn't really asking for a job, because he told me, "I need a job," and he turned around and left. He wasn't thinking I was the manager or a person with some type of control over the possibility of giving him a job. It was obvious I wasn't the owner because I was actually doing laundry, and it was right after I put my laundry in the washing machine. I put my laundry in the washing machine, and when you are in the laundromat you cannot go anywhere. I had to sit in there, and I was grading [papers]. There are these stereotypes that exist in this country about Asians and laundry, believe it or not, and it was really clear he wanted to bother me. He was harassing me as if I were taking something from him, and that's exactly what he was insinuating.

There was not much I could do about this situation because when I realized what he had done to me, he was already gone. [Initially] I was in a good mood, but after that, I really didn't want to go to the laundromat [anymore]. Going to the laundromat [already] is not a great experience because the laundromat itself is not a really happy place. It's a place where you go to do chores basically, and while you are washing and drying the laundry you can't really do anything else. As a grad student, I was always busy, so I had to find a way to use the time more productively. I used to bring grading—students exams to grade. But I always thought that it was kind of wasted time, and that incident made things even worse. [Eventually, I started] putting my clothes in the washing machine, and then I would leave [rather than] stay in the laundromat. I would go have coffee or pizza, or I would just stay in a nearby park.

Incidents like this happened several times. Another instance occurred when I used the bus in that same town. Because my school was in [a different town], I had to commute by bus. It was not a long commute—it was about a fifteen-minute ride. But there was a White male somewhere between [the ages of] thirty-five and forty-five who was a regular customer on the bus, and he started to ramble about many different things, many things that were not really proper. What made me really angry was his loud, rambling exchange with the bus driver. Basically, what he said was the country is not the same as it used to be, and he was deploring how the country has changed. He was talking about how now he has to watch what he is saying, and sometimes when he tries to communicate there are some other people who cannot understand English. That made me really upset. He also talked about some of the clerks in the supermarket who are not U.S. citizens, and how they cannot speak English, and how things like that shouldn't happen. While he was saying these things, he wasn't making eye contact because many undergraduate and graduate students who used that bus were international students. [The university I attended] is supposed to be a really liberal university, so there were many students who were angry with him, and they asked him to stop. When the bus driver started to interact with him and basically agreed with him, there was a kind of verbal exchange between the students and the driver and the guy. And one day it got [really] bad; the students asked the bus driver to stop the bus and they got off the bus in protest. I [recall that] most of the international students and several White students got out of the bus, and the White students were angry as well. I didn't feel as angry [in this situation] as in the laundry case. [But] it makes you realize that bigotry is still there. It also made me think that one thing in common between the bus and the laundromat situations is these are the kind of places where usually the lower middle-class or working-class people [frequent]. It makes you think that maybe bigotry is stronger among those who are poor and those who are underprivileged. So, things like that, and thoughts like that, make me really sad because the reason I came to [that university] and studied [in my field] was because [my graduate school department was] supposed to be a more progressive, sometimes radical, program that firmly believed in workers' rights, and that inequality's a problem we have to find a way to fight. I had to interact quite frequently among realms of public spaces.

It is hard to tell what we usually know among [East Asians] living in the United States, but we usually say during the first two years that the United States is great. Then gradually we start to detect the small differences in attitude [that] during the first two years we don't really detect. When you shop in public places or when you go to a restaurant during the first two years you are just acting like a tourist. So, you don't really see the differences in attitude. But gradually you will see that the attitude of the people toward you and toward other people is sometimes different, and it takes time to realize that. So, we usually gradually say that living in the United States becomes worse and worse, because you get to see that more easily and more often. So, it's not really easy to tell how many times I experienced things like that [at] first, I didn't think that anything like that was really happening. Maybe even if it had happened, I didn't know; I might not have picked up on it. During the first two years, you are learning how people react in a subtle way, in every different kind of situation. You don't really know if the way they react is a conventional reaction or an unconventional reaction, so you are going through this learning experience. After a little bit of learning, now you can pick up something really unusual. Unusual stares, unusual turning away, unusual silence, things like that.

All you can do is hope that things like this don't happen. But suppose there are 5 percent of people who have bigotry [inside of them], and every day you interact with more than a hundred people? Five percent can determine your day. So, I don't know if there's really anything that I can do or say. I cannot say you are not supposed to use the bus or that you shouldn't go to the laundromat, because these are places people have to go.

Even though I have lived in the United States for many years, I still sometimes wonder whether someone's reaction is because I am the minority, the "foreigner." Or is it just because that person is a person with bad manners. For example, when I shop and I am waiting for a clerk to assist me, and no one shows up even though I can see some of them doing different [things], I'm not sure whether they are avoiding me or they are really busy. [Another example,] when I enter some shops and things become suddenly quiet. You don't really know whether it's because of you, or it's just the moment. Things like that are always in the back of my mind, and that's what bothers me the most because I'm quite sure some of them are just a coincidence. The problem is I have no way of telling whether it is just a coincidence or it's a subtle kind of discrimination. So, the fact that I even have to think about things like that bothers me, especially because I have two daughters now. Whenever anything happens to me, I instantly think about my daughters and [whether] they have to go through this. My children are really young, so they have a long way to go, [including] middle school and high school. This can be really crazy. [Therefore,] I'm still struggling every day to try to figure out what was meant by somebody's behavior. [On the other hand,] maybe not every day, because I am in a really protected environment—[a] college environment. The college environment is a really good environment for any kind of foreigner or minorities, compared to the open society.

THINGS THAT PART II'S STORIES CAN TEACH CONSUMERS AND MARKETERS

STRATEGIES CONSUMERS MIGHT CONSIDER TRYING

- Document the incident(s) with whatever legal or approved processes or resources you have for doing so (photos, video, receipts, witnesses, etc.).
- Consider making use of library and online information for researching rights, legal policies, or portals for speaking up, complaining, appealing, or protesting how you are being treated, or for collaborating with shoppers who have experienced the same or similar treatment.
- Some who have experienced disparities in the marketplace have found it helpful to self-reflect and to seek life lessons that can assist them in emotional processing, action-taking, and self-care or health integration. This will be even more apparent in parts III and IV.
- Some have focused on their emotional awareness and responses by recognizing the ignorance they are facing, staying calm, creatively diffusing the situation if they can, or appropriately exiting or removing themselves from the situation to study their options for protesting. For example, a customer, Will Mega, approached a local Lowes to engage them on his observations regarding differences in how White and Black consumers were being treated with the showing of their receipts as they exited. He strategically thought about how he would approach

the situation, and utilized all the resources that he could locate to help him, resulting in a change in Lowes's policy.[1]

- Some have found helpful the process of sharing with family, friends, and support groups that also have had experiences with such disparities.
- Others have suggested journaling, blogging, or otherwise writing out or bringing "voice" to the experience, and even writing alternative endings as a therapeutic measure.
- Some have suggested relying on one's spirituality, voice, the good manners you were taught in your upbringing, or coping skills for initially responding to mistreatment in the marketplace, until you can rally your resources.
- You can move up the chain of command when trying to resolve suspected discrimination—from cashier to manager to store manager to district manager to corporate, depending on your energy level. If you don't have the resources or energy for all of that, you might just go straight to corporate.
- When speaking with personnel and managers, you can ask whether they treat all of their customers like this, or if there is something about you that inspires them to treat you like this. This is a question that I find forces people to think about their own behavior and biases, and sometimes they tell on themselves with their reactions.
- You can seek support from justice-seeking organizations: the ACLU, Commission on Civil Rights, NAACP, and so on, in your city, region, or state. If you go this route, try to approach them as soon as possible because some of them allow only a limited amount of time after an incident for filing a complaint. You also can reach out for support from your local, state, and federal regulators such as mayors, city council, state representatives, state attorney general, federal attorney general office, health department, Environmental Protection Agency, Federal Department of Consumer Affairs, and so on. You also could put pressure on legislators to develop and approve laws to criminalize the inappropriate calling of the police on people of color.[2] For example, the City of Grand Rapids, Michigan, could become the first to develop legislation that is being processed through their channels of approval to make it illegal to call the police on people of color for "participating in their lives."[3]
- As discussed in part I, "Monitoring," you can write letters of complaint to local, state, and federal certification offices that oversee the business with which you have a concern.

- If you have tried everything and nothing has worked, you can check community and online resources and hashtags with respect to organizing boycotts, reporting to news sources and news action teams, and so on, for example, your local Black Lives Matter organization.
- You can hold businesses accountable for their service and contributions to the communities that support them. What have they done for the betterment of the community? How often? How did they involve the community in designing and developing their contributions? And what has been its impact on the community?
- You might examine the reading resources and suggestions at the end of the other parts of this book.

STRATEGIES MARKETERS MIGHT CONSIDER TRYING

- Model diversity and appreciation for diversity in your administrative and supervisory leadership. Make diversifying your administrative leadership and staff at all ranks a top priority. In conjunction with that, develop a pipeline process strategy through middle school, high school, and college internship programs. Develop both recruitment and retention strategies in order to attract and maintain a staff that mirrors the diversity of the United States and world populations.
- Consider where you want to invest your money—in good, preventative diversity training for yourself, your hopefully diverse administration, and your hopefully diverse staff, or, alternatively, in public relations damage control and lawsuit settlements.
- Make your business's diversity values, standards of service, and complaint process easily visible (prominently posted) in your store, webpage, and so on, so that when consumers have concerns, they have an opportunity to come directly to you first and hopefully have their concerns resolved. Consider adopting a consumer bill of rights that make explicit your store, business, or corporation's stance against racial profiling. The National Action Network offers free downloadable templates for such postings.[4] However, don't just say it, print it, or post it, but also be able to back it up with policies and actions.
- Consider including diversity standards questions on customer feedback evaluations at the bottom of customer receipts or in their email.
- Be aware that Black people especially, and other people of color who statistically have tended to experience generational oppression and disenfranchisement, also tend to have a greater affective orientation.

This means that we may heavily focus on, study, and pick up on language, emotional tone, and body language cues in order to determine our safety from situation to situation. This takes up more of our energy (some scholars estimate an additional 25 percent of daily energy) than our White counterparts, just trying to figure out the possible meanings of the behaviors of people to avoid jumping to conclusions. It also makes many people of color very aware and acute at knowing when someone is patronizing us or behaving in a condescending or otherwise insulting way. These kinds of behaviors are a quick way to lose business, increase tensions among your business and the community, and for your business to end up with public relations dilemmas.

- Be aware that critical thinking scholars[5] have noted that cultural humility, or not thinking that your way of looking at the world is the only way, helps humans to not think in stereotypical or rigid ways toward those who are different in background than they are.
- Resources are available online to assist retailers and the general public in figuring out in advance what kinds of situations warrant police involvement and which ones do not. If involving security staff or police, be sure that involving them is for a legitimate reason. For example, is someone's life or health is in danger.[6] Ask yourself, would you be making this call if this were a White person?[7] You might also consider whether you would make this call if this were a person of a higher socioeconomic status, a different LGBTQIA+ status,[8] a different first-language status, and so on. The only way to really know yourself concerning these questions is to take the time to do serious self-reflection work as recommended in other places among these lists.
- I once heard a lawyer say that if people humbly apologized for and truly learned from their mistakes, 90 percent of lawsuits would not happen. "The goal of an apology is not to prevent lawsuits, it's to do what's right."[9] When people of color experience discrimination, and they try to address it and get invalidating denials, defenses, lies, blame, and so on, in return, it only makes the matter worse both for them and potentially for those in the marketplace to whom they are trying to address their concerns.
- Strive to assess, reassess, and revise policies, practices, and procedures to achieve greater equity among your staff and among your customers. Regularly reconsider your written and nonwritten policies and procedures to be sure they are able to be equitably implemented and assessed.

- Do not engage in exploitive practices that take advantage of disenfranchised communities and their vulnerabilities.
- Be sure that your business contributes in services, fiscally, sponsorships, and so on, to the communities that support it. Seek community input on how your business can help support it.
- Free online resources are available that offer strategies that are good for retailers to use with all consumers, including customers who are LGBTQIA+.[10]
- You might examine the reading resources and suggestions at the end of the other parts of the book.

INEQUITIES

Reflection Questions and Related Readings

1. How different or similar have your experiences in the consumer marketplace been to the ones shared thus far? How do you explain these differences?
2. What ideas do you have concerning how people of color and White allies—and both consumers and marketers—can play a greater role in advocating for equity in all divisions and ranks of the marketplace?
3. Responsible engagement requires self-reflection. Where are you in terms of self-reflection on these issues? What do you need to do or what can you do to think further, more responsibly, and more critically in order to consider the inequities that these stories, news accounts, and poems suggest exist in the consumer marketplace and in society in general? What healthy reflective steps and actions might you personally be able to take to help strategically interrupt such inequities?
4. What questions, comments, thoughts, and further processing do you still need to do concerning each of the stories that you read in this section? Who can you partner with to work together on getting a better understanding of what you have read? On what appropriate resources can you draw?

RELATED READINGS

Henderson, G., A. M. Hakstian, and J. Williams. *Consumer Equality: Race and the American Marketplace.* Santa Barbara, CA: Praeger, 2016.

Sue, D. W. *Microaggressions in Everyday Life: Race, Gender, and Sexual Orientation*. Hoboken, NJ: Wiley Press, 2010.

III

TRAUMAS

Many go out into the marketplace just hoping to make it home safely and soundly, and with no trauma for themselves and their loved ones to have to process and overcome.

FangXiaNuo/iStock/Getty Images

POEM 4

#IfIWasGunnedDown

Malik S. Champlain

One day I remember asking my mother why my father didn't want me.
She looked me in my eyes and said "Baby You're a blessing and you come from me."
"I named you Malik which is a name for a King. So never doubt yourself, look every man in the eye, and always hold your head up high."

When they look at me what do they see.
The pain the struggle of who I used to be.
I didn't say my first word until I was four, and then spoke with a stutter for ten more.
Back then I remember everyone that laughed, kicked me when I was down, and the tears I cried.
Because deep down inside there was a little boy that died.

When they look at me what do they see.
Can I walk to the store without being shot and left to bleed?
Or will you squeeze a little tighter if I told you I can't breathe?
Is my hair too nappy, are my pants too baggy?
Mr. Officer are my hands high enough for you to see?
If I was gunned down?
Would FOX or CNN show a picture of me as a gangsta, a thug, or just view me as worthless.

When they look at me this is what they should see.
A father, a son, a man without fear.
A dreamer like Martin

A fighter like Malcolm
A thinker like Garvey
A speaker like Mandela
Judge me not by the color of my skin, but by the content of my character.
I have more to give than you believe, I have more to give than you can see.

When I look at me this is what I see.
All the people in the community that told me I can be anyone I want to be.
How I went from homeless to a homeowner.
Speechless to a Public Speaker.
Labeled Special Ed to earning my Master's Degree.
I want you to admit it what you see is not me.
What you see is yourself, your bias, your prejudice, your fear.
But it doesn't affect this man.
Because my mother raised me a King, so like a King I will STAND.

POEM 5

Brown Girl Shopping

Arakcelis Gomez (age seventeen, twelfth grade)

I'm leaving the store with my mom,
and some guy yells out
"l'il bitch . . . I'm loving that ass!!!"

I hoped it wasn't
towards me
or my mom

so we kept walking
and the guy kept yelling.

Sad shit is,
I was the only dark girl
in the lot

So "aye yo, let me get a taste
of your sweet chocolate"

I already knew he was fucking white . . .

I swear black guys

just give me flirtatious looks
and tell me they love my smile

white guys

just be testing me
like they're picking me up

from the corner

INTRODUCTION

This section concerns the manner in which everyday efforts to secure the things that we need for our very survival can turn into an ordeal that makes us feel so vulnerable that it changes our life forever. Some incidents that people of color experience when engaging out-and-about in the world go way beyond minor inconveniences, microaggressions, anxieties, and minor or major frustrations, and instead escalate to the point of becoming a potential threat to our emotional, physical, or mortal survival—even in stores and other consumer marketplaces. Some experiences are so intense that they would be considered physically or emotionally traumatic. Therefore, even when trying to do something that should be simple, something that most people seem to take for granted such as shopping can be extremely complex and beyond life-altering.

For example, after a very long, hard day at work I stopped at the grocery store to pick up food to prepare for my family for dinner. It was the evening of February 28, 2017, and as I exited a local grocery store and began to load my car with my groceries, I heard loud shouting of racial epithets coming from the other end of the parking lot. "N____r! Jiggaboo! . . . N____r! Jiggaboo!" I sat my groceries down and looked across the parking lot to see two White men in a red Jeep, yelling out of their windows toward a small car parked next to them. The seemingly panicked woman and man of color in the car appeared to be trying to move their car as quickly as possible from their parking space as the men continued to howl the racial epithets in between laughing and whooping. I did my best to move in a way that would allow me to get the license plate number of the red Jeep while simultaneously dialing 911. My heart was beating very quickly, and my breathing became shortened as my hands also shook. Do they have a gun? I worried. I could see the panicked faces of the driver and the passenger as they tried to back up their car while being blocked by the Jeep and continuing to be inundated with loud, threatening-sounding curses. Will the Jeep-riders shoot into the little car? Will they shoot at me? As much as this incident rattled me, I can only imagine what it must have done to the people in the little car trying to escape these threats. The 911 dispatcher picked up, and I tried to control my breathing as I spoke and as my hands continued to shake. Nervously I gathered my thoughts and detailed what I was observing as I tried to inch my way closer to get a license plate number. The little car managed to pull out of its space and burn rubber taking off, apparently in a panic as the men in the truck continued to yell racial insults at them. Then, they also screeched off speedily, perhaps in pursuit of the little car. I was frightened for the people in the little car, and I worried that something worse was going to happen to them down the road. I wasn't able to get close enough to get the license plate, but I did get a good description of the truck as I spoke with the dispatcher. The dispatcher said that in order to make a report of what I witnessed, I would have to wait for the police to arrive and file an official report. I did. Another witness, a White man, also observed the incident and expressed his concern to the police when they arrived. Forty-five minutes later I made my way home, even more tired, and now shaken, as I kept reminding myself that it's 2017, and not 1917. Really, can't people go to the grocery store in peace, without being verbally assaulted with racial epithets and threatened and followed? I thought to myself over and over. It took me a few days to shake off the disappointment and upset of hearing such a breach of peace, especially coming from a space where you would least expect something like that—the grocery store. Mostly I wondered how the incident impacted the people in the small car at whom the racist remarks were angrily and threateningly directed. Unfortunately, even days later, there was no clear follow-up from the police. As related examples, poem 4 illustrates the trauma experienced by a young man in today's society as he, like many Black men, fears losing his life at any moment. In poem 5, a teenager speaks of a traumatizing experience that occurred as she and her mother in 2019 exited a predominantly White grocery store that exists in the midst of a somewhat diverse and "liberal" community in New England. She speaks of her embarrassment and even humiliation as a man hurls sexist and racist comments at her—comments heard often that may be difficult for this teenager to get out of her head, maybe for as long as she lives, given the retraumatization that may lie ahead for her as a woman of color in this society.

The experience of shopping, which the majority of our society may take for granted, is a regularly complicated and often an exceedingly life-altering event for many people of color, their families, and sometimes even their communities. In the past decades since the mall experience with my young relative, which initially inspired this book, I have observed, read about, or otherwise heard of innumerable accounts of shoppers of color being followed; insulted by clerks, other staff, and fellow customers; stopped by security and police for questioning; arrested; and assaulted by authorities. These experiences more and more have alerted me to the disparities in how people of color are handled in shopping venues, based on reasons that seemed to have more to do with the color of the shopper's skin, their style of dress, or their apparent socioeconomic status than any crime they had actually committed.

HOMICIDAL TRAUMAS IN THE MARKETPLACE

Another traumatic incident that initially helped to inspire me to compile this book took place in my hometown of Detroit. It was alleged that thirty-two-year-old Frederick Finley was murdered by Lord & Taylor security officers who put him into a chokehold when he protested his eleven-year-old daughter and his senior-citizen mother being arrested and handcuffed for the eleven-year-old attempting to steal a $4 bracelet.[1] This horrifying incident not only irreparably destroyed this family, but also resulted in the filing of a $600-million-dollar lawsuit against Lord and Taylor, the arraignment of security guards on manslaughter charges and thousands in fines, as well as protests about the incident from the NAACP and other Black leaders and community organizations. Investigations revealed that the murdered victim was not under the influence of any drugs or alcohol and posed no serious threat to the security guards, but rather was simply advocating for his daughter and mother when he noticed them being arrested in the mall parking lot as he was waiting for them. Unfortunately, such cases are not isolated instances. Alecia Thomas and Travis Shelton, who also lived in Detroit, both died in separate but similar scuffles with security within a year of the Finley case.[2]

As has been pointed out previously, even getting to the consumer marketplace at times has been humiliating and hazardous for people of color—and for celebrities of color as well. Traveling America's roads at times can be demoralizing, dangerous, or outright life-threatening, especially for people of color. For example, Black national weatherman Al Roker reported on Twitter his disappointment when—while attempting to rent a taxi—he and his thirteen-year-old son were passed up in favor of a White passenger standing in the next block.[3] And to a far and horrible extreme, former New York Jets running back, Joe McKnight, was shot and killed in a road-rage incident that occurred with a White Louisiana driver.[4] Such incidences unfortunately are not rare, and taken all together, they illustrate that just getting from one place to another is hazardous, and then when or if disenfranchised people arrive to the marketplace, they may be in for more humiliations or even threats to one's life.

BLACK AND BROWN WOMEN IN THE MARKETPLACE

Girls and women are not immune to being harmed or even killed in marketplaces and beyond. Scholar Brittney Cooper and others note how Black woman frequently get interfered with and abused on trains, buses, and in the streets as they try to get to where they need to go in order to sustain themselves.[5] Reflecting on the interference, abuse, and murder of Sandra Bland and other Black women minding their own business, Howard University administrator Elsie Scott explains: "We are seeing increasingly more cases where Black girls and women are being subjected to abuse and over enforcement. . . . We must start placing more attention on the plight of women in the criminal justice system."[6] For example, when twenty-seven-year-old mother of two, Shelly Frey, was suspected of shoplifting, she fled a Houston Walmart and was killed by authorities.[7] The brutality that girls and women experience at the hands of police and other law enforcement has been grossly underestimated and even overlooked in the media and in scholarship. Professor Kimberlé Crenshaw's #SayHerName movement[8] is devoted to helping the world to not forget Tanisha Anderson, Sandra Bland, Michelle Cusseau, Megan Hockady, Aura Rosser, and hundreds of other often overlooked women victims.

VOICES OF TRAUMA

Racial incidents, if they haven't taken one's life, can take days, months, or years to get over, if ever. In this section, several very unnerving incidents are described. An African American man speaks of a disillusioning, life-altering experience when trying to simply return some vitamins at a local grocery store that he had frequented all his life. A gay African American PhD behavioral scientist discusses an incident that occurred at a mall where he went with his partner to celebrate defending his dissertation proposal, an incident that so upset him psychologically that for years he had to receive treatment. An African American woman speaks of an experience that she and her teen son experienced at a grocery store, and the emotional isolation, abandonment, anger, but also resources that it fostered. I speak of the emotional trauma that I experienced seeing what appeared to be a reenactment of a lynching at a community fall festival amusement. An African American woman speaks of her experience being humiliated and assaulted by security guards at a department store. These contributions, taken together, illustrate that for people of color, negative consumer marketplace experiences can escalate past the territory of monitoring and inequitable treatment and into the territory of physical or severe emotional hazard, trauma, or mortal danger. Thus, something taken for granted by many as simple, leisurely, even fun—for people of color can be emotionally or physically traumatizing, violent, or otherwise significantly threatening.

TARGETED

"The Book of Robbers, Scammers, and Fraudulents" (Finley's Story)

Finley's story concerns the potential complexity and inequity of minor transactions for people of color, especially for Black men. I was traveling out of town to visit a loved one in the hospital, and was able to arrange meeting Finley for an interview while there. A relative of his had referred me to him after learning of the work I was doing on this topic.

To make things logistically easier for both of us, Finley agreed to meet me at the hospital I was visiting, which was not far from his office. Although I had never met this young man, I did feel eerily like I had met him before, and I think it was because of his resemblance and mannerisms, similar to his family member who referred us. Finley was a soft-spoken young man apparently in the age of adulthood that reminded me of the ages of my adult nieces and nephews in their mid- to late twenties and early thirties. He was coming from work, so he still had on a pressed shirt and tie. I wondered if he might be tired, having rushed to the interview, straight from work. But he seemed totally engaged and ready to talk.

I explained that I thought I saw a small café area up on the second floor—it seemed that it might be quiet enough for conducting the interview. We took the elevator up, found an empty table, and both sat and chatted a bit to try to break the ice before delving immediately into the interview. We were surrounded by amazing art and sculptures as the café was nuzzled within a mezzanine that overlooked the lower floor. There were gigantic hanging origami, sculptures, and large oil paintings. A live pianist tinkled piano keys in a distance. I thought to myself, this must be the new age of patient- and community-focused hospitals. The atmosphere of the hospital, and all that we could see overlooking the mezzanine gave us plenty to chat about to break the ice.

Finley seemed happy to have a moment to just sit, and he appeared to be further collecting himself as I tried to size up his comfort level to see how much time to take to gently move into the task at hand. There had been quite a long period of on-and-off phone tag and such, and I wasn't 100 percent sure whether he really wanted to be here. I had persisted because I had heard snippets of his story from his relative and felt that it was potentially extremely important. So, my first goal was to confirm that his heart was really in this. I began by going over the purpose of my project, the informed consent paperwork, stressing that this is completely voluntary, and that he can say no now or even stop the interview at any time, even if he has signed the consent form. He assured me that he was good with everything and signed the papers, and we proceeded. Every now and then there was a little more hustle and bustle going around us than we had wanted, but for the most part it was quiet. I gave him some moments to settle a bit more, we chitchatted a little about the city, the weather, and so on. As he spoke, he seemed relieved that I genuinely wanted to know what happened and how it impacted his life. But I did not want to exasperate him, so I tried to proceed very carefully and he seemed to appreciate that.

Before we gradually made our way toward the horrible marketplace events that brought him here, we first spoke of Finley's accomplished educational background, his lucrative but highly competitive job, and a little bit about the sports that he played in high school some years ago. As I noticed him getting more comfortable, I gathered my recorder, notebook, and pen, and asked if he was ready to begin telling his story. He was.

Finley told me that just as his new career and economic security was getting started and his life seemed to be gaining some sense of predictability, he had a jolting, life-altering experience at a grocery store that he has frequented pretty much all of his life. While trying to simply request a small refund at a customer service desk in a large, but local, grocery store, his sense of comfort was turned upside down. He spoke of the heart-wrenching events that were difficult for him to fully perceive in the moments they occurred; therefore he was in a state of shock initially. He described how over a period of days and weeks, that shock turned into cynicism as he began to remember that these are the frequent experiences of many people of color in the United States.

Finley speaks . . .

* * *

I'm thirty-two years old, and the incident happened when I was twenty-eight, and I have the paperwork and the response letter, which was even more offensive. I work as a sales consultant for a residential construction firm, and I'm constantly in and out of people's homes. I've been doing that awhile and plan on staying there for quite some time. Things are really going well as far as the job.

One day I'm in a particular town where I grew up—a predominantly White, upper-middle-class town with a very, very small amount of minorities. I went to the [major grocery store] in that town. There's also a very small amount of minorities that work there as well—maybe one or two at a given moment. At the time I lived literally within a mile of the place, and I had gone to high school in that town. I would frequent this store all the time. On the day of the incident, I was wearing a solid navy-blue sweatshirt with no hood and navy-blue khaki dress pants. I also was wearing some brown casual Polo work boots. So, my attire was blue on blue, with some boots.

I went in there to return some vitamins, and I also wanted to get some gas at that same store because at my job I drive around everywhere. I didn't have a receipt for the vitamins because I had gotten them from my girlfriend—they were some kind of women's vitamins, I don't know. But she was like, you can return these and get some gas money, essentially. Like I said, I had no receipt and I was going to get gas at that same grocery store anyway, so I'm first in line at the customer service desk when I walk up to it. I walk up to the [White] lady who is closest to me, and she's in her thirties or forties, brunette. There's a [White] lady who is behind me with a rug. As I go to the [clerk] lady directly in front of me, I say, "I'm here to return these vitamins." She asks me for my driver's license. I give her my driver's license. Then she proceeds to grab this folder and starts writing my driver's license number in the folder. I'm just sitting there looking around, and going on with my day. The lady behind me, a middle-aged—probably in her fifties, White woman with blondish gray hair—she comes around me to the next [clerk] lady. The woman [also White] who was waiting on the [rug] lady was probably sixty years old. The woman comes up with the rug, and they are like, "Oh, a rug." And I'm also thinking like, oh, a rug, interesting—I didn't know you could get rugs at a grocery store. And [the clerk for the rug lady] says, "I didn't know you could get a rug at the grocery store." And the [rug] lady says, "Yes, we got it for my son in college, and we got this for his dorm room, and he doesn't want it. . . . So, we're returning it." Her clerk asks, "Do you have a receipt?" She says, "No." And her clerk says "Okay," and gives her cash, "There" (gesturing, giving cash). So, I looked, and I said to myself, wait a minute. That's when I said, "What are you writing in this book, first of all?" And she said, "Don't worry about it." And she proceeds to give me a gift card. I said again to myself, wait a minute! And I ask, "So, why am I getting a gift card if she just got cash?" And my clerk responded, "Well, she had a receipt." And I said, "No, she didn't have a receipt, I'm sitting here and I heard the whole thing." And she goes, "Well." I said, "And still, what are you writing in this book, and what is this book?!" And again she says, "Don't worry about it." She also says that the clerk next to us did it wrong. She determines that the lady [customer] next to us also did not have a receipt by talking to her [clerk] coworker. So, I inquire, "If she doesn't have her receipt either, what's the difference? . . . You gave her cash, and I have to get a gift card, and you are also writing in this book." The lady [clerk] I'm dealing with says [again], "Well, she did it wrong! . . . She did it wrong!" So, then I said, "Well, why don't you do it wrong with me too, if that's the case." And she said, "No, I won't do it like that." And I'm like, "What is this book anyway?!" She closes the book, and I see on top of the book, type-written, *"THIS IS A BOOK OF OUR 'FAVORITE CUSTOMERS': ROBBERS, SCAMMERS, FRAUDULENTS."* So, I say, "Are you kidding me? . . . Are you kidding me?! . . . I can understand that I'm a little darker than everybody else in here, but I don't want to be a 'favorite customer' in my favorite store. . . . I live right up the street, I come to this store all the time. . . . Seriously?!" And she goes, "Sorry, that's just the way it's going to be!" I go, "You've got to be kidding me, are you serious?!" At this point the [rug] lady has gone away with her cash. I said [again], "So seriously, you are going to give me a gift card, and you are going to put me in that book?" She said, "Yes!" [Her attitude] was totally condescending, totally refusing to do anything for me. She was treating me as if I'm crazy, totally in the wrong—that she's completely in the right, and that this is the way that it's going to be. The other clerk had an apprehensive, scared, let-me-stay-out-of-this kind of look. I said, "I have to talk to a manager, this is crazy." My clerk basically huffed and puffed, and then went and called for the manager. The manager comes down, he's a White man probably in his fifties. There's a line that has built up by this point. As the manager comes down, the first thing he says, looking puzzled, is, "Where did that rug come from?" That's the very first thing that comes out of his mouth, and no one really responded to that. Then he looked as if to ask, "So what's going on over here?" I told him basically what happened, explaining the situation to him. He's listening to me, and he's listening to her. She's basically telling him over and over, "That's the way we do it!" Initially, his response [addressed to me] was like, "So what's wrong with the gift card?" I responded while nodding toward the rug lady, "She just got the cash." I had mentioned that I was trying to get gas, so he felt that the [store's] gift card [inclusive of the gas station] should be fine. "But no," I said, "It should not be fine, it's exactly the same situation as her, and I shouldn't have been put in the book in the first place, and I don't want the gift card—if she got cash, then I should get cash." He's standing there frustrated, and he's like, "Fine, just give him the cash!" I took the cash, like, "Thank you." He had almost the same affect that she had. You know, like he was doing it just to get me out of the place. After he gave me the cash, he persisted to say something to her and to just go on with his day. Then as I started to walk away, I turned back around, and I said, "You know what, actually, take me out of that book too, because I don't deserve to be in that book." I had to come back and say I want to be taken out of that book! But his response was like, "Where's the book?!" as if annoyed. He seemed frustrated, like he's got to now do this too—deal with the book. He's like, okay, and he grabs the book, and he flips to my page, because it's in alphabetical order or something like that. He rips me out of the book and he throws [the page] in the garbage. As I'm leaving there, there's a crowd, and everything has built up at this point. Like I said, I go to this store all the time, so literally, I couldn't believe it—I was in shock at this point.

And it gets even "better" [gesturing quotations]. After this happened, I immediately knew this wasn't right. I started looking into what I could do, right off the bat. Either that day or the next day, I was talking with [a] human rights [agency] about what's going on. What they do is they take a deposition, and then they contact [the] employers who do [inappropriate] things of this nature. So, they reached out to the grocery store. The grocery store, in their reply, said that the rug cost $19.99, but my vitamins cost $20.01. I'm pretty sure that the vitamins cost in the range of $14 to $15—that's what I got back. But they said that the rug cost $19.99 on the dot, and my vitamins cost on the dot $20.01. Like, it's in writing—I have the letter that says that! Because my purchase was [supposedly] above $20, I was given the gift card, and because her purchase was below $20, she didn't get a gift card and was given cash. Also, they said that I was ranting and raving saying, "This is because I'm Black! . . . This is because I'm Black! . . . This is because I'm Black!" In their letter they said that! [What I actually said was], "Just because I'm darker than everyone here, doesn't mean. . . ." They also said nothing about the book . . . nothing—not one word—not one iota—not one thing about the book, at all! This is the *"BOOK OF OUR 'FAVORITE CUSTOMERS': ROBBERS, SCAMMERS, FRAUDS"*—that's imprinted on my brain—every detail of the book! They didn't put anything about the book—they acted like that never happened. I wrote a response letter, basically responding point by point by point by point about how they are literally categorizing me as that stereotypical, angry Black man running around the store acting a fool—when that's not the way that I was. I'm college-educated, I have a good job, I've done things right my whole life, and they're just putting me in this stereotypical basis that says that young Black men like to act crazy.

What ended up happening is that finally I got an actual lawyer for the case. Even though the human rights [agency] took on my case, because the monetary [discrepancy] was not above $5,000, essentially that meant that I should get a lawyer. They also said that the grocery store can do whatever they want essentially, and that I'm better off getting a lawyer. All that the human rights agency could do was obtain an apology, and perhaps very small damages. So, the grocery store could do whatever they want—deny, and so on—and I never got an apology.

So, I got my lawyer, and we talked and discussed. She was a White woman who had done some cases for [employees of a large business in town] about workplace discrimination. She was all for this case. She said I could pay her a retainer later, once the case is settled. But the case slipped through the cracks. I didn't hear from the attorney for like a year and a half to two years. In the meantime, my girlfriend and I talked about "the book," and she asked if I had seen it. I said that I saw it the one time, but I barely go back there anymore. Soon after, out of frustration I'm there at the grocery store with my girlfriend with a video camera, and we are like, "Oh, can we see the book?" And they're like, "What book?"

Then out of the blue, like six months ago, the lawyer, she calls me up and says, "Oh, I just realized you haven't been getting my emails." She's like, "I thought you were cc:'d on all of them—and we have a hearing like, tomorrow!" She said, "You probably thought this was gone, but we do have a hearing tomorrow!" I said, "I'll be there!"

We had the hearing the next day. The grocery store's [same] manager was there, and their lawyer was there. A deposition or mediator guy was there who made it known that he was a former police officer. We were telling him what was going on, and my lawyer said to me, "It's great that you remember all of these facts—you remember what people were wearing, even what people were saying after all of this time." But the manager is like omitting most of what happened, like, "Ahh, I don't remember. . . . Ohh, I don't recall. . . ." His lawyer would stop him from saying anything that could be the truth. The manager was like, "I've been working for this grocery store for like twenty-five years, I know all their policies." And the next sentence, with the lawyer's intervention, "I don't know anything about anything." In one sentence he's saying he's worked for the grocery store all of his whole life and knows all of its policies. And then you say something about "the book," and he's like, "Ohh, I don't know anything about a book—I don't know anything about that." My lawyer requested, "We'd like to talk to your clerk employee, how can we arrange to talk with her?" He responds, "How can we find an employee two years later?" And two seconds later he'll contradict himself again.

The former police officer/mediator, an Asian man from a nearby suburban town, said that there's a lot of troubling things that were said as far as what happened that day at the grocery store. Concerning "the book," the mediator also had asked, "Was it like a handwritten thing that the employees put together, or was it like a type-written, store-policy type deal?" "No, it was official!" It turns out that I had actually taken a cell phone picture of the book from a distance, and I emailed it to my lawyer. That is, as I said earlier, after that original visit, I had gone back a second time with my girlfriend to take a picture or video or whatever I could. The way that the customer service desk is, it's like an "L," and then there's Western Union stuff on the side. You can actually see behind the desk [from the Western Union kiosk]. It was a picture where you would definitely have to blow it up so that you could see the letters on it, because it was taken from five to ten feet away. The book was still sitting there, and it's stated right on the side—"*THIS IS A BOOK OF OUR 'FAVORITE CUSTOMERS'* . . ." And it's type-written. The judge—the former cop—he said, "You can't do that, that's illegal! . . . You can't take pictures of people without their consent!" He literally chastised me right there. It wasn't even a picture of a person. My lawyer, when we left, she was like, "That's not even true, that's not even true, at all." But the deposition/mediator jumped on me for that, it was crazy. When he said that about the camera thing, that sounded just like a police officer saying, "Get that camera phone out of my face!" My lawyer even said she felt the "cop" come out of him right there—that was a cop, that was not a mediator. Previous to that point the mediator/cop was asking, "What's going on with this book, that doesn't sound right. . . . It's a book, a type-written book, so it's a company policy, I would like to see that book." And then, I say, I have a picture of the book, and he says, "Oh yeah, how did you get a picture of the book?" I said, "I went there on my own." He responds, "How did you do that, you went behind the counter?!" "No," I say, "the counter is in an area where you can see behind it." The grocery store manager interrupts, "That's not true!" I said, "It is true, it's an 'L,' and the Western Union stuff is right there." "No! That's not true!!" they say. And then the mediator/cop says, "Well, it's illegal for you to take a picture like that." I asked him—not to argue or anything—but I asked him, "What if I go in there and I take a picture of some steaks, not to buy them, but just to see if these were the steaks that I wanted—that would be illegal because that's the store's property?" I explained that I was just posing it as a question, for the future. The mediator/cop didn't really have much to say on that one. But he went from wondering about all the inconsistencies with the grocery manager's story, and also the book, and the policies about the book, and how something even gets into the book, to basically just saying it's illegal to take a picture.

Also, it turns out that they don't actually have to produce anything. So, after the hearing, the mediator/cop says, "I suggest you guys settle, if you can get a settlement, you should settle because they don't have to produce anything, and they know that they don't." When we walked out of there, my lawyer was furious, saying, "They perjured themselves about eight times over the course of the hearing. . . . We should sue the chain legit—like right now!" She was ready to go to court, and she was venting, "This is crazy, this is ridiculous, I'm ready to go to court! . . . Let's battle this and let's do this thing!" The mediator/cop set us up for a follow-up visit for the store to produce the book, for them to produce some of the facts that they omitted—so he could go through all of these things. Low and behold, I never went for that follow-up visit—I never heard about that. I get a letter in the mail saying that basically the store produced nothing because they didn't have to do it. The human rights [agency] said that they found that the store doesn't have to produce anything. Soon after, my lawyer said that she's "getting too old for this" and basically she's gone as far as she can go. I thought this was quite the surprise—quite the reversal; what happened to "everyone perjured themselves"? She had even had a monetary amount—"You're this age, and if they gave you damages for just this or that amount of time. . . ." All of that gone, just three to four weeks later, a totally different woman! I was like, "Is there anyone you can refer me to or something like that?" She was like, "I'll try." So basically, she wasn't having any luck with referring someone. So, I suggested, "At this point, what if we just go to the next mediator?" That was something she had talked about that first day, and we could just tell the story. "Nah, you could be sued for libel," [she said]. I said, "If they sued me, that would put me in the courtroom, that would actually be better—they would actually have to produce the books and everything, and prove that I was lying and that I was slandering them." She was like, "Basically they can sue you, and I wouldn't feel comfortable. . . ." I was like, what on earth is going on? So that's how she left me. I was like, "Okay, Miss [lawyer]—wow!" That was about two or three months ago [in the summer of 2016]. No apology, no anything from anyone. In a letter, it also said that we missed a court date, but then she and the mediator/cop guy both said that was a typo and wasn't supposed to be there. I had called, and said, "Wait a minute, I didn't miss any dates." And they were like, "No, no, that wasn't supposed to be there." I'm like ". . . Okay. . . You just send an official letter, and that's not supposed to be on there?"

If somebody's life was on the line, I would say that the CIA has gotten ahold of some people or something (slight chuckling). Literally, it was like it was totally two different lawyers I had talked to. She was ready to sic the dogs . . . "They perjured themselves eight different ways!" This abrupt change was crazy! Hearing the grocery store's response, in that open discussion with the mediator/cop disgusted her just as much as it disgusted me—because it was just disgusting what they were saying. It's just like, you can look someone in the eye and say that a rug cost [less] than a [bottle of] vitamins?! But then also that vitamins magically cost right at the threshold where this did not matter? But also, what made me be fraudulent, and a robber, and a burglar? I don't return stuff there. I've never returned anything there before. So then, what's the criteria to be put in that book? Does it take five returns? Does it take being Black? What does it take? They were supposed to produce the book, but they didn't. I was prepared to put the attorney on retainer and pay the original court fees to get this thing going, because as I expressed to my lawyer, "This is something that really happened—this is truth—this is a true discriminatory case, and I will fight for it if it is what we need to do." But then later she [responds] she's "too old for this."

Over all I felt embarrassed, I felt discriminated against, and I definitely felt upset that this was happening in a town that I call home. Maybe the clerk is just a summer person that spends her summers there? I live there 24/7. I felt embarrassed, kind of hurt, and kind of just shocked. That reminder just kind of slaps you in the face when something like this happens to you, and you are just like this is unbelievable . . . unbelievable! Stumbling on the book, that was just pure shock . . . pure shock—like my jaw dropped—like, are you kidding me? . . . Are you kidding me?! And then I felt sarcastically surprised—like, it doesn't surprise me that you guys would have this type of policy at this store. I guarantee that more than half of that book consists of minorities—or Black people—when only about 2 percent of the customer population of that store is minorities.

I actually had a panic attack a couple of weeks after the [book] incident. I'm sitting like directly with [White] people in their homes and talking about big business and things like that. But in my head I was thinking about this whole thing, and I just had to go out and get some air, and I felt like I was going to pass out. And that wasn't the only panic attack—without a doubt I've definitely been a lot more emotional—again, especially with the way that the climate of the world is going. All these racial issues are happening. I work and live in an area of predominantly White people, and I'm usually with White customers. At the time, I worked with only two Black guys who work at my job doing what I do—now there's three—that's out of fifty. And it's not that it opened my eyes, because my eyes were already opened—I knew. But I also avoid that grocery store chain. The few times I go back there it's late at night because that's when I get off work late, and it's either McDonald's or try to get some actual food. Even when I go to other franchises of that same grocery store, I literally just can't escape the anxiety, the feeling that they are watching me, checking my credit card and seeing if I am actually shopping at their place, so that perhaps they can use it against me if this case proceeds—"We saw that you came to our grocery store." "Yeah, so I could get some food in me, and this is a grocery store." I actually feel more comfortable when I go to other grocery stores because it's uncomfortable in there. Even today, when I go in there, using my credit card, I'm wondering, because of my name and all that. They already have my name, my address—not just from the driver's license they took that day because they got rid of that—but because of all the things we've been through, documents, and so on. I've been in the room with their corporate lawyers, and things like that. I don't feel very trusting of them, and I even feel very threatened—sitting in the room with those guys. If this were a bigger situation than it is, I would definitely feel much more threatened. But that's the way that they come off, and that's the way that they handle it. Basically, you are nothing, you are nobody, and what you are saying is a lie. Their attitude is, "If we are lying, it doesn't matter, because we don't have to prove ourselves to you—you are just wrong."

[To take care of myself], I tried to fight it, that's what I tried to do. I tried to fight it and stand up for what I could do. I was more than willing to go to the media with my lawyer and fight it all that we could through the court systems. So, once again, when the lawyer said she is getting too old for this, I had to just kind of shake my head and say "Wow!" I thought about trying to find another lawyer. Fighting it was my first response and what I thought I should do. I also think this situation has changed me because with all this nonsense that's going on in the world today, I now have a piece of it. Unfortunately, I'm one of the people who is actually in the situation, and I never would have put myself there. I feel like my story should be out there—it's not killing or anything like that—but it's happened to me. Like the small amount of people who find a dead rodent in their fast food or something like that—it's a weird analogy, but . . . I'm a very diverse person, I have a diverse set of friends, and unfortunately, I'm in a situation where it's bigger than me . . . much bigger than me. That's not where anybody wants to be, especially these days—all the guys that got shot. Instead of just being who they were, they're now one of those names on the T-shirt or something like that. People who know me—family and friends—have seen similar incidents in the news and things like that and have brought that to my attention and reminded me.

TRAUMATIZED

"Wouldn't You Want to Hear My Story If You're Ready to Shoot Me?" (Kenrec's Story)

Kenrec's story concerns what I call the unpredictable predictability and aftermath of race-based trauma experienced while shopping, in this case, in a store inside of a mall. Kenrec's story, once I heard it and other similar stories, became my third inspiration for this book.

Kenrec is an openly gay African American man in his mid-forties living in the Midwest. He recently had earned his doctorate degree in a behavioral sciences field, the first in his immediate and extended family to obtain such a level of achievement. I had heard of his story through mutual contacts, and when I contacted him, he seemed not only willing to tell his story but also he seemed to find an added comfort in knowing that his story meant that much to me and my potential audience. Since Kenrec was living in the Midwest, I connected with him while passing through his town on a connecting flight. He agreed to meet me at the airport of my connecting flight. This meant my having to go through security again, but I didn't care if it meant that I could get his extremely important voice for revealing Black marketplace experiences in the "free" United States.

Kenrec lived within an hour's drive of my connecting airport, and he had already arrived at the airport by the time I arrived. I made my way from my initial plane and through the long corridors of the huge airport to the main lobby. I spotted him right away as he waved his arms and stepped at a fast pace toward me, ever the gentleman, grabbing my carry on from me as we warmly greeted each other. As always, I surveyed the area to try to find the quietest spot. We located a spot that seemed to not have much activity and made ourselves comfortable. We started first catching up on Kenrec's new life in academia, and then making note of the time, we decided we had better get to the business at hand so that I could make my connecting flight.

Kenrec has a way of speaking that is rather animated and often full of humor. A tall, robust man, he has a bombastic, infectious laugh and a characteristically big smile when he is comfortable. However, when recounting this story, I did not see much laughing. In fact, at times his eyes often rapidly blinked, his breathing became fast-paced and sometimes labored, and his hands shook. I checked in with him frequently to be sure that he was okay, and had it not been for his reassurance that he wanted to tell his story, I might have stopped the interview to ensure that his recounting his story did not impose an undue burden on his health. My heart was grieved to know what a toll this incident took on him, and even how much it appeared to take out of Kenrec's energy to retell it. But an important retelling it was, like all of these stories.

It is known in most Black circles that many parents of children of color socialize our children concerning mall and other shopping venue behavior. We warn them not to reach into their pockets for even a pencil while shopping, and we may tend to follow those same rules ourselves. Further, we tell them not to wear bulky clothes that may make a shopper appear suspect. We may warn our children to not even *look* or appear like they could be doing anything wrong.[1] It's becoming better understood how these legitimate, added, intense worries may cause some parents of color to be extremely supervisory and strict with children of color, sometimes to levels that could be considered by outsiders to be unhealthy for children's emotional development. Meaning that, historically, fears of what can happen to children of color in the hands of an often biased, White supremacist society may cause some parents to go overboard in applying discipline and punishments, sometimes even corporeal, in an attempt to teach their children to be ultra-well-behaved. However, such tendencies are out of parental fear of punishments far worse than these, including unnecessary death for children, teens, and young adults when they are outside of the home (e.g., the senseless murders of Emmett Till and Trayvon Martin, combined with no accountability for them).[2] However, parents also are learning that the strictest of discipline cannot protect our children from what they may face beyond the safety of home—instead, it is the social structures, procedures, and policies outside of home that need to change so that there is room for all children to be children.

In the following memory-telling, a grown man explains all of the trauma that he experienced over his reaching into his pocket to get a mint while browsing in a store at a mall. Kenrec describes a life-changing shopping experience that occurred on the same day that he defended his dissertation proposal in a northern New England town, about a year before his relocation after earning his PhD. Thus, the situation occurred on what should have been one of the happiest days of his life. But unfortunately, this otherwise happy day turned into a day that has taken Kenrec years to overcome, if he yet has. His story illustrates the tension that many people of color may feel in the marketplace where at any given moment, a happy or relaxing day can turn into a nightmare based on the inaccurate, even delusional, stereotypes that exist in other peoples' heads.

Kenrec tells his story . . .

* * *

When I talk about my experiences with racism, I can go on and on and on. I have a PhD in [an underrepresented field], so that's twenty years of racism right there. I also am an adjunct instructor at a large university, as well as at another university. I teach graduate courses in advanced statistics, as well as courses involving [behavioral] disorders in children. I am African American, and my ethnic background is diverse, with my mother's grandfather having been White, and my father's great-grandfather having been White. I'm also a gay man—an openly gay man who teaches.

My partner, well, he's a White man. This plays into the story of what happened to me at the mall. We've been together for fourteen years. So, what happened is that I was shopping after defending my dissertation proposal. My partner and I went to a particular [household goods retail] store in a suburb of New England. We were going to go to dinner afterward, so we were killing time before the movies and dinner. We entered the store to just kind of browse. We noticed that there was a White [female] store manager that kept looking at us suspiciously. I knew then that there was probably a problem. I said to my partner that the people were following us, and they also were excessively asking, "Can I help you? Can I help you?"

So, we left the store, and after a little while three police officers surrounded us. Two police officers were in front of me, and I was talking to them. But I also was asking them why they had stopped us. They said there was a report that we had stolen something. So, I volunteered to have them check me. I said, "You can check my person." As they were checking me, I was talking to them, and you could tell they were agitated. The only thing I could remember doing in the store is I had my own box of Certs mints. I had popped one in my mouth and put them back in my pocket. You replay the questions in your mind.

I had never been stopped like this before. I was in a different mental or emotional space, because I was very happy that I had just successfully defended my dissertation [proposal]. It was a really wonderful moment in my career. After going to graduate school, this was a defining moment for me. So, I started to explain to the officer that this was my dissertation [proposal] defense day, and that my partner and I were here to celebrate. The officer's response was that I didn't need to tell my life story—he said it in a way that I felt was sort of escalating the situation. I was trying to explain how I got there, who I was. So, when he said I don't have to tell my life story, I just took out my pen, and I started to write down his badge number because at this point I didn't know if there was going to be more trouble. At that point, he motioned by raising his head—and I thought he was raising his head to me—but in fact, there was another officer behind me to whom he was motioning. I didn't realize there was another officer behind me. So, I turned around and was startled that there was another officer right behind me. This was quite threatening—in fact, very threatening. At this point, I said, "I'm going to go to the police department. I need directions to the police department because I want to complain because I don't think this is right that you're stopping us for something that you're not even going to follow through on."

It was definitely a power thing—the police officers and their stares and the tone of voice they were using. And oh, I was very frightened! There were two officers in front of me, and they were speaking with this tone like I had done something wrong. And then when I tried to explain my whereabouts, he had said, "Don't kill the messenger." So, I'm thinking, why go there? You're escalating the situation when I'm trying to share with you what's going on. Furthermore, when he motioned his head, like the old southern motion of "turn around, there's somebody's behind you," I was frightened. From my perspective he was saying, "Look n[_____], you keep talking to me, I've got something for you that you're unaware of." My partner was right next to me, so he saw the third police officer as well. When I turned around, the other officer was looking like, "Yeah, I'm right here for you." So, I recognized that I was surrounded by three officers. I was thinking, "I'm six-foot, and 270 pounds . . . maybe." But they had guns. It was that, plus it was the White woman who had called. I didn't know what she said, but I knew that this is how they're responding to me. Further, they were saying, "I don't need to hear your life story," [which] was their way of saying, "You're just a stereotype anyway." I was trying to explain who I was, how I got there, and they didn't care anything about that. "Look sir, we got a phone call. . . ." And they asked for my license, and not my [White] partner's. I pull my license out and [my partner] snaps to it, and he pulls his license out too. This whole time, he's in shock, because he's never had an experience like this. So, it was fascinating for me.

The police officers involved were young, probably rookies just starting out in the force. One was in his twenties, one was maybe [in his] forties, another was maybe [also in his] twenties. They could hear in my storytelling that I was very upset. They never ended up holding me—they were just in front of me, asking me what I was doing there, and so on, after they had gotten a report from the store manager. At this point I was upset because I felt like they had three police officers, for what? There was no reason for it. I was upset, and I wanted to go back into the store to find out from the store manager what she saw that made her determine that the police should be called. So, if I had just walked away after they said I could go, maybe that probably would have been the end of it. But when they started with "Don't kill the messenger," I said to the officers, "Come back into the store with me." And I think that's when they realized this is not some ordinary Black person who in their mind was going to just accept it and hurry along. By now it was nighttime, and I also was worried the officers were going to harass me further. That's the other part—I was scared.

The officers saw that I wasn't just going to walk away at this point, and instead I went back into the store. I don't know if I asked the officers [again] to go back in with me, or whether they took it upon themselves to follow me, but they went with me. My partner and I confronted the manager, and asked her "Why did you call the police, and what did you tell them on the phone?" I was trying to clarify what they were told by the manager when she called. I wanted to understand what she said on the phone to make the police come with such force. I also asked her about the store policy, which is customary, and she declined to talk. So, one of the officers requested to know why they were called and asked, "Well, what was it?" At that point, the officer was indicating that he was really beginning to understand my question to her, and he said something like, "He is making a good point, why did you call?" She was beating around the bush and procrastinating in her answer. My partner was all worked up, and was pressing her, "Why would you do this?!" Then at some point, one of the officers took her alone, and he said something like, "This guy is over here, and you did a wrong thing, and you should apologize." I think at this point she just shut down, and she would not apologize as I can recall. I think at that point my partner and I decided that this is nuts, and we just left.

Although she never disclosed to me what she actually said [in her 911 call], I later found out what she said from a tape-recording that I was able to get my hands on from the police department because it's a public record. She basically said she was afraid. She was afraid and made an alarming phone call that there was a Black man in the store, one of her employees saw something and she was scared that some harm was going to come. Well, what had they seen? She couldn't say. When I had confronted her about it with the police, she didn't say to me, "Well, when you were over here, you did this." She was so uncooperative about expressing what her fears were. But I had felt this tension when we first walked into the store. When we walked into the store, I remember she acknowledged my partner, who is White, but looked at me in sort of a dismissive way. I knew right then, by the way that she had spoken to my partner and not to me, there was probably going to be some trouble. I could tell she didn't like the fact that he was with a Black man. I don't know if she could sense that we were together or not, but I definitely know she didn't feel that I had a right to be in that space, so she was going to assert her power to let me know that she had the power to defy my space in there. That's really why I went back into the store with the police. Because I wanted her to understand that you just can't do this to people because you have the power to do it.

The subsequent follow-up of all of this is that I called [the store's] corporate office. I spoke with the district manager to find out what their store policy was [concerning] someone who is suspected of shoplifting. My understanding of what was said is that the store's policy was not to call the police, but to use the manager for your own sort of security. In other words, the store manager was within her right to approach me and say, "Sir, my employee saw something, or I saw something, and before you leave the store we need to have you empty," and I would have certainly done that if she had proceeded in that way. But she chose to escalate it, and call the police, reporting that she was afraid of something. And I was like, "Afraid of what?" Eventually she was reprimanded as I do recall. She was reprimanded for going outside of store policy.

In the meantime, I talked to the police chief, I talked to the town manager, and I called the Better Business Bureau (BBB). The BBB in that community would not take my complaint—as a racial complaint—over the phone after I explained to them how I was treated based on race. They would not accept it as a racial complaint. So, I said to the person on the phone, "Well, what if I left out the race part, and just complained, would you accept that as a complaint?" And she said, "Yes, we would." But there was no space in the Better Business Bureau complaint form to mark it as an incident of racism.

When I called [the regional] office of civil rights to talk about what possible claim of action I can have, I spoke to an African American woman attorney. She didn't exactly say this, but she inferred that I should be glad, or that I am lucky, that they didn't hit me or hurt me in some way. There was no recognition of the sort of psychological damage that occurred.

It was an interesting experience, so much so that I sent an e-mail out to people in my graduate school just letting people know what had happened and how upsetting it was. And I received e-mails from all across the country about this experience. For example, there was a White woman who had lived in that [same] community and she explained to me that a year prior, there had been some problem with an African American at that store. That helped me to somewhat understand what was going on. As another example, a Black woman e-mailed that I was probably in the store with a White woman anyway, so what was I doing there? So, I received multiple types of responses from people asking what I was doing in [that particular household goods store] anyway. It certainly informed my thinking about [the behavioral sciences] because at that time the majority of my [student practitioner] clients were White. With the police officers being White, my assumption was, wow, I could have been seeing their sisters, their nieces, their other family members as their clinician—I'm the person who's caring for their community, their family. Yet, here they were being dismissive and noncaring about who I was. It was a very powerful, defining moment in my life because at that point, I didn't know if I could even finish my degree, because I felt like I had given so much to my field [within the behavioral sciences]. I had been the only African American and gay man in the program for the last twenty years or so, and there was a tremendous struggle. Here I was, and what was I working so hard for—what was the use if I couldn't assert that I was an educated person or that I was a person who didn't steal. That didn't seem to matter, so it greatly shook me.

This situation made me question my role of being a helper. I had never had police surround me. Some people said I was lucky to be a Black male and not have had that experience [until then]. And other people suggested that my psychological pain was not worthy of further talking about because I wasn't hit upside the head. Others thought I was stupid for allowing the police officers to check me, because they said the police officers could have planted something on me. I didn't know any of these things. All I knew was that I didn't steal anything, so I figured I should be honest and say, "Look, I didn't steal anything, so you have my permission to check me."

The other part of the story I want to tell is that when I called the corporate office of the store, there was a woman who was the assistant to the CEO with whom I spoke. All I wanted at this point was to have a conversation with the head of [the company] to let him know that this is going on in his stores. This conversation was never allowed to happen. What they did do, was they had a Hispanic man who was the treasurer of the corporation [speak to] me. At this time, I think the corporation was earning $217 million dollars [annually]. The assistant to the CEO, she was very rude. She was like, "Look, we don't care if you're white, green. . . ." Picture this, she's the assistant to the CEO, and she's a White woman. She's a White woman! She was saying that this was not a racial incident, and they threatened to sue me if I didn't get the people off of [them]. A lot of my supporters—the dean, and the professors of the school, and so on, had called and said things like, "This man who you're messing with is of good character, he's nice." Eighty-five people called them to complain. So [corporate] threatened to sue me if I didn't get the people to stop calling them. My response was that I have no control over these people calling. After that, the Latino man called me, and he wanted me to back down. I told him, "This is a corporation that you're working for . . . so now they're putting you on the phone to talk to me, and that is not what my request is . . . I'm asking to speak to the CEO." See, this is all I wanted out of this, so I told him, "No, [and] look, don't call my house anymore, and don't call me anymore." I have a tape-recording of everything, and I let people know that I was taping the conversations and [making] transcripts of everything.

This was a very powerful moment in my life, a very powerful moment. I just couldn't believe the resistance that I was getting trying to just get some form of acknowledgment on the corporate level about the experience, beyond the store manager being reprimanded. The district manager did reprimand her [the clerk]. He told me, he did speak to her. He was a good person and he listened, perhaps because I asked him what the store policy was. Also, when I asked questions about the store policy he gave me the information I wanted to know. He understood that I was a customer, and he respected the fact that I was African American. He understood that I had a right to ask about the store policy and to find out what the store policies were, and to examine the question of whether the store manager followed them. And if she didn't follow them, then shouldn't she be reprimanded? And further, why is it that your store is using the local police department as security detail? I had worked in retail. You don't just pick up the phone and call the police. So, she had potentially behaved unethically in this situation where I could seriously have been hurt. So, he listened.

I reflect back on my experience with the Black people in the regional civil rights office, where they encouraged me to be thankful that I did not get beat. I recognize that this whole experience is illustrative of [the] African American experience. We essentially are living our lives on [the] Middle Passage. We have left the shore[s] and the next thing, the bank[s], but we don't know where [freedom] is. This is part of our psychological experience. By this, I mean that unless something happens to us physically, the realm of psychological pain is not to be expressed or acknowledged. This is where I was at that point. . . . These people weren't trying to address Black pain. They told me that it didn't merit acknowledgment. They couldn't see how this was my beating. And what most people overlook is that this happened on a day that I defended my proposal for my dissertation—that this was one of the happiest days of my life, or should have been. And it wasn't. That part of it is also overlooked. But it illustrates that this is the Black male experience, and we don't necessarily have access to talk about psychological pain. So, people were saying, "Did you get hit in the head? Because my cousin got hit in the head." If that had happened, I probably would have garnered more support. But it also illustrated to me that there are places in America where I should not go because some people will ask, "Why would you pull off a highway?" Or, "Why were you there?" In other words, people will suggest that you went to a place that you didn't know. So, you chose it, and you took your chances. These were Black [people], and [they] had the notion of the precariousness and the notion that one just has to protect oneself and watch the spaces and also watch your actions. I also consulted with the ACLU, and I found out in that state, store owners can call the police. I also consulted with several different lawyers, and they said I probably would have gotten $3,000 or something if I took it to court. But by law, [the store] had a right to do it.

The impact of all of this was devastating. This messed me up. I couldn't sleep. Not being able to sleep was a huge issue for me. I also couldn't eat, and I had a lot of intrusive memories. When the police would drive by our house—I know this is crazy—but I thought, "Oh my goodness, how did the police from that state get here?" I was very nervous around police. I went to see a psychiatrist. I felt a sense of violation I had never felt before. And this was complicated, because I was trying to get my doctorate degree in a mental health field. When I went to the emergency [room] to see the psychiatrist, he gave me some medication to help me sleep. I think the part that traumatized me the most was there was an officer behind me. That's what scared me the most. That at any moment, if something had gone wrong, then something [detrimental] would have just happened because he was ready. He looked at me like . . . bring it. I felt that I was being given the message that because you're physically big, if we got to "take you down," we will. And at that moment I'm thinking, well what happened to bring all of this on? I'm thinking whatever the manager said on the phone, she must have really sounded alarmed. She must have said something on the phone that made them come in force—three of them, in force.

In the aftermath, after reaching out to the Better Business Bureau, [civil rights office], and so on, I also reached out to my friends and my family. And I kept telling my story. It got easier to tell my story about what happened to me and what happened to us. Talking about it, and not just stuffing it, helped me a lot. It also helped me in my work to get my degree. And my partner was very supportive. He was not going to let me not finish. He said, "No, you've come too far." One day, someone also told me that the best way to get back is to teach. I'm teaching White students now about racism at one of the top universities in the country. So, I channel that negative experience into one where I've to some extent dedicated part of my life to talking about racism and white privilege, how it plays itself out, and how people's fears can harm others. I think that's how I healed—by talking about it and then, luckily, I did get some sleep. Being able to sleep was a big step forward.

As I continued to reflect on the situation, I began to think about the degree to which White supremacy played a part in it. It's not just racism, it's also this idea that Whites are superior. And because the idea is that they're superior, their words are sort of taken as bond and trusted. I began to think about it in terms of White supremacy and ideology. That is, there's White supremacy in the way that the Black attorney and the civil rights office said, you know, this is a White supremacist society so anything could happen to you in this society. And the people who are Black who said, well you shouldn't have been there, this is part of what White supremacy does. There are demarcated places, that if you're Black you should be fearful of these places.

And when the police officer said, "I don't have to hear your story." Well, wouldn't you want to hear my story if you're ready to shoot me? Wouldn't you want to hear the person that you're trying to [potentially kill]? There's an ideology that, to some extent, if I were White, I may have been treated differently. My partner [who is White] who was with me, did not get treated in the same way that I did. This is what I mean by the idea or assumption that Whites are superior and trustworthy. The [White female] manager's fears weren't clearly articulated. Yet when you try to deconstruct them, and you ask her, "Well what was fearful for you in this experience?" she couldn't say, "Well, because you're Black." But that was essentially what the whole thing was. This is the idea of superiority: I can look at you and designate you as fearful. And you still see that today also. They were ready for action, or they would not have had the three officers around, and one of them, initially I was unaware that he was there.

TERRIFIED

"This Is What You Put Me Through as a Mother—as a Black Mother and Her Son—in This Community" (Latasha's Story)

As mentioned earlier, an idea circulates from time to time that racism is a mental health disease because it does involve delusional beliefs and behavior that can cause people to respond to people of color in bizarrely negative ways that can have severe consequences, with no real prior evidence to support the delusional beliefs and actions. This story is an illustration of that—where someone's perceptions had been distorted by negative, inaccurate beliefs and stereotypes, causing them to misperceive what they were seeing and then to behave in an unfounded and outrageous way. Latasha's story illustrates some White folks' apparent obliviousness to, dismissal of, or inability to easily understand why we and our allies would be upset at such life-, safety-, and peace-threatening behavior.

Latasha, like many of our memory-tellers, relived traumatic memories as she tells her story of isolation, the abuse of power and privilege, and the presence of ally-ship in a race-based grocery store horror. Latasha is a self-employed consultant who is master's-degree educated and highly sought-after for her expertise. I met her recently through a White woman colleague who would speak of her often, and who was insistent that Latasha and I meet the next time that she was in our area on business. My colleague suspected that we were kindred spirits, and she made it her business to eventually get us connected. I received an email from my colleague asking if she could bring Latasha by the office on a particular day, and I said "Of course." Upon meeting Latasha and speaking a few minutes with her,

I understood why my colleague wanted us to meet so urgently. My colleague is a constantly self-reflective White ally who perceives that it can be challenging for a woman of color to live just about every day of her life in a predominantly White environment. She also perceived not only cultural similarities, but also personality similarities between Latasha and me. Upon meeting Latasha, we were like two grown-up versions of our little girl selves meeting at a pajama party. I could feel a sister-ship with her right away, and our bond was instantaneous. After about ten minutes, my colleague left us alone and said she would come back to pick Latasha up in about a half hour. That was perfect for us; it gave us a chance to learn a little more about one another, our professions, and our lives as mothers. When I happened to mention the book, she connected right away with the topic and began to tell me of her experiences. Finding myself very interested in what she had to say about her shopping experiences, I asked her if she would be willing to be interviewed. She said yes, and we set up a time to meet during the next time that she would be in our region. When my colleague returned to pick up Latasha, she was elated to see how we had connected. Her spirit had known, and she would not let go until she had connected us. I appreciate allies for tuning into the many nuances that would allow them to know how to help women, and especially women of color, to network.

Latasha's interview touches on many important points. For example, she acknowledges through her memory-telling the role that self-reflective White allies can play in our lives, as three White allies and an extremely supportive Black male had critical roles in the memories that she shares. Further, her story illustrates how White-ally sympathy is nice, but showing up and putting White comfort, and not just Black or Brown comfort, on the line in the name of equity and justice when we are being perpetrated against, is even nicer.[1]

On the other hand, this story also illustrates the presence of what many in the community, and even some academics, call "White tears" and especially "White woman tears."[2] The expression, "White woman tears," is the experience that some men and women of color have had when they have attempted to address offensive behavior of White women, and in response, the offending person plays the victim card by resorting to tears, teariness, anger, distress, upset, hysterical offense, chastisement, or other apparent overreactions, as if they have been attacked or otherwise threatened.[3] We saw a version of this in Kenrec's story, just prior to this one. Such "tears" also were evident in the May 2020 Central Park incident in which Amy Cooper placed a distressed call to police on a bird-watcher named Christian Cooper as if he was attacking her. These tears and other expressions of distress, supposedly at the hands of Black people, wouldn't be a problem, except that historically, such tears have resulted in dangerous consequences for people of color, such as loss of jobs, homes, freedom, or life.[4] Sometimes such behavior on the part of White people is actually a distraction or defense that allows them to not have to be responsible or accountable for insensitive or discriminatory behaviors, because then the issue becomes about their upset or other emotional displays, rather than about whatever offensive behavior was being addressed.[5] Such tears historically have launched the lynchings of men, boys, and sometimes women and girls. Therefore, some scholars and commentators see such behavior as potential acts of violence against already vulnerable people.[6] In the 1950s, fourteen-year-old Emmitt Till was dragged through the streets until he was both dead and unrecognizable, all launched by a White woman's "tears" combined with and propelled by White men's toxic masculinity, anger, and violence. Those tears, we have learned five decades later, apparently were a lie.[7]

Just recently, a father watched in horror as his fourteen-year-old African American teen was accused and assaulted in a hotel by a woman erroneously convinced that he stole her cell phone. Similarly, a nine-year-old boy and his family were traumatized in a local store by a White woman who vehemently accused their nine-year-old of touching the rear-end of her body. Video footage was able to confirm that the boy himself did not touch her, although his backpack did, but not before the boy and his family were severely traumatized.[8] Sojourner Truth and Zora Neale Hurston in centuries past have spoken of the tendency for Black women to not enjoy the same protections, concerns for their comfort, and attentions to their discomfort as White women. So, Latasha's story is particularly compelling in that it demonstrates the power of the upset White woman juxtaposed to the disenfranchised Black woman. But then, when that Black woman in this story on her resources to bring the White woman to accountability, the White woman "gets teary." However, that same teariness combined with her accusatory voice could have caused Latasha to lose her freedom, even if just temporarily; her reputation, forever; or even her life, if she happened to pull a bad hand in terms of the luck of the draw that comes with interacting with individual law enforcement officers of varying degrees of "wokeness" (e.g., #SayHerName: Breonna Taylor and Sandra Bland, among a large number). Latasha's story is particularly interesting because it illustrates both loving, caring White woman tears from her allies, and useless White woman tears from her delusional, accusatory perpetrator after she herself had been exposed.

Latasha also offers extremely powerful messages on how she used the incidences to help socialize her children, and especially her son, on the extra survival burdens that Black children have concerning law enforcement and getting home without incident. Her story reveals a great deal on the preparation that parents of children of color tend to share with their children to get them ready at an early age for the real, unkind world that they likely will face.[9] All of this and much more, as Latasha shares with us a life-changing event that she and her son experienced, in a grocery store that they had frequented for years, in a community where they lived for decades.

Latasha speaks . . .

* * *

An incident that stands out above all was a summer shopping experience a few years ago [in the northeast United States] at a large, [franchised] grocery store in the community where I live, and my son was with me. My son was about thirteen or fourteen. . . . He had played sports throughout the years [ever since] we moved into the community, and we had lived there a good decade or more. It was early evening, between 6:30 and 8 p.m. It was summertime and still light outside when we arrived to the grocery store. I was just very comfortable coming back from my Zumba class, and my son came with me to the grocery store where we had shopped every week for years. My son had our cart, and I had a basket. I threw my basket into the shopping cart and left him and the baskets in the aisle to [urgently] go to the ladies' room. [As] I left him, [I] told him that I would be right back.

When I went into the bathroom I observed that there was a child, a little girl, playing with a Spaulding ball outside of the stall, while someone was inside of the stall. [They] were on the right, so I went into the stall on the left. [Eventually,] I heard them leave. Then I heard the main door of the bathroom opening and shutting, opening and shutting. I thought that was strange. When I came out, immediately this [staff] person—this woman—is standing in the doorway, and she screams for security. I'm looking at her, and she's staring at me, glaring at me, and just continues to call for security. I asked her what was going on, and she said that someone had seen me stealing. So, I said to her, stealing? What are you talking about? Actually, I said to her, "You can check me," because all I had on was my tank top, capri pants, sneakers, socks, and my purse—a very small purse. That's it. I had nothing in my hands except [the] purse. It was summer [and] there was not anywhere for me to hide anything. I offered her to look into my bag. [She didn't]. [But] imagine someone standing in the doorway about six feet [away] from the stall, just screaming at you as you are coming out of the bathroom stall. She continues to yell, "I saw you stealing!" and I'm pretty sure she said someone in the community, [i.e.], "someone who lives in this community, saw you stealing!" So, I asked her repeatedly, "Can you tell me who these people are, I'd like to see these people?!" She then left the bathroom. So, I washed my hands, and I went out. Again, this was a store where I had shopped for years, so I knew people at the deli counter. As I came out of the restroom, the workers and the customers at the deli counter were both staring at me. In my head I'm thinking, where is my son? I just wanted to know that he was fine. I followed her, and then she just went behind the deli counter and into an office behind the deli section. There was a gentleman working there behind the deli counter, and he knew me. I didn't know him by name, but he knew me. I said to him, "I'd like to see the manager." And I actually had started to, like, follow her [the lady accusing me], because I was thinking that security was coming. She was walking away from me in the deli area as I was following her, and the fellow in the deli section, he actually stopped me, and said, "You can't come back here." I said [again], "I need to see the manager." While he went to get the manager, I quickly went to find my son. He was still where I had left him. I said to him, "You need to come right away because I've been accused of stealing." He looked at me like "What is this?" So, he brought the cart with my [smaller] basket inside of it. When we got back, she had come out of the back by then—and [the accuser], she's the nighttime manager! It was kind of like one of those shows, I forget the name of the show—but I was surprised when she came out [of the back] as the manager. [And, I was like], oh, hell no! So, I continued to ask her, "Can you tell me why you are accusing me of stealing?" And again, she told me, "People who live here, saw you stealing." I said, "Tell me what they saw, who are these people, where are these people?" Again, she would not produce anybody. Now, she started to walk to the front of the store—and she's walking away from me. There were people that we knew in that area of the store because my son had played baseball and football and ran track. There were friends—parents who were in the area—and nobody, not one person offered to me, "Are you okay?" It was almost as if they were thinking, "Oh, she must have done it."

So, I'm following the nighttime manager who would not answer my questions. I'm irritated, and she says to me, "Why are you getting so upset; why is your voice raising?" [She said this] as if I should be calm through all of this. So, my son and I went to the front of the store, and I asked her for her name, and I said I wanted to call the corporate office. She said, "You can go to customer service and they will give you the number to the corporate office, and you can get my name from them." She couldn't even give me the decency of giving me her actual name. So, I went over there and got the corporate number. My cell phone at that time had very little charge to it, so I'm thinking that I'm in this situation, and I'm wondering if my battery is going to last? [Right there] I got the corporate number, and I called the store and talked to somebody who was not within the state and told them what I had experienced and was basically told, "Well, I'm taking your information, I can't help you tonight, but call back tomorrow, okay?" I said that I wanted to make sure that it was on record that I called you tonight.

In the meanwhile, my son called his father, who was in [another state], and his father's brother is an attorney. We also called my sister who lives in [a neighboring state], and she's an attorney. They both were giving us some guidance on what to do. Bottom line was stay there, because I'm thinking security is coming, police are coming, stay there, groceries are in the cart. So, we are waiting. And we literally waited for probably about a half an hour. And the woman, I even saw her pass by me a few times and I said, "What is going on?" and she totally ignored me at this point. So, I ended up talking to a friend who lived in the community, and this is a good friend with whom I've worked, and we have this personal connection. She is a Caucasian, and [on the phone] she said to me, "Go straight to the police station." The police station was not far from there, so I did not buy any groceries. I rolled the cart right up to one of the cashier's registers. I told the cashier, "I am not buying anything, I am going to leave it right here." My son and I went straight to the police station, [and by then it was] dark when we arrived [there]. I will never forget, I walked in and I said [to the officer at the desk], "I was accused of stealing at this store, I just need help to know how to process this, and I want to file a complaint." I didn't even call it a complaint—I wanted to tell my story. The first thing out of his mouth—and he was White—a White, Italian man—the first thing out of his mouth was, "Do you think it was racially motivated?" I just looked at him and said, "I can't say it was, but it sure as hell felt like it!" It definitely felt like it. He [responded], "The store has not called us, so they are not filing any kind of complaint, so we will verbally take your story." He [went on to say,] "And if you want to come back and make a written report, you can do that [also]." He took my information, and I just remember my son and I, we just felt like we were all alone in this community where we lived all these years. [I began to think,] "How am I going to walk out of here?" I was just weak. I'm like, I have to drive home, and I'm crying, and I'm sad. And I'm trying to be strong for my son. I kept checking in with my son. I was fine, but I kept checking in to see that my son was fine. And I remember when I turned around in that police station, when we turned to leave—again feeling like I was on this island in a community where there aren't a lot of people of color, there aren't a lot of Black people like us—and I remember turning around to leave, and my [White] friend [whom I called earlier] had arrived, and she was standing at the doorway of the police station. She had left her home and didn't even tell me that she would be there. When I turned and saw her, you know it was like, you came for me. I could say it on a Biblical level, I mean, she was standing in the doorway. This is a woman who I have known all these years, [and] she had tears in her eyes, because she knew how painful it was [for me]. And I just felt like, this connection, that literally, somebody gets this.

So, from there, the next day, I called my [White] divorce attorney, told him the situation, and asked for guidance. What he explained was that he had some very particular questions [such as] where's the store, and I told him the situation. [It turned out that] he had had a similar experience with this store, but it was discrimination against the elderly. He told me about [this] situation he knew of, and he said it's a case he could help me with, but it would be years. [He] recommended that I go to the state's [civil rights office or "CRO"[10]] office, so I called them. [Thus,] the divorce attorney recommended CRO, a friend suggested the ACLU [American Civil Liberties Union], my sister and my son's father['s brother], both attorneys, also made recommendations. So, I got advice from different people. I did some Googling on my own as well, and there was one other agency that I reached out to at that time. I just got busy doing some research. The more that I was feeling about it was that, one, I was very grateful that my son was fine. But, [two], I was thinking this should not happen to anybody, and what action can I take to hopefully ensure that this doesn't happen to others. That was my big focus. I remember the American Civil Liberties Union, I got some guidance from them, but I ended up going to CRO. I was able to explain my situation over the phone, and then I had to write my story. My story was many pages long. They even asked my son to write his experience. So, even at his age, he wrote it out. And I watched him, and I remember sitting with him and wondering if this was paining him to have to relive this and to think about the fact that his friends' mothers didn't even look his way or my way. It was a whole several-months-long ordeal. It went way through early summer and into the late fall, so it was a good six months before we had the hearing at the CRO. I went and met with them, we wrote our experiences, they submitted it to the [store's] corporate offices. Corporate offices did not return my calls at all, even the next day after the incident I called them. I had called them twice the night of the incident and left my information, and then I called them the next day as well and left information. It wasn't until they got the written deposition; then they wanted to talk to me, which is really interesting. But I was like, no, I'm not talking to you at that point.

[The store] wrote a rebuttal—their side of the story. There might have been like fourteen categories or items [to address]. And [their response] was like, "Well, yes, this happened, BUT, there's no recollection of parts B and C, so yes, you were in the store, but there's no recollection of parts B and C." Item 3: "Yes, this happened, but we don't remember this and that." I think they even wrote a rebuttal to my son's testimony. Then I had to write a response to that. So, I had to live it, and then I had to keep responding to it so I felt this pain, this anguish [over and over again]. I said [to myself], I don't ever need to go to the store again! We had moved into that area when my daughter was going into the first grade, so I had been living there in the community for a good twelve years when this happened.

When we finally had the hearing, the CRO attorney explained to me what this would be about. She said you can bring whomever you want. I remember when I told each [White ally friend what happened,] they were immediately in shock. "How did they do that to you?!" They had never experienced anything like that, and they knew me, because we were on the same level of working and commitment to all [people]. And they agreed, "It's because you're Black." That was very comforting, that they could agree. [Thus,] not one of those three women looked at me like, "Oh no, you're ridiculous, that's not true!" They knew that's what it was. I felt supported, acknowledged, respected by them. I definitely did. And my boss at the time, a White Jewish man, when I told him, again, reacted similarly. I mean, you could see the pain in their faces, that this happened to me. [So,] the White woman who showed up at the police station, she was one of the three [White] women who came [to the

CRO hearing]. So, I [had] called my friend [who previously had come to the police] station. I also called two friends who work with me. All three of these women were Caucasian women who knew my character, who [also] knew my children. I called and asked a gentleman from my church, a Black man, and he had known my son for many years as well.

I just asked [them], and they came, it wasn't even like they had to say, "Let me think about it." They just said, "Tell me what day and what time." I was advised by CRO to bring whomever I want, because they can speak to my character and credibility, so that's what I did.

I showed up [to the hearing] with my son, and [the] four other adults. [The three store representatives] kind of looked at us like, why do you have all of these people. It was really interesting. The grocery store chain, they had hired a Black gentleman to be the attorney. It just all made sense, right? A common strategy, right? When they saw the people that were with me, the supermarket, which was represented by the attorney, the night time manager, and one other person for the store, requested a private meeting with just my son and me and the CRO attorney. They did not want to have everybody in the room, and they wanted to make a deal. We sat, and we listened to them. After we heard their story, I said, "No, no, no, I came with others and they want to speak as well." So, we separated, came back together, and had perhaps an hour-long meeting. There were other things that came out that were further cutting, further insulting. One, there was no security [at that store], so she [the manager] put me through this mental emotional torment. She said there was no security coming, she just yelled it [a lie, in that moment]. That was to intimidate me and to scare me, but the fact was that there were no security or anyone coming [all along]. Nobody was ever coming! Because she had walked away from me and wouldn't talk to me, she never [admitted] that there [was no] security at the store. To psychologically and emotionally do that, was just wrong. And then to say that people who live here saw you stealing. Like I was compassing through the community. There were some other [such] comments that she had made. I said to her, "The fact that you couldn't even give me your full name—you accuse me of this—and then when I ask for your name. . . ." And she's sitting right across from me [in the hearing]. And she wanted to get teary-eyed, and she did end up apologizing for what she put me through. But I said to her that there is no [amount of] money that you are going to give to me that is going to do away with or ease what I have lived [because of your actions]. And I told them that, "[When the situation happened that] I was most concerned about my son—I was worried and very concerned—was he in handcuffs, had I turned the corner and you had accused him of something? This is what you put me through as a mother—as a Black mother—in this community." I was very clear in those words.

It was when she admitted [that] there was no security coming [all along], I think it was at that point I slammed my hand on the table and said, "I['ve] got to get up and leave here for a minute—to put me in that and you were just crying wolf, you just put something out there that was fake!" What I [also] learned from their attorney was that they had done their homework—"We understand . . . and we have reviewed your records . . . and you have been a customer for all these years . . . and we are so pleased that you have been a customer with us." So, they had done their research. I also know that they probably had Googled my name. If they Googled my name, they would have found my father's name; and if they have found my father's name they would have found [a human rights advocate] to whom my father was like a father. So, at one point I said, let me call [him], who is like a brother to me because my father was like a father to him. At one point I said, "Let me call him and let him know what happened because this is just wrong." It was very evident that they had researched who we were.

My son had to speak as well, and what ended up coming out is—my son said in his testimony—that when I left him in the [shopping] aisle, he saw this woman [the manager] at the other end of the aisle look down, and then start running. And then he finds out [later] that it was her! So, they were watching me, that's what we figured out, they were watching me. And they ended up saying to me in this meeting, "Well, you ran to the bathroom." And I said yes, what did you all see? And she actually said to me, "You were in the bathroom too long." Actually, [hearing this] may have been what made me slam my hands on the table. So not only was I shopping while Black, but I'm also using your bathroom, and there must be a time limit—and, I'm running to the bathroom. I started to put this together while I was sitting in this hearing, and I'm thinking, okay, who's in the bathroom? But in the meanwhile, she had already been watching me. And then I'm thinking when I was in the bathroom, I had nothing with me, [except for] a sanitary pad. And I'm thinking, when I unwrapped it, did they think I was eating food in the stall? I mean, all these things are going through my head [as I'm listening to their side]. Did the mother with the little girl, did she go out and report something? "I think somebody has food in the stall, they're sneaking in food?!" And if I was sneaking food, then maybe there's a need to help somebody. It was just all bizarre. She told me, she literally said it in the hearing, "You were in the bathroom too long." I was just trying to piece this together, did you hear me taking the sanitary napkin out of the wrapper and think . . . ? [This] was not in any of their [written] rebuttals. I did say, "Oh yeah, oh yeah, I did rush to the bathroom." I said, "I have very heavy bleeding, where it can just soak through, that is why I had to rush to the bathroom, and that is why I was in the bathroom for a long time." And they're looking at me, and I'm saying this in front of a male attorney and our [male] friend who has come with us. But I said, you wanted to attack me, but you need to know what happened here. That is, I think, when I slammed my fist on the table, and I said, "I cannot believe that I stayed in the bathroom for too long, and I had to take care of a personal matter, and you put me through this hell!" And my son is sitting [there] too, and he's hearing it. So, I walked out [of the hearing] and went into the [hearing] restroom, and I prayed and asked God to help me to know how to handle this one. I came back in, and then she was sitting there looking all sad, "I never meant to put you through this." I said, "But you did."

CRO asked [me] the whole time, both in my written request and in my testimony response, "What is it that you want?" What I said was, "I'm not trying to get money from this corporate chain, but what I want is to make sure that other people do not get put through this." Not that I can guarantee it. I said I think there needs to be orientation for all new employees. Every year there needs to be annual training on cultural competency. I gave them specific terms from my own [knowledge]—that it's ongoing, not that you can check off a box saying I had this cultural sensitivity and competency training somewhere. There were several things that I put in writing, almost like demands. And [CRO] did say that there would be some kind of compensation, "So what is it that you would like?" So, I stepped out with my team of people, and they say, "Go for it!" (chuckles). And I'm like, I'm not here to get rich or anything like that. So, when I go back in, they actually thought they heard me say something more than what they gave me. It was fine, we took the money. It was an undisclosed cash settlement with the promise that they would do the things that I requested, and that I would not . . . disclose them [by name] as having perpetrated against us. They gave me half, and they gave my son half. He had identified a [summer educational enrichment experience] that he wanted to do that summer and didn't know how he could do it, and then that [settlement] happened. So, there were blessings that occurred from the money we received. They [also] gave me a shopping gift card, with some high limit although I told them that, "I will never go in that store again. . . . [Again,] I will never go in that store, I don't even drive down that street anymore." And they were looking at me like, please [come back]. I ended up giving the [gift] card to my children, so my daughter [and I] went to [another branch of] the grocery store, just that one time, to buy hair products in preparation for [her] leaving for college. I said, "Here, go use this card to get what you need."

I hope that they put into place what I requested. There were some other things I requested [as well]. They never followed up with me, and I never followed up with them, I just never went back into that store. When you're in a community, and you think you have people who are your friends, you spend all of this time together because your kids play sports—and my daughter also played sports in that community. You think you know people, people who are at the store and who work there, the deli counter where you've been ordering your meat and standing in line and having small conversations. Having shopped there for probably ten years, and then to experience, well, like, you were all alone, and people turning their heads. I literally felt and saw people turning their heads, to not make eye contact. You feel again alone. I didn't feel ashamed because I knew I hadn't done anything. But I also felt angry, that I was being accused. I'm told that "people who live here [saw you]"—so you are assuming that I don't live here—and then not only are you ignoring me, but so are the people who do know me or our family—they are ignoring us. These are people who I thought at least had a relationship with my son, who might say, "You're his Mom, can I help you, are you okay?" Nothing like that came. That was immediate, feeling abandoned, and, like, what do I do in this situation but stay calm?

I remember days after, just waking up, like, "That was really painful." I didn't want that to happen to other people, and I knew that there were other people who might not speak up, who might just say, "oh well." I'm sure that this has happened to other people who have just walked away from it. And then having to write it all out, that took it to another level of pain. You must be very specific in what happened. And I know that I do have the times, I do have the dates, I do have the calls that I made to the corporate office, so all of that was being tracked. The fact that I had to do that. . . . And I was always watching to see how my son took it. Fortunately, he didn't seem too phased, but I am going to go back . . . because I wanted him to realize that, you know, everybody's accepted [the ordeal], but in this situation, being Black, it was almost like they [the community] accused us too. The people who were observing this [and staying silent, were accusing us also]. For the police to ask me, "Was it racially motivated?" that was like, whoa, even the White man sees it. And then it was like, whoa, have there been other incidents [in our community]? Why was that the first thing out of his mouth? And then, just again, having to go to trial and confront this person, those six months leading up to the trial were just so heavy. But we got through that, and I was so grateful to the people who came. I can remember taking the money and giving gifts to them, and giving gifts to all of my family, because it wasn't something that I was expecting. I said, "I am going to give this to others and say, thank you." But I would never want anyone to go through that. There are people who don't have voices who will walk away, and they'll say, "Oh well, they treated me this way."

My son and I talked about [the impact of all of this] while we were going through the writing of our testimonies, [and] as we prepared to go to the hearing. We [also] talked about it when there was this compensation—what was the value of the compensation and speaking up, advocating, getting this compensation, and helping him to grow further with [his educational enrichment experiences]. Sometimes it would come back up over the years, linking it to other situations, as a Black mom, a single mom, because his father had lived out of state since my son was eight years old. Being a single, Black mother raising a Black son, and also raising a Black daughter, but trying to prepare your son for the world. And what I would always tell both my children is that no matter what, with all of this multiculturalism, equity, and all of this "talk," you are always going to be Black in America. And that is [considered] the lowest on the pole. When I say that, I am not putting myself there, but that is how people see you. . . . As they were growing up, they experienced [racist] situations. So, for my son, with this [grocery store] situation, and then as he went through his school years, I would always say, just remember how that [grocery store] situation has helped to prepare you for what is to come. That was part of the big lesson; you can always go back to that and think about how you handled it. You had to give a written testimony, and you had to give what was factual for you. Think about how I handled it, and just keep [all of] that with you.

When he was taking driver's ed, I was so excited all the days when I was driving him there. And the day that he got his license, all of that, no matter what, I always had to say to him, "So what do you do when you get stopped? . . . Where are your hands [(gesturing), visibly on the steering wheel or dashboard]?" That was a message, not that I enjoyed saying that to him, but that's a reality for helping him to be prepared. And we've talked about that, "Do you understand why I have always said that to you? Do you understand this?" We would always link it back to this situation. He now has a model—stay calm, call people, because my biggest fear—I would have lost it—had I seen them rough handling him, and I told him that. My son and I had had many conversations while we wrote our testimonies. We would talk about it every now and then. "What did it feel like, that none of your community came to our aid?" These people looked away from us—they looked at us like we were thieves, like we were beneath them, that was kind of the feeling that we had. "How do you take care of yourself. . . . How are you responsible for yourself?" You know, that PSA, "Just get home?" Well, I tell my son, "Just get home . . . we'll deal with it when you get home. . . . Just do what you are told to do, and just get home, and we will deal with it then." So, that is what I have connected back to my son from this incident.

I am fine today, and I'm hopeful. If telling my story and retelling it now helps anyone else, then that is fine.

TRIGGERED

"My DNA Remembers, Even if My Conscious Mind Doesn't" (Michelle's Story)

An emotional trigger is something that causes a person great anxiety or other upset because it contains elements that are reminiscent of a very negative event in a person's life. There have been instances where marketers did not put as much thought as we would have wished into how their advertisements, exhibits, and so on, may impact people of color. Historical, sociological, or other oppressive messages in a campaign may embody physical or emotional triggers for groups of people who themselves or their ancestors have experienced genocide, enslavement, been otherwise exploited, abused, or oppressed in the past. Recently this has been an issue with modeling and advertising concepts of several high-profile designers who have used nooses, blackface, and other props, sparking emotional upset and outrage.[1] For example, in the Netflix biographical documentary, *Miss Sharon Jones!*, an accomplished middle-aged R&B singer speaks of her own childhood years growing up in Augusta, Georgia.[2] In the course of talking about her life, she shares a story about a local store that she and her siblings would frequent. The storeowner had a parrot that was trained to yell, "Nigga's stealing!" as soon as any Black person would enter the store. Such instances may seem unfathomable by today's standards, but they leave a triggering impact that lasts a lifetime when one is exposed to similar sounds, visuals, or circumstances. Likewise, Ms. Eleanor, in a previous story in this book, spoke of a coded intercom announcement that she would hear signaling that a Black person had entered into a particular store. She would hear it over and over, each time she entered that store, and it became deeply etched in her memory as a reminder of the low expectations that society had of Black people. In this day and age, such a parrot and intercom message have been replaced by video monitors and security personnel who may have an inaccurate, stereotypical "tape" in their heads causing them to respond on autopilot pretty much the same way the parrot did when Black people enter their stores and other business establishments. Right away, they may rush to ask, "May I help you?" On the surface, this is a nice thing to do. The only problem is that sometimes such help is code for asking, "Why are you here?" or "How long will you be here?" or "I am watching your every move" or "Please leave as soon as possible." Discerning the intent of "May I help you?" can be taxing and even triggering, depending on one's past experiences. Kenrec, in an earlier story, spoke of repeated offers of assistance that made him uncomfortable and caused him to leave a store. Both hovering and ignoring can signal that Black and Brown bodies do not belong in a space or at least are not trusted there. The racism of today sometimes may or may not be subtler, but it's never less insidious, as demonstrated by the many stories and news reports cited in this book. As a consequence of the tapes that play in other peoples' heads, many mature people of color in recent years have experienced severe traumas in the marketplace that they still live with today.

Thus, emotional triggers are what this story is about. Actually, it's a journal entry, and it has a photo to accompany it that I took with my camera when it happened while on a visit down South. It is a memory-telling of a not-so-amusing event that took place at a local amusement event. The event ended up emotionally triggering vicarious lynching trauma somewhere within me and my historical/generational memory. I have found at times in my life that an incident reminds me of things, if not in my own past, then in the past of my ancestors. It is as if the memory or the trauma is embedded within my cultural "DNA" or at least my Jungian archetypal consciousness. If nothing else, it may be a vicarious memory passed down and held by cultures who historically have experienced trauma, or alternatively, the memorial elaboration of historical facts learned at some point in our lives. Whatever the origin, the following incident describes one such intense reaction to an event. The incident occurred while I was a consumer of a leisure activity for families, for which I paid a fee so that my son and I could attend. It was marketed as a family and community harvest festival that also had a Halloween-ish fright trail component to it. My younger son was eight years old, and I thought that he might enjoy it, as it was occurring during the Halloween season. As expected, the trail event had its share of ghoulish looking characters, miniature graveyard scenes, and so on. But there was one display for which I was not prepared, and when I saw it, I felt as if I was metaphysically reliving an experience that happened long before I was born. It was one of the most emotionally traumatic instances I have ever experienced, in spite of observers around me appearing to find the display merely entertaining, even funny. I believe that I found it exponentially troubling because my young child was present to observe it also.

Originally, I titled my journal entry, "Microaggression #10,592." It happened almost a decade ago, and it is a reminder that the world, even the consumer world, revolves around what is comfortable for those traditionally in power. That is, the consumer movers and shakers traditionally have not had to consider the impact that their products, exhibits, advertisements, and so on, may trigger for those from groups still experiencing the generational impact of violent, exploitive histories. Thus, the journal entry goes like this . . .

* * *

Why did I have to take my eight-year-old to the "Haunted Woods" Halloween fright trail rented on an Indigenous land preserve? While on the fright trail, I came upon the final scene, which consisted of a life-like, adult-sized barefoot human figure hanging from a tree with a noose around his neck. He was repeatedly and quickly dropped, and then over and over suspended mid-air to be dropped again. These repeated gestures occurred as one spotlight was shone on him just enough that no one could miss this scene and well enough that it looked like something out of the back woods of the early to mid-1900s. A local municipality rented the Indigenous land preserve for the event to raise money for their youth sports programs, and so on. It was not the Native Americans who sponsored this trail. And I did not see any minorities among the organizers, nor did I see any other adults of color in attendance, although I did see several youths of color there.

This dark night of lynching reenactment took me back somewhere that my DNA remembers, even if my conscious mind doesn't, and my hands shook and my heart pounded as I stumbled, feeling nauseous inside. I tried to find my way away from the path with wobbly legs that felt as if they may give out on me. I surely just expected some ghouls and ghosts and "things that go bump in the night" as they say, but I wasn't expecting a reenactment of a public lynching. Right away I grabbed my child and, once I was done stumbling, we left for the home where we were staying with family.

After I took my young one home, I went back up there to the trail and snapped pictures. As I snapped photos, the White man controlling the rope seemed proud to pose the effigy at different lynching points (i.e., suspended high, suspended low, dramatically dropped or hung from the branch on which it was hanging, etc.), one of which is depicted in the photo below.

When I complained to the [White] organizer about the display, she tried to comfort me by assuring me that the figure was "completely White." What the bleep?! Somehow, I didn't feel any better. I spoke with her from 9 p.m. to 9:25 p.m., and before I was done explaining all the historical reasons why I was traumatized, they shut the trail DOWN! During that time she apologized several times, and when we were done talking, like I said, she shut the whole trail down (at 9:27 p.m.)—a half hour earlier than the posted time, but kept the rest of the park open (the food, games, hay rides, etc.).

I'm still kind of shook, although many of the children and adults seemed to think that was the most exciting trail display of them all. . . . The posters and flyers billed the program as "a good, fun scare." I didn't see anything good or fun about a reenactment of a lynching. When this harvest festival is offered again, I hope there will be no reenactments of lynchings or other genocidic events.

A fun time at a "Harvest Festival" turned into a traumatizing experience for this book's author and her 8-year-old.
Photo courtesy of Michelle R. Dunlap

TORMENTED

"I Lifted My Sweater Just Enough for Them to See I Had Stolen Nothing" (Priscilla's Story)

Priscilla's story is one concerning a Black mother who was suspected of shoplifting and held captive in the dungeons of a department store. It demonstrates that the self-consciousness that people of color may feel often extends even to our sense of privacy. People of color often speak of the entitlement that some White people think they have when it comes to examining Black and Brown bodies closely, even touching our hair or our pregnant bellies, and so on.

Priscilla struck me as a strikingly lovely woman, perhaps a doppelganger of the famous singer/actress Diahann Carroll. Her demeanor seemed to be very soft-spoken, yet very thoughtful and clear in all that she had to say. I was traveling in the Midwest on other business and was delighted to be able to schedule this interview as well. So that I would not have to travel far out of my way, we met at her relative's home, which was very near where I was staying in my travels. Upon my arrival, Priscilla's family member greeted me kindly and ushered me to a large room where she said I would be able to meet with Priscilla upon her arrival. She began putting on her coat and grabbed her purse, and she assured me that Priscilla would be arriving soon, but that she herself had to head out for a baby shower that she had helped to organize. I am not a fan of flying and then driving long distances, so I welcomed the opportunity to relax after my journey. I put my head back in the loveseat on which I was sitting and pretty much dozed off. When I heard the doorbell ring, it startled me, and I was sure that at least an hour had gone by. As I walked to the front door, I was amazed to see that I had napped for only about fifteen minutes, if that. I peeked outside to be sure that it was her by asking, "Who is it?" When she answered Priscilla, I swung open the door, and we greeted each other warmly.

Priscilla is a sixty-five-year-old African American medical professional still very engaged in her career, and living in the midwestern United States. Her family had made me feel right at home, and they gave us a private, quiet spot where we could talk without interruption. Priscilla sat in a cozy chair facing me, and I also was in a comfortable chair. A small table was in between the two chairs, and I had placed my tape recorder and paperwork upon it. I could hear the phone ringing in the distance and an answering machine pick-up with a recorded greeting, but as Priscilla began to speak, all distractions seemed to fade far into the distance.

Priscilla speaks of an incident that occurred a few years earlier. She was accused of shoplifting in a department store and eventually was assaulted by department store security when she could not produce the goods they were accusing her of stealing. Her story further illustrates for us a lack of respect for Black bodies in public spaces—be these bodies young or mature. It also illustrates that not only do Black parents have to worry about their children, but also Black children—even adult ones—have to worry about their parents as they move about in the world—even in the "leisurely" marketplace. As I have asked throughout this book, how much does this added stress cost Black people over the course of their lives?

Priscilla shares her story . . .

* * *

I went shopping at a local [large, franchised] department store. It was a weeknight, and I had just gotten off of work. I was working twelve-hour shifts, and I think I had gone to one store already, because I already had at least one bag. This was during the winter, and besides having at least one bag prior to entering the store, I also was wearing a long coat. I felt that as soon as I went into the store that [the all-White] security assumed I was there to steal. I especially felt this because of my being a Black woman, and I had long Nubian-styled [hair] locs and an African scarf stylishly tied on my head—plus the one or two bags in my hands.

I began to shop around, and I was looking specifically for bras. I [selected] a couple of bras, and I went into the dressing room to try them on. They did not fit right, so when I left the dressing room, I put them on a shelf or counter, and I continued to look around for other items.

As I left the store, a couple of security officers came up to me and said, "Miss, can you come back into the store?" I said "For what?" They said that they felt that I had merchandise on me, and that they wanted me to come back into the store. I think they said precisely either, "You have merchandise on you," or "Can you come back into the store?" Whatever they said, I knew that they thought I had merchandise on me. As we went back into the store, they took me to their security office—it seemed like it was way downstairs, down a long corridor—a very dark and very long way. I began to become very frightened.

We ended up in this dark cubbyhole-type room. There was a female security guard in there and one of the guards who first stopped me. They said, "We know you have merchandise on you, in your clothing." I said, "Oh no, I do not have anything on me that is not mine." Then they said "You might make it easier on yourself and save a lot of time by just confessing." And I said again, "I do not have anything on me." They said, "Okay, if you don't confess we'll have to call the police and have a female officer search you." They said they would call the [local] police department to come and search me. So I said, "Well, I've already told you I don't have anything on me. . . . I can show you I do not have anything on me," and I opened my coat. I felt that they thought I had a bra tucked down in my clothing. I opened my coat and I lifted my sweater just enough for them to see I had nothing under my shirt, and as I was doing that, they said, "Don't bother, because we are going to have a female officer check you out." In all, there were about four people in the room when this was going on. All four were security, and only one was female. All four of these security officers were White, three were men, and one was a woman. They were all behaving very authoritatively, as if they had made a big "win."

They kept pressuring me to make it "easier" and to go ahead and confess. This went on for an hour to an hour-and-a-half, back and forth, for that long. They wouldn't go ahead and call the police. It seemed that they wanted me to confess and give up the merchandise. It seemed that it would be simpler and easier if I would just go ahead and confess—it seemed that is what they needed me to do, but I wouldn't.

Then one of them left the room for maybe twenty or thirty minutes, although it seemed like an hour. The other three remained in the room with me. I was becoming very tired, afraid, and it was very late. Not only was I becoming very afraid and tired, but also hungry. I was afraid because it was such an isolated, hidden-away area. I felt very vulnerable because of the situation. It was my going back there with them, knowing that I was back there, that scared me. Thank God I didn't have anything on me stolen. If I had, I wonder if they might have been angry and beaten me. So, the fourth fellow returned and said, "We've decided to let you go." And I said, "I'm not going anywhere." I said, "You call the [local] police and let them examine me." I said, "You detained me, accused me, and so on, and now you are saying you are going to let me go like you are doing me a favor. No, you call the police and let them examine me." So, then they got very angry, and one of them took his [paper] tablet and threw it on the floor. I think it was getting near closing time for them to go. But what happened was that the one who went and came back and said he was going to let me go, when that fellow went, he went and looked at the video because I am sure they thought they saw me putting something in my clothes in the dressing room.

Later, I asked someone whether you can be watched on video while you are trying on bras in a dressing room. She said she thinks it might be [possible]. In any case, when the fellow came back, I recall hearing one of them say that he reviewed the video again for a second time. The other three looked surprised when he said I could go. I am not sure if he was one of the ones who first approached me, he might have been the one who was originally watching the cameras and dispatched the others; I'm not sure.

I said [again], "I am not leaving and going anyplace." I need to make a call to my niece who works for [a nearby municipality's] police department. And they said, "We don't deal with [the nearby municipality's] police." I said, "Well then, I want to call my son." They said, okay, you can call your son. So, I did, and I left him a message. By this point, one-and-a-half to two hours had passed. I told them I was not going anywhere, that I was going to wait for the police, and that my son would be coming.

They had this desk, and I was sitting in a chair. On this desk I had my bags, my purse, and so on. My purse was opened because I had pulled everything out to show them that I had nothing in it. But I also had put my stuff back in my purse. The female officer jumped toward the desk and said, "You are going, you are getting your ass out of here!" She then grabbed my purse and my bag, but not my coat. She took my items and started out the door with them. So, I jumped from out of the chair and followed her out of the door because my purse had my paycheck, money, ID cards; everything was in the purse. Knowing the stuff that was in my purse, I followed her out of the door, and I grabbed for my purse because I did not know what she was going to do with it. I didn't know if she was going to take it and throw it on the street or in the garbage or what. So, I grabbed it from her. When I grabbed the purse, she then tried to grab it back, and we started tussling. She went to grab for my hair, and I had just had these Nubian locs done. And you can't be tearing at those. I had been working on my locs for a year. When she tried to grab my locs, I tried to push her away. And I remember her calling me a bitch; she said, "You bitch!" We continued to tussle and we ended up on the ground tussling. She was younger than me, about maybe [age] thirty. She was a young Caucasian woman with a bad attitude, and she seemed very stressed because [the store chain] was in a condition where many of its employees were going to be losing their jobs. Later, when I thought about it, I wondered if the current affairs of the store with impending layoffs had added to their stress. Anyway, back to the tussle: She and I were rolling around in the hall, and all of my stuff was falling out of my purse everywhere. A security guard was standing there watching the whole thing and never tried to stop it or intervene. Then she got up and said, "You crazy bitch!" and she started walking very fast away from me down the hall. Then she went on down the hall, and I started taking off my boot, because I didn't know where she was going or what she was going to be doing. So, I took my boot off in case I would have to defend myself. I also started getting my stuff together. One of the security then said a [local] police officer was coming (because I had asserted earlier that I was not leaving until I saw a police officer). The female security officer never came back, and it still took another half hour, but the police finally came.

At this point, the police wanted me to write down the whole thing, and said that they would have her do the same so that they could hear her side. They said that she said that I hit her and broke her glasses. Therefore, I would have to go to the [local] police department and make a report. And she also would have to do the same. They appeared to be avoiding taking either side. I had never in my life been in any type of trouble—not even a car accident. Here they were saying that she said that I hit her and broke her expensive glasses. So, they were saying that it was my fault, and I was saying it was her fault. The police were saying all they could do is take my statement. The officer was saying I could make a report at the police department. It was late, the main store had closed, and the mall had closed. The police had taken their report and left. In fact, it was very late. They had to let me out through a special back door because it was so late. Out of desperation, I asked one of the same four security officers to walk me out to my car. It was dark, late, snowy, and so on, and I was still scared. Not to mention I had been in a fight. Two of the same security officers walked me out.

I drove home. I didn't get home until after 11 p.m. (the mall closed at 10 p.m., or maybe later since it was near the holidays—right before Christmas maybe or Thanksgiving, or maybe it was just a snowy weekend, but it was definitely in the dead of winter).

My grown son met me at the house. I told him what had happened. My son took pictures of my face, which was all bruised and swollen. He told me we would contact a lawyer the next day. So, the next day I called a couple of lawyers. I called my brother. I called my special friend, and he told me to call a [particular] big, well-known lawyer. I called [that attorney's] office, but they told me they only handle big criminal cases where you have lost an arm or leg or something like that. Then I contacted another lawyer and went to see him with my niece who is a police officer, and he took the case. [Then he] got back with us, and said [that particular chain] had filed bankruptcy, so there was really nothing that could happen. Otherwise, I would have tried to sue them for as much money as possible. And [again,] I think it was the impending bankruptcy that might have contributed to the security guards' behavior. When I inquired as to whether I could press civil charges for assault, I was told by the police detectives that it was basically her word against mine, plus she was asserting that I had broken her expensive glasses.

So, in this situation I was frightened, very fearful that I was fighting—possibly for my life—over something that I did not do. I was fighting with a person of another color—a White person, and all of these people were White, and again, I was fighting for something I didn't do. My captors were White, even the police were White, all of that made me fearful, especially as I was being accused of things I did not do with little recourse for defending myself legally, much less physically. And I have prayed that I would never get into a situation like that again, because I feel that if I had been guilty, that I possibly could have lost my life. I have no idea what they could have done to me back up in that dark hole, and no one would have ever known the difference. So, we all have to be aware of our surroundings, what we are doing, and where we are. It's sad, but it's the truth. As far as I know, they could have tried to plant something on me, they could have killed me, and then said that I was resisting them. Although the security officers did not appear to have guns, and they were dressed in plain clothes, they still felt very threatening and aggressive. The police officers, of course, had guns.

After the incident, I felt beaten and abused. When I would look at my face, I couldn't believe what had happened. My face was bruised and swollen, and I couldn't believe how and why it happened. And the fact that it all happened over *assumptions*! I may have looked like a bag woman or something when I came into the store. They can't assume that every Black woman who comes into the store who is not dressed in their Sunday best is a thief!

It took me a month to get over the physical aspects—my legs, feet, back, and so on, were sore. If it were not for the fact that it was winter and I had on heavy pants and a sweater, and even heavy thick thermal underwear, I would have been hurt more. Thank God she didn't tear out a chunk of my hair—my hair was very beautiful, and I think she thought, "I'll show you," when she grabbed my hair. It would have been very difficult to replace or repair damage to my hair if she had pulled out a chunk. It took me so long to grow my hair.

At times I still think about it. I was hesitant to tell this story because I knew of the emotions that it would bring up. It's very distressing. You would think that things like this wouldn't occur, but they do occur all over the world, and it's sad. It made me depressed, anguished, anxious, and I have never really totally gotten over it. It still comes up sometimes. It was probably the worst encounter of that nature that I have ever had; and all over assumptions. It all could have been avoided if the fellow had said, "Miss, I made a mistake, and I'm sorry." If only they had said it nicer, I probably would have just left. But when they said they are going to "let me go," and so on, it made me very angry. If they had just said, "We are sorry," I would have just left.

I feel [people of color] encounter prejudice in many places, and [we] have to know what it is. But when you have to deal with it on a mental and physical level like that, you see how serious and deadly, and uncalled-for and unnecessary [it is]. There are so many things now for the world to be focused on. It's a shame we have to take time out of our lives to focus on something like that. It would be nice if all the races could come together. I just think everyone should pray. I have been blessed to live sixty-five years, and I think the time has come for us to pray more, and that might be what's going to save us. We must continue to pray and pray and pray. We all need to pray more. We need to teach the children to pray more. And thank God for everything and everyone we have.

THINGS THAT PART III'S STORIES CAN TEACH CONSUMERS AND MARKETERS

STRATEGIES CONSUMERS MIGHT CONSIDER TRYING

- The interviews suggest that when the participants were experiencing a trauma in the consumer marketplace, it was important for them to observe carefully and rely on their appropriate instincts and resources.
- Observing the names of staff, officers, and others, and documenting these details during or immediately following the incident may be important. Recent current events have suggested that if observers of the incident can videotape, that may be helpful. As many recent incidences have illustrated, videotaping may be one of the best things that allies can do if they are safe to do so and if there are no laws against videotaping. One question for potential allies to consider if you are in a situation that is safe for you, but maybe not for someone else: If you can't be an ally when or after someone is being unjustly traumatized in the marketplace, when can you be an ally?
- Go to the hospital if necessary, and again, collect documents on everything related to the impact of the incident on you and your family.
- Be aware that interviews suggest that trauma in the marketplace can result in recurring intrusive memories, replaying the event and related questions over and over in your mind, Post-Traumatic Stress Disorder (PTSD), a sense of helplessness and self-doubt, feeling as if there is nowhere to turn for support, and uncertainty and confusion

about one's rights. Therefore, it is important to seek support as soon as possible and to draw on resources. Most communities have a 211 Information Hotline that is accessible either by phone or internet for assisting anyone with time-sensitive counseling or other community resources for assistance.

- When "shopping while Black and Brown" emotional trauma happens, please give yourself the same time to heal as you would if you were (God forbid) kicked all over your body. Emotional and physical threat are the same to the body's alarmed limbic system when cortisol, adrenaline, and the flight, flight, and freeze responses have been activated. Therefore, be kind to yourself, and balance your advocacy with your energy level needs. Take things only as far as your health and energy levels will allow. Seeking emotional support from family, friends, community members and leaders, support groups, and online groups may be very important for your short- and long-term self-care, especially if you find yourself not talking about the incident at all or, at the other extreme, talking about the incident incessantly. Seeking help from your medical provider(s) also may be important for ensuring your physical and emotional health as your recover from a race-based marketplace trauma.
- It also may be helpful to seek faith-based, medical, psychological, psychiatric, or other therapeutic supports. Other supports, such as meditation practices, routine, ritual, or ceremony, that allow time and processes for assisting in healing physically, emotionally, and spiritually may be not only helpful, but essential. One upcoming interviewee suggested that you should not "stuff it," but rather "get the poison out" in productive ways. Current and past events, the interviews shared throughout this book, and the strategies at the end of each of the other parts of this book, suggest that self-care may be extremely important before, during, and after engaging with the consumer marketplace, especially if a breach of trust has occurred for you.
- Drawing on resources also may be very important for your physical health because it helps the body to put the upset outside of itself instead of holding it within to wreak havoc on the internal body. Reaching out by phone, letters of complaint, and meetings with attorneys, legal aid, community organizations and agencies (e.g., NAACP, ACLU, Commission on Civil Rights, local and national Black Lives Matter organizations, etc.) may be other options. Also, reaching out to regulatory agencies that govern that particular business, (e.g., each state usually has regulatory agencies that govern contractors, medical

professionals, and other occupations) may be helpful. You can research and access the appeal or complaint processes for whatever entity with which you are dealing (medical, corporate, contracting, insurance, etc.).

- To add insult to injury, you may face unsympathetic, clueless acquaintances. Further, when trying to take action, you may encounter corporate offices, law enforcement, and agencies for complaint, who have no framework or complaint "checkbox" for racial and other profiling. Nonetheless, you might keep examining your resources and pressing forward to have your voice heard.
- If you do not mind yourself or your family being in the public light, then with the help of your resources, consider writing editorials, organizing boycotts, contacting news action team outlets, and so on.
- Asking community members to call or write to complain to corporate or to prosocial organizations (BBB, ACLU, etc.) may help spread awareness of the traumas that you and other victims may be experiencing in particular areas of the marketplace.
- Putting the incidents into the context of historical and White supremacy ideologies and frameworks rather than taking them personally may be helpful. More on this is found in the philosophies section. One interviewee in the current section suggested that in spite of the trauma she was experiencing, she managed to consider the employees' impending layoffs and the stress that it may have been having on them. She did not hold them any less accountable, but she seemed to find it helpful to consider what social, structural, and economic factors may have been impinging upon the staff.
- Concern for those with fewer resources to address these kinds of situations is a theme that arises throughout some of the interviews throughout this book. It suggests that blowing the incident off for yourself might not release you of the burden that you may feel for those who may be less powerful or have fewer resources than you.
- One interviewee's story suggests that if it is possible, it may be good to secure the children first, and then go back and try to speak with the managers, organizers, and so on. On the other hand, another story illustrates for us that, depending on the child's age and maturity level, modeling for them your appropriate and strategic efforts to speak up against mistreatment may be useful to them as they move forward in their own lives.
- The interviews suggest that resistance may take many forms: requesting the store manager; inquiring about and requesting copies of store

policy; complaining to the district manager; or calling or writing to complain to the business's corporate office's department of consumer relations, legal department, or other such offices. One of the interviewees suggested that district managers can be helpful for explaining store policies and possibly reprimanding workers who have violated those policies.

- There are many possible strategies outlined in these endings to each of the parts of the book; therefore, you might examine or reexamine the suggestions at the end of the other parts of the book as well.

STRATEGIES MARKETERS MIGHT CONSIDER TRYING

- Your boards, executives, managers, and staff might consider saving yourself the negative publicity, public relations campaigns, clean-up and damage control, lost revenue, costly lawsuits, and expensive settlements by doing the right thing by the community, as proactive rather than reactive measures.
- Being aware of the importance of ongoing, effective diversity training is extremely important for any organization and has been discussed extensively in the two previous section lists, as well as in some of the interviews.
- Be aware that you should ensure that your business or organization does not negatively and inaccurately stereotype, single-out, or traumatize your consumers, which creates emotional upset, anxiety, anger, shock, and fear for one's life, health, and safety.
- You might encourage among your staff the thought process of whether security, police, or other law enforcement are being involved for actual criminal activity or as "personal valets."[1]
- Be aware that "tone-policing," where staff involve law enforcement not for what a person did or said, but rather for their perception of the direct, confident, or perturbed tone used to say something, can also be a problem. Thus, more attention ends up being given to the tone than to the issue that is of concern to the customer.[2]
- Be aware that taking the time to listen to consumers who feel they have been treated unjustly and giving your attention and consideration to their concerns is important. Consumers know when their concerns have not been taken seriously.
- Please be aware of the power that an apology often has. One participant said that "It all could have been avoided if the fellow had said,

'Miss I made a mistake, and I'm sorry. . . . I probably would have just left. . . . But when they said they were going to 'let me go,' and so on, it made me very angry. . . . If they had just said, 'We are sorry,' I would have just left."

- Be aware that you should think very carefully about the role of physically assaulting and even restraining customers, given that people have been seriously harmed and killed. In addition, serious lawsuits and expensive settlements have resulted over situations that amounted to a few dollars and no threat to others. This is not just a financial issue; it's a moral and ethical one.
- You might examine the reading resources and suggestions at the end of the other parts of the book.

TRAUMAS

Reflection Questions and Related Readings

1. What was one of the worst things that has happened to you in the consumer marketplace, through no fault of your own? Was it preventable? If so, how could it have been prevented? How did this occurrence impact you, your health, your mental health, and your life moving forward? How were your loved ones affected by what happened?
2. To what resources did you reach out for support? How did those resources respond and assist you? What resources were most helpful, and what resources were least helpful? If you could rewrite this entire event, how would you change it? What resources might you still need to access for dealing with the situation, and how can you reach out to them?
3. What is the one thing that you think needs to be changed within the structures that govern society so that no one will suffer marketplace traumas? For that one thing, what is the ladder of influence (people, agencies, governing bodies, or steps) that can begin to influence a change? To what degree would fixing this one thing also repair the impact of past exploitations, inequities, and so on?
4. How can academia or other research portals contribute to our understanding of race-based disparities and traumas in the consumer marketplace? What are the questions that you have that you would like to see academia or other research portals pursue in order to better our

understanding of these issues? To whom can you present these questions (e.g., reference librarians)?

5. On a regular basis, we should do self-analyses in order to be held accountable to ourselves for our own behavior. We can ask ourselves, did I do this particular action because it is fair and equitable, or did I do it because of the stereotypes in my head or the racism in my heart (or because of other factors, if applicable)? Can you think of a recent situation where you might ask yourself these questions?
6. "Internalized racism" is when historically oppressed people respond out of the White supremacist notions that we have allowed ourselves to believe, so people of color may be able to benefit from asking these questions (in question 5) of ourselves as well, in case we are struggling with internalized stereotypical or racist notions that have been adopted through the White supremacist context that promotes the idea that whiteness is always right.
7. What is your "so what" after having read all that you have thus far? What questions, comments, thoughts, and further processing do you still have to do about each of the stories that you read in this section? Who can you partner with to work together on getting a better understanding of what you have read? On what appropriate resources can you draw?

RELATED READINGS

Goff, P., M. Jackson, B. Di Leone, C. Culotta, and N. DiTomasso. "The Essence of Innocence: Consequences of Dehumanizing Black Children." *Journal of Personality and Social Psychology* 106, no. 4 (2014): 526–45. https://www.apa.org/pubs/journals/releases/psp-a0035663.pdf.

Williams, Terrie M. *Black Pain: It Just Looks Like We're Not Hurting.* New York: Scribner, 2009.

IV

PHILOSOPHIES

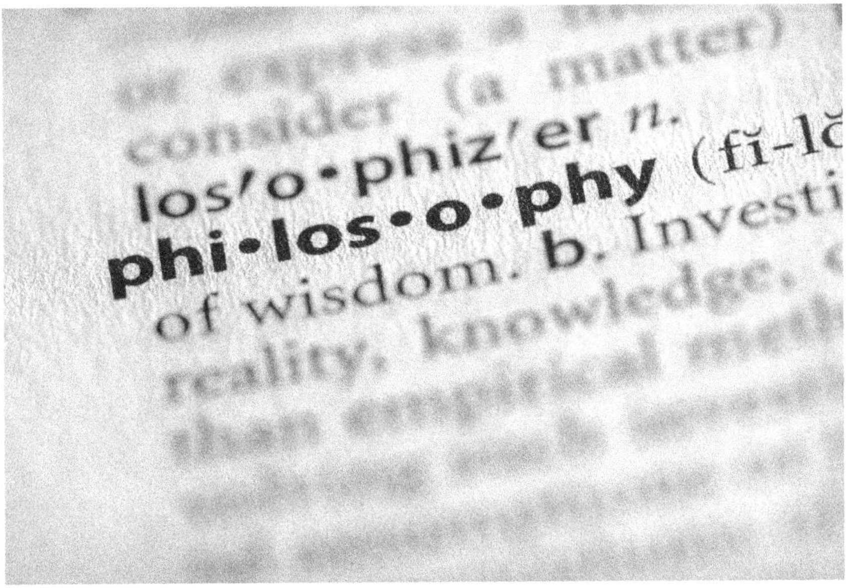

How we might explain, try to come to terms with, and continue to resist the "shopping while Black and Brown" experience.

firebrandphotography/iStock/Getty Images

POEM 6

The Invisible Pause

Denise M. Keyes

Followed in the high-end store I frequent
Sales clerks anxious
"May I help you?"
Shadowing
Before my two feet are fully in the store

Or
worse?

I'm invisible
No offer of help at all
But no . . .
not invisible
'cuz they look me up and down
Side eyed
Can she afford to shop here?

I'm dressed in the best
from previous purchases
at this very establishment
That's how we prepare
to be disrespected where we spend our money
They see the clothes
I see the question

Stolen?
Thrift?
Surely!

Tap it down
Don't get mad
they can't help themselves
they're only being
what they've been taught to believe

I still recall
the time
buying three coats at once
that's how you do when pleasure is made painful;
Get it done

Two fabric coats,
One suede.
Maxis
as the times demanded

The clerk failed.
She couldn't hide her anger
I don't know that she tried
Jealous
I could make this purchase
She
Could not
What was affirmative about this action?

Stalling,
rage exploding in red angry neck blotches
searching the long list of unacceptable credit cards on the roll under the register.
Carefully
Hopefully
For my name to be rejected.

Maybe it's because I'm young?
Looking for an escape hatch for the ritual racism

But

that very night
I saw

White high school girls
Make expensive purchases
Without this "slowdown to a stall" rebellion.

Irritated now and feeling my responsive rage oozing.
Problem? I ask
Vacuous eyes raise from thrice scanned reject list
I feel the smile I have mastered
teasing the corners of my lips
(not my heart)
Sickly sweet I hear my voice
"I understand your questioning. . . .
I know on your salary
You couldn't afford such a purchase,
So, I guess that makes you doubt
I can."

The purchase now expedited
I escape
the store
but
the resentment lingers
with some slight shame
that
her prejudice and assumptions
Brought out the mean in me.

Still I was glad to have
The survivalist wherewithal
To express the sentiment.

Conflicting?
Yes,
Both emotions felt
At the same time
Deeply

Damn
sometimes you feel their hate so strong
Decisions about whether to spend,
or not
Get all twisted

Not buying something you want
'Cuz you're pissed,
Or buying something you don't;
To show you can

Poor,
not Poor
Black skin ensures
our journey and pain are shared
the tie that binds

My white classmates say,
"I don't think there's any
Prejudice . . . that happens to all of us."
Yes,
that's why you ask me to go to the mall with you . . .
to
decoy.

POEM 7

Whitney in the Purple Dress

Michelle Dunlap

As I stood in line
at the store yesterday,
I looked over
at the magazines . . .

And there, I saw copies
of a national magazine,
with the dead body
of Whitney Houston
on the cover.

There she lay
in clear focus—
purple dress,
lipstick,
pretty hair,
and at peace.

Did I also see
a pearl necklace
or something similar?

I tried not to
soak in too much
& I looked away.

I realized I had
been staring
& I felt guilty.

Though I tried
not to look,
it seemed the magazine
was everywhere—
to the right,
to the left,
at the top,
& at the bottom.

I prayed that my little one
would not notice,
and it seems
he didn't . . .
or at least he
didn't talk about it.

A human
body,
a woman's
body,
& especially
a black woman's
body—
even when
dead—
is not considered
sacred.

This ought
not be . . .

INTRODUCTION

Medical scientists are now trying to document the cost of racism, stress, and health disparities on people of color.[1] Community activist Enola Aird speaks to the emotional toll of these added burdens and how they can wear a person down emotionally:[2]

> the daily wearing down of spirit—the "mini-aggressions" and chronic stress of being belittled and misperceived, that most blacks endure every day, some of which may almost be invisible: being followed in a store, or of constantly being suspected of being incompetent or dishonest, or violent; being ignored in restaurants or when waiting in line.

Adding to these burdens, people of color not only have had the burden of worrying about being accused of stealing, but also of being accused of unruly conduct in the marketplace. For example, with regard to mall breaches of peace, one report reveals that the Columbia Mall in Columbia, South Carolina, had policies still in place as late as 1990 to discourage Black patronage by disproportionately banning Black visitors for unruly conduct. The NAACP became more involved in 1990, citing the unconstitutionality of disproportionately ejecting Black patrons for offenses such as "blocking smooth traffic flow," "being loud and boisterous," "being part of a group of three or more," "going in too many stores," "staying in the mall 'too long,'" "fraternizing with White people," and "wearing an 'extreme' ethnic hair style, such as a high-top fade." With these policies, if a patron refused to leave when ordered to do so, or returned within six months of a trespass warning, they could be "fined $200 or imprisoned for 30 days."[3] Such policies are likely code for being able to easily eject primarily Black and Brown bodies. While many mall and consumer venues in the new millennium no longer have formal policies geared to control participation of consumers of color in marketplaces, Black and Brown patrons, and especially Black and Brown youth patrons, may still feel informal policies and inequitable tensions that signal not being entirely welcomed in some establishments.[4] Such policies, whether still formal or informal, can have the impact of keeping a consumer experience or venue predominantly White. For example, even in this decade, using "cover charge racism," a group of African American lawyers reportedly were charged significant entrance fees into a club while none of the White patrons were.[5]

AMELIORATING MARKETPLACE RACISM

Led by pressure from Reverend Al Sharpton and an outpouring of community pressure, some stores and other vendors have tried to ameliorate damage done by discriminatory policies. For example, both Barneys and Macy's, which previously have been embroiled in accusations of racially based "shop and frisk" and related policies,[6] have begun to post Al Sharpton's "Customers' Bill of Rights" in their stores.[7] These downloadable posters review for customers what their rights are, beginning with: "[Store name] is committed to ensuring that all shoppers, guests, and employees are treated with respect and dignity and are free from unreasonable searches, profiling, and discrimination of any kind in our store. . . ." Over the years, stores such as Lord & Taylor and the Gap came on board with these posters.[8]

Along with such strides, when people of color and allies are not consciously and strategically resisting poor treatment in the consumer marketplaces, we are at least critically analyzing it. Marketplace racism is situated within the larger context of social, societal, and historical prejudice and racism targeted at people of color, and therefore it has been situated within social movements such as the reconstruction movement, Jim Crow resistance, civil rights movement, Occupy Wall Street, Black Lives Matter, #SayHerName, #MeToo, and other major social justice movements. It could easily be argued that besides fighting general human rights violations, fighting marketplace racism has played a role in every social fight that Black citizens have started or had a major role in. As with earlier movements, such as the civil rights movement, there frequently is nothing passive about how people of color and our allies are looking at and responding to these incidents.

While some stores and other consumer entities are getting better sensitized to equity issues related to the treatment of consumers, many haven't begun to scratch the surface. The following memory-tellings illustrate a variety of types of treatment that consumers of color still endure, such as the common being overly monitored, ignored, accused of stealing, overcharged for services, or otherwise mistreated. However, these particular memory-tellings illustrate that often recollections of people of color about and responses to such incidences are viewed from and framed within a complex and deeply historical, economic, and social perspective.

VOICES OF PHILOSOPHIES CONCERNING MARKETPLACE RACISM

The following stories speak not only on a variety of other incidences but also on how those who experienced them made sense of them, and put their marketplace experiences into both a modern and historical perspective. An African American woman speaks of her developmental progression over the years within marketplace experiences, as well as how she has come to understand such experiences within the African American historical experience and overall context. An African American and Indigenous young man offers his philosophy for why such exclusionary, discriminatory, and exploitive practices still occur, and how people of color can keep from internalizing such incidents and move themselves psychologically beyond them. A young, White college student discusses white privilege and her upset with her brother as she tried to explain to him his privilege after he did not get arrested when he was caught stealing from a department store. A White remodeling contractor shares his frustration with insurance companies that he has noticed do not fully support the claims of less privileged groups. And lastly, an African American woman speaks on the exploitive practices and difficulty of making ends meets in marketplaces that cater to and take advantage of people of color, and offers her thoughts about fixing it.

PLAGUED

"It's a Wonder [Black People] Live to Fifty" (Rekia's Story)

Rekia shares her story of the emotional costs of and survival strategies for shopping while Black. Rekia is an African American woman, perhaps somewhere in her sixties, who holds multiple advanced degrees. She recently retired from her higher education position and currently teaches as an adjunct professor. Meeting with Rekia was very inspiring for me because of her strong presence and many accomplishments. Our paths had first crossed briefly at a community event at a state capitol. I sensed the spirit of a mentor in her right away, and I was drawn to her wisdom. She seemed accomplished, composed, and very aware of the challenges that are going on in our communities. Her straightforwardness in her communication style and her confidence drew me to her, especially as I could tell from those drawing around her that she was a natural memory-teller with a lot of important information to relay about what is going on in the world. I made sure that I got her card, and I made up my mind that evening that I would follow-up with her. I knew from what she briefly had mentioned experiencing that I had to ask her if she would allow me to interview her. She did not hesitate in saying yes, and we set up a meeting.

I would be driving some hours to get to her, so I asked for directions the evening before the day of our meeting. As I pulled up in front of Rekia's home, I noted that it was a 1960s ranch style that I suspected she and her husband purchased in their younger years when it was new or near-new. It had that familiar feel of houses I had seen and been inside of as I grew up in

Detroit. These houses tended to be brick, with medium-sized three-paned living room windows, and three cement stairs in the front yard leading up to a small porch that may or may not have awnings. There tended to be iron-screened doors with designs on them, and then a wooden door behind that which led into the house. The wooden door usually had some kind of small clear or stained glass toward the top of it. Walking inside of those homes, there was carpet on the floors and on the left, a set of stairs leading to the second floor. My mind went back to where these homes also had a good deal of gold- and amber-toned furnishings and lighting, with huge bureaus and cabinets that held the "good China" to be used on the occasions when special guests came over. I had been in such houses many times in my Detroit upbringing when visiting cousins and friends whose parents worked in the factories and made pay that was substantial enough to live in houses like this—provided that they or their loved ones didn't have any monkeys on their back such as substance abuse, gambling, or perhaps a longterm affair of some sort, which, if they did, might zap any ability to keep up the house payments. Such houses usually had a station wagon in the driveway, the one with the large wood strips of panel on the side. These are the things of which I was reminded as I pulled up in front of Rekia's house. These were memories that came flooding back to me, memories from before the factories abandoned Detroit and moved overseas to exploit and pay workers a tiny fraction of what the unionized Detroit workers were getting paid. And there fell the Detroit that I had known. After just sitting for a moment thinking on these recollections of home, I got out of my car and went up the small cement stairs and knocked on the iron-designed outer door, and I watched the wooden inner door with the decorative glass open, revealing the predicted carpet and stairs inside.

Rekia was a short, stout woman oozing a spunkiness of personality that I could feel all the way from my car to her door. She stepped outside before I could get inside the house and greeted me with a hug, inquiring as to whether I had any difficulty finding her place, and calling me "Dr. Dunlap." In response, I told her that the journey was relaxing, even enchanting at times, and I asked her to please call me by my first name. I knew that request may not be honored with her being a bit older than my generation. Many of the African Americans of my generation or older refuse to call me by my first name. Minority PhDs and other terminal degrees are so disproportionately rare in the Black community in comparison to our White counterparts, that the elders *love* to make it known when someone has excelled in education. In my effort to honor those like themselves who have trail-blazed before me, I ask them to call me by my first name, but in their effort to honor my trailblazing, some refuse, and call me Doctor anyway. I have tried to accept that that is just how it's going to be sometimes, and to take it as an honor and symbol of the push for education for which many people of color and allies have fought and even died.

Miss Rekia (as I called her) offered me something to drink, and I accepted as she headed toward the kitchen to draw water for hot tea. I sat quietly as I waited for her return and relaxed as I settled in. Out from the kitchen Miss Rekia came. She exuded a pride in me, as if I were a long-lost sister or niece who had come to visit, whom she could brag on—one of "us" who has "made it." Although she appeared proud, she also appeared discerning. She looked into my eyes, studied me a bit, as if knowing or having some sense of what academic trailblazing and professional success really costs Black people. She let me know right away that although she is not a tenured professor per se, she's been in academia many years. She let me know in her own way that she knew me and much about me without me even opening my mouth, and I could feel in my spirit that this was true. Through her warmth, Miss Rekia let me know that she was receptive, and we started our interview once our initial chatting was done.

Rekia discusses the anger that she has felt when being both stereotyped and ignored in the consumer marketplace, and the friction that one of her responses created between her and her husband. As she prepares to enter into the late-adulthood phase of her life, she puts some of her past and present experiences in the consumer retail marketplace into a larger philosophical context and perspective that only time and experience can provide.

Rekia's story illustrates for us that the marketplace is not necessarily any different from other contexts of Black life within American culture. Her story is a reminder of the things that perhaps we must not forget, if we are to keep our momentum to resist and overcome the microaggressions and structural hindrances that we face on a daily basis as Black people.

Rekia tells her story . . .

* * *

I had observed that when I would go to the general store—you know, the large grocery store. At the time this happened in [the northern United States], about ten years ago. I would notice that when White customers were ahead of Black customers in line, the clerk would automatically say to the White customers, "Do you have any coupons?" And then when it came time for the Black customer to come through the line, they would say, "Any coupons, food stamps?" Well, I figured, let's see what they do with me. And they did exactly that. They asked me if I had any food stamps. And then they asked me if I had any coupons. And then I noticed again that with the White customers, they would just ask if they had any coupons. I felt that they were making a difference, as subtle as it may have been to some people. Most people didn't seem to notice, or maybe they noticed and didn't react. But I reacted. I reacted in two ways. [For one,] fortunately, I had a $100 bill to pay for my pack of cigarettes. I gave the $100 bill to the clerk as a sign of protest. This was no big deal—they broke the $100 bill. It was no big deal because they do thousands upon thousands of dollars of business. But the other way I reacted was I told some of my [Black] friends who live around here to go to the store. Ironically, [my friends] had been talking about improvements in race relations. I said to them, "We are still considered n[_____]s to the White people here." And they said, "Oh no, no, no. . . . No one would . . . they don't react that way." I said, "Well go to [the local grocery store franchise]." We were middle class Black people—this was the Mercedes, BMW, floor-length mink coat and the whole bit, group. And I said to them just like that, "Go to the store and see if they don't ask you if you have food stamps." And one of them, my husband's cousin, she went. And they asked her for food stamps. So, she came back and said, "You were right." And it wasn't that long ago, as I said. At first I had not noticed, and a lot of people don't notice it. It's because you're preoccupied with what you're doing, and you are trying to get out of this store, and you are thinking about a variety of things. I didn't notice it for a long time, but it became very blatant, and then it dawned on me. [When I presented] the $100 bill, to be perfectly honest with you, it would have been nice if she had reacted, like with a gasp. But there was nothing. And I did not feel anything. I thought I was being cool. But it really didn't make an impression on her. She was oblivious. Because [I thought] I was putting myself in her mindset, which is only conjecture because I can't really be there [in her mind]. . . . And then I thought about it, and I said, "Well, I probably can buy and sell her. . . . Why should I worry about her?" And I didn't care anymore. I just chalked it up to her being ignorant, and biased, and I felt sorry [for her]. Actually, I sort of felt sorry for her because she was stuck in saying, "Coupons, food stamps . . ."

Another incident that occurred—and I'm ashamed to say it—[involved] a dog chain. I was buying a dog chain for my dog at that same store, about fifteen years earlier. [I tried to make my purchase] and give my money to the cashier, who was a relatively young, White female. I tried to be waited on, but they wouldn't assist me; they just continued to ignore me. So, I said to myself, "Oh well!" and I just took the chain and walked out the store. Nobody ever stopped me. You would have had to have seen my face. I don't think they wanted to bother with me. They didn't know what I would do because I was very angry [and it showed on] my face. I made a big deal out of taking that chain out of the door, and I verbalized it [through my] nonverbal communication. [Specifically,] I took the chain and I jerked it! It was all body language that said, "I'm angry!" And I just took the chain. I suspect that I felt violently angry, and I'm being honest with regard to my . . . personality. This is putting it simplistically, very simplistically, but I tend to divide people up into homicidal and suicidal personalities. There are people who really will shirk, or shrink, and do more harm to themselves than to others. Well, I'm on the homicidal side. I honestly, might have been afraid of my own anger. And, that's the truth . . . I might have hit them! Because you see, when I was as far back as age two, my father taught me how to box. If I hit you, I could hurt you—and very badly. I know that I'm capable of that, so I've learned through high school and college, especially in college, to curtail that. So, I'm very obedient now, to myself. Actually, during meetings, when I get angry, I remind myself to sit on my hands. That's just me. It's nothing to do with racism or anything. That has to do with my own anger management.

To be honest with you, I didn't think about it. I just went home. I put the chain on the dog when I got home. And I said to my husband, "You know what those people did?!? . . . Blah-blah-blah-blah! . . . I just took the chain and walked out!" Now, my husband's reaction was—he was horrified! He felt that I did something that I should not have done, point blank. He thought that I should've handled it differently. He was embarrassed and horrified at the thought that I could have been arrested, I could've been beaten up, I could've gotten hurt, I could've gotten [taser] shocked, anything! All of it [could have happened]. But I knew nothing was going to happen. I just felt somehow justified in taking it. My husband kept telling me that was wrong, and he was right. But I didn't care. Because it was either do that, or take it and strangle her with it. If I could do it over again, I would have said, "I've been trying to get your attention!" But knowing me, and my personality, that was it.

Not everyone would've done what I did. And, not all would have felt the same way [about it]. It's like the chicken and the egg, which came first? What I thought and interpreted as racist behavior, [was it] really? Given my personality, I sort of fed into it too, in a way, by saying, "I dare you!" It was triggered by a racist act; however, somebody else might've responded totally differently. My husband would've said, "Hey, Hey! . . . You know? . . . Pay some attention to me . . . I'm trying to give some money to you! . . . What's wrong with you?" or something. Don't forget this happened some time ago, so some other young man or young woman today might've said [otherwise]. I know kids who would just say, literally, "Boom!" [as in gunfire]. It depends.

This is why I say to people, and very specifically to my grandchildren, no matter what happens, you have to think what will be the result of your actions. And you can't trust the mental state of people, all the time. So, when somebody cuts you off on the road, and you think you're going to do something by sticking your hand up and giving them the finger or flipping them the bird, you might be killing yourself. You never know. You have to really think it through, if I take this action, what will be the impact? What will I cause? You've got to think, so I've learned to think. I would not do that today. I would've just driven down there, but I wouldn't have taken the chain. I would not have taken the chain at all. I would've just given it back. I would have just thrown it on the counter and kept going. Today I would be much more calculated, and much more circumspect, in my behavior. I would just put it down, and keep it moving. I've learned something the hard way: After many years of living, it isn't about me. Well it is, and it isn't. I mean, it's their problem. My biggest coping mechanism years ago, quite frankly, was to strike out. I mean that's one way for me to cope, but there's so many other ways for me to cope. I have to deal with mine. I have to deal with whatever I have, it's not about them anymore; it just isn't. I don't care. And I can only do what I can. I can only control me; I can't control the other.

I've always been, as far as I can remember, somewhat better off economically than many Blacks, and more than even my mother and my father. I just was. But [racism] still made me angry, make no mistake about it. Oppression, no matter what economic group you are in, or how much education you've attained, when you are oppressed, there are certain characteristic ways in which you behave, and usually anger is at the very base of it. I don't care if I was Rockefeller, J. P. Morgan, or Joe Blow in the ghetto or on the Bowery [a section of lower-Manhattan in New York], I would've gotten angry in all [these] instances.

[You see it] the minute any Black male or female steps out the door, they know that they have to put on another coat of armor in order to protect themselves and to cope. When you talk to your Black son, and I talk to my Black son, and all of us Black mothers talk to our Black boys, we all say the same thing—we whisper, "don't do this, don't do that, because you'll get killed there, and so on." We all do that. And I say to my students, all the time, "Many Blacks go home, shut their door and say, 'Thank God! Now I can be myself.'" Sad, isn't it? When we go out, we have to operate in a dual manner. Simple things like, what's that kid, T.I., the rapper, who says, "What 'cha know about that?! What 'cha know about that?!" And I also say to them, "I can talk, and teach you, and speak the King's English. And when I get home, and I talk to my daughter, I say, 'I ain't gonna do dat.'" I'm always speaking in a dual way. I also tell my students this all the time, I say, "Now look, do you know what I want most out of life?" And they say, "What [Ms. Rekia]?" I respond,

> I want to be able to get up in the morning, maybe brush my teeth, but not necessarily. At least comb my hair. Put on my running clothes, and run out the door, and run free, not having to worry about being run over by a car, or being bit by a dog, or spat upon. White people have to worry about those things too, but not like I do. When a cop comes up behind me, I can't take for granted that cop's not going to hit me. I have to get on the side of the road, you know up on the grass, to make sure I don't get run over.

And that had a lot of impact on the people in class. [Connecting this] back to my feelings about the incidents in the supermarket, how I respond is a function of my economic status, my educational level, and my psychological make up. But I venture to say, no matter what it was, or no matter what those variables are, if a person comes out of oppression, if they [perceive] any bit of racism, discrimination, or any type of bigotry when they encounter it, they're going to feel anger. When you are White, do you have to think about going into a restaurant, and how you're going to be received, where you are going to be seated? When you're White, when you go into a shoe store, do you worry how they are going to treat you—are they going to put the shoe on your foot, or only on the foot of the White women? When you buy a dress, do you have to worry about how do they stand around and watch you? Over and over and over again, we [Black people] have to do it, and many people don't understand that. People come to see you at your workplace, and they'll say to you, "May I see the boss?" And I'll say, "Ok. I'll go get him." And I'll say to my secretary, "Show them to the office." And then when I meet them at my office, they [sputter, confused], "But I wanted to speak . . . can I . . ."

My son said to me, "Ma, how do you cope with racism? How do you react to it? What do you do [with it]? How do you live with it"? And I said to him,

> Son, the only way I know is to become the boss, which is what I did for thirty years. You treat them with kindness and goodness. Those who are guilty, they self-destruct. The others [who are not guilty], they learn and spread it. They learn and spread [the ideas that], "Yes, yes I can do this; Yes, I work with Blacks; Yes, I can work with a woman; Yes, they are competent people out there; Yes, we can have fun; Yes, I can understand."

My son has never forgotten that. And he still remembers that. He says it every now and then, because now he's the boss.

[To offer advice,] the first thing I would say, is know yourself, and that is know your strengths and your weaknesses. Know who you are. And that will help you to determine where you need to build up, tone down, and so on—that's first, know yourself. Second—and this is hard to do—but don't take [things] personally. Because anybody who attacks you, or in any way threatens you, or tries to put you down or make you feel less than themselves, it's their problem, not yours. Not unless you know you started it. And the only way you'll know that you started it is if you know yourself. So, know yourself, and don't take anything anybody says personally. The third is, and this may sound awfully trite, small. But to me it's the most important thing: gain knowledge. You have power when you're armed with knowledge. . . . Knowledge is power. So, read as much knowledge as you can about everything. It is not enough to listen to rap; it's not enough to listen to popular music; it's not enough to listen to rock and roll. You have to know and appreciate the genius, not only of Duke Ellington—it's not enough. You need to know the genius of Chopin, Mozart, Bach, and Schumann. And you need to be able to relate what they did to what is happening now in rap music. I don't hear any difference. You may think that's crazy, but it really isn't.

Read about those dry, somewhat pale people in England, Great Britain—don't turn your nose up at that. "Oh, they're dull." Dull to whom? Find out about them. Read about those African kings and scholars, who, before Western civilization, really understood what they were doing. Understand how they really set the base for Western civilization and many of the things that Western Civilization is built upon now—it came from Africa. Understand the beauty and tranquility of a Japanese society. Understand the heartbeat—the rapid heartbeat—and yet civility of a Chinese society. You need to know the world. You can now reach out and touch the rest of the world, just like that. It's no longer isolationist. There's no longer big gaps in space and time. Know your environment, and occasionally look up in the sky at night, on a clear night, with all those magnificent stars, and figure out where the hell you are in this universe, and [acknowledge] the power of a great spirit that pulled it all together. Groove till you move!

So again, you have to know yourself. I told you earlier that I'm on the homicidal side [when it comes to racism], and I've learned not to immediately react, unlike when I was younger. When I was twelve years old, my father and mother sent my younger brother and I down to Georgia, and that was the time of real separation—we're talking about the 1950s. And we went to a movie, and Blacks at that time had to go up in the balcony. Coming from New York, going to the balcony was a pleasure, and sitting down stairs was like [crowded and nasty], so we always went up to the balcony anyway. In fact, everybody fought to go up to the balcony. When I went downstairs to leave, as we were walking out of the movie, this White boy called us "n[_____]." Being a New Yorker, and being a fighter and a boxer—see, know yourself—my reaction was to smack, boom, and knock him out cold. Well, all the Black kids were mortified, and they ran screaming away. My brother and I just looked and walked out. When we returned and told my Aunt what had happened, she and her husband sat up all night in a rocking chair, holding a gun, waiting for the White people to come to attack us. That's how bad it was. But they didn't come. We found out later in town that it was being said, "Oh, those kids were visiting from the North, they didn't know any better." [But you still] have to know yourself. To know yourself, it is important. I know I overcompensate [for this] by being overly nice, and by not allowing people to see that if they do something that I really don't like, their life is in danger. I know me, so I control that. My mother also helped me to do that because she would say, "Now you cannot go around knocking out people, you can go to jail for that because you're eighteen years old and [considered an adult]." I [began to understand that] I'm not a kid anymore, and I can't just hit somebody and get away with it. I have to control it, so I do.

When this book is written, somebody will say, "Well, Black folks are angry all the time!" because we're accused of being angry all the time. But [the truth] is that oppression causes anger. . . . Oppression is really bigger than anger. However, the difference between Blacks and Whites, and even the French-Canadian women, and the Jews, and the Italian and the Irish, is that their white skin allows them to escape every now and then. But we [Black folks] can't escape! We can't escape! We're always, always mindful and reminded that we are people of color.

What a lot of people don't realize is that the Irish came over in ships, in the hold—the H-O-L-D—of a ship, just as Black slaves did. And they urinated and defecated on themselves, just like the Blacks did. A lot of people don't know that. And when they got off at Ellis Island, the people that received them, who had just come off Ellis Island a couple of years before they did, they looked their nose down at them and said, "Ugh, they're the unwashed." And that's how the Irish got the name of the Unwashed. It's like the kids in high school who encounter teachers who have low expectations for them, and the kids will say to their teacher, "I may not live till twenty," or "Oh! I can't do that!" or "I can't go to college!" Or they will say, "The only thing I want to become is a correction officer, because all my friends will be in prison and I can take care of them." [These are] expectations. We can say, "Oh, I get this all the time, it doesn't bother me anymore," or "I ignore it, or I dismiss it," but I become angry, and no matter what, it does bother me. It really does bother me. It's a wonder [Black people] live to fifty.

PRECONCEIVED

"[I'm] the Bull's-Eye!" (Stephon's Story)

Stephon's story is a common one of being young, gifted, Black, and targeted in the consumer marketplace and beyond. Initially, as I reflected on this story, I was reminded of a scene from the satirical Comedy Central sketch show Key and Peele, where Key and Peele sang a song, "Negrotown." Negrotown was a mythological place where store staff were not afraid of Black people and did not follow them while shopping. It was a place where Black people were not judged for what they wear, where they did not have to fear the luck of the draw in terms of which negative and inaccurate stereotypes might be in the heads of law enforcement officers if encountered, and where loan applications and other business transactions were treated fairly.[1] Their depiction of a mythical Negrotown was comically sarcastic, yet pretty much sums up the whole of all these pages in their one song, because, unfortunately, the stress-free Negrotown does not exist. When Negrotown came close to existing, often they were violently burned down or otherwise annihilated—for example, Rosewood, Florida, and at least fourteen other Black towns.[2] So, what do Black and Brown people do in the face of a nation and often a world that offers the opposite of the utopian Negrotown? How do we make sense of the stress, the injustices, the pain, and the anger? Stephon offers his insights on this—on how he has come to terms with the injustices of the consumer marketplace and its larger contexts.

Stephon is an Indigenous and African American man in his thirties who works in the field of auto repairing in New England. I was familiar with his extended family, as they are many and well-known in the communities where I live and work. Meeting him, I was reminded of a number of the young men in my own family—educated, proud, dignified. We decided to meet for coffee on a Wednesday after he got off of work. As soon as he walked into the coffee house, I recognized him because of his family resemblance. I greeted him and we began by chatting about his family—who is related to whom, and whom I know, and whom I didn't know was related, and so on. That helped to break the ice between us. Finally, I asked if we might get started, as it was snowing outside, and we both seemed a little concerned about what direction the weather might take. So, I did my routine of going over the informed consent, and the tape was already set up and ready to roll, so we were able to jump right into the interview.

As I listened to Stephon, I realized that he seems to be a young man wise beyond his years. He offers up philosophies not only concerning the minoritized experience in the consumer marketplace, but also for minoritized life in the larger context of life in America. He offers his insightful perspectives on shopping while Black, the media marketplace, colorism, and internalized racism. He also speaks of how he and his family have learned to cope with and resist discrimination in the retail consumer marketplace and beyond. Stephon teaches us important lessons on how to not internalize the racism imbedded within our society, while also working to resist and change it.

Stephon tells his story . . .

* * *

Anybody who is of color has experienced discrimination. . . . It's America. As a man of color myself, there have been a lot of times that I have experienced discrimination. You go out to the stores, and it doesn't matter if you go to Walmart or wherever. But it does seem like the more trendy the establishment, the more you're discriminated against. But it doesn't matter whether you are shopping, banking, or eating—it doesn't matter, it's all the same. They blend in after a while. There is no one particular moment that strikes me, but it's all the same—people follow you, people look at you, or you don't get served.

I don't know if you become callous to it, or if you just get used to it. It used to upset me when I was younger, maybe because when you are young, you are always looking for something [in situations], but as you get older, [not so much] . . . I like to turn it on [the] people themselves. So, if someone is following me, I may walk up to the manager and report it. Even though I know that the person following me works at the store, I will say that I think that the person is getting ready to rip me off or something. I will hold my wallet. If I am walking with a woman, I will have her hold her purse real close to her. Because when you walk by individuals holding their wallets and purses as if you are going to rob them, that always struck me as weird. I don't know if you want to say White, European—Americans, or whatever—they always have these body movements, grabbing their purse, looking at you in a certain way like you're the aggressor, looking at you like they're the victim. I guess if you read a lot about history, you begin to understand where they come from, where that type of attitude comes from, where that type of ideology comes from. We can establish ourselves historically, so I kind of play with it now. I don't feel threatened by it as much as I used to. To me, it's just a game that they play among themselves—it has nothing to do with me.

It has taken me many years to figure this out, and it didn't really become clear to me until maybe in the last five years. I don't know if I ever thought it was about me as much as it was a threat to me. I was always offended by it, I was always ready to battle it, I was always ready to attack it, and I was always looking for it. Because that is what happens; if you keep hitting someone with the same stick sooner or later they expect to be hit with that stick and they also become calloused to that stick. I mean, how many times can you hit the same person over the head with the same stick and think you are going to get the same reaction? Sooner or later that person is going to hit back. I'm meaning that figuratively, not literally. I'm talking about a mental thing. I guess you sometimes have to do that to protect yourself mentally because you could go crazy in this country with racial discrimination and things like that.

When it comes to being a shopping consumer, because I am light-skinned, I'm not as much of a target as somebody that's darker than me in the store. To White Americans, if you're light, you must have a trace of White in you, or at least that's my concept of what they think. So, if you have a trace, in America, if you're one-sixth, or one-sixteenth African American blood, you're considered Black. But they do that; that's weird because in Africa, they do just the opposite. If you're one-sixteenth White, you're considered White. And that's to break everybody up. So, instead of a fist, it's just individual fingers that can break off. But here in the United States, I think that in a store, or in a restaurant that was full of only White Americans, and I was the only one—or there was me and some other people at the table—we're the target. But if I was in one area of the restaurant, and at a table in another area had a darker couple, whether they're Spanish or Native American, it doesn't really matter, they would get singled out—they would be the target. It's how you look, it's whether you have more European features and characteristics. The less [European features] you have, the more you're the target. You're the bull's-eye.

There are a lot of good people that, if you look throughout history, and even today, if you walk around, they are very angry. We've lost a lot of good people not just to shopping, but to racism in general in this country. A lot of good people just can't deal with it. And everybody that is exposed to it on a daily basis—and it is a daily basis—it is something that when you walk out your door in the morning you know you are going to experience. You must build, more or less, a coat of armor. You must have your shield up, your armor on, and you must put your "sword" on. I guess when I was young, I didn't realize I was waving a paper sword. I call it a paper sword because it really did nothing to verbally attack discrimination, [that is], without any knowledge. To clarify, a paper sword is pulling out something, looking tough, acting tough, not wanting to admit that it hurt you. Or it's pulling out something verbally or even physically thinking that it is protecting you when it's really not. [Thus,] society has you beat all the way around, disenfranchised in every aspect of society. You can take a piece of wood and sand it down, and until you get to the last piece of wood, you are still going to get the grains inside of the wood. That's society, that's racism in this country, it is ingrained in every fiber of our being. Looking mean, acting mean, saying, "What are you looking at?!" That's a paper sword. Being young and not knowing how to react, being young and not knowing the historical aspect of where they're coming from, that's it also. The paper sword has caused me many problems, all the time. Well, sometimes you get thrown out of the store, which is funny, because that's what they want. That feeds into their ideology.

The funny thing is, you sometimes have other people of color, and when I say people of color, I mean all people of color. So, I'm not just talking about Black people. I'm also talking about Native Americans, Spanish, Latinos, African Americans, whatever. When we talk among each other about these experiences, we could be in a group, and there could be some White Americans there. By the way, I don't know anyone—do you know anyone—that calls themselves European Americans in this country? In any case, we can refer to them on a politically correct level as European Americans, but they don't refer to themselves as that, so how is that politically correct that you call somebody something that they don't even refer to themselves as? Anyway, here we are talking among ourselves about what we experience on the day-to-day. And if there are White Americas sitting there—and they're welcome in the conversation, they really are—there's no problem with that, but they don't understand that. They think that you're exaggerating, they think that we're making these things up because if it doesn't happen to them and it doesn't exist in their lives on a daily basis, they have no clue. And they look at [us] like we're strange, like we're the Martians. But this is their ideology, this is their concept. And there's some that say, "Yeah, okay, maybe it does exist." But until they experience it, and I think they experience it to some point a little bit when they visit another country, but I'm not going to say they experience it a lot, because they can always leave. And I'm not going to say they're the minority, but they're not the ruling government [there] either. Under these circumstances, when you go to different countries and there's another race of people who run the government, who own the stores, who make the rules, who make the laws and they're in that country, and they speak a totally different language, that's when they get a hint of this experience. They become very paranoid, and I noticed that about White Americans, they're very, very paranoid. If you come into a room, and let's say you're an African American, and you're speaking Swahili [to each other]. Say I understand Swahili, and you and I start speaking Swahili, watch all the White Americans stare at you. They become paranoid, because it's a control thing with them.

I know these things although I only have a high school education. I've done a lot of reading and studying—for years and years. I study constantly, everything from history to economics, as well as math, science, and geography. It's all self-taught to me. I am financially poor, but culturally rich. When I was growing up, we didn't have a lot to eat, and we shared a lot of food with family and community. But we always knew where we came from, we always knew where we were going, and we always knew what we were trying to do—not only as a family, but as a community. Racism, the ideology of racism, will try to break the family, because by breaking a family, you break the culture. By breaking the women, you break the family. And, by making the men angry and feeling "less than," you break the future of the younger men coming up. So, one of the things my family did was a lot of talking, and they felt strongly about that, especially my mother, my grandmother, and my grandfather. And I have a very large family, so it's a lot of touching and hugging, and "I love you," and things like that. And when you had a bad day, it wasn't uncommon to come home and discuss it and to look at it for what it is, and not for what you perceive it to be. So, it was nothing really, as long as you would try to get that anger out, so it doesn't turn you into something that you shouldn't be. But once you get it out, it's like a poison that can no longer harm you. And this is what my grandfather said: It's almost like being bit by a snake; you take the poison, and you suck it out. If you love that person, you get on your knees and you do what you got to do, you suck it out. Because if you let it sit there and fester, it's going to kill you. It may not kill you physically, at first—that's usually the last step; but spiritually, and then mentally, it'll take you out. Every day, that's what I think about. This is everything. These are the things I think about when [racism] happens. These are the things that keep me calm. Because every time they behave in a racist way, they're trying to inject you with their poison, not your poison, it's their ideology.

I think when it first started out, the people who started the concept and the ideology or racism knew it was poison, and that's why they started it. It was to poison the race and the culture and everything else. The people nowadays just take it. If you do something long enough, it's just [poison] now. But who can just walk around giving poison to other people? If you administered poison in a hospital, you'd get arrested. What's the difference? You'd be killing them then. Whether you would be killing them fast or slow, what's the difference? Even the victims—it doesn't matter if the perpetrator knows it's poison or not, because the cure comes when the victim realizes it's poison. Because then, figuratively speaking, he'll push the perpetrator away. He won't allow either him or her to do that.

The "poison" comes in many forms, like, for example, television. If you look at Disney, for example, even in today's terms they've made *Beauty and the Beast* and other movies more diverse by including Middle Eastern and other minority characters. [However,] there's still racism. They're depicting a certain character in a certain light that you perceived them to be, and you want everyone else to perceive them that way. That's racism. Because [the depictions have] nothing to do with you; you don't know anything about their culture, you know nothing about their language, you know nothing about the people, you know nothing about the history, and yet you want to depict them in a certain light. In contrast, the old cartoons from way back, they're much more blatant. They used to have the monkeys running around, with the big lips, and the bulging eyes, and the little jockeys in front of them. I went up to Canada last year, and somewhere along the line we made a wrong turn. We were heading up to Nova Scotia, but I made a wrong turn, and I don't know what I was doing, but anyway we wound up in this neighborhood, and every house had one of these jockeys in front of their homes. These little Black jockeys with big red lips and it started getting to me. Because the mentality, it's very prevalent. BET (Black Entertainment Television) is another example. I'm not going to say there aren't some programs on BET I would allow my son or little daughter to watch. But, there are some self-hate programs, such as many music videos where youth are using degrading terminology, they're degrading themselves, they're degrading women, they're getting caught up in the Eurocentric aspect of life, and getting away from what made them strong as a unit and enabled them to stand.

There had to be a strength and a unity within the Black community—the African American community—to survive slavery. It was one of the most treacherous periods of the United States. There had to be a network. But, one of the slickest things they've done—and I've read a lot of Malcolm [X]—one of the things he says is that they took the shackles off of our hands and our feet, and put them on our mind. You know, and that is so true because whenever you look at a video and you see a young woman, beautiful young Black woman, and she's scantily clad in clothes, and she's shaking everything at the same time, and he's hitting her bottom or whatever—that's self-hate. I also understand that *Vogue* and other magazines depict the White women, and put them on pedestals, and left women of color out. I understand that aspect, but you can't take one extreme and beat it down with another. We were left out, and so we started our own magazine, which is great. We now have women of color depicted in certain ways that are more positive. They're not invisible. So, for young people nowadays to just take that—[to take] what a lot of pioneers, African Americans, Native Americans, Spanish, and Asians have done and sacrificed for, and, in a lot of instances, died for, and to turn it into what we see on BET and MTV, is insulting. Not only is it insulting, but in a very different spectrum, I don't think [the networks] really understand it. And if they do understand it, that's even worse. If they understand—and despite their understanding and knowledge—they still do it, that means they're just going for the almighty dollar, and they will destroy their own people to do it.

[So, when discriminated against,] we are sitting there trying to figure out why do they personally pick on me, why me per say? I don't know. Maybe they're having a bad day that day, maybe they just want to, maybe they're feeling nasty, maybe they're feeling mean, or maybe they have low self-esteem. See you take, for example, the Irish, the Scottish, and the Italians, to start with. They were the down[trodden] of the European society, so the only way for them to feel free, they had to pick [on] somebody else. So, whom did they pick? It wasn't until slavery was enacted that they started to feel better. Because remember, when White people used slaves, first was the indentured servant and then slaves, but [at first] they were all White. This was when it first started in Europe, before it started to expand out. It wasn't until the dark-skinned individuals started coming in, that they were able to feel better about themselves. So now, they had to pick on somebody else. And don't forget the English [colonizers] at the time. But it's still prevalent right here. Because if you have ten people who are blonde and blue-eyed, and you see two White people with dark hair, if you were invisible, you'll see all those blonde people look at those people with dark hair differently. Why does TV portray a blonde-haired, blue-eyed White women like she's the queen of all women of the world? That's a ridiculous concept. She's so busy trying to look like people of color, she's so busy trying to be ethnic, she's so busy trying to find a way to look like women of color, dress like women of color, act like women of color, walk like women of color, talk like women of color; if the women of color just took a moment and just looked, that's like telling somebody their [suit is] ugly and the next day coming in with the same suit. Don't tell me my suit is ugly when you're trying to get my suit! You're [just] trying to beat me.

So, I'm sitting in the restaurant being treated poorly, trying to figure out why someone is having a bad day on me. I've come to understand more [about racism] by teaching myself and asking questions. I've come to understand what they're doing [in the marketplace]. I've come to understand that they're hired, so I haven't changed my shopping patterns—I've changed my thinking and mentality. The truth is that we need to study about who we are, first of all. That builds our self-esteem, our self-pride, and our inner peace. We need to study what's around us, and I'm not saying what's around us here—this man-made stuff. I'm talking about nature—I'm talking about Mother Nature and the spiritual things. And you [will] come to peace with yourself. That's a very powerful weapon. And then you study them, and you learn why they did it. First you have to realize they did it to themselves and they were only looking to push it off on somebody else. That's all—that's all they've done.

Sometimes I'm afraid—I'm terribly afraid, because we have very few options. We can be sucked into it, and we can become a person that hates themselves and anybody that looks like us, and that's like a keg of dynamite ready to explode. For example, there are a lot of policemen of color who go around harassing people and who are a lot more dangerous than the so-called White cops. [Again,] they're a lot more dangerous. So, that's very dangerous. And I'm not picking on the police like that; I'm just using that as an example. You could have anybody in a position of authority who behaves like that. You could have a teacher that is African American, Hispanic, Asian, that has grown up in a racist society but really hates themselves. And they weren't born like that, they didn't come out saying wow, I don't really like myself. That was made—and imagine a teacher like that, teaching children of color. That's scary. But they make them, and they purposely put them in these positions. So, racism against minorities is not limited to White people. In this country, when you have people of color like that, that person didn't do that to themselves. They had a point in time in their lives when they felt so low about what was happening around them, that something snapped and they tried to be something that they're not, and they want to knock everything else down.

PRIVILEGED

"Just Because I'm White Doesn't Mean It Does Not Matter" (Heather's Story)

Heather's story is one of recognizing white privilege and its significance in the consumer marketplace. At one point, as I reflected on Heather's story, I was reminded of a time that my teen son and I went out to dinner. A Caucasian woman sitting in the booth right in front of us was talking so loudly that I felt as if I was sitting at a table of six instead of a table of two. Uncensored, she was expressing her thoughts about Colin Kaepernick being "stupid" for taking a knee; how he should have "stayed standing" for the flag; how he should have "done only what he was getting paid for"; and most importantly, how "He should have kept his big mouth shut!" She was shouting, almost purposefully it seemed, in the direction of me and my precious seventeen-year-old Black prince's direction. She shouted loudly enough for us to clearly hear the racism dripping and oozing from her mouth as she was framing the issues in terms of disrespecting the flag, disrespecting the military, and people inappropriately doing so for no good reason or cause—and how dumb it is, and so on. I don't recall ever feeling that I had the privilege to sit in a public space, a restaurant no less, and just start spewing my views so loudly that I could disturb those around me. But this woman had no restraint. She said whatever she wanted, appeared to not care that she was sitting almost right in front of people of color doing this and that her voice was going in a straight-line of harassment right to our ears and the other customers sitting in that section (who appeared to all be White). She seemed to have no sensitivity to how an obvious woman of color and young man of color might feel as we tried to eat, hearing all her negative bashing of what some consider to be a very important social justice movement for many of the reasons pointed out in this book. She was certainly entitled to her opinion, but I did not have to pay to hear it while my son and I were having quality time together over a nice dinner. I was looking around for our waitress—in fact, any waitress—so that I could report the discomfort that her behavior was causing my son and me, but to no avail. She did not appear intoxicated as far as I could discern. What struck me most about this situation was the freedom or privilege she seemed to feel to be disruptive to other patrons. I would never feel as free to behave that way in a nice restaurant, or any restaurant for that matter. To behave that way would be risky—it could involve the police being called on me for creating a public disturbance, breach of peace, harassment, and so on. I did eventually respond, but I felt a great possible risk to my freedom for protesting her offensive behavior if someone were to code me as being the aggressor—or even if not. I sensed a great difference in the personal freedom that we each felt in the restaurant space. This next interview is about the differences in the freedom to err, the imbalances in the social privileges of whiteness that people of color tend to observe in marketplaces, and how one young woman makes sense of it all.

Heather is a twenty-one-year-old White woman and college senior from the most northern parts of New England. I was speaking about my book project on the campus of a small college, also in New England. When I finished, Heather approached me to tell me of an exchange she had had with her teenage brother, also White, after he *wasn't* arrested or otherwise officially processed in any manner when he was caught shoplifting in a department store and was addressed by police as a result. As she spoke to me about the situation, her hands shook a bit and she was visibly upset, as she expressed her frustration with his—at least at that time—not being able to understand that the handling of his shoplifting by the police was, in her opinion, a white privilege. I asked her if I could get an interview with her about this situation for my book, and she agreed. We set up a day and time for me to drive back up to her university to speak with her.

I met with Heather a few weeks later at one of the smaller libraries on the campus of her university. We sat at a large, heavy, wooden table with chairs that had straight backs and comfortable padded seats. In all honesty, the vintage look of the room looked like something my beloved grandmother would have enjoyed sitting in, and that, combined with the eager and sincere welcome of Heather, made me feel very comfortable. Heather seemed ready and equipped to speak of experiences in ways that illustrated that she was putting her education and critical thinking skills to good practical use—even within her own family.

In her interview, Heather tries to bring enlightenment to how disparities in the consumer marketplace is an issue that should concern everyone. By reflecting on the experience her brother had in the marketplace, she processes it through the lens of white privilege and acknowledgment of disparities in law enforcement. As Heather continues, she offers an earful in terms of what she feels people who identify as White can do to self-analyze and accept greater responsibility for fixing the structural inequities and day-to-day disparities that exist for people of color. Heather offers perspectives that the woman spouting insults at justice-seekers in the direction of my family's table needed to hear. Heather's story provides an example of the application of the understanding that unearned privilege plays in the consumer marketplace and beyond, and how often it is juxtaposed with the inequitable monitoring and adjudication of youth of color.

Heather tells her and her loved ones' story . . .

* * *

My brother is now seventeen and a junior in high school. The incident [involving him] happened when he was sixteen and in the tenth grade. We are from a relatively affluent neighborhood; it's majority White people, not much diversity. So that's my background. I was away at college when the incident actually occurred. I was talking to my mom on the phone, and she was just like, "Oh, we had something happen with your brother, and I don't think he'll be visiting this weekend." They were coming down to visit me that weekend at school, just to say hi. I ended up going home that weekend instead of my parents coming to visit me. My brother, my mom, and I were sitting on the couch, and she said, "Do you want to tell your sister what happened?" I thought it was something minor or stupid that he had done at school or with his friends or something. [But] he told me he had shoplifted. My first reaction was, "Why? Mom and Dad will buy you something if you need it, within reason." He was like, "I don't know, I just felt like it." I also found out that my parents had kind of gone through his things and found little things that he had stolen in those past few weeks—really little stupid things that he would not actually use or wear, like women's necklaces or little trinkets and things like that. These were things that were pretty easy to steal and slip in your pocket. When he told me the story about what had happened that weekend—he had gone to the mall with a friend, and they were in a store—I can't remember which one it was. He walked past the front of the store and had something in his pocket and the alarm went off. He started freaking out saying, "It wasn't me, I didn't steal anything!" And he hadn't even tried to leave the store yet [but the alarm went off]. The store associates asked to see what was in his pockets, and he was trying to steal a wallet. He had the wallet already, so they called the real cops, and they showed up and they talked to him. They asked him, "Where are your parents?" And he lied and said, "My parents are away for the weekend." Which, you should never lie to a cop! The cops said, "Well, I'll have to put you in juvie for the night until we can contact your parents." My brother was like, "Oh, no, I'm just kidding, they're at home." So [to reiterate,] he lied to the cops. Then they called my parents, and they said, "We have your son down here at the mall, and he's been shoplifting." And then the cop said, "Do you want me to put him in handcuffs, just to scare him?" And my dad said, "You know, no, that's okay, you don't have to." So, my parents showed up [to get him], and he went home with my parents with just a lecture from the cop. He's banned from the store for the rest of his life and from the mall area for a year, but that's all the punishment he received for shoplifting [an approximately] $40 item. When he told me this, I was angry with him because he doesn't need to be shoplifting. My parents can buy him what he wants or needs. If he needs a wallet, I'm sure my dad would have said, "Okay, we'll go get you a wallet." [My brother] said, "Oh, well, it was kind of a cry for help," and things like that. For me, I said to him, "This would have been much different if you weren't White. . . . You would not have had a cop asking your dad if it's okay to put you in cuffs, just to scare you. . . . You would have been put in cuffs and brought to juvie regardless of whether you parents were there. . . . You probably would have been much more uncomfortable in the situation, and they probably would have been much more physical with you, especially if it was [again] a White cop." I guess for him, that didn't register. He was like, "Well, I'm White, so it really doesn't matter does it?" And that was just really frustrating for me, because I think that as a young person growing up in the United States, he should be aware of what's going on outside of his bubble. So, for me, that was very frustrating, how he reacted to it, and also how the cop reacted. For a cop to call a parent and say, "Should I put him in cuffs just to scare him?" I think that's just definitely a sign of White privilege right there. If White people are noticing that there's an issue, then there really is quite an issue. I was aware of my brother's privilege after it happened, and then I think this just kind of reiterates why I was so angry after I found out my brother shoplifted.

When I said [to my brother], "This would have been different if you weren't White," and he was like, "Well, I am White, and so, nothing happened to me," he was definitely feeling uncomfortable when I said that to him. Being a teenager, I think he knew that it was wrong, and he knew that if he wasn't White it would be different, but I think he was kind of feeling a little defensive because I called him out on that. He [defensively responded], "Well, it doesn't matter, I'm White and nothing happened!" [It was] a little bit of sass back at me. I don't know if he meant it in an "I deserve that privilege" kind of way. I think it was just a "nothing happened, so why do you have to bring up race?!" kind of thing. . . . My brother is so young that all of his information is from social media—what Facebook and Twitter say about current events. And they don't talk about it in our high school—I went to the same high school—and as far as I know they still aren't talking about current events and racism in general any more than when I was there.

I first learned about racism in third grade, not because I went to a private school, but because my third-grade teacher there, she was Black. One day, she was like, "I'm going to read you slave narratives." Yes—in third grade! And she told us stories about being called racial slurs when she lived [down south] and feeling physically threatened and things like that. I learned that very early on—however old you are in third grade—and that really stuck with me for a really long time. As far as I know there weren't any repercussions for this brave teacher, and people seemed to really respect her. She also was married to a White man who also worked at the school, so I don't know if that changed how things [normally would have been].

Race [is something that] my family talks about. I definitely have had some frustrations with my father when we talk about race, especially when it comes to incarceration and the police brutality that has been happening recently. . . . I'm very open [with my dad], and he'll kind of like just joke back with, "Oh, you go to [a certain kind of higher education institution], so you are all open-minded." I think it's just that people don't like to be told that their views are wrong. . . . I think it's a lack of—not education necessarily—but just a lack of knowledge about the situation since we live in such a bubble. And since we live in such a bubble you don't have to actually go out and look for that information. You can just live in our town forever and pretend that everything is okay. . . . So, when we talk about race, it's never a very intense, long discussion. It's usually just we butt heads a little bit. . . . With my brother and my mom, my mom kind of stays out of it. I know she and I kind of share more similar views, especially because she is [an educator]. . . . She's seen racism at its finest I guess, for lack of better words, so she understands what's going on in our country. Whereas my Dad has never had to work with it, like head-on. I don't think [it's] what I know that he doesn't know, I think it's how we interpret it. [If I could really talk in-depth to my dad about what's really going on,] I would say to him, "Do you think that it's that they are committing more crimes, or are they being accused of committing more crimes because of the color of their skin?" I would say, "I know that you are an educated man, so I know you know that racism still exists." I don't know if he sees it in his workplace. I know that he has worked with people of color before, but I don't know if he's ever experienced [seeing] racism at work. So, I don't know, [I might say], "Think about do you know any one you have worked with at work, who seems to [have experienced anything] different than yourself?" I would just try to frame it in the context of his own life. I would kind of try to talk about scapegoating, and why [it happens]. I would not want to offend him, and pull out all of these facts and kind of shove it in his face. What I've learned best with my dad, personally, is planting the seed, and he'll think about it. So, I probably would say, "If a crime were to happen at the office, and you were working with an African American man, who do you think the police would talk to first?" "Neither of you committed the crime and both of your fingerprints are [at the scene or on the evidence], who do you think is going to get blamed?" I would kind of let that sit there, and he would probably be like, "Hmm, okay."

[When it comes to police brutality], the seeds I would plant in conversation with my dad would include asking, "When was the last time you've heard of a twelve-year-old White kid being shot because he had a nerf gun, or a bee-bee gun even?" "When's the last time you've heard of a twelve-year-old being shot ten times by the cops?" You only need to shoot someone one time, the right way, and you don't even need to shoot people if their hands are up; you don't shoot. I would say, "When was the last time you heard a story about a young, Black man being murdered by the cops and it didn't seem kind of sketchy?" "When was the last time that you didn't hear the cops say, 'Oh, they were holding something, or they reached into their car or their pocket, or they looked like they had a gun, or they ran away'?" I would just be like, "Why do you think that's happening—take a step back and look at it, the whole picture. . . . This isn't happening with all cops and to all races, it's happening to a very concentrated population, just look at the facts for this one. . . . Read the facts, read the articles, read what the cops have to say after the fact." For me, it's kind of like, how can you not see what's going on? But I would not want to say that to him. I would just be like, "Think about it from a more open perspective. . . . Do you really think these twelve-year-olds are really carrying guns?—Or maybe, why are they carrying guns?—Or, why are they running?" Because of what has happened to people in the past. Even if they put their hands up, there's no guarantee anymore. So, I would run, I would be out of there, it's just natural instinct, I guess. So, that's probably what I would say to him.

Honestly, I have lived in such a bubble that these things didn't really start coming to light to me until I started college, not because I wasn't aware of them, but because no one else was talking about them. And it just kind of seemed like news stories to me—it seemed so distant to me—just another thing you see on the news. . . . Obviously, I [already] knew that racism existed, but it didn't affect me. . . . I was in my small, 99.9 percent White town. . . . Nothing really sparked that seed that was planted in third grade. . . . And then I came to [the university]. . . . You know, everything you learn about racism in high school they say it's all "history." You learn about the Jim Crow laws, and you learn about civil rights. But then you don't really talk about it after that. You don't talk about what's going on [now]—and it's not [just] history. . . . Just because I'm White doesn't mean that it doesn't matter. . . . I wish that everyone could receive some kind of diversity training or exposure to diversity. For a lot of people who don't really think about race or their privilege, it is really due to a lack of exposure. I would want people to have that exposure in a positive way, positive experiences with people of color, rather than just hearing about it in the news. Some sort of universal diversity training, bringing it back to the history classes, teaching kids that racism doesn't stop with Martin Luther [King], it keeps going today. Civil rights is still a thing, and people are still not treated equally as much as we claim that everyone is equal. So, that would be the first thing, universal diversity training, if I could put it into one phrase. The second thing, I think it would help if authorities and all of the higher-ups weren't just White people, and if the media wasn't just White people. I know there are exceptions, but when you have all of these things happening, and it's mostly White cops, and it's mostly White reporters, you know they are just reporting, and I feel they don't have the experience. I know that people get emotional when they talk about it on the news, but if you are listening to a White person tell a story about something that happened to a Black kid, does that really do it justice? Maybe if there were just more people of color in law enforcement and working in jails, and reporting to the news, that would maybe kind of equal out the playing field, and maybe people would hear these stories from someone other than a White guy sitting behind a desk. And if police are working with other police of color, maybe if they pull up to a scene, and one of the cops is Black, maybe they aren't going to pull out their guns immediately, maybe they are going to think, "My partner is Black, so why should I just assume that this Black twelve-year-old is committing a crime?" Maybe that exposure, and more people of color in everything, [would help]. A third thing, that's tough, and I wish this was all possible. I guess a third thing would be education from the get-go, preschools having more books about and with more diverse families—and that's not just for race, that's for everything. And movies that are not so White-washed. Advertisements and everything, from when we are young, so that growing up in America you are not just seeing that the beautiful people or the smart people are the White people. The main characters of all your favorite Disney movies and of all your favorite books are all White. So, from the get-go, just exposing kids, because some of the things you learn when you are young, that sticks with you forever. That's similar to the first thing; it's okay to talk to young kids about these things and not shield them from reality. Of course, you wouldn't tell an eight-year-old that people are being shot, but maybe if they are given that opportunity to read different books and watch different movies in elementary school, then maybe when they grow up, they will question why all of this is happening.

[Thankfully], my brother is on the right path [now]. This past summer he did a food project, which is where a bunch of young adults from all over farm together for the whole summer. It was really his first time hanging out with Black people, and he instantly made friends. Something that this food project did was they talked about race. They talked to young adults about what's going on, and they had workshops weekly. One day he came home and he was so upset, and I asked [him] what's wrong. And he said, "today we did the privilege checklist, and I'm not unprivileged in any way. . . . I'm a White, cis-gender male, and I have everything!" He felt guilty, and then he was angry because he felt like people were judging him. He was like, "I shouldn't have to feel guilty because I'm not like gay and I'm not Black." That was very interesting, and I think it sparked something in him. I said to him, "How do you think people feel when they check-off that checklist and they're not privileged? . . . If you feel so upset, how do you think they feel?" At the end of the year there was a cookout, and they did all of these skits. I didn't get to go, but my dad said—my dad said this, which was awesome—he said, "You know, they did all of these skits about gender and race and prejudice and stereotypes . . ." And I think that it definitely changed the way that my brother thought. I don't know what they talked about out in the field, I don't know if they told him about experiences that they had. I doubt he told them about the shoplifting. But I think that was so helpful to him, and I'm jealous—I wish that I had gotten to do that, but I was too old. But I think they did a really good job with that, so I don't even really need to say anything to my brother. He's a year older now, and I think it's also a part of just being an adolescent, and that whole kind of "I'm more important than anyone else." I hope that as he gets older, whether or not he attends college, I hope that experience with the food project kind of sticks with him and that he thinks about that the next time he's confronted with the desire to shoplift, or when reading an article about it in the news, using that as a new context. I'm lucky enough that he went through that [food project] experience, and now is aware of his own privilege and how it relates to other people. Maybe he will think about what he can do to spread that knowledge to his other friends who are White.

PERTURBED

"I Am No Fan of Insurance Companies, Pure and Simple" (Vernon's Story)

Vernon is a fifty-seven-year-old, White remodeling contractor who has owned his own business for thirty-five years. Vernon shares his philosophies on insurance companies' systemic treatment of the disenfranchised. It is well documented that women and people of color maneuvering in the consumer marketplace pay more for homes, automobiles, and services than their male and White counterparts. It's also been demonstrated that the property values of Black homeowners are significantly less than those of their White counterparts living in comparable dwellings due to past inequitable banks' mortgage loan and redlining practices.[1] These past policies and practices have kept many people of color out of the family milestone of home ownership, which is the number one way that families accumulate generational wealth over time. People of color even pay more in loans and interest for less-valuable automobiles than White counterparts.[2] Therefore, the inequitable marketplace experience of people of color is inclusive of housing, banking, loans, traveling, and so on. So, while Vernon's story does not involve the store-shopping experience per se, it does involve a consumer marketplace experience on a larger shopping scale that potentially greatly impacts people of color and their ability to hold onto and accumulate wealth.

Vernon has noticed disparities in how homeowners' insurance companies treat his customers who live in poor and working-class communities, and it makes him very angry. Initially, I met Vernon at the home of an African

American friend who was having several rooms of her house remodeled due to a flood that occurred when a pipe burst in her home. When I arrived, she was upset about her insurance company trying to settle her claim for $5,000 less than what the contractor estimated the repairs would cost. And the contractor was responding by telling her of his own frustrations with the insurance companies when he is contracted in working-class communities like hers. He was telling her that he can pretty much predict when any insurance company will write a check right away for the full estimate, compared to when they will try to settle for thousands less—and he can predict it based on the socioeconomic profile of the community. Hearing of the systemic problem only made my friend more upset. Her voice was escalating, and his face was turning redder as they continued to commiserate. They both were fuming-mad (not with each other) as they grappled with what they both were experiencing at the hands of her insurance company. Either she was going to be out of $5,000 that she already didn't have or he was if he adjusted his estimate; one or both of them were going to have to make up the difference so that the job could get done correctly. Another alternative would be for Vernon to use cheaper materials and less-skilled workers, and he prided himself on not doing that. Any of these options would not be fair or equitable in comparison to what the contractor had observed and experienced with his wealthier clients. In his experience with the wealthy, the insurance companies write the check—boom—no questions asked. This is reminiscent of many banks' racist housing-loans practices and redlining that existed formally up until the 1970s, and informally perhaps even now.

While the two of them were expressing their frustration about all of this, I recalled that this same friend has a sister who also lived in a working-class neighborhood when she experienced a fire some years back. She had had quite a time fighting with her insurance company, even to the point of filing written complaints, to get them to minimally put her house back together to the standard that it was before the fire occurred. But she refused to back down, and she fought back at every opportunity to try to hold the insurance company accountable for restoring her home back to how it was—as an insurance company should. And they did. I recommended to my friend that she speak with her sister and get her advice for appealing her insurance company's proposed adjustment.

In terms of filing formal complaints, I myself had had an experience where I filed a complaint in order to get movement on an issue where I was not reaping the benefit of something for which I had paid. I shared this information with my friend, and explained how a medical professional had conducted a particular medical assessment for a member of my family, but would not send us the report in a timely fashion. After asking repeatedly for this much-needed report, I contacted the State Department of Health and filed a complaint. Within thirty days of filing that complaint, I was surprised to see that not only did I receive the report I needed, but I also received a total refund of my payment and a heartfelt written apology from the provider. The provider received sanctions from the state as well, because other complaints previously had been launched concerning this provider's services.

This knowledge helped encourage my friend to check into the appeal process for the adjustment that her insurance agent was offering her, which, again, was $5,000 less than the contractor's estimate. My friend did just that; she asked the adjuster for the name of the person within the insurance company to whom she could write an appeal. However, before she could get that info from him and write her appeal—that is, within hours—the adjuster magically came through at 100 percent of what the contractor had estimated. Not every family knows that there is a strategy to negotiating with insurance adjusters as well an appeal process. Seeing how quickly my friend was able to resolve this by just asking the question, I began to wonder how many people may be negatively impacted by insurance companies or other entities who have less sympathy for families in poor or working-class communities or who don't mind exploiting them. I also could not forget what the contractor had said about his being able to predict an insurance company's response by the location of the home. I asked my friend if she could ask her contractor if I could possibly interview him for my book. She did, and I was thrilled to learn that he was willing.

Upon meeting Vernon for the interview, he confirmed that the challenge for him is that, in his experience dealing with insurance companies, the least economically privileged of his customers are offered less support for their claims than the more economically privileged of his customers. However, somewhat to my surprise, Vernon wasn't able to connect his observations directly to racism per se—because, as he explained to me, the insurance companies do not use racially laden language in their explanations to him. However, he is able to connect his findings to occupation, socioeconomics, or neighborhood. Whatever the case, he acknowledges that even in this modern day, he perceives subjectivity in insurance companies' adjusting process that may negatively impact consumers, depending on the community in which they live. This has significant implications for working-class and poor people, whom Vernon does not realize, statistically and disproportionately, are Black and Brown people.

Nonetheless, Vernon passionately shares his concerns about the inequitable observations that are very familiar to him . . .

* * *

[The way that I got into this business], I call it an "Irish affliction," [aka] "lack o' bucks," that's why I didn't go to college. I tried to go to college, but I couldn't afford it. So, I had worked summers as a teenager for contractors, and my last full employment was with a [Black] commercial floor and window-cleaning services contractor. He was a great guy; we are still the best of friends although we don't talk that often anymore, but we love to catch up with each other. After one year of working for him I realized that I didn't want to be in the cleaning business; I really wanted to be in the remodeling business. I had more tools in my arsenal as far as carpentry and painting, and that's when I started my business. I was twenty-two years old when I started my business.

My [business's] adopted hometown is a very diverse community. I've had the privilege of working with Greeks, Jews, Gentiles, all different kinds of religious sects of Protestants, all minorities, Vietnamese, Cambodian, Jamaicans—who by the way don't consider themselves Black, they are Jamaicans, they are a nationality, and very proud—and very hard-working—people I might add. But my point is that I've had the opportunity to work with many, many people over the years, either as customers or as employees or as tenants. I mean, I can shoot the gamut just because of the diverse community that I [engage] in. I grew up in [a predominantly White part of a nearby New England state] so as an adult, I adopted this [more diverse] hometown—all adults do it. I don't live in that [more diverse] town, but I own property there, and my business is there, and that's where I started my business. I worked [there] and in other nearby towns. So I've seen a lot. [One thing] I've seen nine out of ten times is when I submit a claim for someone who is upper-middle class or upper class, no questions are asked [by the adjusters or insurance company]. It's only, "When can you start? The check is in the mail." There's no negotiating, only, "Thank you, we needed this information, thank you for helping us to piece this together." But whenever it's middle class or working class, I get beat up. And the homeowner is the one who gets caught in the gears, waiting and waiting for this and that and this and that, and it seems they always stretch things out.

I have to disclose that I am no fan of insurance companies, pure and simple. I'm to the point that my personal belief is that they are bigger than the government. In many cases they are bigger than small countries, as far as their financial power. When you are looking at this interview, you have to understand that my bias is against insurance in that regard because it warps capitalism. . . . The problem with insurance is, when they step in and say to a consumer, before they ever have a problem, we are going to solve your problem. [They say,] you pay us a premium, and if you ever have a problem, we'll take care of you. In theory, that sounds nice, warm, and fuzzy. I can sleep at night knowing that I've got insurance. Everybody wants insurance. Personally, I've got life insurance, I've got health insurance, I've got retirement insurance, I've got insurance up the wazoo. I'm not saying don't get them—but my point and issue is how, for lack of a better word, corrupt insurance companies can be. . . . This is not a jealousy issue—this is just an observation that their money is in the market, and churning in the market. Their money is making money. That's their business—I get that. I also understand that every nanosecond—right down to the nanosecond—that they can hold your money, the more money they can make off of it. So, where's the incentive for them to close [the loop]?

When it comes to homeowner's insurance, oh yeah, your insurance company is here for you, but they are going to try to dictate what it costs. Their incentive is to keep the cost down. I get that, in a perfect world, I'm sure they would like to have multiple bidders, so that they can keep cost down. But the dirty little secret about the insurance company is that they have their own preferred vendors. It's only at the corporate level that [particular vendors] negotiate prices. Once they come into the field and they send their guys, there's no negotiating. [The vendors are] just like, "Mr. and Mrs. Homeowner, you just sign here, and the check will come directly to us." . . . What I have seen though, is that the insurance company comes up with these so-called rates that are impossible for the contractors to meet—it's so low it's ridiculous. You would literally have to have people working for you that have no benefits—that you literally didn't have [registered] on the payroll—in order to meet some of these [rates] because it's just so unrealistic.

Over the years, I also have seen two types of [homeowner] policyholders out there. There's the upper-middle class to upper class, and then there's the middle class and working class. This has been a constant for me for thirty-five years—I have seen this over and over again for the most part—when I submit an insurance claim—[but] not always. I can think of one exception where we submitted a claim for a judge who was definitely upper class [and the claim was not completely supported]. For the most part [upper-class claims] are accepted by the insurance company. I give the same rates no matter where you are on the economic level—I don't base my rates on how much you can afford, I base my rates on what it costs me to make a living. These are my rates for everybody, it doesn't matter what color you are, it doesn't matter what ethnicity you are, what religion you are—those are my rates! And for the life of me, I get looked down upon by certain [insurance] adjusters who think that I'm just trying to steal from the insurance company. I can't get through to them that [I'm not]! Is my estimating subjective—yes, it's not completely objective. There is subjectivity in the estimating process, as there is in everything, but it's a minimal amount. I don't start by saying, "Oh, they've got lots of money, I'm gonna put the screws to them!" Morally, ethically, I'm not wired that way, personally. This is just me talking personally. I had an instance where I was absolutely dumbfounded, but it's an instance that has stood out in my mind as such a violation of ethics, in my opinion, for what it's worth. I actually had two claims on my desk at the same time with the same insurance company and the same adjuster. I just thought it was uncanny. One was for an officer in the [military]. Officers, in my world, are considered upper-middle class and upper class, depending on what they are [in position] and in terms of their years of service and compensation, and so on—[no less,] definitely white-collar. An enlisted man had a very similar claim. We're talking in the bigger scope of things—peanuts [in value]. Two claims, both were less than $5,000, [so] we're not talking big dollars here. Both submitted their claims to a certain insurance company, and it was ironic that they both fell on my desk at about the same time. One officer did not know the other, and the claims were for approximately the same amount of work. The officer's [claim]—approved! The enlisted man had to reach into his personal pocket because he wanted us to do the work. We impressed him as a company that did reputable work that he was willing to go above his deductible and reach into his own pocket for the extra thousand dollars that the insurance company shorted him. I begged him, "You really need to talk to these [insurance] guys, they really shouldn't be doing this to you." [He responded,] "I really want to get this done, I'm tired of fooling around, I don't want to wait for 'their guy' who can do it for this [their quoted] amount of money, and your reputation precedes itself, I want you[r company]." I shrugged my shoulders and said,

"Okay." I got paid my rate on both jobs, but it was just ironic to me. Yes, [these were both White men]. For me, my experiences about prejudices that I've seen in my lifetime have never ever—very little—has it been about racial [prejudice]. It's more been about economics, that's where I see people taken advantage of—is economics. Because they figure the lower you are on the economic scale, you're not as bright. . . . So, I've always seen it as an economic thing, for me, more so than racial. If you have a large racial population—and we do—have a large racial population that is undereducated for a variety of different reasons that I am not qualified to even comment on [but] I've observed. . . . The reason I say that I haven't seen racial discrimination [in my line of work] is because anyone I've ever dealt with, despite differences in estimates and stuff like that, never, ever, ever have I heard a racial slur; I've never heard, "Well this is the best they deserve . . ." I've never heard those terms, never—thirty-five years I've never heard that. [But still,] why do [my estimates] get challenged when it's not an upper-middle class or rich person? Why do those [upper-class] numbers not get challenged? It just boggles my mind!

I'm talking about the inequities that I've personally experienced. . . . The insurance company sees what they can get away with. I've talked to my competitors that only do insurance claims, and they've all told me the same thing. [They say,] "What we do is we simply start at a higher number that we know we can live with, and we negotiate in-between—they think they've beaten me up, but I know that I've gotten more than I really wanted to begin with, [and] everybody goes away happy." From a moralistic compass, I can't go there, I just can't. They ask me to come down on my prices, and I'm like, hold on a second—"Let me get all of my employees on the phone and find out who's willing to work this job for a dollar less an hour for the privilege of having this job." I'm never going to get a "yes" to that.

Another thing that galls me the most involves service; what we are offering is mostly service. . . . What they are trying to do, in my opinion, is they are trying to take a service-based industry and negotiate it for the lowest price. When they drive the price down, there's only one thing that [can] go, and that's quality! That has to go. Because now the boss has to come in and say, "I can't hire the good guys, I have to hire the mediocre guys." And what's the product you get? . . . A mediocre product! If you are willing to accept that—and I have yet to find a client willing to accept that, no matter where they are on the economic scale—that's out the door; everyone wants it done right! Can you blame them? I haven't yet had a homeowner come and say, "Slap some crap on the walls so that it looks nice . . ." Really? I don't think so! They don't exist—everybody wants it done right. It's nice when you get an adjuster who understands all of the moving parts and includes them. I've just witnessed over the years—and I keep coming back to it, and I'm going to stick to it—that it's just more about the working class/middle class, for whatever reason—maybe it just comes down to attorneys. . . . Because [insurance companies] may be afraid of the upper class and the very rich because [the wealthy's] attorneys can beat up [the insurance companies'] attorneys. [Then the question is,] "Are you sure you want to go this way?"

My point is, why does it have to be so hard? That's just my personal opinion. [And] the most vulnerable people are the ones who are impatient. I've said this for years: Emergency dollars outspend planned dollars three-to-one, any day of the week and twice on Sundays! Why? Because when it's an emergency we've got to get it done now. When people [haven't saved up for an emergency] or aren't patient, that's when a lot gets lost. I think that all of us in the marketplace are at a disadvantage when we don't know the ways of the market or a particular market. . . . And then what it comes down to is: Who in the market are you going to deal with? Are you going to deal with someone who is really fast at selling, [who will] size you up real quick, who is out to make a buck fast, fast, fast, fast? Or are you going to find a sales person who is an educator, who wants to educate you before you make a purchase so that they know that you will feel comfortable with what you are purchasing? They also will know that you decided because your arm wasn't twisted. Whatever I'm shopping for—whether it's a mattress, or it's car repairs, or it's a new vehicle, or a used vehicle, or a new dentist, I want to find the person who is going to educate me first before I purchase. That inspires confidence, and it also inspires me as a consumer to deal with someone who is not anxious to make a sale. If they are all about making a sale, you might have some bigger problems. I don't want to underwrite your problems. That's what I see in the marketplace, when you are impatient—and that can happen to anybody on all economic levels. . . .

Now, have I [ever] settled for less? Absolutely, I'll be the first to admit that as a contractor, if they said, "Would you do it for a thousand dollars less? Would you do it for five-hundred dollars less?" Sure, to settle a claim, absolutely! But when [the adjuster] comes back and says, "We're five-thousand dollars different, what can you do?" That's my number dude! I'm not cutting that number in half. I'd be giving the store away! I'd be doing a disservice to my employees! But if they come back at a little less—less than one percent or something like that, I just make less profit, but I've got a job. But I don't want to negotiate large gaps like that, and I can't get over the fact that my numbers get challenged in a certain neighborhood and not in others.

PROVOKED

"I Try to Go to Stores That Cause the Least Stress" (Yvette's Story)

Yvette's story is a reminder of a James Baldwin quote that says, "Anyone who has ever struggled with poverty knows how extremely expensive it is to be poor."[1] When it comes to food, unlike other items that we may buy, disproportionately poor people of color may not have as many alternatives for acquiring it. We can make a new dress or pants if we are able to sew. If not, we can live without them, or we can buy them in a thrift store or in an online auction. But food often we cannot—our options may be more limited, depending on our space, regional climate, and so on. Therefore, often there are limits to even growing our own food. Yvette's story is one of the ways that many stores position themselves in economically disenfranchised neighborhoods and communities of color. In the United States, especially a little more than a decade out of a recession, people from many socioeconomic backgrounds may suffer economically to one degree or another. However, because African Americans have an average individual net worth that is roughly one-tenth that of our White counterparts, we may feel the impact of this to at all socioeconomic statuses.[2] Because of North American genocide and enslavement, exploitive share-cropping practices, Jim Crow laws and practices, and discriminatory and exploitive marketing practices, Black and other people of color may be less likely to own homes rather than renting them. We also may live in communities with less access to competitively priced marketplaces, healthy foods and grocery stores, and preventative care medical facilities. We also are less likely to have stocks and bonds, or a reserve of saved funds for emergencies, private school, or college educations, down payments for a home, legal consultations, insurances of all kinds, and funerals. Thus, we may have observed situations where, for example, funerals have been delayed for weeks, months, or years due to finances while fundraising occurs, for example, through GoFundMe.

Yvette is an African American woman in her early fifties who runs a nonprofit community youth-development program in the southern United States, in a community that has seen its share of disenfranchisement over the generations. Although her town is bustling, like many towns, it also is fraught with divisions: racial, educational, and socioeconomic, with people of color living disproportionately among the poor. A poised, stately woman, Yvette wears her hair in a very natural, ethnic style that is simply beautiful. Her complexion is rich, with little indication of her years. Her demeanor is serious, but her smile also is warm when she shares it. On the day of her interview she was wearing a flowing cotton skirt, a matching T-shirt, and hiking sandals. I noticed her style right away because it's just the way that I like to dress. Upon meeting her, she seemed so much taller than I had envisioned her on the phone. We met for the interview at her office at the community youth-development program. The goal of her program is to help supplement, enrich, and guide the development of teen youth who hail from underserved communities in her area. Befitting, the nonprofit where her program is housed is named after an ancestral pillar of the community.

When I arrived at her office, Yvette came from behind her desk to greet me, and we both sat in chairs next to her desk and directly across from one another. Her office was bright and quaint, with lots of windows, and it felt comfortable and airy to me. She had warned me ahead of time that she would be on-call to her community, and therefore she might have to bring our interview to an early end if necessary and reschedule the remainder. I reassured her that that would be fine. Her work, her memory-telling, her ways of surviving, I thought might be the kind of stories that often go unheard in our society in favor of negative and inaccurate stereotypes of people of color, so I was willing to take a chance on getting whatever I could of her story. I observed her in her space as she got comfortable—she exuded natural—there was nothing commercial or fake about her it seemed. Her confidence, hair, nails, non-made-up face—everything just spoke "earth" from where I was sitting. I imagined what kind of role model she must be for the youth with whom she works, and I wished for such a program for the youth in my community.

Like some of our earlier interviewees, Yvette discussed the stress involved in being frequently monitored in stores, the game that she and other loved ones have made of the shopping-while-Black experience, as well as her desire to be able to one day shop for something other than just her bare necessities. Her story illustrates that there can be many competing complexities for the shopper of color—the racism of monitoring and inequities, historical and generational economics, transportation and access, health, and so on. These together combine to often make the shopping while Black and Brown marketplace experience a consistently very difficult one.

Yvette tells her story . . .

* * *

Although I was born and raised in a rural community, I would not say that I was born poor or perceived some kind of poverty. My family all owned property that had been passed down from my grandfather. I can't say I have much memory of shopping when I was younger. There weren't too many places to shop in such a rural area. There was a general store about five miles away to buy gas and eggs and canned foods and things. Going to the store was never easy. We had a car, but we didn't drive it too much except to go to church or to the store sometimes. About once a month we drove to the grocery store. I don't have a very vivid memory of shopping when I was younger, but I know there weren't many Blacks there [in shopping venues]. People who know me don't really know what my financial situation is or has been. My best friend missed part of my life and therefore doesn't know how hard it's been for me. I think that what I am doing is rewarding, and I enjoy doing it. I probably make my job look like it's not that hard, and I am probably the lowest paid. I have probably made one-third of what everyone makes. I wasn't raised poor, but I take what I have and do what I can with it. I have learned to take what little I have and to make the most of it. People are always asking, "How do you do that?" I can make a meal out of anything, even a can of beans. Maybe I still have aspirations, but I don't hope that I'll be rich. But I do still hope that I will make enough money, and have enough money, to get everything I need. The aspiration that I have is to maybe be able to get some of the things that I don't need.

Shopping for poor people is different than it is for people who don't have to worry about prices. My dream is to go to the grocery store and buy some healthy food and not have to worry about how much it costs. For example, recently tomatoes have been $2.49 per pound, but only the year before they were $1.49 per pound. Tomatoes are just one ingredient that goes into my salad. That is my healthy diet choice, but then, there are other things, for example, broccoli and spinach. Spinach is a medicine for a woman like me who is going through menopause. In short, you could end up using $10 just on salad, and that doesn't even include the rest of the meal. For the rest of the meal, often it's just not happening. The rest—I'm either not having it, or I am just trying to have it. So I just do without a lot. I don't even end up getting all of my vegetables. Especially for organic vegetables—those are expensive. Regular vegetables have all sorts of chemicals in them, which in return isn't good for you. Unless it's payday of course; then, I don't care what gets into my shopping cart. I think the grocery store is the biggest place I go when I get paid. I buy junk food that I usually don't get a chance to buy otherwise. Payday is the day when I can go out and get Chinese food, Jamaican food, and all that kind of thing. I try to buy enough items to last until the next payday.

I get paid every two weeks. There are certain foods and vitamins that I have to take. Vitamins are very expensive, and this has an economic impact on me. Because of finances, I can't take all of the vitamins that are necessary for me at this age. About a month ago, instead of four doses a day of a particular vitamin, I started taking only two doses a day so that I would not have to buy more. I have to cut back on that, but it's important that I get certain foods into my system to balance out the side effects of menopause. I, and other women who are taking a hormonally based treatment, find that menopause probably hurts the budget too. I try my best not to use medications to deal with menopausal symptoms. I try to get by with vitamins instead. I am one of those people who is overly cautious about it, but I don't think you should mess with Mother Nature too much. Menopause is a natural thing, it is a natural process that the body is going through, and you have to let the body do what it does or else something could happen, such as cancerous things. I also had some aches and pains once, and I went to a health center. They suggested surgery and some additional things, but I could not afford them. So, I just resorted to other things like meditation and diet. I was fortunate that it worked, and I did not have to have a surgery.

[Purchasing] clothing is a bit easier because I can go to stores that have reduced racks, and I can still find good quality clothes. The worst thing, however—other than not being able to eat healthy—is buying household appliances. I am lucky enough to have my own house, so I don't have the option of calling a landlord when things break; I have to figure out a way to fix it myself. When my fridge broke, I went to buy a refrigerator with cash because I have such terrible credit. Initially I had to use [portable chest] coolers to keep things cold, and that was tough. My washing machine also broke at around the same time. Making new purchases like that is probably what I dread the most. I don't really do that much shopping unless there's an urgency. Getting the appliances that I need is a sacrifice I have to make, which I do by putting one paycheck together with another paycheck in order to buy the cheapest appliances. My refrigerator was the first and only new appliance that I ever had, and I am fifty-two years old! I can't remember anything else that has come out of the box like that. Well, maybe something else—I bought a 13-inch television once, but it wasn't a major appliance like a refrigerator. My washing machine was secondhand, and I was really lucky that it lasted so long.

Credit is another thing that affects our shopping experiences. If you are like me, you are denied credit for anything you want to buy. I was in the shopping mall at Sears, and they were offering a credit card to their customers. They ran a check right there, and I was declined. When one paycheck doesn't go far enough to pay for bills, they begin to add up. One of my worst experiences that attributes to my bad credit is that I had a credit card from a store that was $300 in its limit. Well, I got behind in the payment, so not only was the $300 due, but the interest rate also piled up. The interest rate was ridiculous, so in a year's time that [$300] turned into $800, and then the $800 turned into $1,600. And then they offered to take care of it for a mere $1,200 instead of $1,600; however, I would have had to pay it within 30 days in order to clear my account. I have had two credit cards like that—one from my bank and the other from a department store. I believe that credit cards end up hurting poor people the most because of the interest rates. For example, I fund my grandson's account, and one time I opened it to check on it. I noticed that he was $42 in debt, so I called him to tell him, and he said that all he bought was a fruit juice drink. Well, he was already at $0, so he got charged $40 for overcharging his account by $2. So he got charged $42 for a drink. To offer another example, when my refrigerator and washing machine broke at the same time, I was able to go out and buy a refrigerator, but I had to rent a washer and dryer from [an appliance weekly rental store] for $40 to $50 a month. They told me at [the weekly rental store] that if I paid outright then it would cost $800, but if I went along with renting them and paying the monthly bills it would have ended up being $1,700. I had no choice but to rent these items. It was so horrible.

The [weekly rental store] truck ended up coming at 11 a.m. the day they told me it was due back, when they initially told me that I had until 5 p.m. I definitely didn't get my money's worth. Only poor people use those [weekly rental stores] anyway, and I definitely felt poor.

As far as my current shopping experiences, over in the area where I live now, they seem to single out Asians. They think all Asian people are Chinese, and they just follow them. I would say that the store is about 90 percent African American customers [and 10 percent Asians], so they are suspicious of and watch everyone, including me. I've also had suspicion [toward me] happen in stores where I wasn't quite sure if it was happening. The store personnel would move in the same direction I was, but I never knew what was really going on. But at this store, when you walk in the door—it is as if there is a sign posted saying you are being watched. They don't just stand there and watch you. Instead, sometimes they will walk around fixing things, or dust, or something like that. I'm sure it happens in other stores too, but it just doesn't stand out. I think as Black people we become numb to it. We can tell ourselves that it doesn't matter for so long that we lose feelings about it.

When my nephew and I go into the store to get things for his hair (he is always changing how he wants to wear his hair), we watch them watching us. It's like we almost make a game out of it. He has to get used to it because he used to resent it when he first realized that they were doing it. He used to say things like "Dang man, why are you watching me like that?" Now we just have to prepare ourselves for it. We just go in, get what we need, and get out.

I think we as a society of Black people have gotten so used to being discriminated against. I just try to go to stores that are not as hard to handle in terms of prices or where security would watch me. I try to go to stores that will cause the least amount of stress. It's hard to put my finger on the nature of the stress. However, the store around the corner, for example, doesn't seem to be as intense. They are White owners, and the prices are comparable to other places. But I prefer to shop with local and Black storeowners because it makes me feel better to shop and give them my money because I know they are working harder for their money. I know that my money is going to people who need it more, and therefore I want to support those local places. I do not think that most people from the Black community are thinking like this. For example, I was talking to a friend about how I was surprised that they are getting rid of a locally owned fresh fruit and vegetable market, and she just didn't understand why I was upset about it. We also had a hardware store down the street, but other big commercial places came in and just drove it right out. She and I were talking about that as well. She just said "Oh." There is also an issue when buying haircare products. When you go to the White stores, they are much more expensive than if you go, for example, to the Asian stores, because the Asian stores buy in bulk. The White stores buy individually, so in order to make a profit they have to charge more money. Our community is trying to keep locally owned businesses open, but then we have people telling us that we are antibusiness. That just isn't true. We want to keep our locally owned businesses open because they are less expensive and also are supporting our own people.

THINGS THAT PART IV'S STORIES CAN TEACH CONSUMERS AND MARKETERS

STRATEGIES CONSUMERS MIGHT CONSIDER TRYING

- Interviewees talk about what might be called "diplomatic confrontation," such as when an interviewee pulled out a $100 bill in protest of being suspected of stealing, or when I proclaimed "DEBIT!" when given only the option of cash or food stamps for paying for my and my children's snacks. Another example is when, in the previous section of this book, an interviewee demanded that the police accompany him to confront the clerk who called the police on him.
- This section and the previous sections have offered many strategies, depending on the situation, such as ignoring it (or not!); using humor; verbal or nonverbal protest; changing how you think about it; making greater efforts to support local and small businesses; in consultation with your medical professionals, considering homeopathic and natural remedies; likewise, considering appropriate do-it-yourself (DIY) projects using YouTube and other educational sites; changing shopping patterns or not; making a game of shopping; shopping online; evaluating whose problem it is—yours or theirs; engaging the community; seeking complaint or appeal processes; seeking legal, consumer, or civil liberties agencies counsel, and so on.
- If you have tried communicating your concerns to management, or have not felt safe to do so, and none of the other recommendations

seem suitable in the four parts of this book, you might also consider checking online for an appropriate office or agency for initiating a formal complaint process.

- Consider taking greater steps or measures to support minority-owned businesses, designers, and so on. Nonminority businesses, with diverse staff or products, that have found ways to be supportive of disenfranchised communities or at least have a welcoming climate for its array of customers and are supportive to the community also may be worthy of support. For example, articles are available online that encourage people of color and allies to support clothing designers that support us.[1] Similar lists may be available concerning other aspects of the marketplace.
- It might be worth asking some businesses or governmental agencies about their contractor bidding processes to see if they are attempting to include minority contractors in those processes. If not, that may be an issue worth complaining about, and it could also be worth finding providers who do attempt some equity in the structures of their businesses or agencies.
- If at all possible, you might work on developing your resourcefulness for not having to depend on exploitive marketers. Financial advisors such as Dave Ramsey offer free online advice and a free online radio show to help people from all walks develop their competencies for budgeting, stretching their money, investing, and building assets and wealth for the short- and long-term so that exploitive businesses cannot easily take advantage. For example, some of my closest friends and I have used Dave Ramsey's concept of "debt snowballing" for our personal budgeting, which is a method that is explained for free online. We all have found it extremely helpful for assisting us in decreasing our debt ratios. Many Black financial advisors also can be found by Googling the Association of African American Financial Advisors.
- One of the participants spoke of how her responses to unjust experiences in the marketplace created friction between her and her husband. These instances can end up impacting the entire family and community; therefore it is important to reach out for support, not only for oneself but also perhaps for your entire household. Even the community may need support working through what has happened. Some of the ripples of these instances have extended nationally and internationally and vicariously have impacted people across the world.
- It is important to not internalize racist notions of who we are, and for allies—or really everyone—to not participate in such perpetuation of

racism. When people of color begin to subconsciously or consciously embrace negative, inaccurate stereotypes and racist ideologies, it is called internalized racism.[2] The interviewees suggest that the consumer marketplace can pose a threat to how we perceive ourselves; therefore it is important that we realize the historical context in which the marketplace exists. This is important so that we do not allow the marketplace to negatively impact our self-concept or sense of self and self-worth. Self-care and reaching out for the support are crucial, as noted in each of these lists.

- Minority participation in profit and nonprofit boards, regulating agencies, and the political ranks of law and government are greatly needed. Such participation is encouraged so that structural changes can be developed within the executive branches to make the marketplace more equitable for all participants of it.
- Reviewing the lists at the end of the previous parts may be helpful.

STRATEGIES MARKETERS MIGHT CONSIDER TRYING

- In addition to not stereotyping customers, consumers, and potential clients, it also is important to take consumers' of color and allies' complaints involving racism, bias, and harassment very seriously—just as seriously as you would take complaints of spoiled food, broken glass, or of any other consumer.
- It is helpful to have contact persons among your personnel and appropriate protocol for responding to and dealing with complaints of bias.
- Even small disparities in treatment, such as asking for food stamps versus coupons, cash, and so on, may inspire consumer anxiety, anger, and negative opinions about your store, services, or other consumer marketplace.
- Be aware that participant interviews suggest that, while many customers have the desire to be able to one day shop for more than the bare necessities, it does not mean that they want to steal what they cannot buy.
- Historically, not only have people of color dealt with economic and consumer marketplace disparities but also with exploitive consumer practices (e.g., high credit rates and rent-a-centers). Therefore, if people of color have any awareness of this (which increasingly we do), we may be very sensitive to unfairness and exploitation in the consumer marketplace, and it can engender negative feeling and distrust against your business and business practices.

- Some stores, designers, and other marketplace entities have developed diversity or equity advisory boards, councils, and so on, or have taken great measures to diversify their boards, administrations, and workforces in order to get regular input from people of color with regard to practices and policies. This is to ensure that their policies and procedures are equitable, nonexploitive, nonstereotypical, and so on.
- Businesses and corporations should keep records of bias-related complaints in order to weekly, monthly, or annually assess and identify the nature of problems that are occurring so that they can deal with them swiftly and proactively (e.g., provide training and discipline).
- Post in visible locations a climate statement and how and where concerns and complaints can be filed.[3]
- Get connected in mutually beneficial ways with the community with which your business is engaged. Further, give back to the community by supporting educational and cultural programs that will mutually benefit the local disenfranchised communities and beyond.
- Regularly revisit and revise your hiring, mentoring, employee, family, business policy, and customer support practices as needed in order to make them more equitable.
- You might examine the reading resources and suggestions at the end of the other parts of this book.

REFLECTION QUESTIONS AND RELATED READINGS

1. What parallels and differences do you see between experiences of people of color in consumer marketplaces and experiences in other major realms of society? What parallels or differences do you see between experiences of people of color in the historical consumer marketplace and the contemporary consumer marketplace?
2. List in order, by the power that they hold in society, who you believe or feel should be held accountable for inequities in policy or practice and disparities in traumas that occur in the consumer marketplace?
3. Many interviewees in this book assert that self-reflection or examination of oneself and one's own behavior is an important part of understanding anything involving culture, diversity, disparities, and so on. Do you agree with that, and why or why not? Do the stories in this book support the notion that self-reflection is important? If so, can you point to some specific examples from inside or outside of this book?
4. What could the stores or businesses in this book have done differently? What could the consumers have done, if anything, beyond what they already did to address the situations?
5. Where do you stand with all that you have heard? Where are you in the grand scheme of things you are learning? To what in society and your personal experience do you attribute where you stand or where you would like to stand?
6. You've read this book. Now what? What are your next steps?

RELATED READINGS

Gabbidon, S., and G. Higgins. *Shopping While Black: Consumer Racial Profiling in America*. New York: Routledge, 2020.

Rankine, C. "The Condition of Black Life Is One of Mourning." *New York Times*, Jun. 22, 2015. https://www.nytimes.com/2015/06/22/magazine/the-condition-of-black-life-is-one-of-mourning.html.

V

CONCLUSION

As an act of resistance, $20 bills were popping up across the nation stamped with Harriet Tubman's image in response to the Trump Administration nixing the production of the Harriet Tubman $20 bill.

Photo by Teala Elise Avery

POEM 8

Shopping While Black

Frances Shani Parker

Shopping in a navy suit,
my school principal attire,
I notice a white woman
approach me like a Cadillac,
then hit me sincerely
with these crashing words:
"I'm so glad to see you!
Would you or your friends
be interested in some
extra hours of maid work?"

Some people wake up and change.
Others just roll over.

CONCLUSION

The memory-tellers and other contributors of this book—whom I consider to be the collective heroes of this book—reveal that people of color and allies are not in any way, shape, or form, passive consumers and observers, whether dealing with minor inconveniences, daily hassles, or life-altering traumas. These amazing memory-tellers use their own humor, resistance, justice-seeking, trauma, exclusion, pain, monitoring, economic struggles, shopping practices, creative responses, and hope for the future to give us just a taste or a profile of what shopping *looks and feels like* for people of color. Thus, the many stories and poems of this book illustrate that oftentimes people of color don't feel welcomed—except (even as an acquaintance once said) "except welcomed to spend our money!" But often we can't do even that in peace. We would desire to be able to spend our money for the essentials of life without some discriminatory or traumatizing incident to remind us that we still have not reached social equity. People of color know what is going on, and we try to fight inequity in a variety of ways—some more conventionally than others. Some pick battles carefully, some confront, some boycott, some use humor in confronting, some call on widespread resources, some write complaints, some try to bring lawsuits—resistance has come in many different forms, even if it's just avoiding the marketplace as much as possible (thus, likely less money spent or more spent online). Their stories reveal every stage of Elisabeth Kübler-Ross's model of adjusting to significant loss, from denial to anger to bargaining to depression to acceptance, and everything in between, as people of color and allies try to cope with what a manmade "race" brings to our daily lives and the structures that hold us.[1]

As I reflect on the current state of affairs when it comes to the process of retail racism or shopping while Black, I am reminded of observations that give me hope. For example, I have a millennial African American relative who is still in her twenties. I have a lot of admiration for how she chooses to spend or not spend her money, be it concerning which stores to patronize (or not) or in terms of other aspects of the consumer marketplace. There are particular stores at which she refuses to shop because of the racist policies and practices those stores have. But then again, she has the transportation, time, and resources for shopping selectively, whereas not everyone does. But when and where people of color and allies can, we often do take a stand. For example, my young relative reported to me that she personally observed that one store at which she used to shop employed a locked, glass showcase to store their section of Black haircare and grooming products, while the mainstream haircare and grooming products were not stored in locked, glass showcases. Once she saw that, she expressed her concerns to the management of the store, and she found other places to shop that would not subject her to such inequities. Similarly, Walmart had a public-relations challenge on their hands, as they were being sued by a California woman, Essie Grundy, for this exact same thing.[2] With African Americans having a minimum of $1.2 trillion of annual buying power but only one-tenth of the individual net value of our White counterparts, if every Black person or ally shopped or otherwise engaged in the marketplace this way, by refusing to buy from vendors that do not appropriately respect shoppers of color, we would have every marketplace's attention. My young relative, like many people, realizes that disenfranchised shoppers of color are being financially compromised on retail purchases, check-cashing and other banking, credit cards, mortgage loans and home ownership, home values, automobile loans, and our ability to comfortably retire—if we can retire at all. Our resources are compromised before we are even born—before our ancestors were born—making it significantly more difficulty for us to competitively educate our children and to have the widespread ability to save for emergencies and financially protect ourselves even in a consumer marketplace that we disproportionately support. Our resources and wealth have been compromised for four-hundred years, and even longer in the case of Indigenous people. Here we are, not just in a new century, but in a new millennium, and still the average net value of the average African American is one-tenth of our White counterparts, in spite of the fact that the enslavement of Africans built this nation. Even efforts to get just one piece of currency, the Harriet Tubman $20 bill in the year 2020, to recognize and remind us of the Africana blood, sweat, and tears that created the backbone of the U.S. economy, was thwarted.[3]

In terms of retail racism, those who are able can resist and demand equitable practices. If a good portion of people of color and allies were to more often take a financial stand in terms of what businesses to support when spending money, perhaps businesses would be clamoring throughout their organizations and industries to be sure that they are equitably adopting, changing, and adhering to policies of equity. Rosa Parks and communities of color and allies all over Montgomery, Alabama, used such strategies and changed the course of history. The grassroots community, as a whole, and especially the younger generations, are beginning to mobilize on this issue through the sharing of information through efforts such as #shoppingwhileblack on social media platforms. While these efforts are growing, greater interest in this topic also is growing among scholars, newspapers and reporters, and other writers and media outlets. For example, ABC's "What Would You Do?" among other network and cable outlets have devoted episodes to this topic. To reduce marketplace racial profiling and other such inequities, Shaun Gabbidon suggests:

> "Requir[ing] clerks and security personnel to receive education on the perils of racial profiling"; 2) "Encourag[ing] victims of profiling to sue retailers who engage in these practices"; 3) "Work[ing] with civil rights groups to organize boycotts"; 4) "Urging federal officials to increase current levels of funding to study and remedy these discriminatory practices."[4]

What is particularly wonderful about Gabbidon's list is that it offers suggestions at every level of the social system from the most intimate and immediate, out to the larger surrounding circles of social life, such as governmental legislation and Resourceful lists also are offered by other scholars.[5] The nineteen stories presented here offer parts and strands of these strategies, and the end of each part of this book offers long lists of such strategies for both consumers and marketers.

For each of the many memories told in this book, there are thousands of other stories from consumers that are far worse. Undoubtedly, there are stories that range the full gamut of much worse and also less harmless than the many told here, and everything all along that range. However, the memories shared here offer a provocative start. This book attempts to be a starting point for anyone interested to hear a sampling of the real-life experiences, emotions, and resources of consumers of color. But it also is a call to action in its many recommendations that the memory-sharers, recommended readings, and resource lists offer, both for consumers and marketers, to resist the patterns traditionally so strongly engrained in our marketplace.

For those who might think they already know everything they need to know about diversity and equity, I would like to share the following. One of the things that I reinforce with my students is that when it comes to understanding multicultural and diversity issues, I find it helpful to not let ourselves think that we "have arrived." I encourage not letting ourselves think that just because we have taken that class, attended that workshop, or read that particular book that we are now "woke."[6] I see the journey of understanding our own selves, and others, as well as the structures that have and still impact all of us, as a lifelong one. And just as importantly, the moment that we think that we "have arrived" is the moment that we potentially become a danger to those with whom we interact, especially if we might have power and privilege on our side for creating and executing policies. Further, I warn them that making ourselves believe that we are "colorblind" is also likely to make us a danger to others as well, because it disables us from the ability to see and examine our own biases.[7] Having said that, consumers, marketers, clinicians, including medical professionals and therapists, and research scholars need to include the impact of marketplace racism, trauma, and so on, when considering what is inequitably burdening people of color, making us sick, and killing us. Marketers should make this issue a top priority for improving customer relations—not for higher sales, but because, morally and ethically, it's the right thing to do.

Does everyone matter in the consumer marketplace? Do Black and Brown bodies and other disenfranchised groups matter in the consumer marketplace? These are questions for every corporation, every business establishment, every staff member, every security person, every law-enforcement officer, every educator, and for the United States and the world. This is the crux of the matter, equitable respect of Black and Brown bodies, as well as other disenfranchised groups, and not just related to advertising, but related to customer service, and in the ethical impact of every aspect of one's business or corporation. Even if a person steals, is their life not worth more than a $4 bracelet,[8] an energy drink,[9] a soda,[10] a beer,[11] or a cake?[12] Some officials realize that those who are hungry—of all backgrounds—matter, and may go as far as to buy or otherwise provide food for people apparently stealing it for survival, or at least direct them to resources to help meet their individual needs. For example, some law-enforcement officers, restaurants, and other establishments make it their policy to avoid arresting the hungry and instead bond with and give back to communities by providing food at least once a month, if not more frequently.[13] On systemic levels, governmental structures are asking why, for example, people in their communities have the need to steal food and how those needs can be more appropriately addressed on a structural level, with, for example, jobs and education.

In all, these stories and spoken-word/poems, and hundreds of recent news accounts, confirm that Black and Brown bodies and other people of color should matter, and should have long ago. The time is hundreds of years overdue within the marketplace, just as in all aspects of Black and Brown life. Black and Brown bodies and other disenfranchised bodies need to be safe, valued, and protected, just as much as anyone else in this world.

The spoken-word/poetry in this book reveals the perception of even our youth concerning the objectification, oversexualizing, pornification, harassment, and even desecration of Black girls', boys', men's, and women's bodies, even in death, in the marketplace. So, what about life? The poetry also reveals the assumption of Black and Brown bodies as dangerous, lethal, needing to be controlled and extinguished or needing to be exoticized and demeaned, which is nothing new to those living it who carry the generational memory of those horrors in our cultural "DNA."

Interestingly, most of the nineteen interviews occurred in the North and Midwest, the areas that are expected to be more liberal and tolerant, less racist. But the stories from the North seemed to be just as heartwrenching as the stories from the South. A warning for us not to forget how insidious racism, sexism, homophobia, and so on, are throughout the world. It also is clear that some of the participants had to deal not only with concerns for themselves but also with concerns for their children—an anxious concern for them as parents. Newspaper accounts also suggest that there are few places where marketplace racism does not reach, and anyone can be touched by its racism. This begs the question of what can be done to make the consumer marketplace a safe, wholesome place and experience for everyone. Marketers, security, law enforcement, management, and policymakers can begin by attending to the lists at the end of each of the sections of this book and by reading the recommended readings at the end of each of the sections as well. Those lists and readings are a starting point to following up, but they are not at all exhaustive. The rest is for marketers to figure out, hopefully with input, in collaboration, or by demand, with diverse consumer advisory panels, boards, or communities. Like my young relative shopping for haircare products has demonstrated for me: dignity, respect, health, and equity are the moral imperatives for which we can strive concerning the spending of the Black, Brown, and otherwise disenfranchised dollar, like any other dollar. Hopefully we can strive for nothing less.

POEM 9

In Her Image

Kenneth E. Watts

Please don't be offended but
I have worked really hard
to maintain my superiority.

I went as far as to capture
a generation of people
and labeled them inferior.

On their backs
they built my world
and I stood at the top
of the mountain
and called myself king.

Somehow you managed
to escape
my stronghold
and began to elevate
in all arenas.

I fought, I fight, I fear,
trampling on every sprout
and grain of guilt
that the land of America
brings forth.

How dare you motion that
your image be placed on
an article of wealth.
For it was that very image
that defied my enslavement
of you
and helped others escape
to freedom.

How great the risk
should the bank teller
hand me a twenty
and there you are,
the image of possibility,
the "Shaw Shank Redemption."

The humiliation felt when today's
KKK member picks up
his robe from the cleaners
and pays the cashier
with currency
with her face
staring at him.

Those things that were
out of sight and
out of mind
will be in every home,
every town,
every city,
every county,
every state,
EVERYWHERE!!!

Justice on hold . . .

NOTES

PREFACE

1. See, for example, P. Goff et al., "The Essence of Innocence: Consequences of Dehumanizing Black Children," *Journal of Personality and Social Psychology* 106, no. 4 (2014): 526–45.

2. M. Concepcion, "Police Release Report on Shoplifting Incident as Family Seeks $10M from Phoenix for Alleged Excessive Force," *12 News*, June 18, 2019, https://www.12news.com/article/news/local/valley/police-release-report-on-shoplifting-incident-as-family-seeks-10m-from-phoenix-for-alleged-excessive-force/75-73fd4494-9cfe-447b-8bdb-8f7f987c8c92.

INTRODUCTION

1. A. M. Harris, G. Harris, and J. Williams, "Courting Customers: Assessing Consumer Racial Profiling and Other Marketplace Discrimination," *Journal of Public Policy and Marketing* 24, no. 1 (2005): 163; See also G. Henderson, A. M. Hakstian, and J. Williams, *Consumer Equality: Race and the American Marketplace* (Santa Barbara, CA: Praeger, 2016).

2. C. Pittman, "'Shopping While Black': Black Consumers' Management of Racial Stigma and Racial Profiling in Retail Settings," *Journal of Consumer Culture* (2017): 1–20.

3. E. F. Davidson, "Shopping While Black: Perceptions of Discrimination in Retail Settings" (PhD diss., University of Tennessee, 2007); S. Gabbidon and G.

Higgins, *Shopping While Black: Consumer Racial Profiling in America* (New York: Routledge, 2020); S. Gabbidon and G. Higgins, "Consumer Racial Profiling and Perceived Victimization: A Phone Survey of Philadelphia Area Residents," *Springer Science and Business Media* 32 (2007): 1.

4. Gabbidon and Higgins, "Consumer Racial Profiling," 1–11.

5. G. Schreer, S. Smith, and K. Thomas, "'Shopping While Black': Examining Racial Discrimination in a Retail Setting," *Journal of Applied Social Psychology* 39 (2009): 1432.

6. Harris et al., "Courting Customers," 163.

7. G. D. Johnson et al., *Race in the Marketplace: Crossing Critical Boundaries* (New York: Palgrave MacMillan, 2019).

8. E. McGirt, "raceAhead: A New Nielsen Report Puts Black Buying Power at $1.2 Trillion," *Fortune*, Feb. 28, 2018, http://fortune.com/2018/02/28/raceahead-nielsen-report-black-buying-power/.

9. L. Carlozo, "Black Americans Donate to Make a Difference," *Reuters*, Feb. 23, 2012, https://www.reuters.com/article/us-usa-blacks-donors/black-americans-donate-to-make-a-difference-idUSTRE81M1WI20120223.

10. M. Baradaran, *The Color of Money: Black Banks and the Racial Wealth Gap* (Cambridge, MA: Belknap Press of Harvard, 2017); R. Weems, *Desegregating the Dollar: African American Consumerism in the 20th Century* (New York: New York University Press, 1998).

11. B. Chapman and L. Greene, "Outrage in Brooklyn Over '40 Ounce' Water Bottle that Looks Like Malt Liquor," *New York Daily News*, Mar. 6, 2019, https://www.nydailynews.com/new-york/brooklyn/ny-metro-forty-water-marketing-20190305-story.html; S. Chowdhry, "Michigan Mom Launches Petition to Remove Candy and Magazines from Meijer Checkout Aisles," *WXYZ Detroit*, Jan. 4, 2017, https://www.wxyz.com/news/michigan-mom-launches-petition-to-remove-candy-and-magazines-from-meijer-checkout-aisles; J. Ravitz, "Black and Hispanic Youth Are Targeted with Junk Food Ads, Research Shows," *CNN*, Jan. 15, 2019, https://www.cnn.com/2019/01/15/health/junk-food-ads-black-hispanic-youth/index.html.

12. Pittman, "'Shopping While Black.'"

13. Pittman, "'Shopping While Black.'"

14. J. Miller, "Couple Stopped by Police Files $4M Lawsuit against Costco," *WBALTV*, Nov. 8, 2018, https://www.wbaltv.com/article/couple-stopped-by-police-files-dollar4m-lawsuit-against-costco/24845419.

15. K. Harsha, "Class Assignment at Mall Takes a Dangerous Turn during Racist Incident," *Fox 31 Colorado News*, Nov. 9, 2018, https://kdvr.com/2018/11/09/class-assignment-at-mall-takes-a-dangerous-turn-during-racist-incident/.

16. J. Bennett, "Store Clerk Calls Cops on College Student for Being 'Arrogant & Black,'" *Ebony*, Aug. 9, 2018, https://www.ebony.com/news-views/store-clerk-calls-cops-on-college-student-for-being-arrogant-black.

17. L. Beck, "Woman Shot Dead by Walmart Security Guard on Suspicion of Shoplifting," Jezebel, Dec. 10, 2012, https://jezebel.com/5967072/woman-shot-dead-by-walmart-security-guard-on-suspicion-of-shoplifting.

18. N. Warikoo and M. Owen, "Death Angers Family: Brutality Alleged as Man Dies in Mall Scuffle with Guards," *Detroit Free Press*, June 24, 2000, https://crimeindetroit.com/documents/Death%20angers%20Family.pdf.

19. T. Wofford, "New Video Emerges of Police Shooting Kajieme Powell in St. Louis," *Newsweek*, Oct. 20, 2014, https://www.newsweek.com/new-video-police-shooting-2nd-man-st-louis-emerges-266041.

20. J. Bihm, "Say Her Name: LaTasha Harlins." *Los Angeles Sentinel*, May 3, 2017. https://lasentinel.net/say-her-name-latasha-harlins.html.

21. K. Bazzle, "Gas Station Owner Arrested After Killing Man Who Stole $36 Worth of Beer from Lakeland Store." *WFTS Tampa Bay*, Jul. 18, 2018. https://www.abcactionnews.com/news/region-polk/gas-station-owner-arrested-after-killing-man-who-stole-36-worth-of-beer-from-lakeland-store; Fox News, "Store Clerk Allegedly Killed Teen He Thought Stole a Beer," *New York Post*, April 2, 2018, https://nypost.com/2018/04/02/store-clerk-allegedly-killed-teen-he-thought-stole-a-beer/.

22. S. Nelson, "Homeless Man Killed by 'Stop n Shop' Employees for Allegedly Stealing Cake," *Atlanta Black Star*, Apr. 19, 2018, https://atlantablackstar.com/2018/04/19/homeless-man-killed-stop-n-shop-employees-allegedly-stealing-cake/.

23. B. Hutchinson, "'My Son Was Murdered,' Says Father of Man Mistakenly Shot by Police in Alabama Mall," *ABC News*, Dec. 3, 2018, https://abcnews.go.com/US/son-murdered-father-man-shot-police-alabama-mall/story?id=59574450.

24. C. Danner, "Everything We Know about the El Paso Walmart Massacre," *New York Intelligencer*, Aug. 7, 2019, http://nymag.com/intelligencer/2019/08/everything-we-know-about-the-el-paso-walmart-shooting.html.

25. B. Patterson, "That Racial Profiling Incident at Nordstrom Rack Apparently Wasn't a First," *Mother Jones*, May 9, 2018, https://www.motherjones.com/crime-justice/2018/05/racial-profiling-nordstrom-rack-apparently-wasnt-a-first/.

26. M. Harriot, "'White Caller Crime': The Worst Wypipo Police Calls of All Time," *The Root*, May 15, 2018, https://www.theroot.com/white-caller-crime-the-worst-wypipo-police-calls-of-1826023382.

27. See, for example, T. Gettys, "Eavesdropping White Woman Threatens to Call Cops on Black Woman: 'We're Going to Build this Wall,'" *Raw Story*, July 24, 2018, https://www.rawstory.com/2018/07/eavesdropping-white-woman-threatens-call-cops-black-woman-going-build-wall/.

28. T. Kenney, "Detroit Owner Apologizes for 'Despicable' Behavior after Spitting on Black Man during Dispute," *Atlanta Black Star*, Jul. 19, 2018, https://atlantablackstar.com/2018/07/19/detroit-store-owner-apologizes-for-despicable-behavior-after-spitting-on-black-man-during-dispute/.

29. M. Stevens, "CVS Fires 2 for Calling Police on Black Woman over Coupon," *New York Times*, July 16, 2018, https://www.nytimes.com/2018/07/16/business/cvs-coupon-manager-black-woman-police.html.

30. T. Jan and E. Dworkin, "A White Man Called Her Kids the N-word. Facebook Stopped Her from Sharing It," *Washington Post*, July 31, 2017, https://www.washingtonpost.com/business/economy/for-facebook-erasing-hate-speech-proves-a-daunting-challenge/2017/07/31/922d9bc6-6e3b-11e7-9c15-177740635e83_story.html?utm_term=.dbd7892de85e.

31. A. Branigin, "Exclusive: New Report Shows Gentrifiers Use Police to Terrorize Communities of Color—Without Even Calling 911," *The Root*, Jan. 8, 2019, https://www.theroot.com/exclusive-new-report-shows-gentrifiers-use-police-to-t-1831576262.

32. *USA Today*, "Joe's Crab Shack Apologizes for Using Photo of Lynching as Table Decor." *USA Today*, Mar. 11, 2016. https://www.usatoday.com/story/news/nation-now/2016/03/11/joes-crab-shack-lynching-photo-texas-hanging-table-decor/81633822/.

33. A. Randle and J. Robertson, "'This Is What Black People Have to Deal With.' Applebee's Admits to Racial Profiling," *Kansas City Star*, Feb. 12, 2018, https://www.kansascity.com/latest-news/article199781989.html.

34. See, for example, Branigin, "Exclusive"; B. Colangelo, "Cleveland-area Bahama Breeze Calls Police to Make Sure Black Sorority Members Pay Bill," *Cleveland Scene*, June 20, 2018, https://www.clevescene.com/scene-and-heard/archives/2018/06/20/cleveland-area-bahama-breeze-racially-profiles-black-sorority-and-calls-police-over-bill-dispute; D. Criss, "A Waitress Asked Some Black Teens to Prepay for Their Meal. A Fellow Diner Wasn't Having That," *CNN*, March 16, 2018, https://www.cnn.com/2018/03/15/us/maine-ihop-race-trnd/index.html; K. Morgan-Smith, "Police Called on 'Suspicious' Black Family Enjoying Meal at Subway," theGrio, Jul. 4, 2018, https://thegrio.com/2018/07/04/police-called-on-suspicious-black-family-enjoying-meal-at-subway/.

35. A. Kringen, "Oklahoma Restaurant Owners Says Doesn't Want 'F*ggot, Freak' Customers," *Oklahoma News 4*, Feb. 6, 2014, https://kfor.com/2014/02/06/graphic-language-enid-restaurant-owner-gets-heat-for-alleged-discrimination/.

36. M. Walsh, "Muslim Girls Harassed at Chicago-area Mexican Restaurant: 'If You Don't Like This Country, Leave.'" Yahoo, Jun. 6, 2017. https://www.yahoo.com/news/muslim-girls-harassed-chicago-area-mexican-restaurant-dont-like-country-leave-195929028.html.

37. B. Edwards, "White Man Who Yelled 'Shut Up, Slave!' at Black Man during Altercation at Chicago Starbucks Now Faces Hate Crime Charges," *The Root*, Sept. 13, 2017, https://www.theroot.com/white-man-who-yelled-shut-up-slave-at-black-man-durin-1806113872.

38. B. Sanders, "I 'Don't Like Serving Blacks': Olive Garden Awards Comedian $6,000 After Server Comment," Black America Web, Dec. 4, 2016, https://blackamericaweb.com/2016/12/05/i-dont-like-serving-blacks-olive-garden-awards-comedian-6000-after-server-comment/.

39. P. Martinez and J. Carissimo, "Waffle House Shooting Victims ID'd as Worker, Star Athlete, Music Artist," *CBS News*, Apr. 22, 2018, https://www.cbsnews.com/news/waffle-house-shooting-victims-identified-today-2018-04-22/.

40. B. Telusma, "After Police Brutally Arrest Chikesia Clemons at Waffle House Where Is the Outrage for Black Women?" theGrio, April 24, 2018, https://thegrio.com/2018/04/24/wake-of-starbucks-white-fear-racial-profiling-where-is-the-outrage-for-black-women-chikesia-clemons/.

41. O. Jamal, "Eden Prairie Police Arrest Lloyd Johnson, 55, in Connection to McDonald's Gun Incident," *CBS Minnesota*, Nov. 21, 2018, https://minnesota.cbslocal.com/2018/11/21/man-pulls-gun-on-somali-teens-mcdonalds-eden-prairie/.

42. D. W. Sue, *Microaggressions in Everyday Life: Race, Gender, and Sexual Orientation* (Hoboken, NJ: Wiley Press, 2010).

43. G. Higgins and S. Gabbidon, "Perceptions of Consumer Racial Profiling and Negative Emotions: An Exploratory Study," *Criminal Justice and Behavior Online First* 36, no. 1 (2008): 77–88.

44. A. Bennett, K. Daddario, and R. P. Hill, "Shopping While Nonwhite: Racial Discrimination in the Marketplace," *Advances in Consumer Research* 42 (2014): 410; B. Cooper, *Eloquent Rage: A Black Feminist Discovers Her Superpower* (London: Picador Press, 2019); J. D. Williams, "African-Americans: Ethnic Roots, Cultural Diversity," in *Marketing and Consumer Identity in Multicultural America*, ed. M. C. Tharpe (Thousand Oaks, CA: Sage Publishing, 2001), 165–211.

45. C. Dunn, "Shopping While Black: America's Retailers Know They Have a Profiling Problem . . . Now What?" *International Business Times*, Dec. 15, 2015, http://www.ibtimes.com/shopping-while-black-americas-retailers-know-they-have-racial-profiling-problem-now-2222778; A. M. Harris, "Shopping While Black: Applying the Civil Rights Act of 1866 to Cases of Consumer Racial Profiling," *Human Services Today* (HST), 2004, http://www.uwosh.edu/hst/?p=208; Higgins and Gabbidon, "Perceptions of Consumer Racial Profiling."

46. J. Silverstein, "I Don't Feel Your Pain: A Failure of Empathy Perpetuates Racial Disparities," *Slate*, Jun. 27, 2013, http://www.slate.com/articles/health_and_science/science/2013/06/racial_empathy_gap_people_don_t_perceive_pain_in_other_races.html; S. Vedantam, "What Does Modern Prejudice Look Like?" NPR *Code Switch*, Apr. 22, http://www.npr.org/blogs/codeswitch/2013/04/22/177455764/What-Does-Modern-Prejudice-Look-Like?ft=3.

47. T. Cramer, "Nielsen Dives into the Digital Lives of Black Consumers," *EContent*, Sept. 26, 2018, http://www.econtentmag.com/Articles/News/News-Feature/Nielsen-Dives-into-the-Digital-Lives-of-Black-Consumers-127625.htm; S. Whiting, C. Campbell, and C. Pearson-McNeil, "Resilient, Receptive, and Relevant: The African American Consumer 2013 Report," Nielsen, 2013, https://www.iab.com/wp-content/uploads/2015/08/Nielsen-African-American-Consumer-Report-Sept-2013.pdf.

48. Whiting et al., "Resilient, Receptive, and Relevant."

49. J. Reingold and P. Wahba, "Where Have All the Shoppers Gone?" *Fortune*, Sept. 3, 2014, https://irving.fortune.com/2014/09/03/where-have-all-the-shoppers-gone/.

50. Dunn, "Shopping While Black."

51. L. Bayly, "Sears, Once the World's Biggest Retailer, Now Faces Bankruptcy," *NBC News*, Oct. 10, 2018, https://www.nbcnews.com/business/business-news/125-year-old-sears-file-bankruptcy-report-n918446.

52. N. Kristof, "When Whites Just Don't Get It," *New York Times*, Aug. 30, 2014, https://www.nytimes.com/2014/08/31/opinion/sunday/nicholas-kristof-after-ferguson-race-deserves-more-attention-not-less.html.

53. J. M. Lacko, S. M. McKernan, and M. Hastak, "Survey of Rent-to-Own Customers," Federal Trade Commission, April 2000, https://www.ftc.gov/reports/survey-rent-own-customers.

54. M. Corkery and J. Silver-Greenberg, "Prosecutors Scrutinize Minority Borrowers' Auto Loans," *New York Times*, Mar. 30, 2015, https://www.nytimes.com/2015/03/31/business/dealbook/prosecutors-scrutinize-minorities-auto-loans.html; Harris, "Shopping While Black."

55. L. Adelman et al., Race: *The Power of an Illusion*, Episode 3, "The House We Live In," PBS, 2003; A. Austin, "A Good Credit Score Did Not Protect Latino and Black Borrowers," Economic Policy Institute, Jan. 19, 2012, https://www.epi.org/publication/latino-black-borrowers-high-rate-subprime-mortgages; C. Ingraham, "A New Explanation for the Stubborn Persistence of the Racial Wealth Gap," *Washington Post*, Mar. 14, 2019, https://www.washingtonpost.com/us-policy/2019/03/14/new-explanation-stubborn-persistence-racial-wealth-gap/?noredirect=on&utm_term=.066bf14f6088.

56. Whiting et al., "Resilient, Receptive, and Relevant."

57. J. Feagin, *The White Racial Frame: Centuries of Framing and Counter-Framing* (New York: Routledge, 2013); S. M. Poole, S. Grier, K. Thomas, "Operationalizing Critical Race Theory in the Marketplace," *Journal of Public Policy and Marketing*, Dec. 14, 2020, https://doi.org/10.1177/0743915620964114.

58. J. Feagin, *The White Racial Frame*; Poole et al., "Operationalizing Critical Race Theory."

59. C. Lowndes, "The Guidebook that Helped Black Americans Travel during Segregation," Vox, March 15, 2018, https://www.vox.com/2018/3/15/17124620/green-book-black-americans-travel-segregation; D. Moodie-Mills, "The 'Green Book' Was a Travel Guide Just for Black Motorists," *NBC News*, Oct. 11, 2016, https://www.nbcnews.com/news/nbcblk/green-book-was-travel-guide-just-black-motorists-n649081.

60. See, for example, N. Cobb, "Where We Belong. Is There Room for African Americans Outdoors?" *Smile Politely*, Sept. 28, 2018, http://www.smilepolitely.com/opinion/where_we_belong_is_there_room_for_african_americans_outdoors/.

61. See, for example, I. Cummings, "NAACP Issues First-ever Travel Advisory for a State—and It's Missouri," *Kansas City Star*, Aug. 2, 2017, https://www.kansascity.com/news/local/article164851802.html; R. McLean and J. Disis,

"NAACP Warns Black Passengers about Traveling with American Airlines," *CNN Money*, Oct. 25, 2017, https://money.cnn.com/2017/10/25/news/companies/naacp-travel-advisory-american-airlines/index.html.

62. M. Cohen, "FBI Director Says White Supremacy Is a 'Persistent, Pervasive Threat' to the US," *CNN*, Apr. 4, 2019, https://www.cnn.com/2019/04/04/politics/fbi-director-wray-white-supremacy/index.html.

63. A. Picchi, "Shopping While Black: An Old Problem Under New Scrutiny." *CBS News*, May 30, 2018. https://www.cbsnews.com/news/shopping-while-black-an-old-problem-under-new-scrutiny/.

64. Kristof, "When Whites Just Don't Get It."

65. M. Alexander, *The New Jim Crow: Mass Incarceration in the Age of Colorblindness* (New York: The New Press, 2012); *13th*, directed by Ava DuVernay (2016; Sherman Oaks, CA: Kandoo Films), Netflix; Pew Center on the States, *One in One-Hundred: Behind Bars in America 2008*, Washington, DC: Pew Charitable Trusts, Feb. 2008, https://www.pewtrusts.org/-/media/legacy/uploadedfiles/pcs_assets/2008/one20in20100pdf.pdf.; S. K. Shelton, "Community Healing Network Aims to Counter 'Lie of Black Inferiority,'" *New Haven Register*, Mar. 30, 2013, https://www.nhregister.com/connecticut/article/Community-Healing-Network-aims-to-counter-lie-of-11388077.php; S. Sommers and P. Ellsworth, "Race in the Courtroom: Perceptions of Guilt and Dispositional Attributions," *Personality and Social Psychology Bulletin* 26, no. 11 (2000): 1367–79; B. Stevenson, *Just Mercy*, reprint ed. (New York: Random House, 2015).

66. Alexander, *The New Jim Crow*; DuVernay, *13th*; Sommers and Ellsworth, "Race in the Courtroom"; Stevenson, *Just Mercy*.

67. S. Deere, C. Raasch, and J. Kohler, "DOJ Finds Ferguson Targeted African Americans, Used Courts Mainly to Increase Revenue," *St. Louis Today*, Mar. 5, 2015, https://www.stltoday.com/news/local/crime-and-courts/doj-finds-ferguson-targeted-african-americans-used-courts-mainly-to/article_d561d303-1fe5-56b7-b4ca-3a5cc9a75c82.html; C. Rabin, J. Weaver, and D. Ovalle, "The Chief Wanted Perfect Stats, so Cops Were Told to Pin Crimes on Black People, Probe Found," *Miami Herald*, Jul. 12, 2018, https://www.miamiherald.com/news/local/crime/article213647764.html.; R. Robinson, "Locking Up Black People Is Big Business," *The Root*, Mar. 24, 2019, https://www.theroot.com/locking-up-black-people-is-big-business-1833524257.

68. E. Peralta, "Pa. Judge Sentenced to 28 Years in Massive Juvenile Justice Bribery Scandal," NPR, Aug. 11, 2011, https://www.npr.org/sections/thetwo-way/2011/08/11/139536686/pa-judge-sentenced-to-28-years-in-massive-juvenile-justice-bribery-scandal.

69. E. Seslowsky, "Bryan Stevenson Says 'Slavery Didn't End in 1865, It Just Evolved,'" *CNN*, Dec. 7, 2018, https://www.cnn.com/2018/12/07/politics/bryan-stevenson-axe-files/index.html.

70. Bennett et al., "Shopping While Nonwhite."

71. P. Goff, M. Jackson, B. Di Leone, C. Culotta, and N. DiTomasso, "The Essence of Innocence: Consequences of Dehumanizing Black Children," *Journal of*

Personality and Social Psychology 106, no. 4 (2014): 526–45, https://www.apa.org/pubs/journals/releases/psp-a0035663.pdf.

72. C. Woodyard, "Hate Group Count Hits 20-year High Amid Rise in White Supremacy, Report Says," *USA Today*, Feb. 20, 2019, https://www.usatoday.com/story/news/nation/2019/02/20/hate-groups-white-power-supremacists-southern-poverty-law-center/2918416002/.

73. R. DiAngelo, *White Fragility: Why It's So Hard for White People to Talk about Racism* (Boston: Beacon Press, 2018); L. O. Graham, "Lawrence Otis Graham: I Thought Privilege Would Protect My Kids from Racism. I Was Wrong," *Dallas Morning News*, Nov. 2014, http://www.dallasnews.com/opinion/commentary/2014/11/12/lawrence-otis-graham-i-thought-privilege-would-protect-my-kids-from-racism-i-was-wrong.

74. N. Roberts, "Dallas Police Shamed into Dropping Charges against Black Woman Beaten by Racist," *NewsOne*, Apr. 3, 2019, https://newsone.com/3850017/dallas-woman-charges-dropped/.

75. J. Feagin, "The Continuing Significance of Race: Antiblack Discrimination in Public Places," *American Sociological Review* 56 (1991): 101–16; Silverstein, "I Don't Feel Your Pain"; Sue, *Microaggressions in Everyday Life*.

76. C. Colen, Q. Li, and C. Reczek, "The Intergenerational Transmission of Discrimination: Children's Experiences of Unfair Treatment and Their Mothers' Health at Midlife," *Journal of Health and Social Behavior* 60, no. 4 (2020): 474–92, https://doi.org/10.1177/0022146519887347; T. Williams, "Research Shows Entire Black Communities Suffer Trauma After Police Shooting," *Yes!* Magazine, Aug. 3, 2018, https://www.yesmagazine.org/mental-health/research-shows-entire-black-communities-suffer-trauma-after-police-shootings-20180803.

77. M. Franco, "The Science of Why Black People Root for Everybody Black," *Psychology Today*, Aug. 22, 2019, https://www.psychologytoday.com/us/blog/platonic-love/201908/the-science-why-black-people-root-everybody-black.

78. Colen et al., "The Intergenerational Transmission of Discrimination"; Williams, "Research Shows Entire Black Communities Suffer."

79. Pittman, "'Shopping While Black.'"

80. Colen et al., "The Intergenerational Transmission of Discrimination"; Williams, "Research Shows Entire Black Communities Suffer."

81. Colen et al., "The Intergenerational Transmission of Discrimination"; Williams, "Research Shows Entire Black Communities Suffer."

82. Franco, "The Science of Why."

83. M. Santia, "Line-Cutting Mom Drags 81-Year-Old Woman to Ground by Her Hair for NYC 'Dumbo' Showing," *NBC*, Apr. 9, 2019, https://www.nbcnewyork.com/news/local/Mom-Drags-81-Year-Old-Woman-to-Ground-By-Her-Hair-While-Waiting-to-Watch-Dumbo-on-UWS-Police-508344811.html.

84. KCAL9, "Woman Charged with Attempted Murder After Beating 92-year-old with Brick," *CBS Los Angeles*, Jul. 12, 2018, https://losangeles.cbslocal

.com/2018/07/12/woman-charged-with-attempted-murder-after-allegedly-beating-92-year-old-with-brick/.

85. N. Dhaliwal, "Suspect in Custody After Viral Video Shows Elderly Woman Kicked in Face on New York City Subway," *ABC*, Mar. 23, 2019, https://abc7.com/suspect-in-custody-after-elderly-woman-kicked-on-subway/5213608/.

86. World Tourism Organization, "Global Report on LBGT Tourism: AM Reports, Volume 3," World Tourism Organization, 2012, https://www.e-unwto.org/doi/pdf/10.18111/9789284414581.

87. N. Krawczyk, "Out, But Still Not Always Equal, in Retail," *Convenience Store News*, Aug. 14, 2017, https://csnews.com/out-still-not-always-equal-retail; R. Winton, "Hate Crimes in L.A. Highest in 10 Years, with LGBTQ and African Americans Most Targeted," *LA Times*, Jan. 31, 2019, https://www.latimes.com/local/lanow/la-me-ln-hate-crime-la-big-cities-20190131-story.html.

88. C. Fiorini, "Mills Fleet Farm Apologizes for Denying Wheelchair to Disabled Man at Mason City Store," *Globe Gazette*, Apr. 26, 2017, https://globegazette.com/news/local/mills-fleet-farm-apologizes-for-denying-wheelchair-to-disabled-man/article_a460e8da-9bf3-5a5c-8a44-b34e82af7d69.html.

89. Feagin, *The White Racial Frame*; Poole et al., "Operationalizing Critical Race Theory."

90. See V. Newkirk, "The Language of White Supremacy," *The Atlantic*, Oct. 6, 2017, https://www.theatlantic.com/politics/archive/2017/10/the-language-of-white-supremacy/542148/; P. McIntosh, "White Privilege: Unpacking the Invisible Knapsack," Seed: The National Seed Project, 1989, https://www.racialequitytools.org/resourcefiles/mcintosh.pdf.

91. M. Harriot, "Cops Cuff Black Teen Riding with White Grandmother Because Someone Thought He Was Robbing Her," *The Root*, Sept. 6, 2018, https://www.theroot.com/cops-cuff-black-teen-riding-with-white-grandmother-beca-1828853245.

92. R. Martin, "Sybrina Fulton: 'George Zimmerman Has Trayvon's Innocent Blood on His Hands,'" Black America Web, Jul. 19, 2013, https://blackamericaweb.com/2013/07/19/sybrina-fulton-george-zimmerman-has-trayvons-innocent-blood-on-his-hands/.

93. R. Clarke and C. Lett, "What Happened When Michael Brown Met Officer Darren Wilson," CNN, Nov. 11, 2014, http://www.cnn.com/interactive/2014/08/us/ferguson-brown-timeline/.

94. C. Mathias, "He Filmed the Death of Eric Garner. Now He's Getting Ready to Spend 4 Years in Prison," *Huffington Post*, Sept. 2, 2016, http://www.huffingtonpost.com/entry/ramsey-orta-eric-garner_us_57a9edbde4b0aae2a5a15142; R. Sanchez, "Choke Hold by Cop Killed NY Man, Medical Examiner Says," *CNN*, Aug. 2, 2014, http://www.cnn.com/2014/08/01/justice/new-york-choke-hold-death/.

95. J. Hanna, M. Savidge, and J. Murgatroyd, "Video Shows Troops Shooting Unarmed Man, South Carolina Police Say," *CNN*, Sept. 26, 2014, https://www.cnn.com/2014/09/25/justice/south-carolina-trooper-shooting/.

96. T. Stelloh, "Ex-South Carolina Trooper Pleads Guilty After Shooting Unarmed Man," *NBC News*, Mar. 14, 2016, https://www.nbcnews.com/news/us-news/ex-south-carolina-trooper-pleads-guilty-after-shooting-unarmed-man-n538411.

97. J. Jordon, "Jordan Davis, Teen Shot Over Loud Music, Compared to Trayvon Martin," *Huffington Post*, Nov. 30, 2012, http://www.huffingtonpost.com/2012/11/30/jordan-davis-teen-loud-music-trayvon-martin_n_2217444.html.

98. N. Chittal, "Cops Shoot and Kill Man Holding Toy Gun in Wal-Mart," *MSNBC*, Aug. 9, 2014, http://www.msnbc.com/msnbc/cops-shoot-and-kill-man-holding-toy-gun-walmart.

99. J. Jacobs, "Florida Sheriff Cites 'Stand Your Ground' in Not Arresting Shooter in Parking Lot Killing," *WRAL*, Jul. 21, 2018, https://www.wral.com/florida-sheriff-cites-stand-your-ground-in-not-arresting-shooter-in-parking-lot-killing/17713189/.

100. Colen et al., "The Intergenerational Transmission of Discrimination"; Williams, "Research Shows Entire Black Communities Suffer."

101. Bihm, "Say Her Name."

102. R. Graham, "It's Not Just Starbucks: White Fear Is an American Problem," *Boston Globe*, Apr. 16, 2018, https://www.bostonglobe.com/opinion/2018/04/16/blackness-not-about-teachable-moments/V9PHArYOMb4Y71ydEZS4jL/story.html.

103. Y. Callahan, "#CookingOutWhileBlack: White Woman Calls Cops on Black People Cooking Out in Oakland, Calif., Park," *The Root*, May 10, 2018, https://www theroot.com/cookingoutwhileblack-white-woman-calls-cops-on-black-1825920347.

104. M. Dunlap, *Reaching Out to Children and Families: Students Model Effective Community Service* (Lanham, MD: Rowman & Littlefield, 2000).

105. See, for example, Henderson et al., *Consumer Equality*; Johnson et al., *Race in the Marketplace.*

106. D. W. Sue et al., "Racial Microaggressions in Everyday Life: Implications for Clinical Practice," *The American Psychologist* 62, no. 4 (2007): 271–86.

107. Feagin, "The Continuing Significance of Race."

108. C. Rankine, "The Condition of Black Life Is One of Mourning," *New York Times*, Jun. 22, 2015, https://www.nytimes.com/2015/06/22/magazine/the-condition-of-black-life-is-one-of-mourning.html.

109. Sue et al., "Racial Microaggressions in Everyday Life."

110. M. Dunlap, T. F. Shueh, C. Burrell, and P. J. Beaubrun, "Belief in Colorblindness and Perceptions of Minority Children During a Fictionalized Parent-Child Discipline Scene," *Journal of Ethnic and Cultural Diversity in Social Work* 27, no. 2 (2017): 193–213.

111. Higgins and Gabbidon, "Perceptions of Consumer Racial Profiling"; Sue, *Microaggressions in Everyday Life.*

112. N. Chavez and S. Lipp, "Smith College Student Who Was Racially Profiled While Eating Says the Incident Left Her So Shaken She Can't Sleep," *CNN*, Aug.

3, 2018, https://www.cnn.com/2018/08/03/us/smith-college-student-police-trnd/index.html.

PART I: INTRODUCTION

1. S. A. Crockett Jr., "Cover Charge Racism: 3 Black Lawyers Charged to Enter Club While Whites Enter for Free," *The Root*, Sept. 22, 2015, https://www.theroot.com/cover-charge-racism-3-black-lawyers-charged-to-enter-c-1790861178.

2. C. Santi, "Kansas Teen Says He Was Arrested for Sagging Pants at Movie Theater," *Ebony*, May 25, 2018, https://www.ebony.com/news-views/kansas-teen-arrested-sagging-pants-movie-theater.

3. J. Armstrong, "Lowe's Suspends Annoying Receipt-Checking Policy After West Philly Customer Complains," *Philadelpia Inquirer*, Jun. 13, 2018, https://www.inquirer.com/philly/columnists/jenice_armstrong/lowes-suspends-receipt-checking-policy-will-mega-jenice-armstrong-20180613.html.

4. J. Dalrymple, "Safeway Employees Call Police on a Black Woman Who Was Donating to a Homeless Man," *Buzzfeed News*, Aug. 1, 2018, https://www.buzzfeednews.com/article/jimdalrympleii/safeway-employees-called-police-on-a-black-woman-donating.

5. D. Westneat, "'Unwanted Subject': What Led a Kirkland Yogurt Shop to Call Police on a Black Man," *Seattle Times*, Nov. 16, 2018, https://www.seattletimes.com/seattle-news/unwanted-subject-what-led-a-kirkland-yogurt-shop-to-call-police-on-a-black-man/.

6. J. Johnson, "From Starbucks to Hashtags: We Need to Talk About Why White Americans Call the Police on Black People," *The Root*, Apr. 6, 2018, https://www.theroot.com/from-starbucks-to-hashtags-we-need-to-talk-about-why-w-1825284087.

7. S. Nelson, "Maine Supermarket Sends Police to Customer's Home for Questioning Store Policy," *Atlanta Black Star*, Jun. 23, 2018. https://atlantablackstar.com/2018/06/23/maine-supermarket-sends-police-to-customers-home-for-questioning-store-policy/.

8. T. Thornhill, "'It's Not Illegal to Be Black': Cops Complain Online about White People Getting 'Freaked Out' by Their Black Neighbors and Wasting Police Time with 911 Calls," *Daily Mail*, May 7, 2015, https://www.dailymail.co.uk/news/article-3071957/It-s-not-illegal-black-Cops-complain-online-white-people-getting-freaked-black-neighbors-wasting-police-time-911-calls.html.

9. M. Harriot, "'White Caller Crime': The Worst Wypipo Police Calls of All Time," *The Root*, May 15, 2018, https://www.theroot.com/white-caller-crime-the-worst-wypipo-police-calls-of-1826023382.

10. M. Alexander, *The New Jim Crow: Mass Incarceration in the Age of Colorblindness* (New York: The New Press, 2012); *13th*, directed by A. DuVernay (2016;

Sherman Oaks, CA: Kandoo Films), Netflix; W. Gilliam et al., "Do Early Educators' Implicit Biases Regarding Sex and Race Relate to Behavior Expectations and Recommendations of Preschool Expulsions and Suspensions?" Yale Child Study Center: A Research Brief, 2016; W. Schwartz, "School Practices for Equitable Discipline of African American Students," Eric Clearinghouse on Urban Education, 2001, https://www.ericdigests.org/2002-1/discipline.html.

11. Alexander, *The New Jim Crow*; *13th*, directed by A. DuVernay; C. Hartney and L. Vuong, "Created Equal: Racial and Ethnic Disparities in the US Criminal Justice System," Washington, DC: National Council on Crime and Delinquency, March 2009, http://www.nccdglobal.org/sites/default/files/publication_pdf/created-equal.pdf; B. Stevenson, *Just Mercy*, reprint ed. (New York: Random House, 2015).

12. P. Goff et al., "The Essence of Innocence: Consequences of Dehumanizing Black Children," *Journal of Personality and Social Psychology* 106, no. 4 (2014): 526–45, https://www.apa.org/pubs/journals/releases/psp-a0035663.pdf.

13. M. Pearson, "Tamir Rice Shooting: Cleveland to Pay $6 Million to Settle Family's Lawsuit," *CNN*, Apr. 25, 2016, https://www.cnn.com/2016/04/25/us/tamir-rice-settlement/.

14. Alexander, *The New Jim Crow*; *13th*, directed by A. DuVernay; Goff et al., "The Essence of Innocence."

15. W. Henderson, "Racial Profiling," The Leadership Conference on Civil & Human Rights, 2011, https://civilrights.org/resource/racial-profiling-henderson/.

16. Alexander, *The New Jim Crow*; *13th*, directed by A. DuVernay; E. King, "Black Men Get Longer Prison Sentences Than White Men for the Same Crime: Study," *ABC News*, Nov. 17, 2017, https://abcnews.go.com/Politics/black-men-sentenced-time-white-men-crime-study/story?id=51203491; Pew Center on the States, *One in One-Hundred: Behind Bars in America 2008*, Washington, DC: Pew Charitable Trusts, Feb. 2008, https://www.pewtrusts.org/-/media/legacy/uploaded-files/pcs_assets/2008/one20in20100pdf.pdf; S. Sommers and P. Ellsworth, "Race in the Courtroom: Perceptions of Guilt and Dispositional Attributions," *Personality and Social Psychology Bulletin* 26, no. 11 (2000): 1367–79; Stevenson, *Just Mercy*.

17. Gilliam et al., "Do Early Educators' Implicit Biases"; C. Turner, "Bias Isn't Just a Police Problem, It's a Preschool Problem," NPR Morning Edition, Sept. 28, 2016, https://www.npr.org/sections/ed/2016/09/28/495488716/bias-isnt-just-a-police-problem-its-a-preschool-problem.

18. M. Dunlap, T. F. Shueh, C. Burrell, and P. J. Beaubrun, "Belief in Colorblindness and Perceptions of Minority Children During a Fictionalized Parent-Child Discipline Scene," *Journal of Ethnic and Cultural Diversity in Social Work* 27, no. 2 (2017): 193–213; J. W. Schofield, "Causes and Consequences of the Colorblind Perspective," in *Prejudice, Discrimination, and Racism*, ed. J. F. Dovidio and S. L. Gaertner (Orlando, FL: Academic Press, 1986).

19. S. Evans, K. Bell, N. Burton, and L. Blount, *Black Women's Mental Health: Balancing Strength and Vulnerability* (New York: SUNY Press, 2017); A. Fichter,

"The Emotional Toll of Shopping While Black," Medium, Jun. 10, 2016, https://medium.com/the-establishment/the-emotional-toll-of-shopping-while-black-bcda5e51a7fd; C. Steele, *Whistling Vivaldi: And Other Clues to How Stereotypes Affect Us* (New York: W. W. Norton, 2010).

20. G. Henderson, A. M. Hakstian, and J. Williams, *Consumer Equality: Race and the American Marketplace* (Santa Barbara, CA: Praeger, 2016).

21. J. Kiertzner, "Michigan Woman Says She Was Profiled, Accused of Fraud While Shopping at Saks Fifth Avenue." *FOX4*, Dec. 22, 2017. https://www.fox4now.com/news/national/michigan-woman-says-she-was-profiled-accused-of-fraud-while-shopping-at-saks-fifth-avenue.

22. D. Stout, "3 Blacks Win $1 Million in Bauer Store Incident," *New York Times*, Oct. 10, 1997, http://www.nytimes.com/1997/10/10/us/3-blacks-win-1-million-in-bauer-store-incident.html.

23. Reuters, "Black Shoppers Sue Toys 'R' Us for Discrimination," *Reuters*, June 11, 2007, http://www.reuters.com/article/2007/07/11/us-toysrus-suit-idUSN1128989720070711.

24. Minnesota Department of Human Rights, "Case Spotlight: Two African American Customers Allege Racial Discrimination by Marshalls and Walgreens," Minnesota Department of Human Rights, 2012, https://www.reuters.com/article/us-toysrus-suit/black-shoppers-sue-toys-r-us-for-discrimination-idUSN1128989720070711.

25. J. Kopp, "Wet Seal to Pay 7.5m in Discrimination Lawsuit," *Fort Bragg Advocate-News*, May 10, 2013, http://www.advocate-news.com/ci_23215982/wet-seal-pay-7-5m-discrimination-lawsuit.

26. R. Laboni, "HBO Star Files Lawsuit Against NYPD, Macy's, Cites Racial Profiling," *CNN Justice*, Nov. 14, 2013, http://www.cnn.com/2013/11/13/justice/hbo-star-lawsuit/.

27. A. Siff, "Black Teen Cuffed, Put in Cell After $350 Purchase; Second Shopper Says She Was Harassed," *4 NBC New York*, Oct. 24, 2013, https://www.nbcnewyork.com/news/local/Black-Teenager-Lawsuit-Barneys-Belt-NYPD-Purchase-Detain-Fake-Identification-228915061.html.

28. K. Bhasin, "Barneys Pays $525,000 to Settle Allegations of Racial Profiling," *Huffington Post*, Aug. 11, 2014, https://www.huffingtonpost.com/2014/08/11/barneys-racial-profiling_n_5669129.html.

29. A. Green, "Shopping While Black Lawsuits Accuse Portland Area Retailers of Discrimination," *Oregonian*, Jun. 22, 2018, https://www.oregonlive.com/portland/2018/06/shopping_while_black_lawsuits.html.

30. A. Austin, "A Good Credit Score Did Not Protect Latino and Black Borrowers," Economic Policy Institute, Jan. 19, 2012, https://www.epi.org/publication/latino-black-borrowers-high-rate-subprime-mortgages/; L. O. Graham, "Lawrence Otis Graham: I Thought Privilege Would Protect My Kids from Racism. I Was Wrong," *Dallas Morning News,* Nov. 2014, http://www.dallasnews.com/opinion/commentary/2014/11/12/lawrence-otis-graham-i-thought-privilege-would-protect-my-kids-from-racism-i-was-wrong; T. Vega, "For Affluent Blacks, Wealth

Doesn't Stop Racial Profiling," *CNN Money*, Jul. 14, 2016, https://money.cnn.com/2016/07/14/news/economy/wealthy-blacks-racial-profiling/.

31. S. Boboltz, "Trevor Noah Describes Extreme Surrender Whenever He Is Stopped by Police," *Huffington Post*, Jun. 21, 2017, https://www.huffingtonpost.com/entry/trevor-noah-describes-extreme-surrender-whenever-he-is-stopped-by-police_us_594a64d5e4b0db570d37ea60.

32. M. Harriot, "Billionaire BET Founder Bob Johnson Wasn't Allowed to Check In at Florida Hotel," *The Root*, Sept. 4, 2018, https://www.theroot.com/billionaire-bet-founder-bob-johnson-wasnt-allowed-to-ch-1828798705.

33. Laboni, "HBO Star Files Lawsuit."

34. W. Shepard, "Former Canes Football Player Sues Bank for Alleged Racial Profiling," *NBC 6 South Florida*, Nov. 14, 2011, http://www.nbcmiami.com/news/sports/133842813.html.

35. D. Hamill, "From Oprah to Trayon Christian, It's Business as Usual to Racially Profile Blacks," *New York Daily News*, Oct. 23, 2013, http://www.nydailynews.com/new-york/hamill-business-usual-barneys-racially-profile-article-1.1494890.

36. Black Loop, "Gabourey Sidibe Reveals Discrimination at Chanel Boutique Store, 'I'll Buy This Whole Damn Store!'" Black Loop, May 11, 2017, https://www.theblackloop.com/gabourey-sidibe-reveals-discrimination-at-chanel-boutique-store-ill-buy-this-whole-damn-store/.

37. H. Vela, "Justice for Trayvon Rallies Held in D.C., Nationwide." *WJLA*, Jul. 20, 2013. https://wjla.com/news/nation-world/-justice-for-trayvon-rallies-set-for-100-cities-91635.

38. Vela, "Justice for Trayvon."

39. W. K. Bell, "W. Kamau Bell: I Know What It's Like to Get Kicked Out for Being Black," *CNN*, May 28, 2018, https://www.cnn.com/2018/04/16/opinions/philadelphia-starbucks-sounds-familiar-to-me-w-kamau-bell-opinion/index.html.

40. A. Haney, "Actresses Claim They Were Wrongfully Arrested after Using Atlanta Houston's Bathroom," 11Alive, May 23, 2018, https://www.11alive.com/article/news/actresses-claim-they-were-wrongfully-arrested-after-using-atlanta-houstons-bathroom/85-556851943.

41. L. Ferrigno, "Macy's Has First Black Santa, by Special Request," *CNN*, Dec. 24, 2013, https://www.cnn.com/2013/12/24/us/macys-black-santa/index.html.

42. *Daily Mail* Reporter, "'Santa Is White, This One Would Steal Presents': Racists Target Mall of America After They Employed Their First Ever Black Father Christmas," *Daily Mail*, Dec. 4, 2016, https://www.dailymail.co.uk/news/article-3999496/Racists-target-Minnesota-s-Mall-America-employed-black-Father-Christmas.html.

43. N. Manskar, "Mineola Man Says Garden City Cops Racially Profiled, Beat Him," *The Island Now*, Dec. 31, 2016, https://theislandnow.com/uncategorized/mineola-man-says-garden-city-cops-racially-profiled-beat-him/.

PART I: MISPERCEIVED

1. In accordance with informed consent, the names of those interviewed have been changed to pseudonyms, and other identifying information changed or removed, to protect their anonymity. The pseudonyms were derived from murder victims of the civil rights movement and the September 11, 2001, attacks, as well as the names of minority consumers, police- or neighbor-involved youth murder victims, #SayHerName victims, transgender victims, and White allies, who have been murdered.

PART I: THINGS THAT PART I'S STORIES CAN TEACH CONSUMERS AND MARKETERS

1. S. Evans, K. Bell, N. Burton, and L. Blount, *Black Women's Mental Health: Balancing Strength and Vulnerability* (New York: SUNY Press, 2017); A. Fichter, "The Emotional Toll of Shopping While Black," Medium, Jun. 10, 2016, https://medium.com/the-establishment/the-emotional-toll-of-shopping-while-black-bcda5e51a7fd; C. Steele, *Whistling Vivaldi: And Other Clues to How Stereotypes Affect Us* (New York: W.W. Norton, 2010).

2. See, for example, J. Disis, "Starbucks Will Close 8,000 US Stores May 29 for Racial-bias Training," *CNN*, Apr. 17, 2018, https://money.cnn.com/2018/04/17/news/companies/starbucks-store-closings-racial-bias-education/index.html; H. Knowles, "Black Man Trying to Propose to His Girlfriend Interrupted by Security Guard Accusing Him of Shoplifting," *Yahoo News*, Jul. 24, 2019, https://www.yahoo.com/news/black-man-trying-propose-girlfriend-072146612.html.

3. C. Turner, "Bias Isn't Just a Police Problem, It's a Preschool Problem," NPR Morning Edition, Sept. 28, 2016, https://www.npr.org/sections/ed/2016/09/28/495488716/bias-isnt-just-a-police-problem-its-a-preschool-problem.

PART II: INTRODUCTION

1. B. Hughes, "A Man Shouts Racial Slurs in a Seattle Starbucks. The Silence Is Deafening." KUOW, Aug. 6, 2017, http://archive.kuow.org/post/man-shouts-racial-slurs-seattle-starbucks-silence-deafening; I. Raftery, "9 Heartbreaking Responses to 'A Man Shouts Racial Slurs at a Seattle Starbucks,'" KUOW, Jun. 9, 2016, http://archive.kuow.org/post/9-heartbreaking-responses-man-shouts-racial-slurs-seattle-starbucks.

2. See, for example, T. Kenney, "Detroit Owner Apologizes for 'Despicable' Behavior after Spitting on Black Man during Dispute," *Atlanta Black Star*, Jul. 19, 2018, https://atlantablackstar.com/2018/07/19/detroit-store-owner-apologizes

-for-despicable-behavior-after-spitting-on-black-man-during-dispute/; R. Roley, "A White Businessman Spit in the Face of a Black Man Just Doing His Job," *USA Today*, Jul. 21, 2018, https://www.usatoday.com/story/opinion/nation-now/2018/07/21/detroit-mercantile-owner-spits-black-mans-face/799809002/; J. Washington, "Connecticut Woman Resigns after Using N-word, Spitting at Black Man," *Ebony*, Mar. 18, 2019, https://www.ebony.com/news/connecticut-woman-resigns-uses-n-word-spit/.

3. T. Kenney, "Study Suggests White People Are More Likely to Assault Black, Latino People Than the Other Way Around," *Atlanta Black Star*, Jun. 23, 2018, https://atlantablackstar.com/2018/06/23/study-suggests-white-people-are-more-likely-to-assault-black-latino-people-than-the-other-way-around/.

4. M. Eversley, "Reports: S.C. Restaurant Refused to Seat Black Patrons," *USA Today*, Aug. 27, 2013, http://www.usatoday.com/story/news/nation/2013/08/26/south-carolina-charleston-wild-wing-cafe-black-americans/2704125/.

5. S. Jilani, "My Racist Encounter at the White House Correspondents' Dinner," *Huffington Post*, May 7, 2013, http://www.huffingtonpost.com/seema-jilani/racism-white-house-correspondents-dinner_b_3231561.html.

6. P. Gast, "Plea Deal in Beating at Georgia Cracker Barrel," *CNN Justice*, Oct. 23, 2010, http://www.cnn.com/2010/CRIME/10/23/georgia.beating.plea.deal/.

7. C. Bessette, "Offensive Internet Connection in Norwichtown Upsets Residents," *The Day*, Nov. 23, 2016, https://www.theday.com/article/20161123/NWS01/161129626.

8. M. J. Feeney, "WiFi Signal with Racist, Anti-Semitic Slur in Teaneck, NJ Sparks Police Probe; Signal Came from Rec Center Router," *New York Daily News*, Jan. 18, 2012, http://www.nydailynews.com/news/national/wifi-signal-racist-anti-semitic-slur-teaneck-nj-sparks-police-probe-signal-rec-center-router-article-1.1008135.

9. P. Banerjee, "Racial Profiling at Airports Adds a Colour-coded Cost When I Fly on Business." *Globe and Mail*, Jul. 19, 2016. https://www.theglobeandmail.com/life/facts-and-arguments/flying-while-brown/article30979345/; Black Issues in Higher Education, "Racial Discrimination a Reality for Black Tourists, Researcher Finds," *Black Issues in Higher Education*, Oct. 25, 2001, https://diverseeducation.com/article/1709/.

10. Associated Press, "Man Charged with Slapping Toddler Now Out of Job," *KDVR*, Feb. 18, 2013, https://kdvr.com/2013/02/18/idaho-man-charged-with-slapping-toddler-on-plane/.

11. E. Margolin, "Black Female Doctor: Delta Discriminated, Barred Me from Sick Passenger," *NBC News*, Oct. 14, 2016, https://www.nbcnews.com/news/us-news/black-female-doctor-delta-discriminated-barred-me-sick-passenger-n666251.

12. M. Hunter, "Saggy Pants Lead to Passenger's Arrest," *CNN Travel*, Jun. 17, 2011, http://www.cnn.com/2011/TRAVEL/06/16/sagging.pants.flight.arrest/index.html.

13. Boston Globe, "Fliers See Bias as Pilots Move to Bump Them," *Boston Globe*, Nov. 11, 2001; E. Peralta, "Double-standard? US Airways Allows Man

Wearing Panties to Fly," NPR, Jun. 22, 2011, https://www.npr.org/sections/thetwo-way/2011/06/22/137348120/double-standard-us-airways-allows-man-wearing-panties-to-fly#:~:text=Double%20Standard%3F-,US%20Airways%20Allows%20Man%20Wearing%20Panties%20To%20Fly%20%3A%20The%20Two,because%20of%20his%20sagging%20pants.

14. C. Herreria, "2 Officers Fired, 2 Suspended for Violently Dragging Doctor Off United Flight," *Huffington Post*, Oct. 17, 2018, https://www.huffingtonpost.com/entry/chicago-aviation-officers-fired-united-airlines-dragging_us_59e680c7e4b00905bdad5775.

15. B. Cooper, "The N-word on the 4th of July: The Flight Home to See My Family for the Holiday Was a Tearful, Shameful Affair," *Salon*, Jul. 4, 2013, http://www.salon.com/2013/07/04/the_n_word_on_the_4th_of_july/.

16. BGLH (Black Girl with Long Hair), "TSA Officers Will No Longer Stop Black Women to Conduct Hair Searches in Airports," BGLH, Mar. 29, 2015, https://bglh-marketplace.com/2015/03/tsa-officers-will-no-longer-stop-black-women-to-conduct-hair-searches-in-the-airport/.

17. E. Knickmeyer, "California Wine Train Orders Off Black Women's Book Club," *ABC 6*, Aug. 25, 2015, https://6abc.com/news/calif-wine-train-orders-off-black-womens-book-club/956151/.

18. E. Donnelly, "Anne Hathaway Calls Out White Privilege in Passionate Post About 'Unspeakable' Murder of Nia Wilson," *Yahoo Lifestyle*, Jul. 26, 2018, https://www.yahoo.com/lifestyle/anne-hathaway-calls-white-privilege-passionate-post-unspeakable-murder-nia-wilson-104249741.html.

19. D. Mandani and D. Romero, "Retired Firefighter Found Guilty for Shooting at Lost Black Teen on Doorstep," *NBC News*, Oct. 12, 2018, https://www.nbcnews.com/news/us-news/retired-firefighter-found-guilty-shooting-lost-black-teen-doorstep-n919656; C. Sommerfeldt, "Georgia Woman Who Shot 15-year-old Boy Walking by Her House Claims She's Not 'an Evil Person,'" *New York Daily News*, Jan. 19, 2017, https://www.nydailynews.com/news/national/georgia-woman-shoots-15-year-old-boy-walking-house-article-1.2950044.

20. K. Mettler, "Four Black Teenagers Held at Gunpoint by White Woman While Fundraising for Football Team," *Yahoo News*, Aug. 16, 2019, https://www.yahoo.com/news/four-black-teenagers-held-gunpoint-141725967.html.

21. M. Whitaker, "Teens Arrested in NY While 'Waiting While Black' at Bus Stop," theGrio, Dec. 3, 2013, http://thegrio.com/2013/12/03/teens-arrested-in-ny-for-waiting-while-black-at-bus-stop/.

22. Raftery, "9 Heartbreaking Responses."

23. A. Luthern, "No Charges in Donte Hamilton Shooting; Edward Flynn Seeks External Review," *Journal Sentinel*, Nov. 11, 2015, http://archive.jsonline.com/news/milwaukee/dontre-hamiltons-family-to-meet-with-federal-officials-may-learn-of-charges-b99613433z1-344675532.html.

24. R. Riley, "White Mom and Sons Hurled Racial Slurs, Beat, Try to Drown Black Teen at an Illinois Campground," *Atlanta Black Star*, Jun. 2, 2016, https://

atlantablackstar.com/2016/06/02/white-mom-and-sons-hurled-racial-slurs-beat-try-to-drown-black-teen-at-chicago-area-campground/.

25. P. Holley, "'Super Racist' Pool Poster Prompts Red Cross Apology," *Washington Post*, Jun. 27, 2016, https://www.washingtonpost.com/news/morning-mix/wp/2016/06/27/super-racist-pool-safety-poster-prompts-red-cross-apology/?utm_term=.7114a0f4ac2c; A. Welsh-Huggins, "'White Only' Swimming Pool Sign Violated Girl's Civil Rights, Panel Says," Cleveland.com, Jan. 12, 2012, https://www.cleveland.com/metro/2012/01/white_only_swimming_pool_sign.html.

26. R. Erb, "Nurse Sues After Hospital Grants Dad's Racial Request," *USA Today*, Feb. 18, 2013, https://www.usatoday.com/story/news/nation/2013/02/18/black-nurse-lawsuit-father-request-granted/1928253/.

27. W. Lane, D. Rubin, R. Monteith, and C. Christian, "Racial Differences in the Evaluation of Pediatric Fractures for Physical Abuse," *Journal of the American Medical Association* 288, no. 13 (2002): 1603–1609.

28. M. Dunlap, T. F. Shueh, C. Burrell, and P. J. Beaubrun, "Belief in Colorblindness and Perceptions of Minority Children During a Fictionalized Parent-Child Discipline Scene," *Journal of Ethnic and Cultural Diversity in Social Work* 27, no. 2 (2017): 193–213.

29. J. C. Williams, "Black Americans Don't Trust Our Healthcare System—Here's Why," *The Hill*, Aug. 24, 2017, https://thehill.com/blogs/pundits-blog/healthcare/347780-black-americans-dont-have-trust-in-our-healthcare-system.

30. N. Bahadur, "Woman Says She Was Kicked Out of a Bank for Wearing a Hijab," *Teen Vogue*, May 12, 2017, https://www.teenvogue.com/story/woman-kicked-out-of-bank-wearing-hijab-video.

31. S. Chowdhry, "Metro Detroit Bar Accused of Having Cover Charge for Black Patrons, but Not for White," *WXYZ Detroit*, Jul. 25, 2017, https://www.wxyz.com/news/region/macomb-county/bar-accused-of-having-cover-charge-for-black-patrons-but-not-for-white.

32. Black Issues in Higher Education, "Racial Discrimination a Reality"; C. Dunn, "Shopping While Black: America's Retailers Know They Have a Profiling Problem . . . Now What?" *International Business Times*, Dec. 15, 2015, http://www.ibtimes.com/shopping-while-black-americas-retailers-know-they-have-racial-profiling-problem-now-2222778; N. Kristof, "When Whites Just Don't Get It, Part 7," *New York Times*, Oct. 1, 2016, https://www.nytimes.com/2016/10/02/opinion/sunday/when-whites-just-dont-get-it-part-7.html; K. Meeks, *Driving While black: Highways, Shopping Malls, Taxicabs, Sidewalks: How to Fight Back If You Are the Victim of Racial Profiling* (New York: Broadway Books, 2000); N. K. Peart, "Why Is the N.Y.P.D. After Me?" *New York Times*, Nov. 17, 2011, http://www.nytimes.com/2011/12/18/opinion/sunday/young-black-and-frisked-by-the-nypd.html?_r=4; W. Shepard, "Former Canes Football Player Sues Bank for Alleged Racial Profiling," *NBC 6 South Florida*, Nov. 14, 2011, http://www.nbcmiami.com/news/sports/133842813.html.

33. J. A. Quezada, "Driving While Black, Brown, and LGBTQ," *Huffington Post*, Apr. 7, 2014, http://www.huffingtonpost.com/janet-arelis-quezada/driving-while-racial-profiling_b_5105261.html.

34. F. Wells, "My White Neighbor Thought I Was Breaking Into My Own Apartment: Nineteen Cops Showed Up," *Washington Post*, Nov. 18, 2015, https://www.washingtonpost.com/posteverything/wp/2015/11/18/my-white-neighbor-thought-i-was-breaking-into-my-own-apartment-nineteen-cops-showed-up/?noredirect=on&utm_term=.2303f097ab9e.

35. M. Gomez, "White Woman Who Blocked Black Neighbor from Building Is Fired," *New York Times*, Oct. 15, 2018, https://www.nytimes.com/2018/10/15/us/hilary-brooke-apartment-patty-st-louis.html.

36. CBS News/Associated Press, "N.C. Police Pepper Spray Black Teen in His Own Home," *CBS News*, Oct. 8, 2014, https://www.cbsnews.com/news/nc-police-pepper-spray-black-teen-thinking-foster-son-is-burglar/.

37. E. McLaughlin, "'I Thought It Was My Apartment,' Dallas Officer Says 19 times in Tearful 911 Call After Shooting Botham Jean," *CNN*, Apr. 30, 2019, https://www.cnn.com/2019/04/30/us/dallas-botham-jean-911-police-officer-amber-guyger/index.html.

38. H. Yan, A. Vera, and S. Jones. "Former Fort Worth Police Officer Charged with Murder for Killing Atatiana Jefferson in Her Own Home," *CNN*, Oct. 14, 2019, https://www.cnn.com/2019/10/14/us/fort-worth-police-shooting-atatiana-jefferson/index.html.

39. S. Estrada, "Black Man Killed by Cop in His Own Garage for Loud Music Complaint, Jury Awards Family $4," DiversityInc, Jun. 1, 2018, https://www.diversityinc.com/black-man-killed-by-cop-in-his-own-garage-for-loud-music-complaint-jury-awards-family-4/.

40. T. Perkins, "Detroit Judge Tosses 'Gardening While Black' Case Brought by Three White Women," *Detroit Metro Times*, Oct. 18, 2018, https://www.metrotimes.com/table-and-bar/archives/2018/10/18/detroit-judge-tosses-gardening-while-black-case-brought-by-three-white-women.

41. R. Winton, S. Parvini, and M. Morin, "Stephon Clark Shooting: How Police Opened Fire on an Unarmed Black Man Holding a Cellphone," *Los Angeles Times*, Mar. 23, 2018, http://www.latimes.com/local/lanow/la-me-stephon-clark-shooting-sacramento-explainer-20180323-story.html.

42. A. J. Willingham, "Police Officer Pulled a Gun on a Black Man Picking Up Trash on His Own Property. Now, the Department Is Investigating," *CNN*, Mar. 7, 2019, https://www.cnn.com/2019/03/07/us/colorado-police-black-man-picking-trash-trnd/index.html.

43. E. Ortiz and S. Goldstein, "Milwaukee Man, 76, Found Guilty of Intentional Homicide in 13-year-old Neighbor's Shooting Death," *Daily News*, Jul. 17, 2013, https://www.nydailynews.com/news/crime/trial-milwaukee-mom-recounts-shooting-son-13-article-1.1400993.

44. See, for example, T. Kenney, "Georgia Parents Speak Out After Woman Calls the Cops on Black Man Babysitting Their Children," *Atlanta Black Star*, Oct. 10, 2018, https://atlantablackstar.com/2018/10/10/georgia-parents-speak-out-after-woman-calls-the-cops-on-black-man-babysitting-their-children/.

45. M. Eversley, "9 Dead in Shooting at Black Church in Charleston, S.C.," *USA Today*, Jun. 19, 2015, https://www.usatoday.com/story/news/nation/2015/06/17/charleston-south-carolina-shooting/28902017/.

46. F. Jones, "Breathing While Black," *Essence*, 118–19, Sept. 2018.

47. J. Hughes, "What Black Parents Tell Their Sons About the Police," Gawker, Aug. 21, 2014, http://gawker.com/what-black-parents-tell-their-sons-about-the-police-1624412625.

48. Margolin, "Black Female Doctor."

49. See, for example, L. O. Graham, "Lawrence Otis Graham: I Thought Privilege Would Protect My Kids from Racism. I Was Wrong," *Dallas Morning News*, Nov. 2014, http://www.dallasnews.com/opinion/commentary/2014/11/12/lawrence-otis-graham-i-thought-privilege-would-protect-my-kids-from-racism-i-was-wrong.

PART II: INDICTED

1. J. Johnson, "From Starbucks to Hashtags: We Need to Talk About Why White Americans Call the Police on Black People," *The Root*, April 6, 2018, https://www.theroot.com/from-starbucks-to-hashtags-we-need-to-talk-about-why-w-1825284087.

2. A. Branigin, "Exclusive: New Report Shows Gentrifiers Use Police to Terrorize Communities of Color—Without Even Calling 911," *The Root*, Jan. 8, 2019. https://www.theroot.com/exclusive-new-report-shows-gentrifiers-use-police-to-t-1831576262; Johnson, "From Starbucks to Hashtags."

PART II: INVALIDATED

1. See, for example, H. Drake, "Do Not Move Off the Sidewalk Challenge: Holding Your Space in a White World," WriteSomeShit, July 12, 2018, https://writesomeshit.com/2018/07/12/do-not-move-off-the-sidewalk-challenge-holding-your-space-in-a-white-world/; Y. Dzhanova, "University of Florida Employee Manhandles Black Graduates at Commencement," NBC News, May 7, 2018, https://www.nbcnews.com/news/us-news/university-florida-employee-manhandles-black-graduates-commencement-n872116.

2. See, for example, Davis, "White Baton Rouge Judge Calls Black Woman the N-Word at Local Restaurant," The Rouge Collection, Feb. 8, 2017. http://therougecollection.net/therouge/white-baton-rouge-judge-calls-black-woman-the-n-word-at-local-restaurant/.

PART II: THINGS THAT PART II'S STORIES CAN TEACH CONSUMERS AND MARKETERS

1. J. Armstrong, "Lowe's Suspends Annoying Receipt-Checking Policy After West Philly Customer Complains," *The Philadelpia Inquirer*, June 13, 2018. https://www.inquirer.com/philly/columnists/jenice_armstrong/lowes-suspends-receipt-checking-policy-will-mega-jenice-armstrong-20180613.html.

2. D. Mosbergen, "NY Lawmaker Wants to Make Calling Cops on Innocent Black People a Hate Crime," *Huffington Post*, Aug. 20, 2018, https://www.huffingtonpost.com/entry/911-discrimination-law-jesse-hamilton-new-york_us_5b796dbfe4b0a5b1febc2632.

3. J. Hicks, "Grand Rapids Could Make It Illegal to Call Police on People of Color for 'Participating in Their Lives,'" MLive Michigan, Aug. 20, 2019, https://www.mlive.com/news/grand-rapids/2019/04/grand-rapids-could-make-it-illegal-to-call-police-on-people-of-color-for-participating-in-their-lives.html.

4. National Action Network, "Customers' Bill of Rights," National Action Network, 2013, http://nationalactionnetwork.net/wp-content/uploads/2013/12/bill-of-rights-final-draft.pdf.

5. See, for example, L. Elder and R. Paul, "Becoming a Critic of Your Thinking: Learning the Art of Critical Thinking," The Critical Thinking Community, 2017, http://www.criticalthinking.org/pages/becoming-a-critic-of-your-thinking/605.

6. N. Krawczyk, "Out, But Still Not Always Equal, in Retail," *Convenience Store News*, Aug. 14, 2017, https://csnews.com/out-still-not-always-equal-retail; C. Blain, "10 Questions to Ask Yourself Before Calling the Police on Black and Brown Bodies," The Body Is Not an Apology, Dec. 7, 2019, https://thebodyisnotanapology.com/magazine/10-questions-to-ask-yourself-before-you-call-the-police-on-black-brown-bodies/; Touré, "When Calling 911 Makes an Emergency," *The Daily Beast*, May 13, 2018, https://www.thedailybeast.com/when-calling-911-makes-the-emergency.

7. Blain, "10 Questions to Ask Yourself Before Calling the Police on Black and Brown Bodies."

8. Krawczyk, "Out, But Still Not Always Equal"; Blain, "10 Questions to Ask Yourself Before Calling the Police on Black and Brown Bodies."

9. D. Curtis, "Sometimes, an Apology Can Deter a Lawsuit," *California Bar Journal*, July 2010, http://www.calbarjournal.com/July2010/TopHeadlines/TH1aspx.

10. Krawczyk, "Out, But Still Not Always Equal"; Blain, "10 Questions to Ask Yourself Before Calling the Police on Black and Brown Bodies."

PART III: INTRODUCTION

1. N. Warikoo and M. Owen, "Death Angers Family: Brutality Alleged as Man Dies in Mall Scuffle with Guards," *Detroit Free Press*, June 24, 2000, https://crimeindetroit.com/documents/Death%20angers%20Family.pdf.

2. CNN, "Woman Dies After Struggle with Security Guards," CNN Law Center, April 6, 2001, http://www.cnn.com/2001/LAW/04/06/shoplifting.death.03/.Woman dies after struggle with security guards."

3. T. McKay, "Al Roker Says a New York City Taxi Refused to Pick Him Up Because He's Black," *Yahoo News*, Nov. 22, 2015, https://www.yahoo.com/news/al-roker-says-york-city-191044120.html.

4. R. Ellis, "Death of ex-NFL Play Joe McKnight Came During Road-Rage Incident," *CNN*, Dec. 2, 2016, https://www.cnn.com/2016/12/02/us/nfl-player-joe-mcknight-shooting/.

5. B. Cooper, *Eloquent Rage: A Black Feminist Discovers Her Superpower* (London: Picador Press, 2019); J. Holland, "Tough Time for Black Women—Like Black Men—With Police," *The Spokesman-Review*, Oct. 31, 2015, http://www.spokesman.com/stories/2015/oct/31/tough-time-for-black-women-like-black-men-with-pol/.

6. Holland, "Tough Time for Black Women."

7. R. Stanton, "Slain Shoplifter's Family Sues Walmart," *The Houston Chronicle*, March 9, 2013, https://www.chron.com/news/houston-texas/houston/article/Shop-lifter-s-family-sues-Wal-Mart-deputy-4337438.php.

8. H. Khaleeli, "#SayHerName: Why Kimberle Crenshaw Is Fighting for Forgotten Women," *The Guardian*, May 30, 2016, https://www.theguardian.com/lifeandstyle/2016/may/30/sayhername-why-kimberle-crenshaw-is-fighting-for-forgotten-women.

PART III: TRAUMATIZED

1. L. O. Graham, "Lawrence Otis Graham: I Thought Privilege Would Protect My Kids from Racism. I Was Wrong," *Dallas Morning News*, Nov. 2014, http://www.dallasnews.com/opinion/commentary/2014/11/12/lawrence-otis-graham-i-thought-privilege-would-protect-my-kids-from-racism-i-was-wrong.

2. See, for example, K. Laymon, *Heavy: An American Memoir* (New York: Simon and Schuster, 2018).

PART III: TERRIFIED

1. See, for example, G. Martinez, "'Leave These Women Alone!' Grocery Store Customer Defends Spanish Speakers in Viral Video," *Time*, Oct. 4, 2018, https://time.com/5416077/colorado-grocery-store-viral-video-harassment/.

2. M. M. Accapadi, "When White Women Cry: How White Women's Tears Oppress Women of Color," *The College Student Affairs Journal* 26, no. 2 (2007): 208–15; L. Donnella, "When the 'White Tears' Just Keep Coming," NPR Morning Edition,

Nov. 28, 2018, https://www.npr.org/sections/codeswitch/2018/11/28/649537891/when-the-white-tears-just-keep-coming; R. Hamad, "How White Women Use Strategic Tears to Silence Women of Colour," *The Guardian*, May 7, 2018, https://www.theguardian.com/commentisfree/2018/may/08/how-white-women-use-strategic-tears-to-avoid-accountability; K. Seaton, "White Tears Part I: Black Educators Share Their Thoughts on What Happens When White Women Cry in Schools," Urban Joy: The Life and Times of City Schools, Nov. 6, 2017, https://joyofurbaneducation.org/2017/11/731/.

3. Accapadi, "When White Women Cry."

4. ZamaMdoda, "White Women Got This Black Reporter Fired for Sharing Article About White Fragility." AfroPunk, Aug. 22, 2018. https://afropunk.com/2018/08/white-women-got-this-black-reporter-fired-for-sharing-article-about-white-fragility/.

5. Accapadi, "When White Women Cry."

6. Donnella, "When the 'White Tears' Just Keep Coming"; J. Johnson, "From Starbucks to Hashtags: We Need to Talk About Why White Americans Call the Police on Black People," *The Root*, Apr. 6, 2018, https://www.theroot.com/from-starbucks-to-hashtags-we-need-to-talk-about-why-w-1825284087.

7. Equal Justice Initiative, "Emmitt Till's Accuser Admits She Lied," EJI, Jan. 31, 2017, https://eji.org/news/emmett-till-accuser-admits-she-lied.

8. E. Fieldstadt, "Woman Declaring 'I'm White and I'm Hot' Fired From Job After Harassing Two Black Women in North Carolina Parking Lot," *NBC News*, Oct. 30, 2018, https://www.nbcnews.com/news/us-news/woman-declaring-i-m-white-i-m-hot-fired-job-n926151; A. Stone, A. Katersky, and S. Ghebremedhin, "Woman Accused of Attacking Teen in NY Hotel Arrested After Fleeing, Boy's Family Speaks Out," *ABC News*, Jan. 8, 2021, https://abcnews.go.com/US/woman-accused-attacking-teen-ny-hotel-arrested-california/story?id=75124832.

9. G. Yancy, M. Davidson, and S. Hadley, *Our Black Sons Matter: Mothers Talk about Fears*, Sorrows, and Hopes (Lanham, MD: Rowman & Littlefield, 2016).

10. A pseudonym.

PART III: TRIGGERED

1. M. Bulman, "H&M Apologises Following Backlash Over 'Racist' Image of Child Model on Website," *Independent*, Jan. 8, 2018, https://www.independent.co.uk/news/uk/home-news/hm-apology-racist-image-website-child-model-backlash-twitter-monkey-jumper-black-a8147641.html; E. Jensen, "Prada Announces Diversity Council with Ava DuVernay Following Blackface Outrage," *USA Today*, Feb. 13, 2019, https://www.usatoday.com/story/life/2019/02/13/prada-starts-diversity-council-ava-duvernay-after-blackface-outrage/2860422002/; M. McAfee, "T.J. MAXX Removes Noose T-shirt," *CNN*, Mar. 19, 2015, https://www.cnn.com/2015/03/19/living/feat-tjmaxx-hang-loose-tshirt/index.html; R. Picheta, "'Sui-

cide Isn't Fashion': Burberry Apologizes for Hoodie with Noose Around the Neck," *CNN*, Feb. 19, 2019, https://www.cnn.com/style/article/burberry-noose-hoodie-scli-gbr-intl/index.html; C. Sparks, "20 Black Designers to Support Instead of Gucci and Prada," *Rolling Out*, Feb. 12, 2019, https://rollingout.com/2019/02/12/20-black-designers-to-support-instead-of-gucci-and-prada/; C. Stern, "'Hoping Someone Got Fired for This': Twitter Users Slam Online Retailer for Using White Women to Model Shirts that Say Things like 'Unapologetically Black,' and 'I'm a Strong Black Woman.'" *Daily Mail*, Jul. 31, 2017. https://www.essence.com/beauty/teyana-taylor-free-manicures-brooklyn-nail-salon-victim/.

2. *Miss Sharon Jones!*, directed by Barbara Kopple (2015; New York: Cabin Creek Films), Netflix.

PART III: THINGS THAT PART III'S STORIES CAN TEACH CONSUMERS AND MARKETERS

1. J. Johnson, "From Starbucks to Hashtags: We Need to Talk About Why White Americans Call the Police on Black People," *The Root*, Apr. 6, 2018, https://www.theroot.com/from-starbucks-to-hashtags-we-need-to-talk-about-why-w-1825284087.

2. See, for example, J. Bennett, "Store Clerk Calls Cops on College Student for Being 'Arrogant & Black,'" *Ebony*, Aug. 9, 2018, https://www.ebony.com/news-views/store-clerk-calls-cops-on-college-student-for-being-arrogant-black.

PART IV: INTRODUCTION

1. J. Silverstein, "I Don't Feel Your Pain: A Failure of Empathy Perpetuates Racial Disparities," *State*, June 27, 2013, http://www.slate.com/articles/health_and_science/science/2013/06/racial_empathy_gap_people_don_t_perceive_pain_in_other_races.html.

2. S. K. Shelton, "Community Healing Network Aims to Counter 'Lie of Black Inferiority,'" *New Haven Register*, Mar. 30, 2013, https://www.nhregister.com/connecticut/article/Community-Healing-Network-aims-to-counter-lie-of-11388077.php.

3. Columbia State. "Segregation Law Used to Police Columbia Mall." The Columbia *State*, Jan. 28, 1990.

4. See, for example, M. Mitchell, "Water Tower Place to Black Teens Kicked Out of Mall: 'It Was Wrong, Very Sorry,'" *Chicago Sun Times*, Apr. 9, 2018, https://chicago.suntimes.com/columnists/water-tower-place-to-black-teens-kicked-out-of-mall-it-was-wrong-very-sorry/.

5. S. A. Crockett Jr., "Cover Charge Racism: 3 Black Lawyers Charged to Enter Club While Whites Enter for Free," *The Root*, Sept. 22, 2015, https://www.theroot.com/cover-charge-racism-3-black-lawyers-charged-to-enter-c-1790861178.

6. N. Flatow, "If You Thought Stop-and-Frisk Was Bad, You Should Know About Jump-Outs," *Mint Press News*, Dec. 27, 2014, https://www.mintpressnews.com/thought-stop-frisk-bad-know-jump-outs/200247/.

7. National Action Network, "Customers' Bill of Rights," National Action Network, 2013, http://nationalactionnetwork.net/wp-content/uploads/2013/12/bill-of-rights-final-draft.pdf.

8. A. Sutherland and B. Golding, "Stores Adopt 'Customers' Bill of Rights' After 'Shop Frisk' Fiasco," *New York Post*, Dec. 9, 2013, http://nypost.com/2013/12/09/stores-agree-to-customers-bill-of-rights-after-shop-and-frisk-fiasco/.

PART IV: PRECONCEIVED

1. W. Roseliep, "Is 'Negrotown' Smart Satire Or Just Off-Key?" *WGBH News*, May 11, 2015, https://www.wgbh.org/news/post/negrotown-smart-satire-or-just-key.

2. B. Sanders, "History's Lost Black Towns," *The Root*, Jan. 27, 2011, https://www.theroot.com/historys-lost-black-towns-1790868004.

PART IV: PERTURBED

1. A. Austin, "A Good Credit Score Did Not Protect Latino and Black Borrowers," Economic Policy Institute, Jan. 19, 2012, https://www.epi.org/publication/latino-black-borrowers-high-rate-subprime-mortgages/; M. Baradaran, *The Color of Money: Black Banks and the Racial Wealth Gap* (Cambridge, MA: Belknap Press of Harvard, 2017); Velshi and Ruhle, "Homes Owned by Black Americans Are Undervalued by Billions of Dollars," Black Periscope, Nov. 29, 2018, https://www.blackperiscope.com/2018/11/29/homes-owned-by-black-americans-are-undervalued-by-billions-of-dollars-velshi-ruhle-msnbc/.

2. M. Corkery and J. Silver-Greenberg, "Prosecutors Scrutinize Minority Borrowers' Auto Loans," *New York Times*, Mar. 30, 2015, https://www.nytimes.com/2015/03/31/business/dealbook/prosecutors-scrutinize-minorities-auto-loans.html; R. Weems, *Desegregating the Dollar: African American Consumerism in the 20th Century* (New York: New York University Press, 1998).

PART IV: PROVOKED

1. J. Baldwin, *Nobody Knows My Name: More Notes of a Native Son* (New York: Vintage Press, 1961/1992).

2. *Race: The Power of an Illusion*, episode 3, "The House We Live In," produced by L. Adelman, L. Smith, and J. Cheng, 2003, on PBS, VHS; C. Ingraham, "A New Explanation for the Stubborn Persistence of the Racial Wealth Gap," *Washington Post*, Mar. 14, 2019, https://www.washingtonpost.com/us-policy/2019/03/14/new-explanation-stubborn-persistence-racial-wealth-gap/?noredirect=on&utm_term=.066bf14f6088; T. Jan, "White Families Have Nearly 10 Times the Net Worth of Black Families. And the Gap Is Growing," *Washington Post*, Sept. 28, 2017, https://www.washingtonpost.com/news/wonk/wp/2017/09/28/black-and-hispanic-families-are-making-more-money-but-they-still-lag-far-behind-whites/?utm_term=.2503be92ab1e.

PART IV: THINGS THAT PART IV'S STORIES CAN TEACH CONSUMERS AND MARKETERS

1. C. Sparks, "20 Black Designers to Support Instead of Gucci and Prada," *Rolling Out*, Feb. 12, 2019. https://rollingout.com/2019/02/12/20-black-designers-to-support-instead-of-gucci-and-prada/.

2. See DeGruy, *Post-Traumatic Slave Syndrome: America's Legacy of Enduring Injury and Healing*, revised edition (Portland, OR: Joy DeGruy Publications, Inc., 2017).

3. National Action Network, "Customers' Bill of Rights," National Action Network, 2013, http://nationalactionnetwork.net/wp-content/uploads/2013/12/bill-of-rights-final-draft.pdf.

PART V: CONCLUSION

1. M. Dunlap, "Thriving in a Multicultural Classroom," in *Understanding and Managing Diversity*, ed. C. P. Harvey and M. J. Allard (Upper Saddle River, NJ: Pearson/Prentice Hall, 2011).

2. N. Magee, "Walmart Sued for Locking Up Black Hair Care Products in Glass Case," Black America Web, Jan. 29, 2018, https://blackamericaweb.com/2018/01/29/walmart-sued-for-locking-up-black-hair-care-products-in-glass-case/.

3. D. Brown, "Harriet Tubman Is Already Appearing on $20 Bills Whether Trump Officials Like It or Not," *The Seattle Times*, May 19, 2019, https://www.seattletimes.com/nation-world/nation/harriet-tubman-is-already-appearing-on-20-bills-whether-trump-officials-like-it-or-not/.

4. S. Gabbidon, "Racial Profiling by Store Clerks and Security Personnel in Retail Establishments: An Exploration of 'Shopping While Black,'" *Journal of Contemporary Criminal Justice* 19, no. 3 (2003): 345–64, https://doi.org/10.1177/1043986203254531.

5. See, for example, G. Henderson, A. M. Hakstian, and J. Williams, *Consumer Equality: Race and the American Marketplace* (Santa Barbara, CA: Praeger, 2016).

6. M. Dunlap, C. Burrell, and P. J. Beaubrun, "Moments in the Danger Zone: Encountering 'Non-racist,' 'Non-racial,' 'Non-color-seeing' Do-Gooders," in *Black Women and Social Justice Education: Legacies and Lessons*, ed. S. Y. Evans, A. D. Domingue, and T. D. Mitchell, (Albany, NY: SUNY Press, 2019), 201–17.

7. K. Brown-Dean, "The Fallacy of NOT Seeing Race," Diverse Education, Feb. 14, 2019, https://diverseeducation.com/article/138702/; M. Dunlap, T. F. Shueh, C. Burrell, and P. J. Beaubrun, "Belief in Colorblindness and Perceptions of Minority Children During a Fictionalized Parent-Child Discipline Scene," *Journal of Ethnic and Cultural Diversity in Social Work* 27, no. 2 (2017): 193–213; Dunlap et al., "Moments in the Danger Zone"; M. Dunlap, J. Scoggin, P. Green, and A. Davi, "White Students' Experiences of Privilege and Socioeconomic Disparities: Toward a Theoretical Model," *Michigan Journal of Community Service-Learning* (Spring 2007): 19–30; J. W. Schofield, "Causes and Consequences of the Colorblind Perspective," in *Prejudice, Discrimination, and Racism*, ed. J. F. Dovidio and S. L. Gaertner (Orlando, FL: Academic Press, 1986).

8. N. Warikoo and M. Owen, "Death Angers Family: Brutality Alleged as Man Dies in Mall Scuffle with Guards," *Detroit Free Press*, June 24, 2000, https://crimeindetroit.com/documents/Death%20angers%20Family.pdf.

9. T. Wofford, "New Video Emerges of Police Shooting Kajieme Powell in St. Louis," *Newsweek*, Oct. 20, 2014, https://www.newsweek.com/new-video-police-shooting-2nd-man-st-louis-emerges-266041.

10. J. Bihm, "Say Her Name: LaTasha Harlins," *Los Angeles Sentinel*, May 3, 2017, https://lasentinel.net/say-her-name-latasha-harlins.html.

11. K. Bazzle, "Gas Station Owner Arrested After Killing Man Who Stole $36 Worth of Beer from Lakeland Store," *WFTS Tampa Bay*, Jul. 18, 2018, https://www.abcactionnews.com/news/region-polk/gas-station-owner-arrested-after-killing-man-who-stole-36-worth-of-beer-from-lakeland-store.

12. S. Nelson, "Homeless Man Killed by 'Stop n Shop' Employees for Allegedly Stealing Cake," *Atlanta Black Star*, Apr. 19, 2018, https://atlantablackstar.com/2018/04/19/homeless-man-killed-stop-n-shop-employees-allegedly-stealing-cake/.

13. Meredith Digital Staff, "Instead of Arresting an Accused Shoplifter, 3 NYPD Officers Pay for Her Groceries," *CBS 46*, Jul. 5, 2019, https://www.cbs46.com/instead-of-arresting-an-accused-shoplifter-nypd-officers-pay-for/article_3d3a7fb2-d09d-52d3-b209-f26285c8a3d1.html.

REFERENCES

Accapadi, M. M. "When White Women Cry: How White Women's Tears Oppress Women of Color." *The College Student Affairs Journal* 26, no. 2 (2007): 208–15.

Adelman, L., L. Smith, and J. Cheng, producers. *Race: The Power of an Illusion.* Episode 3, "The House We Live In." 2003, on PBS. VHS.

Alexander, M. *The New Jim Crow: Mass Incarceration in the Age of Colorblindness.* New York: The New Press, 2012.

Armstrong, J. "Lowe's Suspends Annoying Receipt-Checking Policy After West Philly Customer Complains." *The Philadelpia Inquirer*, Jun. 13, 2018. https://www.inquirer.com/philly/columnists/jenice_armstrong/lowes-suspends-receipt-checking-policy-will-mega-jenice-armstrong-20180613.html.

Associated Press. "Man Charged with Slapping Toddler Now Out of Job." *KDVR*, Feb. 18, 2013. https://kdvr.com/2013/02/18/idaho-man-charged-with-slapping-toddler-on-plane/.

Austin, A. "A Good Credit Score Did Not Protect Latino and Black Borrowers." Economic Policy Institute, Jan. 19, 2012. https://www.epi.org/publication/latino-black-borrowers-high-rate-subprime-mortgages/.

Bahadur, N. "Woman Says She Was Kicked Out of a Bank for Wearing a Hijab." *Teen Vogue*, May 12, 2017. https://www.teenvogue.com/story/woman-kicked-out-of-bank-wearing-hijab-video.

Baldwin, J. *Nobody Knows My Name: More Notes of a Native Son.* Reprinted. New York: Vintage Press, 1961/1992.

Banerjee, P. "Racial Profiling at Airports Adds a Colour-coded Cost When I Fly on Business." *Globe and Mail*, Jul. 19, 2016. https://www.theglobeandmail.com/life/facts-and-arguments/flying-while-brown/article30979345/.

Baradaran, M. *The Color of Money: Black Banks and the Racial Wealth Gap*. Cambridge, MA. Belknap Press of Harvard, 2017.

Bayly, L. "Sears, Once the World's Biggest Retailer, Now Faces Bankruptcy." *NBC News*, Oct. 10, 2018. https://www.nbcnews.com/business/business-news/125-year-old-sears-file-bankruptcy-report-n918446.

Bazzle, K. "Gas Station Owner Arrested After Killing Man Who Stole $36 Worth of Beer from Lakeland Store." *WFTS Tampa Bay*, Jul. 18, 2018. https://www.abcactionnews.com/news/region-polk/gas-station-owner-arrested-after-killing-man-who-stole-36-worth-of-beer-from-lakeland-store.

Beck, L. "Woman Shot Dead by Walmart Security Guard on Suspicion of Shoplifting." *Jezebel*, Dec. 10, 2012. https://jezebel.com/5967072/woman-shot-dead-by-walmart-security-guard-on-suspicion-of-shoplifting.

Bell, W. K. "W. Kamau Bell: I Know What It's Like to Get Kicked Out for Being Black." *CNN*, May 28, 2018. https://www.cnn.com/2018/04/16/opinions/philadelphia-starbucks-sounds-familiar-to-me-w-kamau-bell-opinion/index.html.

Bennett, A., K. Daddario, and R. P. Hill. "Shopping While Nonwhite: Racial Discrimination in the Marketplace." *Advances in Consumer Research* 42 (2014): 410–10.

Bennett, J. "Store Clerk Calls Cops on College Student for Being 'Arrogant & Black.'" *Ebony*, Aug. 9, 2018. https://www.ebony.com/news-views/store-clerk-calls-cops-on-college-student-for-being-arrogant-black.

Bessette, C. "Offensive Internet Connection in Norwichtown Upsets Residents." *The Day*, Nov. 23, 2016. https://www.theday.com/article/20161123/NWS01/161129626.

BGLH (Black Girl with Long Hair). "TSA Officers Will No Longer Stop Black Women to Conduct Hair Searches in Airports." BGLH, Mar. 29, 2015. https://bglh-marketplace.com/2015/03/tsa-officers-will-no-longer-stop-black-women-to-conduct-hair-searches-in-the-airport/.

Bhasin, K. "Barneys Pays $525,000 to Settle Allegations of Racial Profiling." *Huffington Post*, Aug. 11, 2014. https://www.huffingtonpost.com/2014/08/11/barneys-racial-profiling_n_5669129.html.

Bihm, J. "Say Her Name: LaTasha Harlins." *Los Angeles Sentinel*, May 3, 2017. https://lasentinel.net/say-her-name-latasha-harlins.html.

Black Issues in Higher Education. "Racial Discrimination a Reality for Black Tourists, Researcher Finds." *Black Issues in Higher Education*, Oct. 25, 2001. https://diverseeducation.com/article/1709/.

Black Loop. "Gabourey Sidibe Reveals Discrimination at Chanel Boutique Store, 'I'll Buy This Whole Damn Store!'" Black Loop, May 11, 2017. https://www.theblackloop.com/gabourey-sidibe-reveals-discrimination-at-chanel-boutique-store-ill-buy-this-whole-damn-store/.

Blain, C. "10 Questions to Ask Yourself Before Calling the Police on Black and Brown Bodies." The Body Is Not an Apology, Dec. 7, 2019. https://thebodyisnotanapology.com/magazine/10-questions-to-ask-yourself-before-you-call-the-police-on-black-brown-bodies/.

Boboltz, S. "Trevor Noah Describes Extreme Surrender Whenever He Is Stopped by Police." *Huffington Post*, Jun. 21, 2017. https://www.huffingtonpost.com/entry/trevor-noah-describes-extreme-surrender-whenever-he-is-stopped-by-police_us_594a64d5e4b0db570d37ea60.

Boston Globe. "Fliers See Bias as Pilots Move to Bump Them." *Boston Globe*, Nov. 11, 2001.

Branigin, A. "Exclusive: New Report Shows Gentrifiers Use Police to Terrorize Communities of Color—Without Even Calling 911." *The Root*, Jan. 8, 2019. https://www.theroot.com/exclusive-new-report-shows-gentrifiers-use-police-to-t-1831576262.

Brown, D. "Harriet Tubman Is Already Appearing on $20 Bills Whether Trump Officials Like It or Not." *The Seattle Times*, May 19, 2019. https://www.seattletimes.com/nation-world/nation/harriet-tubman-is-already-appearing-on-20-bills-whether-trump-officials-like-it-or-not/.

Brown-Dean, K. "The Fallacy of NOT Seeing Race." Diverse Education, Feb. 14, 2019. https://diverseeducation.com/article/138702/.

Bulman, M. "H&M Apologises Following Backlash Over 'Racist' Image of Child Model on Website." Independent, Jan. 8, 2018. https://www.independent.co.uk/news/uk/home-news/hm-apology-racist-image-website-child-model-backlash-twitter-monkey-jumper-black-a8147641.html.

Callahan, Y. "#CookingOutWhileBlack: White Woman Calls Cops on Black People Cooking Out in Oakland, Calif., Park." *The Root*, May 10, 2018. https://www.theroot.com/cookingoutwhileblack-white-woman-calls-cops-on-black-1825920347.

Carlozo, L. "Black Americans Donate to Make a Difference." *Reuters*, Feb. 23, 2012. https://www.reuters.com/article/us-usa-blacks-donors/black-americans-donate-to-make-a-difference-idUSTRE81M1WI20120223.

CBS News/Associated Press. "N.C. Police Pepper Spray Black Teen in His Own Home." *CBS News*, Oct. 8, 2014. https://www.cbsnews.com/news/nc-police-pepper-spray-black-teen-thinking-foster-son-is-burglar/.

Chapman, B., and L. Greene. "Outrage in Brooklyn Over '40 Ounce' Water Bottle that Looks Like Malt Liquor." *New York Daily News*, Mar. 6, 2019. https://www.nydailynews.com/new-york/brooklyn/ny-metro-forty-water-marketing-20190305-story.html.

Chavez, N., and S. Lipp. "Smith College Student Who Was Racially Profiled While Eating Says the Incident Left Her So Shaken She Can't Sleep." *CNN*, Aug. 3, 2018. https://www.cnn.com/2018/08/03/us/smith-college-student-police-trnd/index.html.

Chittal, N. "Cops Shoot and Kill Man Holding Toy Gun in Wal-Mart." *MSNBC*, Aug. 9, 2014. http://www.msnbc.com/msnbc/cops-shoot-and-kill-man-holding-toy-gun-walmart.

Chowdhry, S. "Metro Detroit Bar Accused of Having Cover Charge for Black Patrons, but Not for White." *WXYZ Detroit*, Jul. 25, 2017. https://www.wxyz.com/news/region/macomb-county/bar-accused-of-having-cover-charge-for-black-patrons-but-not-for-white.

Chowdhry, S. "Michigan Mom Launches Petition to Remove Candy and Magazines from Meijer Checkout Aisles." *WXYZ Detroit*, Jan. 4, 2017. https://www.wxyz.com/news/michigan-mom-launches-petition-to-remove-candy-and-magazines-from-meijer-checkout-aisles.

Clarke, R., and C. Lett. "What Happened When Michael Brown Met Officer Darren Wilson." *CNN*, Nov. 11, 2014. http://www.cnn.com/interactive/2014/08/us/ferguson-brown-timeline/.

CNN. "Woman Dies After Struggle with Security Guards." CNN Law Center, April 6, 2001. http://www.cnn.com/2001/LAW/04/06/shoplifting.death.03/.

Cobb, N. "Where We Belong. Is There Room for African Americans Outdoors?" *Smile Politely*, Sept. 28, 2018. http://www.smilepolitely.com/opinion/where_we_belong_is_there_room_for_african_americans_outdoors/.

Cohen, M. "FBI Director Says White Supremacy Is a 'Persistent, Pervasive Threat' to the US." *CNN*, Apr. 4, 2019. https://www.cnn.com/2019/04/04/politics/fbi-director-wray-white-supremacy/index.html.

Colangelo, B. "Cleveland-area Bahama Breeze Calls Police to Make Sure Black Sorority Members Pay Bill." *Cleveland Scene*, June 20, 2018. https://www.clevescene.com/scene-and-heard/archives/2018/06/20/cleveland-area-bahama-breeze-racially-profiles-black-sorority-and-calls-police-over-bill-dispute.

Colen, C., Q. Li, and C. Reczek. "The Intergenerational Transmission of Discrimination: Children's Experiences of Unfair Treatment and Their Mothers' Health at Midlife." *Journal of Health and Social Behavior* 60, no. 4 (2020): 474–92. https://doi.org/10.1177/0022146519887347.

Columbia *State*. "Segregation Law Used to Police Columbia Mall." The Columbia *State*, Jan. 28, 1990.

Concepcion, M. "Police Release Report on Shoplifting Incident as Family Seeks $10M from Phoenix for Alleged Excessive Force." *12 News*, June 18, 2019. https://www.12news.com/article/news/local/valley/police-release-report-on-shoplifting-incident-as-family-seeks-10m-from-phoenix-for-alleged-excessive-force/75-73fd4494-9cfe-447b-8bdb-8f7f987c8c92.

Cooper, B. *Eloquent Rage: A Black Feminist Discovers Her Superpower*. London: Picador Press, 2019.

Cooper, B. "The N-word on the 4th of July: The Flight Home to See My Family for the Holiday Was a Tearful, Shameful Affair." *Salon*, Jul. 4, 2013. http://www.salon.com/2013/07/04/the_n_word_on_the_4th_of_july/.

Corkery, M., and J. Silver-Greenberg. "Prosecutors Scrutinize Minority Borrowers' Auto Loans." *New York Times*, Mar. 30, 2015. https://www.nytimes.com/2015/03/31/business/dealbook/prosecutors-scrutinize-minorities-auto-loans.html.

Cramer, T. "Nielsen Dives into the Digital Lives of Black Consumers." EContent, Sept. 26, 2018. http://www.econtentmag.com/Articles/News/News-Feature/Nielsen-Dives-into-the-Digital-Lives-of-Black-Consumers-127625.htm.

Criss, D. "A Waitress Asked Some Black Teens to Prepay for Their Meal. A Fellow Diner Wasn't Having That." *CNN*, March 16, 2018. https://www.cnn.com/2018/03/15/us/maine-ihop-race-trnd/index.html.

Crockett, S. A., Jr. "Cover Charge Racism: 3 Black Lawyers Charged to Enter Club While Whites Enter for Free." *The Root*, Sept. 22, 2015. https://www.theroot.com/cover-charge-racism-3-black-lawyers-charged-to-enter-c-1790861178.

Cummings, I. "NAACP Issues First-ever Travel Advisory for a State—and It's Missouri." *Kansas City Star*, Aug. 2, 2017. https://www.kansascity.com/news/local/article164851802.html.

Curtis, D. "Sometimes, an Apology Can Deter a Lawsuit." *California Bar Journal*, July 2010. http://www.calbarjournal.com/July2010/TopHeadlines/TH1.aspx.

Daily Mail Reporter. "'Santa Is White, This One Would Steal Presents': Racists Target Mall of America After They Employed Their First Ever Black Father Christmas." *Daily Mail*, Dec. 4, 2016. https://www.dailymail.co.uk/news/article-3999496/Racists-target-Minnesota-s-Mall-America-employed-black-Father-Christmas.html.

Dalrymple, J. "Safeway Employees Call Police on a Black Woman Who Was Donating to a Homeless Man." *Buzzfeed News*, Aug. 1, 2018. https://www.buzzfeednews.com/article/jimdalrympleii/safeway-employees-called-police-on-a-black-woman-donating.

Danner, C. "Everything We Know about the El Paso Walmart Massacre." *New York Intelligencer*, Aug. 7, 2019. http://nymag.com/intelligencer/2019/08/everything-we-know-about-the-el-paso-walmart-shooting.html.

Davidson, E. F. "Shopping While Black: Perceptions of Discrimination in Retail Settings." PhD diss., University of Tennessee, Knoxville, TN, 2007.

Davis, T. S. "White Baton Rouge Judge Calls Black Woman the N-Word at Local Restaurant." The Rouge Collection, Feb. 8, 2017. http://therougecollection.net/therouge/white-baton-rouge-judge-calls-black-woman-the-n-word-at-local-restaurant/.

Deere, S., C. Raasch, and J. Kohler. "DOJ Finds Ferguson Targeted African Americans, Used Courts Mainly to Increase Revenue." *St. Louis Today*, Mar. 5, 2015. https://www.stltoday.com/news/local/crime-and-courts/doj-finds-ferguson-targeted-african-americans-used-courts-mainly-to/article_d561d303-1fe5-56b7-b4ca-3a5cc9a75c82.html.

DeGruy, J. *Post-Traumatic Slave Syndrome: America's Legacy of Enduring Injury and Healing*, Revised Edition. Portland, OR: Joy DeGruy Publications, Inc., 2017.

Dhaliwal, N. "Suspect in Custody After Viral Video Shows Elderly Woman Kicked in Face on New York City Subway." *ABC*, Mar. 23, 2019. https://abc7.com/suspect-in-custody-after-elderly-woman-kicked-on-subway/5213608/.

DiAngelo, R. *White Fragility: Why It's So Hard for White People to Talk about Racism.* Boston: Beacon Press, 2018.

Disis, J. "Starbucks Will Close 8,000 US Stores May 29 for Racial-bias Training." *CNN*, Apr. 17, 2018. https://money.cnn.com/2018/04/17/news/companies/starbucks-store-closings-racial-bias-education/index.html.

Donnella, L. "When the 'White Tears' Just Keep Coming." NPR Morning Edition, Nov. 28, 2018. https://www.npr.org/sections/codeswitch/2018/11/28/649537891/when-the-white-tears-just-keep-coming.

Donnelly, E. "Anne Hathaway Calls Out White Privilege in Passionate Post About 'Unspeakable' Murder of Nia Wilson." *Yahoo Lifestyle*, Jul. 26, 2018. https://www.yahoo.com/lifestyle/anne-hathaway-calls-white-privilege-passionate-post-unspeakable-murder-nia-wilson-104249741.html.

Drake, H. "Do Not Move Off the Sidewalk Challenge: Holding Your Space in a White World." WriteSomeShit, July 12, 2018. https://writesomeshit.com/2018/07/12/do-not-move-off-the-sidewalk-challenge-holding-your-space-in-a-white-world/.

Dunlap, M., C. Burrell, and P. J. Beaubrun. "Moments in the Danger Zone: Encountering 'Non-racist,' 'Non-racial,' 'Non-color-seeing' Do-Gooders." In *Black Women and Social Justice Education: Legacies and Lessons*, edited by S. Y. Evans, A. D. Domingue, and T. D. Mitchell, 201–17. Albany, NY: SUNY Press, 2019.

Dunlap, M., T. F. Shueh, C. Burrell, and P. J. Beaubrun. "Belief in Colorblindness and Perceptions of Minority Children During a Fictionalized Parent-Child Discipline Scene." *Journal of Ethnic and Cultural Diversity in Social Work* 27, no. 2 (2017): 193–213.

Dunlap, M. "Thriving in a Multicultural Classroom." In *Understanding and Managing Diversity*, edited by C. P. Harvey and M. J. Allard. Upper Saddle River, NJ: Pearson/Prentice Hall, 2011.

Dunlap, M., J. Scoggin, P. Green, and A. Davi. "White Students' Experiences of Privilege and Socioeconomic Disparities: Toward a Theoretical Model." *Michigan Journal of Community Service-Learning* (Spring 2007): 19–30.

Dunlap, M. *Reaching Out to Children and Families: Students Model Effective Community Service.* Lanham, MD: Rowman & Littlefield, 2000.

Dunn, C. "Shopping While Black: America's Retailers Know They Have a Profiling Problem . . . Now What?" *International Business Times*, Dec. 15, 2015. http://www.ibtimes.com/shopping-while-black-americas-retailers-know-they-have-racial-profiling-problem-now-2222778.

DuVernay, A., dir. *13th*. 2016; Sherman Oaks, CA: Kandoo Films. Netflix.

Dzhanova, Y. "University of Florida Employee Manhandles Black Graduates at Commencement." NBC News, May 7, 2018. https://www.nbcnews.com/news/us-news/university-florida-employee-manhandles-black-graduates-commencement-n872116.

Eberhardt, Jennifer. *Biased: Uncovering the Hidden Prejudice that Shapes What We See, Think, and Do*. New York: Vintage Press, 2019.

Edwards, B. "White Man Who Yelled 'Shut Up, Slave!' at Black Man during Altercation at Chicago Starbucks Now Faces Hate Crime Charges." *The Root*, Sept. 13, 2017. https://www.theroot.com/white-man-who-yelled-shut-up-slave-at-black-man-durin-1806113872.

Elder, L. and R. Paul. "Becoming a Critic of Your Thinking: Learning the Art of Critical Thinking." The Critical Thinking Community, 2017. http://www.criticalthinking.org/pages/becoming-a-critic-of-your-thinking/605.

Ellis, R. "Death of ex-NFL Play Joe McKnight Came During Road-Rage Incident." *CNN*, Dec. 2, 2016. https://www.cnn.com/2016/12/02/us/nfl-player-joe-mcknight-shooting/.

Equal Justice Initiative. "Emmitt Till's Accuser Admits She Lied." EJI, Jan. 31, 2017. https://eji.org/news/emmett-till-accuser-admits-she-lied.

Erb, R. "Nurse Sues After Hospital Grants Dad's Racial Request." *USA Today*, Feb. 18, 2013. https://www.usatoday.com/story/news/nation/2013/02/18/black-nurse-lawsuit-father-request-granted/1928253/.

Estrada, S. "Black Man Killed by Cop in His Own Garage for Loud Music Complaint, Jury Awards Family $4." DiversityInc, Jun. 1, 2018. https://www.diversityinc.com/black-man-killed-by-cop-in-his-own-garage-for-loud-music-complaint-jury-awards-family-4/.

Evans, S., K. Bell, N. Burton, and L. Blount. *Black Women's Mental Health: Balancing Strength and Vulnerability.* New York: SUNY Press, 2017.

Eversley, M. "Reports: S.C. Restaurant Refused to Seat Black Patrons." *USA Today*, Aug. 27, 2013. http://www.usatoday.com/story/news/nation/2013/08/26/south-carolina-charleston-wild-wing-cafe-black-americans/2704125/.

Eversley, M. "9 Dead in Shooting at Black Church in Charleston, S.C." *USA Today*, Jun. 19, 2015. https://www.usatoday.com/story/news/nation/2015/06/17/charleston-south-carolina-shooting/28902017/.

Feagin, J. "The Continuing Significance of Race: Antiblack Discrimination in Public Places." *American Sociological Review* 56 (1991): 101–16.

Feagin, J. *The White Racial Frame: Centuries of Framing and Counter-Framing.* New York: Routledge, 2013.

Feeney, M. J. "WiFi Signal with Racist, Anti-Semitic Slur in Teaneck, NJ Sparks Police Probe; Signal Came from Rec Center Router." *New York Daily News*, Jan. 18, 2012. http://www.nydailynews.com/news/national/wifi-signal-racist-anti-semitic-slur-teaneck-nj-sparks-police-probe-signal-rec-center-router-article-1.1008135.

Ferrigno, L. "Macy's Has First Black Santa, by Special Request." *CNN*, Dec. 24, 2013. https://www.cnn.com/2013/12/24/us/macys-black-santa/index.html.

Fichter, A. "The Emotional Toll of Shopping While Black." Medium, Jun. 10, 2016. https://medium.com/the-establishment/the-emotional-toll-of-shopping-while-black-bcda5e51a7fd.

Fieldstadt, E. "Woman Declaring 'I'm White and I'm Hot' Fired From Job After Harassing Two Black Women in North Carolina Parking Lot." *NBC News*, Oct. 30, 2018. https://www.nbcnews.com/news/us-news/woman-declaring-i-m-white-i-m-hot-fired-job-n926151.

Fiorini, C. "Mills Fleet Farm Apologizes for Denying Wheelchair to Disabled Man at Mason City Store." *Globe Gazette*, Apr. 26, 2017. https://globegazette.com/news/local/mills-fleet-farm-apologizes-for-denying-wheelchair-to-disabled-man/article_a460e8da-9bf3-5a5c-8a44-b34e82af7d69.html.

Flatow, N. "If You Thought Stop-and-Frisk Was Bad, You Should Know About Jump-Outs." *Mint Press News*, Dec. 27, 2014. https://www.mintpressnews.com/thought-stop-frisk-bad-know-jump-outs/200247/.

Fox News. "Store Clerk Allegedly Killed Teen He Thought Stole a Beer." *New York Post*, April 2, 2018. https://nypost.com/2018/04/02/store-clerk-allegedly-killed-teen-he-thought-stole-a-beer/.

Franco, M. "The Science of Why Black People Root for Everybody Black." *Psychology Today*, Aug. 22, 2019. https://www.psychologytoday.com/us/blog/platonic-love/201908/the-science-why-black-people-root-everybody-black.

Gabbidon, S. "Racial Profiling by Store Clerks and Security Personnel in Retail Establishments: An Exploration of 'Shopping While Black.'" *Journal of Contemporary Criminal Justice* 19, no. 3 (2003): 345–64. https://doi.org/10.1177/1043986203254531.

Gabbidon, S., and Higgins, G. "Consumer Racial Profiling and Perceived Victimization: A Phone Survey of Philadelphia Area Residents." *Springer Science and Business Media* 32 (2007): 1–11.

Gabbidon, S., and G. Higgins. *Shopping While Black: Consumer Racial Profiling in America.* New York: Routledge, 2020.

Gast, P. "Plea Deal in Beating at Georgia Cracker Barrel." *CNN Justice*, Oct. 23, 2010. http://www.cnn.com/2010/CRIME/10/23/georgia.beating.plea.deal/.

Gettys, T. "Eavesdropping White Woman Threatens to Call Cops on Black Woman: 'We're Going to Build this Wall.'" Raw Story, July 24, 2018. https://www.rawstory.com/2018/07/eavesdropping-white-woman-threatens-call-cops-black-woman-going-build-wall/.

Gilliam, W., A. Maupin, C. Reyes, M. Accavitti, and F. Shic. "Do Early Educators' Implicit Biases Regarding Sex and Race Relate to Behavior Expectations and Recommendations of Preschool Expulsions and Suspensions?" Yale Child Study Center: A Research Brief, 2016.

Goff, P., M. Jackson, B. Di Leone, C. Culotta, and N. DiTomasso. "The Essence of Innocence: Consequences of Dehumanizing Black Children." *Journal of Personality and Social Psychology* 106, no. 4 (2014): 526–45. https://www.apa.org/pubs/journals/releases/psp-a0035663.pdf.

Gomez, M. "White Woman Who Blocked Black Neighbor from Building Is Fired." *New York Times*, Oct. 15, 2018. https://www.nytimes.com/2018/10/15/us/hilary-brooke-apartment-patty-st-louis.html

Graham, L. O. "Lawrence Otis Graham: I Thought Privilege Would Protect My Kids from Racism. I Was Wrong." *Dallas Morning News*, Nov. 2014. http://www.dallasnews.com/opinion/commentary/2014/11/12/lawrence-otis-graham-i-thought-privilege-would-protect-my-kids-from-racism-i-was-wrong.

Graham, R. "It's Not Just Starbucks: White Fear Is an American Problem." *Boston Globe*, Apr. 16, 2018. https://www.bostonglobe.com/opinion/2018/04/16/blackness-not-about-teachable-moments/V9PHArYOMb4Y71ydEZS4jL/story.html.

Green, A. "Shopping While Black Lawsuits Accuse Portland Area Retailers of Discrimination." *Oregonian*, Jun. 22, 2018. https://www.oregonlive.com/portland/2018/06/shopping_while_black_lawsuits.html.

Hamad, R. "How White Women Use Strategic Tears to Silence Women of Colour." *The Guardian*, May 7, 2018. https://www.theguardian.com/commentisfree/2018/may/08/how-white-women-use-strategic-tears-to-avoid-accountability.

Hamill, D. "From Oprah to Trayon Christian, It's Business as Usual to Racially Profile Blacks." *New York Daily News*, Oct. 23, 2013. http://www.nydailynews.com/new-york/hamill-business-usual-barneys-racially-profile-article-1.1494890.

Haney, A. "Actresses Claim They Were Wrongfully Arrested after Using Atlanta Houston's Bathroom." 11Alive, May 23, 2018. https://www.11alive.com/article/news/actresses-claim-they-were-wrongfully-arrested-after-using-atlanta-houstons-bathroom/85-556851943.

Hanna, J., M. Savidge, and J. Murgatroyd. "Video Shows Troops Shooting Unarmed Man, South Carolina Police Say." *CNN*, Sept. 26, 2014. https://www.cnn.com/2014/09/25/justice/south-carolina-trooper-shooting/.

Harriot, M. "Billionaire BET Founder Bob Johnson Wasn't Allowed to Check In at Florida Hotel." *The Root*, Sept. 4, 2018. https://www.theroot.com/billionaire-bet-founder-bob-johnson-wasnt-allowed-to-ch-1828798705.

Harriot, M. "Cops Cuff Black Teen Riding with White Grandmother Because Someone Thought He Was Robbing Her." *The Root*, Sept. 6, 2018. https://www.theroot.com/cops-cuff-black-teen-riding-with-white-grandmother-beca-1828853245.

Harriot, M. "'White Caller Crime': The Worst Wypipo Police Calls of All Time." *The Root*, May 15, 2018. https://www.theroot.com/white-caller-crime-the-worst-wypipo-police-calls-of-1826023382.

Harris, A. M. "Shopping While Black: Applying the Civil Rights Act of 1866 to Cases of Consumer Racial Profiling." Human Services Today (HST), 2004. http://www.uwosh.edu/hst/?p=208.

Harris, A. M., G. Harris, and J. Williams. "Courting Customers: Assessing Consumer Racial Profiling and Other Marketplace Discrimination." *Journal of Public Policy and Marketing* 24, no. 1 (2005): 163–71.

Harsha, K. "Class Assignment at Mall Takes a Dangerous Turn during Racist Incident." *Fox 31 Colorado News*, Nov. 9, 2018. https://kdvr.com/2018/11/09/class-assignment-at-mall-takes-a-dangerous-turn-during-racist-incident/.

Hartney, C., and L. Vuong. "Created Equal: Racial and Ethnic Disparities in the US Criminal Justice System." Washington, DC: National Council on Crime and Delinquency, March 2009. http://www.nccdglobal.org/sites/default/files/publication_pdf/created-equal.pdf.

Henderson, G., A. M. Hakstian, and J. Williams. *Consumer Equality: Race and the American Marketplace.* Santa Barbara, CA: Praeger, 2016.

Henderson, W. "Racial Profiling." The Leadership Conference on Civil & Human Rights, 2011. https://civilrights.org/resource/racial-profiling-henderson/.

Herreria, C. "2 Officers Fired, 2 Suspended for Violently Dragging Doctor Off United Flight." *Huffington Post*, Oct. 17, 2018. https://www.huffingtonpost.com/entry/chicago-aviation-officers-fired-united-airlines-dragging_us_59e680c7e4b00905bdad5775.

Hicks, J. "Grand Rapids Could Make It Illegal to Call Police on People of Color for 'Participating in Their Lives.'" MLive Michigan, Aug. 20, 2019. https://www.mlive.com/news/grand-rapids/2019/04/grand-rapids-could-make-it-illegal-to-call-police-on-people-of-color-for-participating-in-their-lives.html.

Higgins, G., and S. Gabbidon. "Perceptions of Consumer Racial Profiling and Negative Emotions: An Exploratory Study." *Criminal Justice and Behavior Online First* 36, no. 1 (2008): 77–88.

Holland, J. "Tough Time for Black Women—Like Black Men—With Police." The Spokesman-Review, Oct. 31, 2015. http://www.spokesman.com/stories/2015/oct/31/tough-time-for-black-women-like-black-men-with-pol/.

Holley, P. "'Super Racist' Pool Poster Prompts Red Cross Apology." *Washington Post*, Jun. 27, 2016. https://www.washingtonpost.com/news/morning-mix/wp/2016/06/27/super-racist-pool-safety-poster-prompts-red-cross-apology/?utm_term=.7114a0f4ac2c.

Hughes, B. "A Man Shouts Racial Slurs in a Seattle Starbucks. The Silence Is Deafening." KUOW.ORG, Aug. 6, 2017. http://archive.kuow.org/post/man-shouts-racial-slurs-seattle-starbucks-silence-deafening.

Hughes, J. "What Black Parents Tell Their Sons About the Police." Gawker, Aug. 21, 2014. http://gawker.com/what-black-parents-tell-their-sons-about-the-police-1624412625.

Hunter, M. "Saggy Pants Lead to Passenger's Arrest." *CNN Travel*, Jun. 17, 2011. http://www.cnn.com/2011/TRAVEL/06/16/sagging.pants.flight.arrest/index.html.

Hutchinson, B. "'My Son Was Murdered,' Says Father of Man Mistakenly Shot by Police in Alabama Mall." *ABC News*, Dec. 3, 2018. https://abcnews.go.com/US/son-murdered-father-man-shot-police-alabama-mall/story?id=59574450.

Ingraham, C. "A New Explanation for the Stubborn Persistence of the Racial Wealth Gap." *Washington Post*, Mar. 14, 2019. https://www.washingtonpost.com/us-policy/2019/03/14/new-explanation-stubborn-persistence-racial-wealth-gap/?noredirect=on&utm_term=.066bf14f6088.

Jacobs, J. "Florida Sheriff Cites 'Stand Your Ground' in Not Arresting Shooter in Parking Lot Killing." *WRAL*, Jul. 21, 2018. https://www.wral.com/florida-sheriff-cites-stand-your-ground-in-not-arresting-shooter-in-parking-lot-killing/17713189/.

Jamal, O. "Eden Prairie Police Arrest Lloyd Johnson, 55, In Connection to McDonald's Gun Incident." *CBS Minnesota*, Nov. 21, 2018. https://minnesota.cbslocal.com/2018/11/21/man-pulls-gun-on-somali-teens-mcdonalds-eden-prairie/.

Jan, T. "White Families Have Nearly 10 Times the Net Worth of Black Families. And the Gap Is Growing." *Washington Post*, Sept. 28, 2017. https://www.washingtonpost.com/news/wonk/wp/2017/09/28/black-and-hispanic-families-are-making-more-money-but-they-still-lag-far-behind-whites/?utm_term=.2503be92ab1e.

Jan, T., and E. Dworkin. "A White Man Called Her Kids the N-word. Facebook Stopped Her from Sharing It." *Washington Post*, July 31, 2017. https://www.washingtonpost.com/business/economy/for-facebook-erasing-hate-speech-proves-a-daunting-challenge/2017/07/31/922d9bc6-6e3b-11e7-9c15-177740635e83_story.html?utm_term=.dbd7892de85e.

Jensen, E. "Prada Announces Diversity Council with Ava DuVernay Following Blackface Outrage." *USA Today*, Feb. 13, 2019. https://www.usatoday.com/story/life/2019/02/13/prada-starts-diversity-council-ava-duvernay-after-blackface-outrage/2860422002/.

Jilani, S. "My Racist Encounter at the White House Correspondents' Dinner." *Huffington Post*, May 7, 2013. http://www.huffingtonpost.com/seema-jilani/racism-white-house-correspondents-dinner_b_3231561.html.

Johnson, G. D., K. Thomas, A. K. Harrison, and S. A. Grier. *Race in the Marketplace: Crossing Critical Boundaries.* New York: Palgrave MacMillan, 2019.

Johnson, J. "From Starbucks to Hashtags: We Need to Talk About Why White Americans Call the Police on Black People." *The Root*, Apr. 6, 2018. https://www.theroot.com/from-starbucks-to-hashtags-we-need-to-talk-about-why-w-1825284087.

Jones, F. "Breathing While Black." *Essence*, 118–19, Sept. 2018.

Jordon, J. "Jordan Davis, Teen Shot Over Loud Music, Compared to Trayvon Martin." *Huffington Post*, Nov. 30, 2012. http://www.huffingtonpost.com/2012/11/30/jordan-davis-teen-loud-music-trayvon-martin_n_2217444.html.

KCAL9. "Woman Charged with Attempted Murder After Beating 92-year-old with Brick." *CBS Los Angeles*, Jul. 12, 2018. https://losangeles.cbslocal.com/2018/07/12/woman-charged-with-attempted-murder-after-allegedly-beating-92-year-old-with-brick/.

Kenney, T. "Detroit Owner Apologizes for 'Despicable' Behavior after Spitting on Black Man during Dispute." *Atlanta Black Star*, Jul. 19, 2018. https://atlantablackstar.com/2018/07/19/detroit-store-owner-apologizes-for-despicable-behavior-after-spitting-on-black-man-during-dispute/.

Kenney, T. "Georgia Parents Speak Out After Woman Calls the Cops on Black Man Babysitting Their Children." *Atlanta Black Star*, Oct. 10, 2018. https://atlantablackstar.com/2018/10/10/georgia-parents-speak-out-after-woman-calls-the-cops-on-black-man-babysitting-their-children/.

Kenney, T. "Study Suggests White People Are More Likely to Assault Black, Latino People Than the Other Way Around." *Atlanta Black Star*, Jun. 23, 2018. https://atlantablackstar.com/2018/06/23/study-suggests-white-people-are-more-likely-to-assault-black-latino-people-than-the-other-way-around/.

Khaleeli, H. "#SayHerName: Why Kimberle Crenshaw Is Fighting for Forgotten Women." *The Guardian*, May 30, 2016. https://www.theguardian.com/lifeandstyle/2016/may/30/sayhername-why-kimberle-crenshaw-is-fighting-for-forgotten-women.

Kiertzner, J. "Michigan Woman Says She Was Profiled, Accused of Fraud While Shopping at Saks Fifth Avenue." *FOX4*, Dec. 22, 2017. https://www.fox4now

.com/news/national/michigan-woman-says-she-was-profiled-accused-of-fraud-while-shopping-at-saks-fifth-avenue.

King, E. "Black Men Get Longer Prison Sentences Than White Men for the Same Crime: Study." *ABC News*, Nov. 17, 2017. https://abcnews.go.com/Politics/black-men-sentenced-time-white-men-crime-study/story?id=51203491.

Knickmeyer, E. "California Wine Train Orders Off Black Women's Book Club." *ABC 6*, Aug. 25, 2015. https://6abc.com/news/calif-wine-train-orders-off-black-womens-book-club/956151/.

Knowles, H. "Black Man Trying to Propose to His Girlfriend Interrupted by Security Guard Accusing Him of Shoplifting." *Yahoo News*, Jul. 24, 2019. https://www.yahoo.com/news/black-man-trying-propose-girlfriend-072146612.html.

Kopp, J. "Wet Seal to Pay 7.5m in Discrimination Lawsuit." *Fort Bragg Advocate-News*, May 10, 2013. http://www.advocate-news.com/ci_23215982/wet-seal-pay-7-5m-discrimination-lawsuit.

Kopple, Barbara, dir. *Miss Sharon Jones!* 2015; New York: Cabin Creek Films. Netflix.

Krawczyk, N. "Out, But Still Not Always Equal, in Retail." *Convenience Store News*, Aug. 14, 2017. https://csnews.com/out-still-not-always-equal-retail.

Kringen, A. "Oklahoma Restaurant Owners Says Doesn't Want 'F*ggot, Freak' Customers." *Oklahoma News 4*, Feb. 6, 2014. https://kfor.com/2014/02/06/graphic-language-enid-restaurant-owner-gets-heat-for-alleged-discrimination/.

Kristof, N. "When Whites Just Don't Get It." *New York Times*, Aug. 30, 2014. https://www.nytimes.com/2014/08/31/opinion/sunday/nicholas-kristof-after-ferguson-race-deserves-more-attention-not-less.html.

Kristof, N. "When Whites Just Don't Get It, Part 7." *New York Times,* Oct. 1, 2016. https://www.nytimes.com/2016/10/02/opinion/sunday/when-whites-just-dont-get-it-part-7.html.

Laboni, R. "HBO Star Files Lawsuit Against NYPD, Macy's, Cites Racial Profiling." *CNN Justice*, Nov. 14, 2013. http://www.cnn.com/2013/11/13/justice/hbo-star-lawsuit/.

Lacko, J. M., S. M. McKernan, and M. Hastak. "Survey of Rent-to-Own Customers." Federal Trade Commission, April 2000. https://www.ftc.gov/reports/survey-rent-own-customers.

Lane, W., D. Rubin, R. Monteith, and C. Christian. "Racial Differences in the Evaluation of Pediatric Fractures for Physical Abuse." *Journal of the American Medical Association* 288, no. 13 (2002): 1603–09.

Laymon, K. *Heavy: An American Memoir*. New York: Simon Schuster, 2018.

Lowndes, C. "The Guidebook that Helped Black Americans Travel during Segregation." Vox, March 15, 2018. https://www.vox.com/2018/3/15/17124620/green-book-black-americans-travel-segregation.

Luthern, A. "No Charges in Donte Hamilton Shooting; Edward Flynn Seeks External Review." *Journal Sentinel*, Nov. 11, 2015. http://archive.jsonline.com/news/milwaukee/dontre-hamiltons-family-to-meet-with-federal-officials-may-learn-of-charges-b99613433z1-344675532.html.

Magee, N. "Walmart Sued for Locking Up Black Hair Care Products in Glass Case." Black America Web, Jan. 29, 2018. https://blackamericaweb.com/2018/01/29/walmart-sued-for-locking-up-black-hair-care-products-in-glass-case/.

Mandani, D., and D. Romero. "Retired Firefighter Found Guilty for Shooting at Lost Black Teen on Doorstep." *NBC News*, Oct. 12, 2018. https://www.nbcnews.com/news/us-news/retired-firefighter-found-guilty-shooting-lost-black-teen-doorstep-n919656.

Manskar, N. "Mineola Man Says Garden City Cops Racially Profiled, Beat Him." The Island Now, Dec. 31, 2016. https://theislandnow.com/uncategorized/mineola-man-says-garden-city-cops-racially-profiled-beat-him/.

Margolin, E. "Black Female Doctor: Delta Discriminated, Barred Me from Sick Passenger." *NBC News*, Oct. 14, 2016. https://www.nbcnews.com/news/us-news/black-female-doctor-delta-discriminated-barred-me-sick-passenger-n666251.

Martin, R. "Sybrina Fulton: 'George Zimmerman Has Trayvon's Innocent Blood on His Hands.'" Black America Web, Jul. 19, 2013. https://blackamericaweb.com/2013/07/19/sybrina-fulton-george-zimmerman-has-trayvons-innocent-blood-on-his-hands/.

Martinez, G. "'Leave These Women Alone!' Grocery Store Customer Defends Spanish Speakers in Viral Video." *Time*, Oct. 4, 2018. https://www.msn.com/en-us/news/us/leave-these-women-alone-grocery-store-customer-defends-spanish-speakers-in-viral-video/arBBNXsuj.

Martinez, P., and J. Carissimo. "Waffle House Shooting Victims ID'd as Worker, Star Athlete, Music Artist." *CBS News*, Apr. 22, 2018. https://www.cbsnews.com/news/waffle-house-shooting-victims-identified-today-2018-04-22/.

Mathias, C. "He Filmed the Death of Eric Garner. Now He's Getting Ready to Spend 4 Years in Prison." *Huffington Post*, Sept. 2, 2016. http://www.huffingtonpost.com/entry/ramsey-orta-eric-garner_us_57a9edbde4b0aae2a5a15142.

McAfee, M. "T.J. MAXX Removes Noose T-shirt." *CNN*, Mar. 19, 2015. https://www.cnn.com/2015/03/19/living/feat-tjmaxx-hang-loose-tshirt/index.html.

McGirt, E. "raceAhead: A New Nielsen Report Puts Black Buying Power at $1.2 Trillion." *Fortune*, Feb. 28, 2018. http://fortune.com/2018/02/28/raceahead-nielsen-report-black-buying-power/.

McIntosh, P. "White Privilege: Unpacking the Invisible Knapsack." Seed: The National Seed Project, 1989. https://www.racialequitytools.org/resourcefiles/mcintosh.pdf.

McKay, T. "Al Roker Says a New York City Taxi Refused to Pick Him Up Because He's Black." *Yahoo News*, Nov. 22, 2015. https://www.yahoo.com/news/al-roker-says-york-city-191044120.html.

McLaughlin, E. "'I Thought It Was My Apartment,' Dallas Officer Says 19 times in Tearful 911 Call After Shooting Botham Jean." *CNN*, Apr. 30, 2019. https://www.cnn.com/2019/04/30/us/dallas-botham-jean-911-police-officer-amber-guyger/index.html.

McLean, R., and J. Disis. "NAACP Warns Black Passengers about Traveling with American Airlines." *CNN Money*, Oct. 25, 2017. https://money.cnn.com/2017/10/25/news/companies/naacp-travel-advisory-american-airlines/index.html.

Meeks, K. *Driving While black: Highways, Shopping Malls, Taxicabs, Sidewalks: How to Fight Back If You Are the Victim of Racial Profiling*. New York: Broadway Books, 2000.

Meredith Digital Staff. "Instead of Arresting an Accused Shoplifter, 3 NYPD Officers Pay for Her Groceries." *CBS 46*, Jul. 5, 2019. https://www.cbs46.com/instead-of-arresting-an-accused-shoplifter-nypd-officers-pay-for/article_3d3a7fb2-d09d-52d3-b209-f26285c8a3d1.html.

Mettler, K. "Four Black Teenagers Held at Gunpoint by White Woman While Fundraising for Football Team." *Yahoo News*, Aug. 16, 2019. https://www.yahoo.com/news/four-black-teenagers-held-gunpoint-141725967.html.

Miller, J. "Couple Stopped by Police Files $4M Lawsuit against Costco." *WBALTV*, Nov. 8, 2018. https://www.wbaltv.com/article/couple-stopped-by-police-files-dollar4m-lawsuit-against-costco/24845419.

Minnesota Department of Human Rights. "Case Spotlight: Two African American Customers Allege Racial Discrimination by Marshalls and Walgreens." Minnesota Department of Human Rights, 2012. https://mn.gov/mdhr/news-community/case-histories/case-spotlight/?id=1061-242784.

Mitchell, M. "Water Tower Place to Black Teens Kicked Out of Mall: 'It Was Wrong, Very Sorry.'" *Chicago Sun Times*, Apr. 9, 2018. https://chicago.suntimes.com/columnists/water-tower-place-to-black-teens-kicked-out-of-mall-it-was-wrong-very-sorry/.

Moodie-Mills, D. "The 'Green Book' Was a Travel Guide Just for Black Motorists." *NBC News*, Oct. 11, 2016. https://www.nbcnews.com/news/nbcblk/green-book-was-travel-guide-just-black-motorists-n649081.

Morgan-Smith, K. "Police Called on 'Suspicious' Black Family Enjoying Meal at Subway." theGrio, Jul. 4, 2018. https://thegrio.com/2018/07/04/police-called-on-suspicious-black-family-enjoying-meal-at-subway/.

Mosbergen, D. "NY Lawmaker Wants to Make Calling Cops on Innocent Black People a Hate Crime." *Huffington Post*, Aug. 20, 2018. https://www.huffingtonpost.com/entry/911-discrimination-law-jesse-hamilton-new-york_us_5b796dbfe4b0a5b1febc2632.

National Action Network. "Customers' Bill of Rights." National Action Network, 2013. http://nationalactionnetwork.net/wp-content/uploads/2013/12/bill-of-rights-final-draft.pdf.

Nelson, S. "Homeless Man Killed by 'Stop n Shop' Employees for Allegedly Stealing Cake." *Atlanta Black Star*, Apr. 19, 2018. https://atlantablackstar.com/2018/04/19/homeless-man-killed-stop-n-shop-employees-allegedly-stealing-cake/.

Nelson, S. "Maine Supermarket Sends Police to Customer's Home for Questioning Store Policy." *Atlanta Black Star*, Jun. 23, 2018. https://atlantablackstar.

com/2018/06/23/maine-supermarket-sends-police-to-customers-home-for-questioning-store-policy/.

Newkirk, V. "The Language of White Supremacy." *The Atlantic*, Oct. 6, 2017. https://www.theatlantic.com/politics/archive/2017/10/the-language-of-white-supremacy/542148/.

Ortiz, E., and S. Goldstein. "Milwaukee Man, 76, Found Guilty of Intentional Homicide in 13-year-old Neighbor's Shooting Death." *Daily News*, Jul. 17, 2013. https://www.nydailynews.com/news/crime/trial-milwaukee-mom-recounts-shooting-son-13-article-1.1400993.

Patterson, B. "That Racial Profiling Incident at Nordstrom Rack Apparently Wasn't a First." *Mother Jones*, May 9, 2018. https://www.motherjones.com/crime-justice/2018/05/racial-profiling-nordstrom-rack-apparently-wasnt-a-first/.

Pearson, M. "Tamir Rice Shooting: Cleveland to Pay $6 Million to Settle Family's Lawsuit." *CNN*, Apr. 25, 2016. https://www.cnn.com/2016/04/25/us/tamir-rice-settlement/.

Peart, N. K. "Why Is the N.Y.P.D. After Me?" *New York Times*, Nov. 17, 2011. http://www.nytimes.com/2011/12/18/opinion/sunday/young-black-and-frisked-by-the-nypd.html?_r=4.

Peralta, E. "Pa. Judge Sentenced to 28 Years in Massive Juvenile Justice Bribery Scandal." NPR, Aug. 11, 2011. https://www.npr.org/sections/thetwo-way/2011/08/11/139536686/pa-judge-sentenced-to-28-years-in-massive-juvenile-justice-bribery-scandal.

Peralta, E. "Double-standard? US Airways Allows Man Wearing Panties to Fly." NPR, Jun. 22, 2011. https://www.npr.org/sections/thetwo-way/2011/06/22/137348120/double-standard-us-airways-allows-man-wearing-panties-to-fly#:~:text=Double%20Standard%3F-,US%20Airways%20Allows%20Man%20Wearing%20Panties%20To%20Fly%20%3A%20The%20Two,because%20of%20his%20sagging%20pants.

Perkins, T. "Detroit Judge Tosses 'Gardening While Black' Case Brought by Three White Women." *Detroit Metro Times*, Oct. 18, 2018. https://www.metrotimes.com/table-and-bar/archives/2018/10/18/detroit-judge-tosses-gardening-while-black-case-brought-by-three-white-women.

Pew Center on the States. *One in One-Hundred: Behind Bars in America 2008*. Washington, DC: Pew Charitable Trusts, Feb. 2008. https://www.pewtrusts.org/-/media/legacy/uploadedfiles/pcs_assets/2008/one20in20100pdf.pdf.

Picchi, A. "Shopping While Black: An Old Problem Under New Scrutiny." *CBS News*, May 30, 2018. https://www.cbsnews.com/news/shopping-while-black-an-old-problem-under-new-scrutiny/.

Picheta, R. "'Suicide Isn't Fashion': Burberry Apologizes for Hoodie with Noose Around the Neck." *CNN*, Feb. 19, 2019. https://www.cnn.com/style/article/burberry-noose-hoodie-scli-gbr-intl/index.html.

Pittman, C. "'Shopping While Black': Black Consumers' Management of Racial Stigma and Racial Profiling in Retail Settings." *Journal of Consumer Culture* (2017): 1–20.

Poole, S. M., S. Grier, K. Thomas. "Operationalizing Critical Race Theory in the Marketplace." *Journal of Public Policy and Marketing*, Dec. 14, 2020. https://doi.org/10.1177/0743915620964114.

Quezada, J. A. "Driving While Black, Brown, and LGBTQ." *Huffington Post*, Apr. 7, 2014. http://www.huffingtonpost.com/janet-arelis-quezada/driving-while-racial-profiling_b_5105261.html.

Rabin, C., J. Weaver, and D. Ovalle. "The Chief Wanted Perfect Stats, so Cops Were Told to Pin Crimes on Black People, Probe Found." *Miami Herald*, Jul. 12, 2018. https://www.miamiherald.com/news/local/crime/article213647764.html.

Raftery, I. "9 Heartbreaking Responses to 'A Man Shouts Racial Slurs at a Seattle Starbucks.'" KUOW, Jun. 9, 2016. http://archive.kuow.org/post/9-heartbreaking-responses-man-shouts-racial-slurs-seattle-starbucks.

Randle, A., and J. Robertson. "'This Is What Black People Have to Deal With.' Applebee's Admits to Racial Profiling." *Kansas City Star*, Feb. 12, 2018. https://www.kansascity.com/latest-news/article199781989.html.

Rankine, C. "The Condition of Black Life Is One of Mourning." *New York Times*, Jun. 22, 2015. https://www.nytimes.com/2015/06/22/magazine/the-condition-of-black-life-is-one-of-mourning.html.

Ravitz, J. "Black and Hispanic Youth Are Targeted with Junk Food Ads, Research Shows." *CNN*, Jan. 15, 2019. https://www.cnn.com/2019/01/15/health/junk-food-ads-black-hispanic-youth/index.html.

Reingold, J., and P. Wahba. "Where Have All the Shoppers Gone?" *Fortune*, Sept. 3, 2014. https://irving.fortune.com/2014/09/03/where-have-all-the-shoppers-gone/.

Reuters. "Black Shoppers Sue Toys 'R' Us for Discrimination." *Reuters*, June 11, 2007. https://www.reuters.com/article/us-toysrus-suit/black-shoppers-sue-toys-r-us-for-discrimination-idUSN1128989720070711.

Riley, R. "White Mom and Sons Hurled Racial Slurs, Beat, Try to Drown Black Teen at an Illinois Campground." *Atlanta Black Star*, Jun. 2, 2016. https://atlantablackstar.com/2016/06/02/white-mom-and-sons-hurled-racial-slurs-beat-try-to-drown-black-teen-at-chicago-area-campground/.

Roberts, N. "Dallas Police Shamed into Dropping Charges against Black Woman Beaten by Racist." *NewsOne*, Apr. 3, 2019. https://newsone.com/3850017/dallas-woman-charges-dropped/.

Robinson, R. "Locking Up Black People Is Big Business." *The Root*, Mar. 24, 2019. https://www.theroot.com/locking-up-black-people-is-big-business-1833524257.

Roley, R. "A White Businessman Spit in the Face of a Black Man Just Doing His Job." *USA Today*, Jul. 21, 2018. https://www.usatoday.com/story/opinion/nation-now/2018/07/21/detroit-mercantile-owner-spits-black-mans-face/799809002/.

Roseliep, W. "Is 'Negrotown' Smart Satire Or Just Off-Key?" *WGBH News*, May 11, 2015. https://www.wgbh.org/news/post/negrotown-smart-satire-or-just-key.

Sanchez, R. "Choke Hold by Cop Killed NY Man, Medical Examiner Says." *CNN*, Aug. 2, 2014. http://www.cnn.com/2014/08/01/justice/new-york-choke-hold-death/.

Sanders, B. "History's Lost Black Towns." *The Root*, Jan. 27, 2011. https://www.theroot.com/historys-lost-black-towns-1790868004.

Sanders, B. "I 'Don't Like Serving Blacks': Olive Garden Awards Comedian $6,000 After Server Comment." Black America Web, Dec. 4, 2016. https://blackamericaweb.com/2016/12/05/i-dont-like-serving-blacks-olive-garden-awards-comedian-6000-after-server-comment/.

Santi, C. "Kansas Teen Says He Was Arrested for Sagging Pants at Movie Theater." *Ebony*, May 25, 2018. https://www.ebony.com/news-views/kansas-teen-arrested-sagging-pants-movie-theater.

Santia, M. "Line-Cutting Mom Drags 81-Year-Old Woman to Ground by Her Hair for NYC 'Dumbo' Showing." *NBC*, Apr. 9, 2019. https://www.nbcnewyork.com/news/local/Mom-Drags-81-Year-Old-Woman-to-Ground-By-Her-Hair-While-Waiting-to-Watch-Dumbo-on-UWS-Police-508344811.html.

Schofield, J. W. "Causes and Consequences of the Colorblind Perspective." In *Prejudice, Discrimination, and Racism*, edited by J. F. Dovidio and S. L. Gaertner. Orlando, FL: Academic Press, 1986.

Schreer, G., S. Smith, and K. Thomas. "'Shopping While Black': Examining Racial Discrimination in a Retail Setting." *Journal of Applied Social Psychology* 39 (2009): 1432–444.

Schwartz, W. "School Practices for Equitable Discipline of African American Students." Eric Clearinghouse on Urban Education, 2001. https://www.ericdigests.org/2002-1/discipline.html.

Seaton, K. "White Tears Part I: Black Educators Share Their Thoughts on What Happens When White Women Cry in Schools." Urban Joy: The Life and Times of City Schools, Nov. 6, 2017. https://joyofurbaneducation.org/2017/11/731/.

Seslowsky, E. "Bryan Stevenson Says 'Slavery Didn't End in 1865, It Just Evolved.'" *CNN*, Dec. 7, 2018. https://www.cnn.com/2018/12/07/politics/bryan-stevenson-axe-files/index.html.

Shelton, S. K. "Community Healing Network Aims to Counter 'Lie of Black Inferiority.'" *New Haven Register*, Mar. 30, 2013. https://www.nhregister.com/connecticut/article/Community-Healing-Network-aims-to-counter-lie-of-11388077.php.

Shepard, W. "Former Canes Football Player Sues Bank for Alleged Racial Profiling." *NBC 6 South Florida*, Nov. 14, 2011. http://www.nbcmiami.com/news/sports/133842813.html.

Siegel, R. "Golf Course That Called the Police on Black Women Loses Business, Faces Call for State Investigation." *The Washington Post*, April 27, 2018: https://www.washingtonpost.com/news/business/wp/2018/04/27/golf-course-that-called-the-police-on-black-women-loses-business-faces-call-for-state-investigation/?utm_term=.e4262086dd61

Siff, A. "Black Teen Cuffed, Put in Cell After $350 Purchase; Second Shopper Says She Was Harassed." *4 NBC New York*, Oct. 24, 2013. https://www.nbcnewyork.com/news/local/Black-Teenager-Lawsuit-Barneys-Belt-NYPD-Purchase-Detain-Fake-Identification-228915061.html.

Silverstein, J. "I Don't Feel Your Pain: A Failure of Empathy Perpetuates Racial Disparities." *Slate*, Jun. 27, 2013. http://www.slate.com/articles/health_and_science/science/2013/06/racial_empathy_gap_people_don_t_perceive_pain_in_other_races.html.

Sommerfeldt, C. "Georgia Woman Who Shot 15-year-old Boy Walking by Her House Claims She's Not 'an Evil Person.'" *New York Daily News*, Jan. 19, 2017. https://www.nydailynews.com/news/national/georgia-woman-shoots-15-year-old-boy-walking-house-article-1.2950044.

Sommers, S., and P. Ellsworth. "Race in the Courtroom: Perceptions of Guilt and Dispositional Attributions." *Personality and Social Psychology Bulletin* 26, no. 11 (2000): 1367-79.

Sparks, C. "20 Black Designers to Support Instead of Gucci and Prada." *Rolling Out*, Feb. 12, 2019. https://rollingout.com/2019/02/12/20-black-designers-to-support-instead-of-gucci-and-prada/.

Stanton, R. "Slain Shoplifter's Family Sues Walmart." *The Houston Chronicle*, March 9, 2013. https://www.chron.com/news/houston-texas/houston/article/Shoplifter-s-family-sues-Wal-Mart-deputy-4337438.php.

Steele, C. *Whistling Vivaldi: And Other Clues to How Stereotypes Affect Us*. New York: W.W. Norton, 2010.

Stelloh, T. "Ex-South Carolina Trooper Pleads Guilty After Shooting Unarmed Man." *NBC News*, Mar. 14, 2016. https://www.nbcnews.com/news/us-news/ex-south-carolina-trooper-pleads-guilty-after-shooting-unarmed-man-n538411.

Stern, C. "'Hoping Someone Got Fired for This': Twitter Users Slam Online Retailer for Using White Women to Model Shirts that Say Things like 'Unapologetically Black,' and 'I'm a Strong Black Woman.'" *Daily Mail*, Jul. 31, 2017. https://www.essence.com/beauty/teyana-taylor-free-manicures-brooklyn-nail-salon-victim/.

Stevens, M. "CVS Fires 2 for Calling Police on Black Woman over Coupon." *New York Times*, July 16, 2018. https://www.nytimes.com/2018/07/16/business/cvs-coupon-manager-black-woman-police.html.

Stevenson, B. *Just Mercy*. Reprint edition. New York: Random House, 2015.

Stone, A., A. Katersky, and S. Ghebremedhin. "Woman Accused of Attacking Teen in NY Hotel Arrested After Fleeing, Boy's Family Speaks Out." *ABC News*, Jan. 8, 2021. https://abcnews.go.com/US/woman-accused-attacking-teen-ny-hotel-arrested-california/story?id=75124832.

Stout, D. "3 Blacks Win $1 Million in Bauer Store Incident." *New York Times*, Oct. 10, 1997. http://www.nytimes.com/1997/10/10/us/3-blacks-win-1-million-in-bauer-store-incident.html.

Sue, D. W. *Microaggressions in Everyday Life: Race, Gender, and Sexual Orientation*. Hoboken, NJ: Wiley Press, 2010.

Sue, D. W., C. Capodilupo, G. Torino, J. Bucceri, A. Holder, K. Nadal, and M. Equin. "Racial Microaggressions in Everyday Life: Implications for Clinical Practice." *The American Psychologist* 62, no. 4 (2007): 271–86.

Sutherland, A., and B. Golding. "Stores Adopt 'Customers' Bill of Rights' After 'Shop Frisk' Fiasco." *New York Post*, Dec. 9, 2013. http://nypost.com/2013/12/09/stores-agree-to-customers-bill-of-rights-after-shop-and-frisk-fiasco/.

Telusma, B. "After Police Brutally Arrest Chikesia Clemons at Waffle House Where Is the Outrage for Black Women?" theGrio, April 24, 2018. https://thegrio.com/2018/04/24/wake-of-starbucks-white-fear-racial-profiling-where-is-the-outrage-for-black-women-chikesia-clemons/.

Thornhill, T. "'It's Not Illegal to Be Black': Cops Complain Online about White People Getting 'Freaked Out' by Their Black Neighbors and Wasting Police Time with 911 Calls." *Daily Mail*, May 7, 2015. https://www.dailymail.co.uk/news/article-3071957/It-s-not-illegal-black-Cops-complain-online-white-people-getting-freaked-black-neighbors-wasting-police-time-911-calls.html.

Touré. "When Calling 911 Makes an Emergency." *The Daily Beast*, May 13, 2018. https://www.thedailybeast.com/when-calling-911-makes-the-emergency.

Turner, C. "Bias Isn't Just a Police Problem, It's a Preschool Problem." NPR Morning Edition, Sept. 28, 2016. https://www.npr.org/sections/ed/2016/09/28/495488716/bias-isnt-just-a-police-problem-its-a-preschool-problem.

USA Today. "Joe's Crab Shack Apologizes for Using Photo of Lynching as Table Decor." *USA Today*, Mar. 11, 2016. https://www.usatoday.com/story/news/nation-now/2016/03/11/joes-crab-shack-lynching-photo-texas-hanging-table-decor/81633822/.

Vedantam, S. "What Does Modern Prejudice Look Like?" NPR Code Switch, Apr. 22, 2013. http://www.npr.org/blogs/codeswitch/2013/04/22/177455764/What-Does-Modern-Prejudice-Look-Like?ft=3.

Vega, T. "For Affluent Blacks, Wealth Doesn't Stop Racial Profiling." *CNN Money*, Jul. 14, 2016. https://money.cnn.com/2016/07/14/news/economy/wealthy-blacks-racial-profiling/.

Vela, H. "Justice for Trayvon Rallies Held in D.C., Nationwide." *WJLA*, Jul. 20, 2013. https://wjla.com/news/nation-world/-justice-for-trayvon-rallies-set-for-100-cities-91635.

Velshi and Ruhle. "Homes Owned by Black Americans Are Undervalued by Billions of Dollars." Black Periscope, Nov. 29, 2018. https://www.blackperiscope.com/2018/11/29/homes-owned-by-black-americans-are-undervalued-by-billions-of-dollars-velshi-ruhle-msnbc/.

Walsh, M. "Muslim Girls Harassed at Chicago-area Mexican Restaurant: 'If You Don't Like This Country, Leave.'" Yahoo, Jun. 6, 2017. https://www.yahoo.com/news/muslim-girls-harassed-chicago-area-mexican-restaurant-dont-like-country-leave-195929028.html.

Warikoo, N., and M. Owen. "Death Angers Family: Brutality Alleged as Man Dies in Mall Scuffle with Guards." *Detroit Free Press*, June 24, 2000. https://crimeindetroit.com/documents/Death%20angers%20Family.pdf.

Washington, J. "Connecticut Woman Resigns after Using N-word, Spitting at Black Man." *Ebony*, Mar. 18, 2019. https://www.ebony.com/news/connecticut-woman-resigns-uses-n-word-spit/.

Weems, R. *Desegregating the Dollar: African American Consumerism in the 20th Century*. New York: New York University Press, 1998.

Wells, F. "My White Neighbor Thought I Was Breaking Into My Own Apartment: Nineteen Cops Showed Up." *Washington Post*, Nov. 18, 2015. https://www.washingtonpost.com/posteverything/wp/2015/11/18/my-white-neighbor-thought-i-was-breaking-into-my-own-apartment-nineteen-cops-showed-up/?noredirect=on&utm_term=.2303f097ab9e.

Welsh-Huggins, A. "'White Only' Swimming Pool Sign Violated Girl's Civil Rights, Panel Says." Cleveland.com, Jan. 12, 2012. https://www.cleveland.com/metro/2012/01/white_only_swimming_pool_sign.html.

Westneat, D. "'Unwanted Subject': What Led a Kirkland Yogurt Shop to Call Police on a Black Man." *Seattle Times*, Nov. 16, 2018. https://www.seattletimes.com/seattle-news/unwanted-subject-what-led-a-kirkland-yogurt-shop-to-call-police-on-a-black-man/.

Whitaker, M. "Teens Arrested in NY While 'Waiting While Black' at Bus Stop." theGrio, Dec. 3, 2013. http://thegrio.com/2013/12/03/teens-arrested-in-ny-for-waiting-while-black-at-bus-stop/.

Whiting, S., C. Campbell, and C. Pearson-McNeil. "Resilient, Receptive, and Relevant: The African American Consumer 2013 Report." Nielsen, 2013. https://www.iab.com/wp-content/uploads/2015/08/Nielsen-African-American-Consumer-Report-Sept-2013.pdf.

Williams, J. C. "Black Americans Don't Trust Our Healthcare System—Here's Why." *The Hill*, Aug. 24, 2017. https://thehill.com/blogs/pundits-blog/healthcare/347780-black-americans-dont-have-trust-in-our-healthcare-system.

Williams, J. D. "African-Americans: Ethnic Roots, Cultural Diversity." In *Marketing and Consumer Identity in Multicultural America*, edited by M. C. Tharpe, 165–211. Thousand Oaks, CA: Sage Publishing, 2001.

Williams, T. "Research Shows Entire Black Communities Suffer Trauma After Police Shooting." *Yes!* Magazine, Aug. 3, 2018. https://www.yesmagazine.org/mental-health/research-shows-entire-black-communities-suffer-trauma-after-police-shootings-20180803.

Williams, T. M. *Black Pain: It Just Looks Like We're Not Hurting*. New York: Scribner, 2009.

Willingham, A. J. "Police Officer Pulled a Gun on a Black Man Picking Up Trash on His Own Property. Now, the Department Is Investigating." *CNN*, Mar. 7, 2019. https://www.cnn.com/2019/03/07/us/colorado-police-black-man-picking-trash-trnd/index.html.

Winton, R. "Hate Crimes in L.A. Highest in 10 Years, with LGBTQ and African Americans Most Targeted." *LA Times*, Jan. 31, 2019. https://www.latimes.com/local/lanow/la-me-ln-hate-crime-la-big-cities-20190131-story.html.

Winton, R., S. Parvini, and M. Morin. "Stephon Clark Shooting: How Police Opened Fire on an Unarmed Black Man Holding a Cellphone." *Los Angeles Times*, Mar. 23, 2018. http://www.latimes.com/local/lanow/la-me-stephon-clark-shooting-sacramento-explainer-20180323-story.html.

Wofford, T. "New Video Emerges of Police Shooting Kajieme Powell in St. Louis." *Newsweek,* Oct. 20, 2014. https://www.newsweek.com/new-video-police-shooting-2nd-man-st-louis-emerges-266041.

Woodyard, C. "Hate Group Count Hits 20-year High Amid Rise in White Supremacy, Report Says." *USA Today*, Feb. 20, 2019. https://www.usatoday.com/story/news/nation/2019/02/20/hate-groups-white-power-supremacists-southern-poverty-law-center/2918416002/.

World Tourism Organization. "Global Report on LBGT Tourism: AM Reports, Volume 3." World Tourism Organization, 2012. https://www.e-unwto.org/doi/pdf/10.18111/9789284414581.

Yan, H., A. Vera, and S. Jones,. "Former Fort Worth Police Officer Charged with Murder for Killing Atatiana Jefferson in Her Own Home." *CNN*, Oct. 14, 2019. https://www.cnn.com/2019/10/14/us/fort-worth-police-shooting-atatiana-jefferson/index.html.

Yancy, G., M. Davidson, and S. Hadley. *Our Black Sons Matter: Mothers Talk about Fears, Sorrows, and Hopes.* Lanham, MD: Rowman & Littlefield, 2016.

ZamaMdoda. "White Women Got This Black Reporter Fired for Sharing Article About White Fragility." *AfroPunk*, Aug. 22, 2018. https://afropunk.com/2018/08/white-women-got-this-black-reporter-fired-for-sharing-article-about-white-fragility/.

ACKNOWLEDGMENTS

My first appreciation is to God the Father/Son/Holy Spirit, and then to my ancestors, parents, children, siblings, nieces and nephews, and godchildren, with all my love. Appreciation to all of my family, friends, colleagues, and students who so kindly and supportively listened to me talk about this book and its process. Much appreciation also to the nineteen interviewees who so openly shared their experiences, as well as the spoken-word/poetry artists, and visual artists, who shared their many talents: Teala Avery, Tara Betts, Malik S. Champlain, Arakcelis Gomez, Denise Manning Keyes, Micah E. Lubensky, Lisa Mallory, Frances Shani Parker, and Kenneth E. Watts. Appreciation also to Dan Alpert, John-Manuel Andriote, Terrlyn Curry Avery, Marcus Ballenger, Penny-Jade Beaubrun, Jessica Brown Beckford, Sunil Bhatia, Rhonda Bivins, Don Blake, Scott Brauer, Irvin Brown, Christina Burrell, Mary Cabrini, W. C. Sr., Joan Chrisler, Kaitlin Ciamiello, Rebecca Colesworthy, Connecticut College (Center for the Critical Study of Race and Ethnicity (CCSRE) Research Workshop Participants, Dean of Faculty Office, Holleran Center for Community Action and Public Policy, Dept. of Human Development, and R. F. Johnson Faculty Development Fund), Alice Brown Cunningham, Charles Davis, Frances Davis, Jerry L. Davis, Maya Doig-Acuna, Jeanne Donato, Jim Downs, Mike Dreimiller, R. Danielle Egan, Bianca Estriplet, Stephanie Y. Evans, Joe Feagin, Danny Feliciano, Hannah Fisher, Ashonti Flowers, Naima Gherbi, Pattie Glenn, Rick and Sue Gomez, Donna Graham, Lorraine Gruber, Dina Guilak, Jerome

Guilford, Cherise Harris, Sylvia A. Holladay, Carolyn Holleran, Barbara Holloway, Gayla Holmes, Jeffrey Howard, Bill Howe, Donna Hunter, Sian M. Hunter, Kevin Ith, Charles Jackson, Mike James, Rolf Janke, Candice Jemison, Devin and Charity Johnson, Marcelyn Dallis Jones, Eileen Kane, Jean Kilbride, Julie Kirsh, Benjamin Knepp, Maureen Lee, Gary Lemons, Sarah Lefrancois, Adonnica Malone, Amy Martin, Tarishia Martin, Loren Marulis, Yousuf Marvi, Rosalinda Monsegur, Kyle M. Moore, Jorge and Wanda Morales, Lawrence Morehouse and the Florida Education Fund, Kylar Nelson, Carey Newman, Katheryn O'Connor, RasAmen Oladuwa, Courtney Packard, Sonja Parham, Fred Paxton, Lorraine Perkins, Caroline Peterson, Robert and Patricia Ann Peterson, Poppy and Rye Bakery, Mary Alice Randall, Phyllis Reddick, Bill Rivera, Sarah Rothenberg, Ariella Rotramel, Shamar, Chantelle Sharpe, Charlotte Sheedy, Peggy Sheridan, Paola Sica, Jon Sisk, Michelle Smith, Catherine Stock, Keeanga-Yamahtta Taylor, Paula Torres, CaraLynn Turner, Charity Turner, Ubuntu Storytellers and Consulting, Aracelis Vasquez, Stuart Vyse, Andrew Walker, Frances Williams, Sarette Williams, Marc Zimmer, and the anonymous manuscript reviewers. If anyone is missing, please charge it to my head, and not to my heart; much appreciation to everyone for your help, encouragement, inspiration, and support; I am ever grateful.

INDEX

ABOUT THE AUTHOR

Michelle Dunlap, PhD, earned a bachelor's of science with honors in psychology from Wayne State University; a master's in social psychology with an emphasis on consumer behavior; and a PhD in social psychology with an emphasis on prejudice, racism, and intergroup relations from the University of Florida in 1993. She has taught at Connecticut College in the Human Development Department since 1994. She is author or coeditor of more than forty journal articles, books, chapters, and essays on the topics of cultural competency and family and community engagement; service-learning; multicultural issues and diversity; and racial identity and adolescent development. She has traveled extensively and has presented her work nationally and internationally. Among her travels have been Germany, France, Finland, Russia, Mexico, Canada, South America, and throughout the United States and Caribbean. She has won local, state, and national awards for her community-engaged work, and has consulted for universities, schools, social service and community agencies, and businesses. Also extremely rewarding for her has been raising her children, serving as auntie to a host of godchildren, and engaging in ministry work.

CPSIA information can be obtained
at www.ICGtesting.com
Printed in the USA
LVHW081330150822
725903LV00027B/324

9 781538 137123